PLAZA

Aristotle's *Ethics*

Critical Essays on the Classics
Series Editor: Steven M. Cahn

The volumes in this new series offer insightful and accessible essays that shed light on the classics of philosophy. Each of the distinguished editors has selected outstanding work in recent scholarship to provide today's readers with a deepened understanding of the most timely issues raised in these important texts.

Aristotle's *Ethics*

Critical Essays

EDITED BY
NANCY SHERMAN

ROWMAN & LITTLEFIELD PUBLISHERS, INC.
Lanham • Boulder • New York • Oxford

ROWMAN & LITTLEFIELD PUBLISHERS, INC.

Published in the United States of America
by Rowman & Littlefield Publishers, Inc.
4720 Boston Way, Lanham, Maryland 20706

12 Hid's Copse Road
Cumnor Hill, Oxford OX2 9JJ, England

British Library Cataloguing in Publication Information Available

Library of Congress Cataloging-in-Publication Data

Aristotle's Ethics : critical essays / edited by Nancy Sherman.
     p.   cm. — (Critical essays on the classics)
   ISBN 0-8476-8914-X (alk. paper). — ISBN 0-8476-8915-8 (pbk. :
alk. paper)
    1. Aristotle—Ethics.   2. Ethics, Ancient.   I. Sherman, Nancy,
1951– . II. Series.
B491.E7A76   1998
171'.3—dc21   98-41164
                                                CIP

Printed in the United States of America

Contents

v

Introduction

The ethics of Aristotle (384–322 BC), and virtue ethics in general, have seen a resurgence of interest over the past few decades. No longer do utilitarianism and Kantian ethics alone dominate the moral landscape. Now Aristotelian themes fill out that landscape with such issues as the importance of friendship and emotions in a good life, the role of moral perception in wise choice, the nature of happiness and its constitution, moral education and habituation.

The essays in this volume represent the best of that debate. Taken together, they provide a close analysis of central aruguments in Aristotle's *Nicomachean Ethics*. But they do more than that. Each shows the enduring interest of the complex questions Aristotle himself subtly raises in the context of his own discussions with contemporaries.

The *Nicomachean Ethics* (NE or EN), in addition to the *Eudemian Ethics* (EE) and the *Magna Moralia* (MM),[1] constitute Aristotle's ethical corpus. While Anthony Kenny has recently championed the *Eudemian* as the final and most authoritative of the ethical treatises,[2] the *Nicomachean* (three of whose books—V, VI, and VII—are in common with the *Eudemian*) remains the text most widely used by students and is the treatise in the best state of textual preservation. It is the text most commonly identified as "Aristotle's *Ethics*."

Aristotle, like Socrates and Plato before him and the Stoics after, begins his inquiry with the questions, What is the best life to live? What is a good and happy life (*eudaimonia*) for a human being? What are its parts and the structure of its parts? How much depends on an inner state of virtuous character? How much depends on external goods and fortune, that is, on success? If happiness is virtuous activity and not merely the possession of virtuous states of character, then how can it not depend upon some degree of luck and the contributions of an hospitable world?

These are questions that T. H. Irwin and Julia Annas explore in the first two essays of this volume and further develop in their later writings.[3] The debate puts to the fore the question of the sufficiency of virtue for happiness. On the one hand, as Irwin notes, "most of the *Ethics* is devoted to an account of the virtues" and the assumption throughout that "if we want to be happy, we should cultivate and practice the virtues" (2). On the other hand, Aristotle is attracted to the common view that "happiness is vulnerable to external hazards," that sudden disaster or tragedy can reverse happiness, no matter how virtuous one's life has been. The Stoics are undoubtedly counterintuitive in insisting that happiness is invulnerable to either prosperity or tragedy. Yet, as Annas puts it, Aristotle feels the pull of that philosophical position. At the same time he also clearly indicates that "external goods have value in themselves; when deprived of them your happiness is ruined, even if you are virtuous" (42–43). Where does Aristotle come out on this question? In what sense can he, the great compromiser, chart a stable middle course?

Annas divides the debate on external goods into two camps: the Peripatetic interpretation, defended by Irwin in the above paper and by Martha Nussbaum in *The Fragility of Goodness*,[4] and the proto-Stoic interpretation, defended by John Cooper.[5] On the latter view, external goods are instrumental, affecting the virtuous person's happiness only insofar as their loss or absence detracts from the performance of virtue. To be solitary or childless does not itself mar one's happiness. It does so only indirectly, by diminishing opportunities for virtuous activity. On the Peripatetic view, to lack those external goods is to lack something of intrinsic worth; it is itself to lack a component of happiness. "On [the proto-Stoic view] . . . the virtuous person broken on the wheel fails to be happy only because his prospects or future virtuous activity are dim, not because of any intrinsic badness about being broken on the wheel" (44). Annas argues that Aristotle never firmly decides between the two competing views, leaving it to later interpretors to read him in one or the other way.

J. L. Ackrill and Richard Kraut continue the discussion of what constitutes the happy life. Ackrill raises the question as to whether the virtuous activity of the happy or *eudaimōn* life will be constituted by a broad range of civic and practical activities intrinsically valued for their own sakes as ingredients of happiness or be narrowly construed in terms of just one activity, namely philosophical contemplation (*theoria*). Readers have long struggled with the tension in Aristotle's own text between these options—between the life of practice and the life of divine thought. Ackrill holds that indeed there is a contradiction in Aristotle's view. While Books I–IX seem to expound the first option, dubbed the "inclusive" doctrine of *eudaimonia*, Book X.7–8 abruptly shifts to present the second alternative of a "dominant" or monolithic view of *eudaimonia*—that the end for a human being is in a single, best and most complete activity, *theoria*, and its virtue, *sophia*. Many have worried that if the dominant view is viable, then it reduces good action and the life of virtue to a mere means to the more final good of contemplation. But how could this be? Virtuous action, on Aristotle's view, is supposed to be done for its own sake. It is intrinsically valuable. Others have argued that contemplation may be a supremely valuable pursuit and constitute, though not in an exclusive way, the best life for a human being. "But then the question is unavoidable," as Ackrill states: "If *theoria* and virtuous action are both valuable forms of activity—independently though not equally valuable—how should they be combined in the best possible human life?"

Richard Kraut takes up this question as well as Irwin's and Annas's claims about the role of external goods in Aristotelian happiness. While acknowledging the attractiveness of the "inclusive" view—that happiness is an "all-inclusive aggregate" of intrinsic goods (of practical and theoretical virtue, as well as external goods), Kraut rejects the view in favor of "the thesis that happiness consists in just one type of good—virtuous activity" (79). He claims on textual grounds that external goods will support virtuous activity, but are not themselves "components of the ultimate end of a happy life." "To have these other goods is not to be thought of as making . . . [a] life even more desirable than it is already made by . . . [an individual's] virtuous activity" (85–86).

But what about the apparent contradiction between Book X.7–8 and the rest of the NE? Does the defense of the philosophical life in X.7–8 radically depart from the whole framework of Aristotle's ethical theory? On Kraut's reading, there is no radical departure, since, on his view, Aristotle never conceives of happiness as an all-inclusive composite. Throughout the *Nicomachean*, in Book X as well as Books I–IX, Aristotle endorses, he argues, a non-composite reading of happiness as virtuous activity of the rational soul. Still, Kraut admits that there is a new thesis introduced in Book X.7–8: namely, the claim that "*perfect* happiness consists in *theoria*" (86). "Contemplation is perfect happiness . . . but at the same time a life 'in accordance with the other kind of virtue' is happy 'in a secondary degree' (1178a7–9). That statement can reasonably be taken to mean that both philosophical and political lives are happy and well lived, but that of these the philosophical life is happiest" (87). So on Kraut's view, even if happiness is exhausted by virtuous activity, this still allows for the excellent activities of both practical and contemplative reason. Furthermore, if we take seriously Aristotle's notion of degrees of happiness, then the life of *praxis* and politics will not be unhappy, though neither will it be the happiest. Finally, Kraut reminds us that contemplative life need not be thought of as an isolated life of ascetic retreat. Aristotle's notion of philosophical study requires the sustenance of a community of friends engaged in teaching and discussion (1172a32–4).

With Rosalind Hursthouse's chapter, we move from framing questions about the structure and nature of happiness to questions about the nature of virtuous activity itself. Perhaps the most famous of Aristotle's ethical doctrines is that virtue or excellence of character (*ēthikē aretē*) is a disposition in a mean. In "A False Doctrine of the Mean," Hursthouse criticizes the traditional view, represented by J. O. Urmson, that to hit the mean is a quantitative notion—that, as she puts it (in a paraphrase of Urmson's view), "to have a disposition regarding a certain emotion in a mean is to be disposed to exhibit or feel that emotion neither *too* often nor *too* rarely; about or toward neither *too* many nor *too* few objects or people, for neither *too* many nor *too* few reasons, neither *too* strongly nor *too* weakly" (109; italics added). In what sense is this gloss equivalent to Aristotle's standard formulation that to have a disposition regarding a certain emotion in a mean is to exhibit or feel that emotion *hōs dei* —"on the right occasions, about or towards the right objects or people, for the right reasons, in the right manner"? Examining specific virtues and vices, she presses the question as to whether *wrong* objects must literally connote "excess"; is it always just a matter of "too . . ."? Consider what distinguishes the temperate from the licentious person. True enough, the licentious person is often a greedy guts, but immoderateness isn't the only way to be licentious. One can alternatively be licentious by overstepping the limits of what is honorable or fine, to be slim but wicked by taking the *wrong* objects—e.g., not scrupling to take my food, even if I am starving, or to "happily cheat fellow soldiers of their rations on campaign" (111). The point is clearest in the case of adultery. Adultery is an act of license, Aristotle holds, with respect to sex. But as Hursthouse insightfully interprets, it is an act of license not only when there is an "excess" of sex directed toward the wives and widowed mothers or unmarried daughters of citizens. By Aristotle's lights, "a man who commits 'adultery' just *once* has done an act which 'connotes depravity' and is 'simply wrong' (1107a10ff)." The issue is the appropriateness of the object, not the repeat offense. Where there is excess, then "each 'wrong object' will happen to be 'at least one object too many.' " "Too often" or "too seldom," "too much" or "too little" are accidental features of failing to hit the mean, not essential elements to getting it wrong.

But what is the disposition by which the wise person gets things right? In the next trio of essays, John McDowell, Martha Nussbaum, and Alfred Mele explore the cognitive capacites of virtue and cognitive defects of vice. The theme that links these three pieces is the importance of perceptual sensitivity in making right choices. The virtuous person perceives what is morally salient such that through that perception she knows what a particular situation requires in terms of action. As McDowell puts it, "A kind person has a reliable sensitivity to a certain sort of requirement which situations impose on behavior. The deliverances of a reliable sensitivity are cases of knowledge; and there are idioms according to which the sensitivity itself can appropriately be described as knowledge: a kind person knows what it is like to be confronted with a requirement of kindness. The sensitivity is, we might say, a sort of perceptual capacity" (122). McDowell's Aristotle subscribes to a version of moral particularism, in the sense that to see what is required is not a matter of deductive application of codifiable rules about how to live. Moreover, on his interpretation, perceptual sensitivity is itself motivational, not dependent on a further noncognitive element to motivate action. "If someone takes that fact to be the salient fact about the situation, he is in a psychological state which is essentially practical. The relevant notion of salience cannot be understood except in terms of seeing something as a reason for acting which silences all others" (137). These are issues that have been widely debated independent of Aristotle's texts. For the reader approaching the *Nicomachean* afresh, they force the question of just what place perceptual and practical wisdom have in Aristotle's account of virtue. In what sense is virtue a matter of "seeing aright"? How do we train individuals to notice and become aware of the requirements of situations? Are they morally wanting when they fail to notice?

Issues concerning moral perception are discussed in a lively way by Martha Nussbaum in her "The Discernment of Perception." On her reading, Aristotle rejects the view that the discernment of correct choice is a matter of algorithmic reasoning characteristic of utilitarianism. Aristotle himself, she argues, was aware of such a "science of measurement," notably propounded at the end of Plato's *Protagoras*, and he offers strong opposition to its implicit claim "that there is some one value that it is the point of rational choice, in very case, to maximize" (147). Aristotelian practical rationality proceeds neither by a tidy calculus nor by a top-down deduction of rules. Rather, Nussbaum argues, as McDowell does, the primary deliberative work is in the sizing-up of circumstances. "Practical insight is like perceiving in the sense that it is noninferential, nondeductive; it is an ability to recognize the salient features of a complex situation" (165). Rules may play some role in guiding action, but are at best heuristic summaries of experience and not subsumptive governing principles. In addition, Nussbaum emphasizes that the discernment of particulars is never a purely cognitive capacity but must also include the readings of the emotions and imagination. To capture the concreteness of detail and nuanced shading of situations requires the engagement of the heart and fancy as well as the intellect.

Alfred Mele's account of *akrasia* (i.e., incontinence or weakness of will) further underscores the place of perception in virtue. The akratic's failure, on Aristotle's view, is that he suffers from a kind of cognitive deficiency. Critics have long worried as to how this account differs substantially from Socrates' intellectualist account in the *Protagoras*, which essentially explains away the phenomenon of *akrasia* by claiming that the akratic agent suffers not from lack of control but lack of knowledge of what is the best course of action. For if an agent did know but acted against that knowledge, reason's putative authority would be undermined; it would be to concede that reason could be dragged around by desire like a slave. Aristotle is less concerned with defending that intellectualist thesis than in exploring where a potential epistemic deficiency might rest. Pointing to Aristotle's formal argument in VII.3, Mele locates that deficiency in the agent's relation to a relevant "particular" or "minor" practical syllogistic premise. For example, an agent may smoke cigarettes well aware of the general premises that she desires health and that smoking is bad for one's health. The distorting or cognitive bug is not in the general (major) premises but in the particular premise, that here and now *this* cigarette is bad for me and poses a threat to my general health. As Mele puts it, "the first deficiency is, minimally, a failure to focus one's attention on the relevant 'minor' [premise], a failure to hold it vividly before one's mind . . . (1146b33–35), and the second is a failure (again minimally) to notice the bearing of the 'minor' upon one or more ends of the agent which support his 'right major' [premise]" (198). In short, the akratic "fails to see how the 'particular facts' of his present situation bear upon his happiness" (184). Aristotle may not sufficiently explore the motivated aspect of that failure of focus or connection to overriding ends of happiness,[6] but, as Mele argues, he does signifcantly move beyond the implausible Socratic position that the akratic must always be ignorant of what is best. Once again, here in a negative way, we see how perception of the particular circumstances is crucial to virtuous action and avoidance of vice.

The next three chapters, those of M. F. Burnyeat, Nancy Sherman, and L. A. Kosman, take up the issue of how we become good. What is Aristotle's conception of moral development? In what sense can virtue be taught? The last question, as Burnyeat reminds us, is among the oldest in moral philosophy, yet until recently Aristotle's contribution to the debate went largely unnoticed. Part of the problem is that Aristotle's remarks are scattered and unsystematic. Burnyeat's significant contribution is to reconstruct an account that at once emphasizes both cognitive and emotional dimensions of moral development as well as shows moral development to be a continuous project spanning a lifetime. Central to Burnyeat's view is that one makes progress in virtue by doing things in such a way that one can discover the truth of what one has earlier taken on faith. The moral learner must try to convert "the *that*" to the "the *because*" (the "*hoti*" to the "*dioti*"). This requires, in part, doing virtuous actions in such a way that one enjoys them for their own sake. A person who has developed a taste for virtue for its own sake may not yet "have the good man's unqualified knowledge or practical wisdom," but he is "educable" with the right disposition for deepening his grasp of what is right (215).

Aristotle's notion that moral character is habituated is duly famous. But what is habituation? What does it mean to become just by doing just actions, or temperate by doing what is temperate? If practice is a kind of mindless repetition, then how does it ever lead to the sort of practical wisdom requisite for full virtue? In this excerpt from *The Fabric of Character* Sherman argues that Aristotelian habituation is not rote practice but a cognitive and critical mode of doing that requires appraisal and correction of mistake. One learns virtue by doing virtuous actions, but not in the absence of norms embodied in role models and vigilant teachers who critique one's practice. In addition, Sherman argues, habituation requires an education of the emotions constitutive of virtue. But how do we cultivate appropriate emotions? Here Sherman turns to Book II of the *Rhetoric*. In that work Aristotle propounds an appraisal-based conception of the emotions whereby emotions are partially constituted by beliefs, perceptions, or *phantasiai* (imaginings). The implication of this account is that we change and shape emotions by revising the appraisals constitutive of emotions such that they come to be aligned with our best judgments and perceptions of circumstances. In this way, the judgments internal to emotions are "harmonized" with the considered judgments of reason. Emotions, as Aristotle puts it in NE I.13, become obedient to reason. It is noteworthy that Freud will later turn this view on its head, arguing that a thoroughgoing harmonization of the emotions cannot just be a top-down chastening. Unruly emotions need to be heard from and "owned," if a more enduring resolution of psychic conflict is to take place. The sources and stories upon which conflictual emotions rest need to be reflectively "worked through" as a part of the project of character development.

The theme of emotional education is further pursued by L. A. Kosman in his essay, "Being Properly Affected." The problem explored is this: Aristotle claims that virtue is a *hexis prohairetikē*, a state of character concerned with choice and deliberate conduct. In addition, he claims that virtues are dispositions toward actions *and* emotions: "Aristotle's moral theory must be seen as a theory not only of how to *act* well but also of how to *feel* well." Yet in what sense do we have deliberative agency over our emotions? In what sense are emotions states that we don't merely suffer, but that we choose? In sorting out this puzzle, Kosman explores the notion of indirect responsibility for emotions. We may not be able to choose specific emotional occurrences ("individual moments of emotion") by a simple act of choice, but in making the many choices through which character is constituted, we indirectly choose how to cultivate emotions. "On this view the structure of becoming virtuous with respect to feelings reveals itself to be of the following sort: one recognizes through moral education what would constitute appropriate and correct ways to feel in certain circumstances. One acts in ways that are naturally associated with and will 'bring about' those very feelings, and eventually the feelings become, as Aristotle might have said, second nature; that is, one develops states of character that dispose one to have the right feelings at the right time" (271).

The virtuous person has the right emotions, on Aristotle's view, as well as cultivates appropriate friendships and attachment relationships. So at NE I. 7 Aristotle reminds us that we are discussing the happiness and good functioning of a human being, not a god. Self-sufficiency for a human being requires a life lived with others, in friendships, families and cities. Spending days together, sharing a life, is the best way for a human to live. Aristotle's deep commitment to this claim is evidenced in his devoting two of the ten books of the *Nicomachean* (Books VIII and IX) to a thoroughgoing discussion of *philia*. In "Friendship and Good in Aristotle," John Cooper explores the topic as Aristotle revisits it in IX.9: In just what sense does the flourishing or happy person need friends? In what sense is friendship a constituent of the flourishing life? Why should one arrange a life that leaves ample room for nurturing and sustaining friendships? Aristotle's argument in IX.9 is difficult, but Cooper isolates several key points that emerge from that argument as well as from supplemental texts in the *Magna Moralia*. The first point is that friendship is an indispensable medium for self-knowledge. As Cooper puts it, referring to the MM text, "one recognizes the quality of one's own character and one's own life by seeing it reflected, as in a mirror, in one's friend" (284). A friend, as a mirror, helps one see oneself with a critical distance that self-examination often lacks. Aristotle makes a second claim: Our happiness rests in activity, in being active with regard to things that are worthwhile and that we care about. By engaging in activities with friends who share our interests, we are better able to sustain our activities and are more continuously active in their pursuit.

Aristotle underscores the role of friendship in the good life. In the contemporary idiom of the feminist ethics inspired by Carol Gilligan, Aristotle seems to recognize the importance of a "care perspective." This perspective sits side by side in his texts with an emphasis on the rational life of theoretical and practical reason as the best life for a human being. "The function of a human being is an activity of soul in accordance with, or not without, reason" (1098a8). Is there a tension between the perspectives, much like that echoed in recent debates between care ethicists and impartial reason advocates? In "Feminism and Aristotle's Rational Ideal," Marcia Homiak explores feminist criticism of rational ideals and asks whether Aristotle's ethics ultimately excludes women from its purview by setting up a rational ideal of moral goodness that women characteristically fall short of. Her answer is "no." On the view she proposes, "being caring and compassionate must be expressed within a life lived according to the rational ideal, or else these traits become destructive and unhealthy" (304). That is, healthy, non-servile forms of care require the very exercise of rational activities embraced in Aristotle's ideal model of the *phronimos* (person of practical wisdom). Moreover, the most cultivated exercise of practical reason will be in the shared and cooperative context of democratic deliberation, which in turn will foster civic friendship and the value of affiliation.

The above essays cover a wide range of themes that a careful reading of the *Nicomachean Ethics* poses. Inevitably, any text worth revisiting regularly will raise more questions than it can answer. Aristotle's texts are no exception. The intention of this anthology is not to settle debate on Aristotle's ethics but to invigorate it. These interepretive essays will serve their purpose if they bring to the experienced scholar a fresh and critical look at an old friend, and to the new reader, only just making acquaintance with the *Nicomachean*, the beginning of a long and lasting friendship.

Notes

1. Until recently, the *Magna Moralia* was generally agreed not to have been written by Aristotle, but rather to have been a late compendium of Peripatetic theory. However, of late, Franz Dirlmeir has argued for the authenticity of its content, as has John Cooper. I follow Cooper in viewing the text as reporting in a student's hands lectures of Aristotle that predate the *Eudemian*. See *Aristoteles, Magna Moralia, übersetzt und kommentiert* by Franz Dirlmeier (Berlin: Akademie-Verlag, 1962); John M. Cooper, "The *Magna Moralia* and Aristotle's Moral Philosophy," *American Journal of Philology* 94 (1973): 327–49.

2. *The Aristotelian Ethics* (New York: Oxford University Press, 1978). See also his *Aristotle on the Perfect Life* (New York: Oxford University Press, 1992). Most other scholars date the *Eudemian* as earlier than the *Nicomachean*.

3. T. H. Irwin, *Aristotle's First Principles* (New York: Oxford University Press, 1988); J. Annas, *The Morality of Happiness* (New York: Oxford University Press, 1993).

4. M. Nussbaum, *The Fragility of Goodness* (Cambridge: Cambridge University Press, 1986), chs. 11 and 12.

5. J. Cooper, "Aristotle on the Goods of Fortune," *Philosophical Review* 94 (1985): 173–97.

6. See David Pears, *Motivated Irrationality* (New York: Oxford University Press, 1984) for an insightful discussion of motivated ignorance.

Acknowledgments

T. H. Irwin, "Permanent Happiness: Aristotle and Solon" originally appeared in *Oxford Studies in Ancient Philosophy*, vol. 3, ed. Julia Annas (Oxford, UK: Clarendon Press, 1985), 89–124. Reprinted by permission of Oxford University Press and the author.

Julia Annas, "Aristotle on Virtue and Happiness" originally appeared in *The University of Dayton Review* 19, no. 3 (1988/89): 7–22. Reprinted with permission of *The University of Dayton Review* and the author.

J. L. Ackrill, "Aristotle on *Eudaimonia*" is a Dawes Hicks Lecture delivered to the British Academy, originally published in *Proceedings of the British Academy* 60 (1974). Reprinted by permission of The British Academy and the author. Copyright The British Academy 1975.

Richard Kraut, "Aristotle on the Human Good: An Overview" has not previously been published.

Rosalind Hursthouse, "A False Doctrine of the Mean," originally appeared in the *Proceedings of the Aristotelian Society* 81 (1980/81): 57–72. Reprinted by permission of the author and by courtesy of the editor of the Aristotelian Society. Copyright the Aristotelian Society 1981.

John McDowell, "Virtue and Reason" originally appeared in *The Monist* 62, no. 3 (1979): 331–50. Reprinted by permission of the editor of *The Monist* and the author.

Martha C. Nussbaum, "The Discernment of Perception: An Aristotelian Conception of Private and Public Rationality" originally appeared, in unabbreviated form, as chapter 2 of Nussbaum's *Love's Knowledge: Essays on Philosophy and Literature* (New York: Oxford University Press, 1990). A shortened version of the chapter is reprinted by permission of Oxford University Press, Inc., and the author.

Alfred R. Mele, "*Akrasia, Eudaimonia*, and the Psychology of Action" originally appeared in *History of Philosophy Quarterly* 2, no. 4, (1985): 375–92. Reprinted by permission of the editor of *History of Philosophy Quarterly* and the author.

M. F. Burnyeat, "Aristotle on Learning to Be Good" originally appeared in *Essays on Aristotle's Ethics*, ed. Amelie O. Rorty (Berkeley: University of California Press, 1980): 69–92. Reprinted by permission of the University of California Press and the author.

Nancy Sherman, "The Habituation of Character," is a shortened excerpt from *The Fabric of Character* (Oxford: Oxford University Press, Clarendon, 1989), chapter 5. Reprinted by permission of Oxford University Press and the author.

L. A. Kosman, "Being Properly Affected: Virtue and Feelings in Aristotle's Ethics" originally appeared in *Essays on Aristotle's Ethics*, ed. Amelie O. Rorty (Berkeley: University of California Press, 1980): 103–16. Reprinted by permission of the University of California Press and the author.

John M. Cooper, "Friendship and the Good in Aristotle" originally appeared in *The Philosophical Review*, 86 (1977): 290–315. Copyright 1977 Cornell University. Reprinted by permission of the publisher and the author.

Marcia L. Homiak, "Feminism and Aristotle's Rational Ideal" originally appeared in *A Mind of One's Own*, ed. Louise Antony and Charlotte Witt, pp. 1–17. Copyright 1992 by Westview Press. Reprinted by permission of Westview Press and the author.

1

Permanent Happiness:
Aristotle and Solon

T. H. Irwin

1. Introduction

Satan answered the Lord, "Has not Job good reason to be God-fearing? Have you not hedged him round on every side with your protection, him and his family and all his possessions? Whatever he does you have blessed, and his herds have increased beyond measure. But stretch out your hand and touch all that he has, and then he will curse you to your face."

(Job 1: 9–11)

Many of Aristotle's arguments begin from common beliefs. He does not commit himself to agreement with them; but he recognizes an obligation to explain them—to show the partial truth in the beliefs he rejects, and the grounds for rejecting them (*Nicomachaean Ethics* [*EN*] 1154a22–5).

In his initial claim about happiness he attends closely to common beliefs. When he has defined happiness as an activity of the soul expressing complete virtue in a complete life, he introduces the common view that happiness is rather unstable because it is vulnerable to ill fortune, to external hazards that the agent cannot control. Aristotle remarks that if someone is well off for most of his life, but finally suffers disastrous ill fortune and comes to a bad end, no one counts him happy; this is what happened to Priam at the end of his life (1100a4–9).

Here Aristotle seems to raise a serious difficulty for himself. For he had just argued that if we want to be happy, we should cultivate and

practice the virtues (1099b25–1100a4). Most of the *Ethics* is devoted to
an account of the virtues that Aristotle regards as constituents of the
happy life. But if he admits that happiness is vulnerable to external
hazards, he cannot claim that virtue ensures happiness. How, then, can
he advise us to be virtuous if we want to be happy?

This is a difficulty within Aristotle's theory. But we may think it is a
more general difficulty about his whole approach to moral theory. We
expect an account of moral virtues to prescribe some degree of inflexibility; for we expect an honest and reliable person to stick to his principles even when he is offered some attractive inducements to violate
them, or faces some severe threat for sticking to them. We tend to
agree with Satan's method for testing Job's virtue, by plunging him into
severe misfortune. Job's wife was puzzled that Job remained inflexibly
virtuous in disaster: "Are you still unshaken in your integrity? Curse
God and die!" (Job 2: 9). Though we may also be puzzled, we expect
this integrity from a virtuous person. The Greeks expect it also. It is
rather surprising to us, then, that Greek moralists advocate the pursuit
of virtue by appealing to the agent's happiness, when it seems obvious
that his virtue does not always promote his happiness. The problem
about ill fortune is simply one expression of this general difficulty about
virtue and happiness.

Aristotle sees the difficulty. He wants to solve it not by brusquely
rejecting common beliefs, but by examining them to see what they
imply, and how far they really conflict with a reasonable view of happiness. After the remark about Priam he adds: "Then should we not
count any one else either as happy, as long as he is alive? Should we
follow Solon's advice and see the end?" (1100a11–12).[1] I agree with
Aristotle's view that Solon's advice deserves discussion, and that it illuminates the problem about happiness and fortune. Before considering
Aristotle's views we will find it useful to explore Solon's advice further.

2. Solon's Problem

We learn most about Solon's advice from Herodotus' elaborate account
of it (I. 30–3). The rich and successful Croesus gives Solon a conducted
tour of the palace and treasuries, and then asks Solon to say who he
thinks is the most prosperous of human beings. Solon mentions the
winner and the runners-up, all utterly obscure people, and Croesus is
predictably disappointed, since he could have bought and sold them

all. Solon explains that the obscure people he favours were all permanently well off, though less rich and splendid than Coresus; we know they were permanently well off because they are dead, and so no longer liable to reversals of fortune. Croesus, however, is alive, and we cannot know that he is permanently happy, because we do not know that he will be spared reversals of fortune.

When Solon advises us to see the end of a person's life before deciding about the person's happiness, we see how he conceives happiness. He refuses to consider the apparently natural possibility that Croesus might be happy at one time and unhappy at another time in his life. He must, then, regard happiness as a condition of a person's life as a whole. It is reasonable for him to do this, if he conceives happiness as success. For the success that a person reasonably wants and pursues is not success for a day or two, but his success over his whole lifetime.[2] And that is the sort of thing that, as Solon reasonably observes, you can discover only when you contemplate a person's complete lifetime after it is over.

Solon's conception of happiness was widely shared. It is reflected in Aristotle's account in the *Rhetoric* of common views. Aristotle describes happiness as "doing well combined with virtue" or "self-sufficiency of life" or "the pleasantest life with safety" or "prosperity of possessions and bodies with the power to protect them and use them in action" (1360b14–17). Power and fortune are also parts of happiness because these are the best providers of safety (1360b28–9). It is because we aim at complete and secure success in life as a whole that we need fortune, and cannot be assured of happiness till we are dead; for the fortune that is needed for prosperity is unstable and variable (*EN* 1100b2–7). Not surprisingly, it becomes a Greek commonplace that no one should be called happy until his death.[3]

This shared belief that happiness requires fortune, and fortune is unstable, provokes different reactions; an these set some of the problems for Aristotle.

Since Solon remarks that good and bad fortune can affect happiness, a sensible person might think he needs to be adaptable, so that he can act on reasonable predictions about the future and avoid too serious a loss if things turn out badly. The supremely adaptable Greek is Odysseus, both in Homer and in the tragedies in which he appears.

On the other hand, many find it hard to admire the astutely flexible person. One prominent type of tragic character refuses to be sensible and adaptable, and apparently harms himself and others by his inflexibility and wilfulness. None the less, these characters are presented as admirable, not always without reservation, but often as more admirable than the plastic and adaptable characters. Ajax is the traditional type of the inflexible hero to contrast with Odysseus; and Prometheus, Antigone, and Medea share this trait.

The contrast between the adaptable and the inflexible character is a particular interest of Sophocles, who explores it in the *Ajax, Antigone, Electra,* and *Philoctetes.* The bad aspects of inflexibility are prominent in the *Ajax;* the good sides in the *Antigone* and *Electra;* the *Philoctetes* is much less decisive.[4] The same sort of contrast much later forms some of Plutarch's antitheses in his parallel lives, and through Plutarch shapes some of Shakespeare's characters.[5] We are familiar with the inflexible character of Coriolanus and the adaptable character of Antony.

The contrast between adaptability and inflexibility points to an odd feature of Greek pre-philosophical reflection. Solon's view of happiness seems to support the adaptable person's strategy. Such a person foresees all that can be foreseen, and when something unforeseen happens he improvises suitably.[6] But some Greeks hesitate to advocate this sort of outlook, and find themselves admiring the inflexible person, even though his inflexibility seems to destroy his prospect for happiness. Why should inflexibility seem so admirable? The common conception of happiness offers no answer to this question, and common sense offers no ground for admiration apart from happiness.

A student as sympathetic and critical as Aristotle should be able to identify this conflict in common-sense reactions to Solon's advice; and he should be able to find the true or false beliefs underlying the conflicting views. In his discussion of Solon's advice Aristotle tries to do justice to both sides in the conflict.

3. Aristotle's Agreement with Solon

Aristotle makes it clear that in his view happiness depends on fortune and external conditions, so that to this extent he has strong reasons for agreeing with Solon.[7] Since happiness is the highest good, it must be complete *(teleion)* and selfsufficient *(autarkes).* A complete and self-sufficient good is one that all by itself makes life choiceworthy and lacking in nothing. If it really makes life lacking in nothing, a complete good must be comprehensive; nothing can be added to it to make a better good (1097b8–21).[8] A comprehensive good must extend beyond conditions of the agent himself; Aristotle explains that it must include the happiness of family, friends, and fellow citizens (1097b8–13).

If happiness is comprehensive, and goods dependent on fortune are genuine goods, then happiness must include them. If it did not, then their addition to happiness would produce a good better than happiness alone, which is impossible. Aristotle agrees that goods of fortune are genuine goods; hence he agrees that happiness requires them (1099a31-b8). He sharply rejects the Socratic and Cynic view that virtue alone is sufficient for happiness (1095b31–1096a2, 1153b14–25).[9]

This point needs no qualification when Aristotle defines happiness as activity of the soul expressing complete virtue. For both the acquisition and the actualization of complete virtue require goods of fortune. Some examples make the point obvious. We cannot be magnificent or magnanimous if we are not rich; and we cannot live with our friends if they die at the wrong times. The definition of happiness shows why it is subject to fortune.[10]

Since happiness is an activity of the soul expressing complete virtue in a complete life, external goods have two distinct roles. Aristotle describes them as follows:

(a) In many actions we use friends, riches and political power as we use instruments; and *(b)* there are some things the lack of which mars blessedness.

(1099a32–b2)

Among the remaining goods (i.e. the external goods), *(b)* there are some whose presence is necessary (for happiness), *(a)* others that are by nature co-operative and useful as instruments.

(1099b27–8)

Great and numerous (strokes of fortune) that turn out well make his life more blessed; for *(b)* they themselves by nature adorn it, and *(a)* his use of them proves to be fine and excellent.

(1100b25–8)

In each passage Aristotle distinguishes *(a)* the role of external goods as instruments of virtuous action from *(b)* their role as contributors to happiness apart from *(a)*. The difference between the two roles needs to be explained. In one way all external goods are 'resources' *(chorēgia;* cf. 1099a32–3, 1178a26) that a virtuous person has to use properly;

a vicious person will misuse the goods he has to his own harm (1129b1–4). But still, not all external goods are goods simply because they are used to virtuous action. A temperate person's pursuit of sensual pleasure is regulated by his temperance, but his enjoyment of ordinary sensual pleasures is not good for him simply because it is what temperance prescribes; on the contrary, temperance prescribes it partly because it is the sort of thing that is good for him. Similarly, the instrumental goods that secure these sensual pleasures are not good because they help him to be temperate, but because they secure these pleasures. For similar reasons the magnanimous person values honour, and thinks he deserves it as the appropriate prize for virtue (1123b15–24, 34–6); it is an appropriate prize not because he needs it to act virtuously but because it is the greatest external good in its own right.[11]

Honour is simply the most important of the noninstrumental external goods needed to make a virtuous person's life complete. Aristotle suggests that someone who is physically repulsive (not merely undistinguished) or of low birth, or solitary or childless is a poor candidate for happiness; and remarks that it is even worse for someone who has bad children or friends, or has had good ones who have died (1099b2–6). He does not suggest that the absence or loss of these goods is bad because it causes pain or frustration, or because it prevents virtuous action (though no doubt it may have both of these effects). These are goods that are valued for their own sake, and therefore belong to a complete life.[12]

No external good is a part of happiness if it is isolated from virtue; a healthy, strong, handsome, vicious person has no part of happiness at all, since he will simply misuse the external goods he has (1129b1–4). The external goods that in the *Rhetoric* count as parts of happiness are refused this status in the *Ethics,* because they are not parts of happiness in their own right; it is the virtuous person's correct use of one of these goods, not the good by itself, that is a part of his happiness.[13] Still, the external goods are necessary for happiness, and some are necessary because they are intrinsic (i.e., not purely instrumental) goods.

4. Aristotle's Disagreement with Solon

It is easy to see why Aristotle has reasons for agreeing with Solon's view that happiness is exposed to chance; and if he agrees this far, we might expect him to advocate flexibility. We might suppose that someone is best equipped for the pursuit of happiness if he is able to adapt himself and his aims to circumstances, minimizing the ill effects of misfortune. In fact, however, Aristotle defends a surprising degree of inflexibility, because he thinks Solon is quite wrong on one crucial point.

Solon's conception implies that happiness depends on conditions outside the agent; and Aristotle criticizes such conceptions. He rejects the life of honour as a candidate for happiness, because honour depends on the attitudes of other people, whereas "we intuitively believe that the good is something of our own and hard to take from us" (1095b25). Our intuitive belief is partly satisfied if happiness is controlled by virtuous activities (1100b11–22), since these are our own, in our power and hard to take from us. The external goods are those that, in Job's view, "the Lord gives and the Lord takes away" (Job 1: 21). The Lord does not in the same way take away Job's integrity; it is up to Job himself to retain his integrity, and Aristotle argues that this is what controls happiness.

Aristotle must reconcile these claims with his equally firm belief that happiness includes external goods, and hence depends on fortune. His attempt to reconcile his different views is characteristically compressed and complex:

> Many stokes of fortune occur, differing in degrees of importance. Small strokes of good fortune or its opposite clearly will not tip the balance of his life. If many great strikes of fortune turn out well, they will make his life more blessed; for they themselves are of a nature to adorn his life, and moreover the way he uses them proves to be fine and excellent. But if things turn out the other way, they oppress and mar his blessedness, since they introduce pains and impede many activities. None the less, in these conditions also what is fine shines through, whenever someone bears with good temper many serious strokes of ill fortune, and does this not because he is incapable of feeling distress, but because he is noble and magnanimous. And if it is activities that control life, as we said, no blessed person could ever become miserable; for he will never do what is hateful and despicable.
>
> (1100b23–35).

Aristotle makes two claims about the role of major gains or losses of external goods:

1. Major gains make a happy person happier.
2. Major losses deprive a happy person of his happiness, but do not make him unhappy.

Both claims need to be explained.

The first claim is difficult because it seems to conflict with the assumption that happiness is complete, and therefore can have no further goods added to make a better good. If external goods can be added, then apparently they make a better good, and so the person who lacks them cannot be happy. Aristotle raises the same puzzle for us in his remarks about how events after my death may affect my happiness. These events, in his view, may indeed affect me for good or ill, but only to a degree that neither makes someone happy when he would otherwise not be happy, not takes away the happiness of someone who is otherwise happy (1101b1–9).[14] Aristotle needs to explain how the addition and subtraction of goods can make someone more or less happy without making him cease to be happy, if happiness cannot have any goods added to make a better good.

His claims are consistent if he explains completeness in the right way. The goods that are components of happiness are determinable types of goods; these are exemplified in determinate types of goods and in determinate tokens of these types. My playing golf now is a token of the type playing golf, which is a determinate type of the determinable type physical exercise and the determinable type recreation.

Aristotle probably believes that the complete good is composed of a sufficient number of tokens of some determinate types of each of the determinable types of good. If recreation is a component of the good, and one afternoon's golf and one evening's bridge or bingo are equally good types of recreation, then I can achieve this component of the good either by playing golf one afternoon a week or by playing bridge or bingo one evening a week. It may not matter which determinate type of activity I prefer, as long as I include the right number of tokens of the right determinable types. In saying that no good can be added Aristotle means that no determinable type of good can be added to happiness to make a better good than happiness.

These distinctions certainly raise difficulties of application. How are we to choose the right level of generality to identify the appropriate determinable types? How are we to decide the right number of tokens to count as the realization of a given type? It is not only the problem about degrees of happiness that forces such questions on Aristotle. He must face them in any case once he defines happiness as a realization of human capacities in a complete life. If we count capacities perversely, the fulfilment of my capacities will be too difficult (if they are too specific) or too easy (if they are too generic). We must count them according to the right conception of a human being's physical and psychological nature; and this will not be an easy task. Moreover, Aristotle's demand for completeness seems both unsatisfiable and unreasonable unless it requires an acceptable number of tokens, rather than all the tokens, of a determinate type of action. For however complete someone's life may seem to be, we will be able to imagine some token good activity that could have been added; but Aristotle will not want to concede that such a life is not complete and not happy.[15]

Though further enquiry is needed to see if Aristotle can satisfy us on these questions, we can see who he might draw intelligible distinctions that would solve the problem about completeness. I am happy, he can claim, if my virtue and external conditions allow me to fulfil my different capacities in the right order and proportion—if, for example, I am virtuous, and also rich enough to make magnificent actions prominent in my life. To be magnificent in contributing to the public good I need enough money for the appropriate large expenses. If I am left a large legacy, I will be pleased; for I will be able to do more of the magnificent actions that I enjoy and value. As Aristotle says, the use of these extra goods will be fine and excellent (1100b27). But though they make me happier, they do not produce a greater good than the happiness I previously had; for they do not add any further determinable good, but only add further tokens of some determinate types of a determinable good.

Aristotle can therefore defend his first claim about fortune—that good fortune can make me happier, though it does not give me a greater good than happiness. The effects of ill fortune are more serious. The happy life requires a certain moderate level of external goods (1179a1–17); and if these are lost, the happy person ceases to be happy.[16] He does not, however, become unhappy.[17] Aristotle can defend this claim if he appeals again to the composite character of happiness.

If happiness has several determinable parts, I am happy if I have all these parts, and not happy if I lack at least one of them. But there is still a difference between having some parts of happiness and having none at all. In Aristotle's view this difference is crucial. For the virtuous person always retains one crucial part of happiness, without which none of the other goods is a part of happiness at all. The virtuous person, then, always has some part of happiness, and the non-virtuous person has no part of happiness, however many other goods he may have. The virtuous but unlucky person is not happy; the lucky but non-virtuous person is unhappy.

Since Aristotle believes this about virtue, he regards it as the *dominant* good, and the dominant component of happiness; it is always to be preferred over any other component or combination of components of happiness, and over any other good or combination of goods.[18]

5. The Stable and the Unstable Components of Happiness

Aristotle's arguments imply that Solon's view is either wrong or else seriously incomplete. Solon assumed that because happiness depends to some degree on fortune, fortune can make someone miserable. He did not realize that the dominant component of happiness is stable and immune to fortune. Since Solon requires happiness to be permanent, lasting through a lifetime, he seems to make it unstable; for it is vulnerable to bad luck all that time. Aristotle suggests that happiness is more stable than Solon thought it was, because it is controlled by virtuous actions, and they are controlled by virtue, which is stable and not likely to be destroyed in our lifetime (1100b11–22). If virtue is stable, then happiness is stable to the extent that virtuous actions control happiness; and in so far as it is stable it is permanent.

Aristotle's position may appear to be inconsistent if we consider his claim that virtuous actions "control" *(kuriai)* happiness (1100b11–22); that someone is happy "because of" *(dia)* himself and not because of fortune *(Pol.* 1323b24-9; cf. 1099b20–1); and that happiness is "in" one's own character and actions *(EE* 1215a13–19; cf. 1100b8). These claims may seem to conflict with the admission that happiness depends on fortune. But Aristotle's use of the relevant causal concepts implies no conflict. In saying that virtuous actions control or cause happiness, he does not mean that they are sufficient for it, or that happiness consists only of them and their necessary consequences. He means that in the right circumstances virtuous actions make the decisive-contribution to happiness; we are to assume a reasonable level of external goods and then notice the role of virtue and virtuous action. This causal claim is not easy to evaluate; but it shows how Aristotle's position is consistent, and why he insists in the same sentence both that virtuous actions control happiness and that human life needs external goods as well (1100b8–11).[19]

Since Aristotle's view insists that virtue controls happiness, it implies that we are right to admire inflexible people to some extent, and right to be somewhat suspicious of adaptable people. A virtuous character is stable; and someone who maintains that inflexibility will secure the dominant component of his happiness; inflexibility does not require a sacrifice of happiness.[20] The adaptable person who is ready to change his character and outlook to meet changing fortune does this to secure the aspects of happiness that depend on fortune. If he cares more about these than about having a virtuous and stable character, he chooses subordinate goods rather than the dominant component of happiness. His choice is futile; for without the virtues these goods are not components of happiness at all. In choosing subordinate goods over virtue he shows that he misunderstands the nature of virtue and the nature of happiness. It is better to be inflexible about virtue; and to that extent we are right to prefer the inflexible to the adaptable character.

Aristotle has explained why happiness is in some ways more stable than Solon noticed; why it is complete, though allowing addition; and why it is caused by virtue, though vulnerable to ill fortune. He can now evaluate Solon's advice to call someone happy only when he is dead. The advice rests on the assumption that happiness must be permanent, so that if I lack it at any time in my life, I never have it.

In the *Eudemian Ethics* and *Magna Moralia* this assumption about permanence seems to be accepted, and so Solon's advice is endorsed:

> Since, then, happiness is a complete good and an end . . . it will also be in something complete. For it will not be in a child (for a child is not happy), but in a man, since he is complete [i.e. mature]. Nor will it be in an incomplete time, but in a complete one; and a complete time is as much time as a human being lives. For the many are correct to say that we must judge the happy person in the greatest time of his life, on the assumption that what is complete must be both in a complete time and in a [complete] human being.

> (*MM* 1185a5–9)

> And [there is supporting evidence for us in the claim] that a person is not happy for [just] one day, or as a child, or for each period of his life. Hence Solon's advice is right, not to count anyone happy while he is alive, but only when his life reaches its end. For nothing incomplete is happy, since it is not a whole.[21]

> (*EE* 1219b4–8)

In the *Nicomachaean Ethics,* however, as we have seen, Aristotle insists that complete happiness still allows addition. He is correspondingly careful when he explains that happiness, being complete, requires complete virtue and a complete life:

> Further, [the activity of the soul] must be in a complete life; for one swallow does not makes a spring, nor does one day; nor, similarly, does one day or a short time make one blessed and happy.
>
> (1098a18–20)

This connection between happiness and length of time is explained later. A child, like an ox or a horse, is incapable of happiness because he is incapable of the right sort of activity, and if we congratulate him on his happiness it is because we expect that he will perform the right sort of activity when he is an adult (1099b32–1100a3). Aristotle adds:

> For, as we say, we need both complete virtue and complete time. For many variations and fortunes of all sorts arise in life, and it is possible for the most prosperous person to fall into great disasters in old age, as is told of Priam in the Trojan story; and if someone suffers such misfortunes and comes to a miserable end, no one counts him happy.[22]
>
> (1100a4–9)

As in the *Eudemian Ethics* Aristotle suggests some connection between happiness and length of time; and we might think he regards a "complete time" as a lifetime. On this view, Priam's misfortunes in old age imply that he never was happy.

Eventually, however, Aristotle shows that this is not his view. For he recognizes that a happy person can lose his happiness if he suffers the misfortunes of Priam (1101a6–11). If happiness requires a complete life and a complete time, he must have had these before he suffered the misfortunes; hence a complete time cannot be a lifetime. Aristotle confirms this point when he remarks that someone who has lost his happiness can still regain it, "not . . . in a short time, but, if at all, in some long and complete time, in which he has succeeded in great and fine achievements" (1101a12–13). Though "if at all" suggests that the task of recovering happiness is not easy, it is plainly not self-contradictory, as it would be if a complete time were a whole lifetime.

The different claims in the *Nicomachaean Ethics* explain each other if we begin from the "great and fine achievements." Happiness is complete, and therefore requires a complete range of activities realizing human capacities. A complete time is a time long enough for such a complete range; and since the projects of a virtuous friend or of a magnificent and magnanimous person take some time to realize, a complete time will not be a short time. Moreover, since a child is incapable of the complete range of activities, it cannot achieve happiness. And yet, just as a complete good allows addition, a complete time need not be a whole lifetime; I may be happy if I have had a complete time and exercised the complete range of activities, and then lose my happiness, as Priam did. With enough time I may also regain happiness. When God "blessed the end of Job's life more than the beginning" (Job 42: 12) Job lived another hundred and forty years, and saw his sons and grandsons to four generations. This is presumably rather above the minimum needed for Job's return to happiness; but at least he needed long enough for the restoration of his herds, flocks, and family, and of his standing with his neighbours. As we have seen, Aristotle has assumed that happiness is complete in a way that still allows some sorts of addition; and the same notion of completeness explains his view of a complete length of time. If the parts of happiness are determinable types of action, and I can realize sufficient tokens of all of them in less than a lifetime, then I am completely happy in less than a lifetime, even though I am even happier if my happiness lasts longer than the time needed for completeness.[23]

Aristotle's rejection of Solon's advice, then, is not a casual disagreement. He has looked for plausible assumptions about happiness that might seem to support Solon. He appeals to the correct assumption that happiness is complete; and he argues that the correct assumption, correctly understood, does not support Solon. In the *Rhetoric* Aristotle accepted the common view that happiness must be secure, and recognized this as a reason for including good fortune and power in happiness (1360b28–9). In the *Magna Moralia* and *Eudemian Ethics* the popular demand for security and permanence is defended by appeal to completeness. But in the *Nicomachaean Ethics* Aristotle shows that the relevant sort of completeness needs more careful explanation than it receives in the other works; when we see that completeness allows addition we also see that it does not justify the belief that a complete time is a lifetime, and therefore does not justify the demand for security and permanence. Nothing else justifies these demands either; happiness need not be secure and permanent, and a stroke of ill fortune that ends my prosperity neither ensures that I never was happy nor necessarily deprives me of the prospect of future happiness. Contrary to Solon's view, I may be happy in some periods of my life and not in others.[24]

Though he rejects Solon's demand for permanent happiness, and suggests why he thinks it is wrong. Aristotle still thinks there is something right in the demand for permanence. Solon is wrong to demand that something as unstable as happiness should be permanent. It is better to demand permanence in a component of happiness that is stable and in our power; and virtue meets these conditions. If we are virtuous, we assure permanent success in securing the dominant component of happiness; for virtue is stable, not exposed to destruction by external circumstances, and hence we can count on it to be permanent. Once we recognize this, we can allow that happiness is impermanent, liable to come and go.

Aristotle's view on the relation between virtue and happiness is not an innovation. It is derived from Plato's *Republic*. Plato does not maintain the Socratic claim that virtue is sufficient for happiness.[25] In the *Republic* the unlucky just person loses external goods and suffers genuine harms by his loss. His justice does not ensure that he is happy, but only that he is happier than any unjust person would be.

Though Aristotle does not comment on this doctrine of the *Republic*, he refers in his verses on Plato to Plato's views on virtue and happiness: "He alone, or first among mortals, showed clearly both by his own life and by enquiries in arguments that a man is becoming good and happy at the same time."[26] Aristotle chooses his words carefully here. He does not ascribe to Plato the Socratic claim that the good person *is* happy, but the different claim that someone is becoming happy at the same time as he is becoming good; and this is a claim that Aristotle himself can accept. In saying that Plato is the first to have shown this Aristotle may be implying that Socrates had not shown it. Perhaps Socrates' life was beyond reproach; but he had not shown clearly by his enquiries in arguments that becoming virtuous is becoming happy. Socrates had argued unconvincingly for the sufficiency of virtue, which Aristotle thinks no one would maintain except as a philosopher's paradox. Plato had argued convincingly for the dominance, not the sufficiency, of virtue. This is the position that Aristotle himself defends.[27]

6. Virtue and Reason

We have seen how Aristotle disagrees with Solon because he believes virtue is dominant in happiness. Why then does he believe this, and how good are his reasons? It will not be enough to argue that being virtuous and actualizing virtue as far as possible is a good in itself. It could be that and still be less than a dominant component of happiness. It is hard to find a direct and explicit argument for the conclusion Aristotle needs. Still, arguments can be found, reflecting different aspects of Aristotle's conception of virtue. In this section and the next two I sketch three lines of argument:

1. The rational agent will correctly value rational agency over its external results.
2. He will correctly value rigid states of character and attachment to particular goals over a flexible character adapted to external circumstances.
3. He will correctly regard as dominant those rational and rigid states of character that secure complete happiness in moderately favourable external circumstances.

Though I will speak of "the virtues," and use examples of Aristotelian virtues at each stage of the argument, it is important to notice that only the third stage defines the specific Aristotelian virtues.

Aristotle defines happiness as activity of the soul expressing reason and virtue. Happiness will require the best activities that actualize the person's capacities; and the best ones will be those that best express practical reason. Hence the virtuous person guides his life most of all by practical reason.

Someone who guides his life by practical reason will want to develop and exercise practical reason in his choice of aims and goals. He will regard these as matters for rational reflection, not simply as the products of nature or environment or unalterable desires.

The same concern for the exercise of practical reason will encourage someone to choose goals that allow practical reason in their pursuit, in preference to goals that do not allow it. This means that a wise person will not choose as his primary goals those that leave little or no scope for practical reason because they depend heavily on fortune and external circumstances. If I see this, I will not choose success in winning lotteries, or any other sort of success that depends almost entirely on chance, as my ultimate and overriding end. I will prefer activities in which practical reason determines the end to be pursued, and the means that will successfully attain it.

If someone reflects in this way about preferable ends and activities, he will come to see good reasons for valuing states of character and the activities that express them. Being virtuous and acting as virtuously as possible are in a person's power; they can be developed and preserved by rational reflection. Evidently the virtuous person wants to succeed in doing virtuous action, and in achieving the end for which he does the action; it is a strange just person who does not care at all about whether a struggle against injustice succeeds or not. But since he cares above all about guiding his life by reason, he will want above all to be just and to do just actions, whether or not he succeeds in his further aims.

Character and action will be his primary, not his exclusive concern. He has other capacities than those that belong to him as a rational agent; and he will want to exercise them too. But he will want to be sure that his life allows the maximum development of practical reason; and it will allow this if his dominant aim is character and action, rather than their external results. If he preferred the external results over the character and action themselves, he would be forgetting that he is a rational agent. For he would be willing to subordinate the exercise of the rational agency that is essential to him to some good that is good for some less essential aspect of him. A rational agent who correctly identifies himself with his rational agency will have no reason to believe he could have been better off if he had been less virtuous; while he might have gained benefits that were good for some aspect of him, he could never have benefited himself more. Aristotle claims that the virtuous person will be "just about with regret" (1166a29). This is not because he will always be successful in his aims, or because his failures do not distress him (cf. 1100b32–3). Rather, he will always be pleased that he did what a virtuous person would do, and will not wish that he had been a less virtuous person; for he sees that he would have been worse off if he had sacrificed the rational agency that is the dominant component of his good.

The argument for the dominance of rational agency and character relies on notoriously disputable (or at any rate disputed) Aristotelian claims about the human essence and its relation to the human good. I do not intend to examine these claims further. They deserve our attention here, however, to show that Aristotle's belief in the dominance of virtue is not an anomaly in his theory. His claims about the function and essence of a human being do not imply that rational agency is the whole of human nature; therefore they do not imply that virtue is sufficient for happiness. But they imply that rational agency is primary

and essential in human nature; and therefore they support the dominance of virtue in happiness.

7. Virtue and Stability

To say that rational agency and character are dominant over other
goods is not to say much about the sort of character a rational agent
will have reason to form. Perhaps we can agree that a rational agent
will not want to abdicate his rational agency if (to take relatively simple
examples) the abdication would increase his sensual pleasure or his
wealth or his power over others. But still, we could apparently exercise
rational agency in the prudent planning for these goods, adapting ourselves to external circumstances, and sacrificing our other aims and
ends to secure these overriding ends.[28]

Aristotle, however, takes a different view of the proper sort of character. The virtues he describes are rather inflexible and rather liable to
conflict with external conditions. Someone with the Aristotelian virtues
does not have just one overriding aim, for example power or pleasure,
to which he subordinates his other aims. Nor does he have simply the
schematic end of happiness, waiting to be filled by different specific
ends suited to particular circumstances. He has a series of relatively
fixed specific ends that he pursues inflexibly even when they conflict
with each other and with external circumstances. He is expected to be
brave, and so to risk his life and the other goods he values; he is expected to be just, and so to face the penalties of being just and to forgo
the advantages of injustice.[29]

Someone with these rigid aims and virtues may seem to defeat his
own ends; for he could apparently sometimes secure his ends more
effectively if he had less of a virtue. Justice requires him to be concerned with the good of his neighbour and the common good of the
community; but sometimes he might secure these results better if he
were willing to be less concerned with them. Machiavelli remarks:
"Hence a prince who wishes to maintain his position must learn to be
able *not* to be good, and must use or not use that ability according
to necessity."[30] Reflection on such bad results of virtue suggests that
someone "must have a mind disposed to bend itself (disposto a vol-
gersi) as the winds and variations of Fortune command it, and must
not depart from the good, when he is able [not to depart from it], but

must know how to enter into evil, when he is necessitated [to enter into it]."[31]

In Aristotle's view, the virtuous person with rigid aims is not defeating his own ends. For he attaches dominant value to having this state of character and expressing it, not to the result he achieves by it. Though he has reason to be sorry that being just does not always achieve its anticipated results, he has no reason to think he should care less about being just; for he is better off being just and unsuccessful in achieving the results than he would be if he were successful and unjust.

But we may still wonder why Aristotle thinks the virtuous person should attach himself to these rigid aims and to the dangers of failure, when he could cultivate a more flexible state of character. Aristotle needs to answer that the appropriate sort of rigidity in states of character is itself an aspect of the virtuous person's happiness. When the virtuous person cultivates stable and unchanging states of character (1100b12–22, 1104b32–3), he secures his own happiness. His stability distinguishes him from the vicious person, who is unstable (1172a9), and therefore lacks the benefits of stability. In saying that the vicious person is unstable Aristotle should not mean that he has a less constant and steady ultimate end and rational plan than the virtuous person's; he is unstable in so far as he is more willing to adapt and sacrifice his other ends to his overriding ends (1167b4–16). Aristotle must show that the vicious person's adaptability is itself a reason for preferring virtue.

Aristotle considers a rational agent planning for his own interest. As we have seen, such an agent attaches dominant value to the exercise of practical reason. He also considers himself as a temporally extended rational agent concerned for himself and for his persistence as the same rational agent. Aristotle wants to argue that the right plans for my future will prescribe the persistence, as far as possible, of the aims, concerns, and states of character that belong to my present self. The more adaptable and flexible my character is, the more readily I will destroy myself in trying to achieve the results I value. The adaptable person wants to adapt himself to secure his own interests. But in making himself flexible and refusing to form a fixed character, he allows less of himself to persist into the future. In adapting himself he partly destroys himself; and hence he will fail to secure his own interest.

To defend this argument Aristotle must agree that the persistence of a person depends in some way on the persistence of states of character. We can see that he agrees with this view if we consider three points in his account of persistence.

1. In a natural organism the form is what persists in the absorption and elimination of matter; hence the form is the primary subject of growth and shrinkage. It is compared to a pipe with water flowing through it, and to a measure that remains constant while different particular quantities and pieces of matter come and go (*de Generatoine et Corruptione* [*GC*] 322a28, 321b24).[32] The particular organism persists as long as the form keeps absorbing and eliminating matter in the right way; the form is "a sort of capacity in the matter" (322a29).

2. The form of a living organism is its soul, the first actuality of the living body. The first actuality is, for example, the state of someone who knows French even when he is not actually speaking it, and the second actuality is the activity of speaking it (*de Anima* [*DA*] 412a22–8). A creature's form will not be its second actuality; second actualities are intermittent, but the creature itself is stable because it has the persistent state that is actualized in these intermittent activities. Hence the persistent state is the form and the soul.

3. To conncct these general metaphysical claims about persistence with Aristotle's view of happiness we must attend to the role of states of character. The states of character that we develop when we acquire the virtues are first actualities realized in intermittent virtuous actions; and they arc among the essential states whose persistence is the persistence of the same person. Aristotle's description of the best kind of friendship makes it clearest that he regards these states of character as essential to the person. A virtuous person loves his friend in himself by loving the friend's virtuous character, because the friend is good in himself (1156a7–9). His virtuous character is essential to him, and he is the person he is in so far as he has the virtuous character he has (1156a10–19). Since virtuous people are friends because of themselves and their character, and their character is an essential and persistent state of them, their friendship is also persistent, whereas the friendship of other friends is unstable and transient (1156a16–24, b9-12). It follows that if someone's character changes enough, he is no longer the person he was, and that if I was his friend because of his former character, that gives me no reason to continue the friendship when he acquires his later character. Aristotle accepts, indeed stresses, this result, to explain the dissolution of friendships; if we were friends, but my character changes for the worse, I am no longer the person you were friendly to, and you are released from the obligations special to friends

(1165b20–36). These claims are reasonable only if Aristotle thinks that the persistence of the person includes the persistence of his states of character.

We are justified, then, in ascribing to Aristotle the claims about persistent characters and persistent persons that support his preference for stability and inflexibility. In his view, adaptability fails to secure my future interests, since it fails in some important way to secure my future persistence.

If Aristotle's claim is to be plausible it must be neither indefensibly strong nor uselessly weak. The adaptable person does not literally destroy himself; he still remains the same person. On the other hand, his choices are self-destructive; less of him persists in the future than would persist if he had been less flexible. His prudent planning frustrates itself if it requires the disappearance of many aspects of his present self.

Aristotle's claim requires us to think of an important aspect of prudence that is not always obvious. On his view, the prudent person will plan for self-preservation not only by ensuring the satisfaction of his future desires, but also by ensuring that as many as possible of his present aims and goals, and as much as possible of their present structure, remain in his future self; the more of them remain, the more of himself will persist. If I concentrate on some one overriding end, I may destroy some aspects of myself. A vicious person who regards his power or sensual pleasure as his overriding end will also have subordinate ends; though these are less important to him than his overriding end, they are not merely instrumental to it. He may, for instance, be somewhat attached to his family and friends, and somewhat reluctant to cheat innocent people. But his overriding end requires him to sacrifice those aspects of himself that are attached to his subordinate ends.

Aristotle rejects this degree of self-sacrifice, and urges a rational agent to form plans that allow him to be strongly attached to the same system of ends. The just person does not have to sacrifice his attachment to justice in order to achieve the good of his community; for the dominant component of his good is not the achievement of this result, but the state of character that is concerned with it. Though we cannot achieve incompatible results, we can retain states of character that include concern for incompatible results. By being rigidly attached to particular states of character and to their associated aims and sentiments the virtuous person secures his own interest better than he would if he were more flexible.[33]

These points about stability and self-preservation explain why a rational agent is better off if he cultivates stable and persistent states of character, and does not adapt himself entirely to circumstances. It does not follow that everyone is better off, everything considered, the more stable his character is. If I have a bad character, then I will be better off if I change it; but changing it will itself involve a loss, since less of my old self will persist in my improved character. This is no objection to Aristotle's view. On the contrary, he will argue that it is one further benefit of having a virtuous character; the virtuous person is the only one who can achieve happiness for the whole of the person who aims at it.

The claims about rationality and stability suggest why being virtuous seems to Aristotle to be a dominant component of happiness. Someone who pursues other goods when they require abandonment of goals dependent on rational activity, or when they require dissolution of a stable character, has forgotten that he was concerned with happiness for a human being and for himself as the human being he is. Finding what might be good for another sort of being or for someone other than himself is no answer to Aristotle's question. Since we could not secure happiness for ourselves by sacrificing rationality or stability, we could never have reason to prefer any other good over these, if we are choosing rationally and aiming at our own happiness.

8. Virtue and Completeness

These arguments may show that rationality and stability are dominant in happiness. But they do not yet prove the dominance of the Aristotelian virtues. It is not clear why these virtues are necessary for rationality and stability. For are there not rational and stable states of character that allow, for example, total indifference to the interests of others? Moreover, is it clear that the Aristotelian virtues are even sufficient for rationality and stability? They are defined by reference to the complete good. The complete good has other components besides rationality and stability. How do we know that the demands of Aristotelian virtue will not conflict with rationality and stability?

Someone who regards rationality and stability as dominant even in unfavourable external circumstances might suppose that his plans ought to assume the worst about external circumstances; then he will not be disappointed, and will not have to change his plans or his state of character when things go badly. But is this the rational attitude?

If two stable and rational agents both have good fortune, the optimist who uses the external goods will be happier than the pessimist who refuses to use them for fear that he will lose them. By using external goods the optimist will realize more of his capacities, will have a more complete and self-sufficient life, and will therefore be happier.[34] If both suffer ill fortune, the pessimist's assumptions will have been proved true. The optimist will fail in his more ambitious aims. But, like the pessimist, he regards a stable and virtuous character as the dominant component of happiness; and he still has this character. He is therefore no worse off than the pessimist.

This conclusion may be disputed. The optimist has suffered failures and the resulting pain from which the pessimist is free. Though each of them has the dominant component of happiness, the pessimist seems to have more of its other components, if both suffer ill fortune, and therefore seems to be better off on the whole. Still, we need not agree; perhaps the optimist is better off if he suffers the pain that results from failure in worthy projects than if he suffers no pain as a result of avoiding the projects. Aristotle claims that some pleasures are bad if they are taken in the wrong objects, even if the fact that they are pleasures is a good feature of them (1173b25–8). He might claim with equal justice that suffering some types of pains is on the whole good, even if the fact that they are pains is a bad feature of them. Aristotle can therefore defend the apparently paradoxical claim that when Priam's misfortunes are at their worst, even so (supposing Priam to be a virtuous person) Priam is better off than a pessimist would be who had neither attempted Priam's projects nor suffered Priam's failures.

Aristotle, then, must accept the view that Tennyson has made a commonplace, that failing is better than not trying.[35] His conception of the dominant component of happiness explains the truth of the commonplace. By attempting a worthy project the optimist has exercised his practical reason to make a desirable difference to the world; even if he fails and suffers pain for his failure, he is better off for having exercised his practical reason in this way than if, like the pessimist, he had decided not to exercise it at all. Pessimistic assumptions encourage the agent to narrow the area in which he can exercise practical reasoning; in deciding not to form a plan requiring non-pessimistic assumptions about external conditions, he makes one rational decision, but denies himself the opportunity of making others. He would be justified only if the failure of his attempts would make him worse off than he would have been by not making them. But he cannot reasonably believe this if he attaches dominant value to character and practical reasoning; for in that case he cannot count the harm resulting from failure as greater than the benefit of having made the attempt.

If there were no practical possibility of moderately favourable external circumstances, the choice between optimism and pessimism would make no practical difference. But if there is any such practical possibility, the rational person has reason to be an optimist, and to choose the states of character and the goals that make the best use of external circumstances. The Aristotelian virtues are intended to be those states of character that a rational person recognizes as virtues when he is optimistic. They never leave him worse off than he would be if he were pessimistic, and in moderately favourable external circumstances they leave him better off. They equip us both to use good fortune well and to face ill fortune without disintegrating.

We can be rational and stable in ill fortune even if we lack the specific Aristotelian virtues, but we cannot be well equipped for both good and ill fortune. Nor can we have understood Aristotle's defence of rationality and stability if we refuse to form plans that carry some risk of failure. Once we see why rationality and stability are dominant, we have no reason to fear failure enough to refuse risks.

9. Virtue and Inflexibility

The Aristotelian virtues of character are intended to secure complete happiness, in the right external circumstances. At the same time these virtues include a commitment to inflexibility; they are stable states of character that the agent will retain even in ill fortune. Their inflexibility is beneficial both in good fortune and in ill fortune. To show that the individual virtues of character meet these conditions it would be best to examine them one at a time. But even without doing this we can suggest and illustrate Aristotle's general view. To illustrate it by reference to the Aristotelian virtues, however, we must grant one further assumption—that, as Aristotle says, the good for an individual includes the good for his family, friends, and fellow-citizens (1097b8–11). The direct benefits of the Aristotelian virtues are often benefits to the agent's community, and the agent himself benefits only in so far as Aristotle's assumption is correct. The assumption and Aristotle's ground for it clearly deserve a full discussion; here I will simply try to show how Aristotle's argument works if the assumption is accepted.

Aristotle's doctrine of the mean applies to the use and pursuit of external goods. Two aspects of a virtue define the two errors to be avoided:

1. The virtuous person avoids the pessimistic attitude that refuses to be concerned with external goods or with any aim that requires successful use of them. He has friends, he takes and gives money, and he pursues honour and reputation.
2. He avoids the over-valuation of external goods that leads someone to be excessively adaptable; he will not compromise his virtuous aims and outlook to secure external goods, desirable though they are.

We have already seen why the first component of a virtue is better for securing complete happiness in moderately favourable external circumstances. Some people are ungenerous with money because they are afraid of losing it and being "compelled" to do something shameful (1121b21–8). But they are wrong. If they fell on hard times, and did something shameful, they would be over-estimating the value of the external goods gained by the shameful action; and the virtuous person, recognizing the dominance of virtue, will never do this.[36]

We might think the second concept of virtue is an insurance policy that will pay off in adverse circumstances, but is unnecessary in reliably favourable circumstances; perhaps it is only our belief about the fickleness of external goods that makes it wrong to be too attached to them. Aristotle, however, denies this. He wants to show that in good times as well as bad it is better to be inflexible about virtue and hence reserved about external goods.

The point is easiest to see with bravery. The brave person willingly faces the loss of external goods when bravery requires him to sacrifice his life. His friends and fellow citizens benefit if he is willing to make this sacrifice. Since his good includes the good of friends and fellow citizens, he is better off being inflexible about bravery than he would be if he were more flexible.

The magnificent *(megaloprepēs)* person is not so concerned with honour and reputation that he spends his money in ostentatious and conspicuous displays; he wants to spend it to benefit the community (1122b19–23), not merely to win admiration (1123a19–27). His reserve about external goods benefits the community; and a community of such people will be less likely to admire the ostentatious person, and so will collectively benefit from their collective reserve about external goods.

Aristotle claimed that the virtuous person will take the right attitude to misfortune because he is "noble and magnanimous" *(megalop-suchos)* (1100b31–3); and his account of magnanimity explains that it is the appropriate virtue for these circumstances, since it controls the virtuous person's relative valuation of external goods.[37] The magnanimous person values external goods enough to pursue them vigorously on the right occasions. He wants to be honoured, but only for the right reasons by the right people, precisely for being virtuous and only secondarily for other things (1124a20–6). He is ready to press his own claims, and fear of failure does not restrain him; for failure cannot remove the virtue that is the dominant component of his happiness, and the value of a worthy attempt cannot be overridden by the harm resulting from failure. Even the greatest external good is small by comparison with virtue (1123b32, 1124a19). The magnanimous person pursues the complete good that the pusillanimous person denies himself; but his interest in external goods is not the excessive attachment of the vain person. Hence he is neither too pleased about good fortune nor too distressed about ill fortune (1124a12–20). He cares less about the goods of fortune than about being as virtuous as he can be, and hence he is not prone to lament about them (1129a9–10).

A community of people who lack magnanimity will be both selfish and self-sacrificing in the wrong ways. If they care too much about external goods, they will be ready to cheat each other, or ready to harm their friends for the sake of keeping up the friendship; for they live "with an eye on another" (1124b31), an attitude that Aristotle condemns as slavish. At the same time they may be ready to harm themselves for inadequate reasons, when the magnanimous person will refuse (1124b23–6); someone who cares a lot about other people's opinion or about other external goods may be ready for some foolish and dangerous exploit that the magnanimous person avoids. This sort of person will be too ready to cultivate the adaptable character commended by Machiavelli. Such a person, Aristotle suggests, may make a good mercenary soldier (1117b18–20); but a community of such people will have mistaken views about the dangers that should and should not be faced.

In all these ways Aristotle argues that magnanimity promotes complete happiness better than any different attitude to external goods would promote it. This does not mean that magnanimity always results in happiness. But its contribution to happiness is inseparable from the virtuous persons' attitude to virtue when it does not promote happiness. If he did not believe that being virtuous dominates the other components of happiness, he would not secure the other components of happiness. Aristotle believes that virtue should be chosen when we cannot have complete happiness, and that it promotes complete happiness; and each of these beliefs explains and supports the other.

Aristotle needs this sort of argument if he is to show that the demands of rationality and stability do not conflict with the demands of the other components of complete happiness, and to show that the rational agent's concern for his own good does not conflict with his attachment to the good of some larger community. If Aristotle's theory cannot avoid these conflicts, then we have to face the possibility raised by Machiavelli, that concern for the good of a community requires an agent to cultivate traits that he rightly condemns as vicious. Aristotle will reject the cultivation of such traits as unreasonable self-sacrifice for the benefit of others; and he argues that the conflict that seems to demand such self-sacrifice does not arise in moderately favourable external conditions. In less favourable circumstances Machiavelli may be right to say that the conflict arises; this is one consequence of Aristotle's claim that the good person and the good citizen are identical only in the best political system (*Pol.* 1276b20–35).

The magnanimous person is inflexible in a way, and Aristotle sees that he may easily remind us of the stubborn and self-willed tragic character who refuses to adapt his views to accommodate external circumstances. When the magnanimous person despises something, he despises it justly, from a true sense of worth (1124b5); but people easily confuse him with a contemptuous person (1124a20; *EE* 1232b9). To avoid this confusion it is important to see the difference between the inflexibility recommended by Aristotle and that displayed by Ajax or Coriolanus.[38] Ajax is stubborn and unyielding in ways that harm himself and others, because he is ashamed and afraid of dishonour. Though he despises other people, and seeks to display his superiority and independence, he is not independent after all; he is excessively attached to honour, which depends on external conditions, and especially on other people's opinion of him. Hence he is excessively afraid of failure and dishonour, and tries to escape it no matter what harm he does to himself and others.

The magnanimous person is different. He will not be like Ajax or Coriolanus, because he will not be so attached to honour or to any other external good. Since he sees that virtue is dominant, he will be inflexibly virtuous. But since he sees that other goods are subordinate to it, he will be flexible in his pursuit of them, and has no reason to be sullen or uncooperative or unforgiving as Ajax was. Though we are right to admire something about Ajax and about his reaction to Solon's advice, we are wrong to admire Ajax's inflexible and antisocial attachment to those particular values. When Aristotle accepts part of the common attitude he also corrects part of it.

Our discussion of the virtues of character may suggest how Aristotle tries to show that the Aristotelian virtues are a rational agent's best equipment when he faces good fortune and ill fortune. Hence they are the best stable states of character to acquire; and someone who has them has the dominant component of happiness.

10. Aristotle's Solution

Aristotle is right to attend to Solon's problems; for his answer to the problem illuminates his own conception of happiness. Solon was right to suggest that happiness is unstable because it is vulnerable to chance and external circumstances. But we are wrong if we suppose that chance also determines whether we are unhappy or not; and we are wrong if we decide to make ourselves adaptable to external circumstances. The inflexible response is right, if we are inflexible about the right things. We should realize that the Aristotelian virtues are the dominant component of happiness, and that, though happiness itself is unstable, its dominant component is stable.

Aristotle's answer to Solon's problem is as complex as his answer to most of the traditional problems of Greek ethics that he discusses. He does not totally reject the commonsense outlook. He refuses to follow the Socratic and Cynic solution that ensures the stability of happiness by taking virtue to be sufficient for it. Still, his solution would appear to common sense to be much closer to the Socratic position than to common sense. Here as in his discussion of incontinence Aristotle first rejects Socrates' position, and then argues for one of its most counterintuitive elements.

Aristotle's view did not convince his main Hellenistic successors, who generally agreed with Socrates. It has not convinced most modern moralists either. Even when they want to agree that a morally virtuous person has reason to prefer to be virtuous even at a severe cost to him, they do not normally rely on Aristotle's sort of argument. Many have thought that once Aristotle rests his defence of virtue on an appeal to happiness he cannot succeed. And even if he succeeded, many would reject his as the wrong sort of defence of morality, a defence that the moral person should not seek.

Once we understand Aristotle's argument, however, we may have some reason to resist both these criticisms. We should ask ourselves again more carefully whether his defence of virtue is relevant to the proper concern of the morally virtuous person. He argues that the virtuous person's proper degree of commitment to virtue is explicable and justifiable by reference to a plausible conception of the good of a rational agent. The conclusion is striking enough to make it worth our while to examine the premises.

Notes

Versions of this paper were read at a meeting of the Southern Association for Ancient Philosophy in Cambridge; Cornell; the University of California, Riverside; Colgate; William and Mary; and the University of Vermont. I am grateful to the helpful critics mentioned in the footnotes above, to others who raised questions on these occasions, and especially to Susan Sauvé and Jennifer Whiting for detailed and useful written comments.

1. For Solon's proverb see *Paroemiographi Graeci,* ed. E. L. Leutsch and F. G. Schneidewin (Göttingen, 1839), i, 315: *telos horo biou—touto to apophthegma Solon eipe Kroiso (i).*

2. This demanding attitude is expressed in Sophocles (Soph.) *Antigone* 583–92. It explains the pessimistic conclusion about human happiness in Aeschylus (Aesch.), *Agamemnon (Ag.)* 553–4; Soph., *Oedipus Tyrannos (OT)* 1186–96.

3. See Aesch., *Ag.* 928; Soph., *Trachiniae* 1–3, *OT* 1524–30; Euripides, *Andromache* 96–103, *Trojan Women* 505–10, *Heraclidae* 863–4, *Iphigenia at Aulis* 161–3.

4. Heroic inflexibility; B. M. W. Knox, *The Heroic Temper* (Berkeley, 1964), 10–27.

5. See Plutarch, *Alcibiades* 16. 3, 23. 4–5; *Alcibiades et Coriolanus* 1. 3, 2. 1, 3. 2 (for *oikeiōs* cf. *EN* 1171a15), 4. 5, 5. 1. See D. A. Russell, *Plutarch* (London, 1973), 110–29.

6. This adaptability and foresight is illustrated in Thucydides' presentation of Themistocles, I. 138. 3, and Pericles, II. 65. 6–6.

7. "Auf jeden Fall ist er weit davon entfernt, Schicksalssichläge in ihren

Auswirkungen zu bagatellisieren"; F. Dirlmeier, *Nikomachische Ethik* (Berlin, 1969), 288.

8. Because of 1097b20 I take b16–20 to be an explanation of self-sufficiency, rather than a third condition. On the sense of b16–20 I follow J. L. Ackrill, "Aristotle on eudaimonia," in *Essays on Aristotle's Ethics,* ed. A. O. Rorty (Berkeley, 1980), 21–4. I also agree with his explanation of *teleia aretē,* 27 f. For a defence of the alternative view of 1097b16–20 (happiness is only the best single good) see A. J. P. Kenny, *The Aristotelian Ethics* (Oxford, 1978), 204, well answered in J. M. Cooper's review, *Nous* 15 (1981), 384f. The alternative view, however, responds to a genuine problem in Aristotle's position, that he must allow the possibility of adding goods to happiness. Eustratius (discussed by Kenny and Cooper) seems to be aware of the problem; for he contrasts happiness, taken to include its more important *(kuriōtera)* parts, with the better good that results from the addition of the less important parts (*CAG* XX, 64. 34–65. 17, esp. 65. 3–8). This distinction allows him to cope with the problem of addition (cf. 98. 19–29). The problem, however, does not raise an insuperable difficulty for the first view of b16–20; see s 4 below.

9. J. M. Cooper, *Reason and Human Good in Aristotle* (Cambridge, Mass., 1975), 125, rightly stresses the importance of voluntariness in happiness, and concludes: "On the view I am suggesting, to flourish is not actually to possess a full portion of all the basic good things, but rather to be living in accordance with principles that are rationally calculated to secure them." In commenting on 1153b19–21 (the rejection of the Socratic position) Cooper remarks: "But it is not easy to see exactly how he thought his own theory of *eudaimonia* could accommodate this insight" (126). It certainly would not be easy to see this, if Aristotle held the view Cooper ascribes to him. But the evidence Cooper cites (*Politica* [*Pol.*] 1323b24–9; *Eudemian Ethics* [*EE*] 1215a12–19; *EN* 1099b18–25) does not commit Aristotle to this view. (See n 19 below.)

J. McDowell, "The role of eudeaimonia in Aristotle's ethics," in Rorty (ed.), above, n 8, 340 and n 26, argues: "If we take seriously *(a)* Aristotle's contention that a persons' eudaimonia is his own doing, not conferred by fate or other people, but also try to make room for *(b)* his commonsense inclination to say . . . that external goods make a life more satisfactory, we are in any case required to distinguish *(c)* two measures of desirability or satisfactoriness; one according to which *(d)* a life of exercise of excellence, being—as eudaimonia is—self-sufficient (1097b6–21) *(e)* can contain no ground for regret in spite of great ill-fortune; and *(f)* one according to which such a life would have been better if the fates had been kinder" (reference-letters added). There is no conflict between *(a)* and *(b),* since *(a)* does not imply that fortune has no influence on happiness; see n 19 below. Hence there is no need for *(c)*. Aristotle does not claim *(d)*; the virtuous activity that belongs to happiness must be "in a complete life," 1098a18 (see s 5 below). Besides *(e)* is consistent with *(f);* the virtuous but unlucky person may not regret any of his actions (see n 25 below), but still may recognize that his life could have been better. McDowell's reasons for *(c)* are therefore insufficient.

10. Aristotle discusses Solon's problem more fully and carefully in the *EN* than in the *EE.* Unlike the *EE,* the *EN* rejects the sufficiency of virtue for happi-

ness at the outset, and explains this by an argument to show that happiness must be complete (cf. *atelestera,* 1095b32). The *EE* mentions the completeness of happiness, 1219a35, but has not argued for it, or related it to the insufficiency of virtue. H. Rackham, *Eudemian Ethics* (London, 1935), 238, suggests that *ēn,* 1219a35, refers back to 1218b7–12, which, however, does not include *teleion.* On *EE* 1219b4–7 see s 5 below.

11. The 1153b17–25 Aristotle remarks that external goods are needed for happiness because it requires unimpeded activity and ill fortune impedes activities. This role of external goods is relevant in a discussion of the claim (not endorsed by Aristotle) of pleasure to be happiness; he does not imply that this is the only role of external goods. (He might, however, construe it as their only role, consistently with what we have said about Bk I; for the activities impeded by lack of external goods need not be only virtuous activities, and the goods whose absence impedes activities need not be purely instrumental goods; we cannot have the unimpeded enjoyment of honour without the intrinsic external good of honour.) Questions raised by J. L. Ackrill and Alan Fuchs have helped me to see some of these issues more clearly.

12. A different view of the role of external goods is ably defended by Cooper, "Aristotle on the Goods of Fortune," *Philosophical Review* 44 (1985), 173–96. I believe he underestimates the difference between the two types of external goods, and gives insufficient grounds for denying that a large loss of external goods will by itself deprive a person of happiness (even apart from its effects on his capacity for virtuous action). Cooper rightly emphasizes that Aristotle thinks external goods are the normal consequences of virtuous action, "so that they should not be counted as goods that he needs as *supplements* to virtue if he is to be happy" (195). This does not seem to follow, however, since the normal consequence does not always result from the virtuous action; and when it does not, the virtuous person seems to gain one component of his happiness, but fails to gain another that is rightly described as a supplement to virtue. Cooper denies this, appealing to "Aristotle's central conviction that what determines the character of a person's life is what he does" (195). I doubt if Aristotle believes this in a strong enough sense to secure Cooper's conclusion (see n 19 below, and text). Moreover, if the right action is sufficient for happiness and the results are no part of happiness, why does the virtuous person aim at them? This question raises an issue about Aristotelian and Stoic ethics that I discuss in "Stoic and Aristotelian Conceptions of Happiness," in *The Norms of Nature,* ed. M. Schofield and G. Striker (Cambridge, forthcoming). I have benefitted from reading Cynthia Freeland's comments on Cooper's paper.

13. The *EN,* unlike the *EE* and *Magna Moralia (MM),* actually avoids speaking of parts of happiness, probably to avoid the suggestion that an external good could be a part of happiness all by itself. See Ackrill, above n 8, 29; Cooper, above n 9, 123.

14. I do not think this passage implies post-mortem consciousness. Contrast K. Pritzl, "Aristotle and Happiness after Death," *Classical Philogy* 78 (1983), 101–11, and P. W. Gooch, "Aristotle and the Happy Dead," ibid., 112–16.

15. This objection to the more plausible interpretation of 1097b16–20 (see n 8 above) is raised by, e.g., S. R. L. Clark, *Aristotle's Man* (Oxford, 1975), 154.

16. In I.10, as elsewhere in the *EN* (contrast *EE* 1215a10, M. J. Woods, *Eudemian Ethics* (Oxford, 1982), 55), *eudaimōn* and *makarios* have to be used interchangeably. Unless they are, the argument of 1100b33–1101a11 is unintelligible.

17. "Unhappy" represents *athlios,* used as the contrary, not the mere negation, of *eudaimōn.* Cf. Plato, *Meno* 78a1–9; Soph., *OT* 1204, Seneca, *Epistolae Morales* 92. 22, mentions the appropriate distinction, between *non beatus* and *miser.*

18. This notion of dominance is used by Antiochus in his defence of an (allegedly) Aristotelian view in Cicero, *de Finibus* V. 92. Passages such as 1100b25–6 might have suggested to Antiochus the distinction between being *beatus,* for which virtue is sufficient, and being *beatissimus,* for which external goods are also needed, and encouraged him to ascribe it to Aristotle. His mistake is to suppose that in these passages Aristotle thinks virtue is sufficient for the happiness that can be increased by external goods. On the relevance of these chapters to Antiochus see Cooper, above n 12, n 7.

In considering Aristotle's claims about the composition of happiness and the place of virtue in it, I have assumed that no revision is demanded by his advocacy of contemplation in *EN* X. 6–8. D. Keyt, "Intellectualism in Aristotle," in *Essays in Ancient Greek Philosophy,* vol. ii, ed J. P. Anton and A. Preus (Albany, 1983), 364–87, offers a plausible account of Bk X. If, however, the account in X identifies contemplation with the whole of happiness, Aristotle is still more influenced by the demand for stable happiness than I allow.

19. For a clearer grasp of the causal claims I am indebted to Susan Sauvé and Gail Fine. Cooper and McDowell rely on the causal claims in ways that lead them to underestimate the role of fortune in happiness; see nn 9, 12.

20. In stressing the stability of virtue as a reason for choosing it Aristotle agrees with Solon, who says he will not exchange virtue for wealth, because virtue is stable, *empedon aiei,* while wealth fluctuates. See Plutarch, *Solon* 3. 2 in *Anthologia Lyrica Graeca,* ed. E. Diehl (Berlin, 1949), fr 4. 9–11. There is no evidence to show that Solon connected this claim with his advice about happiness.

21. The scope of "hence Solon's . . ." and "For nothing . . ." is ambiguous; different views are reflected in Woods's and Rackham's translations. The *MM* passage suggests narrow escape for "Hence Solon's . . ." (i.e. referring to "for each period") and wide scope for "For nothing . . ." (explaining that all the previous points rely on completeness). However, we would expect Solon's advice to explain "one day" as well as "for each period"; it should then also explain "as a child," presumably as an example of "for each period"; in that case the point about children and adults is different from that in the *MM,* which offers different explanations of this point and the point about an incomplete time.

22. There is some difficulty in 1099b5, on which see especially J. A. Stewart, *Notes on the Nicomachean Ethics* (Oxford, 1892), i, 103. Aristotle supports the demand for a complete life by remarking that we can, like Priam, be unlucky in old age, and that if this happens no one counts us happy, *eudaimonizei,* 1100a9. If this means (1) "no one thinks we *ever were* happy," then Aristotle

takes the Solonian view. But perhaps it means (2) "no one thinks we are happy *then.*" In that case the point might be only that we need some good luck, and that bad luck can destroy happiness. If only (2) is meant, the position in the *EN* is consistent and different from the one in the *EE.*

23. It is useful (as A. A. Long suggested to me) to compare the notion of a "complete action" in *Poetics* 1451a30–5, which allows quantitative addition that does not increase the qualitative completeness of the complete whole.

24. Some difficulty has reasonably been found in reconciling this view with 1101a16–21. R. A. Gauthier, *Aristote: l'Éthique à Nicomaque* (Paris and Louvain, 2nd edn, 1970), ad loc, finds the difficulty so great that (following Rassow) he condemns the passage as an interpolation. It is unconvincingly defended by J. Burnet, *Ethics of Aristotle* (London, 1900), ad loc. The question "*ē prostheteon . . .*" is asking "Should we agree with Solon after all?" I. Bywater (*Ethica Nicomachaea* (Oxford, 1894)) punctuates so that "*epeidē to mellon . . .*" gives a reason for agreeing with Solon. In that case what does the "*ei d'houtō . . .*" clause mean? The question is whether "*kai huparxei*" (a) concedes Solon's point, or (b) maintains some weaker condition. If (a), then this whole section conflicts with the previous admission that happiness can be lost, and with Aristotle's earlier criticism of Solon in 1100a34ff. But if (b) is meant, what is the argument, when "*ē prostheteon . . .*" seems to have given an argument for (a)? We might perhaps make better sense of the whole passage by reading "*epei dē*" instead of "*epeidē*" in 1101a17, and taking this to support what follows, not what precedes. Then the argument will be: "Should we agree with Solon (*ē prostheteon . . . logon)?* No. Since we think happiness is complete but the future is unclear, we can't make happiness depend on a whole lifetime. We must insist that happiness can be complete without requiring a whole lifetime. Hence we will insist that it must continue *some* way into the future *(kai huparxei),* but should not require a whole lifetime of happiness." If this is right, then the passage will reflect the modified view of "complete life" that marks the disagreement between the *EN* on the one side and the *EE, MM,* and Solon on the other side.

25. I have discussed this in "Socrates the Epicurean?" in *Illinois Classical Studies* (1985).

26. Aristotle, *Fragmenta Selecta,* ed W. D. Ross (Oxford, 1955), 146. "Is becoming" translates *gignetai.* If we take it to mean "has come to be" Aristotle ascribes to Plato a position incompatible with the *Republic (Rep.).*

27. W. Jaeger, *Aristotle* (English translation, Oxford, 1938), 110, finds "tragic resignation" in Aristotle's praise of Plato because "the fact is that Aristotle in his *Ethics* denies Plato's doctrine that man's happiness depends only on the moral power of his soul." See also Jaeger, "Aristotle's Verses in Praise of Plato," *Scripta Minora* (Rome, 1960), 339–45 (from *Classical Quarterly,* 21 (1927), 13–17). Here (342) Jaeger ascribes to the *Rep.* belief in the sufficiency of virtue, citing the *Gorgias* and *Rep.* I. Significantly, he offers no evidence from the rest of the *Rep.* Jaeger doubts if Socrates holds this thesis, but does not consider, e.g., *Apology* 41c–d, *Crit.* 48b9–10. Here Jaeger's positions on Aristotle's view is not clear (344).

28. In this section I have benefited from criticisms and suggestions by Richard Boyd, David Brink, Eugene Garver, Mark Fowler, and William Wilcox.

29. This aspect of the virtues is well explained by Cooper, above n 9, 83–5.

30. Machiavelli, *Prince,* ch 15, ed. S. Bertelli (Milan, 1960), 65. In such passages Machiavelli probably attacks rigid commitment to Aristotelian virtues. See Q. Skinner, *Foundatins of Modern Political Thought* (Cambridge, 1978), vol. 1, 121, 131.

31. *Prince,* ch 18, 73 f.

32. G. E. M. Anscombe, in *Three Philosophers* (Oxford, 1961), 55 f, rightly draws attention to these passages.

33. The Aristotelian views about character and persistence that I have sketched here are evidently connected with issues discussed by D. Parfit, *Reasons and Persons* (Oxford, 1984), esp. 298–306, and B. Williams, "Persons, Character and Morality," in *Moral Luck* (Cambridge, 1981), esp. 12–14. Not being sure exactly what the connections are, I leave them unexplored.

34. I use "optimist" loosely, for someone who is willing to plan on the basis of something more than the most pessimistic assumptions, not for someone who makes unrealistically optimistic assumptions. In this section I have benefited from Hilary Kornblith's criticisms.

35. "I envy not in any moods / The captive void of noble rage, / The linnet born within the cage, / That never knew the summer woods; / . . . I hold it true, whate'er befall, / I feel it when I sorrow most; / 'Tis better to have loved and lost / Than never to have loved at all." (*In Memoriam* XXVII.) The reference to noble rage suggests a reason fairly close to Aristotle's.

36. 1110a4–8, 19–29, requires us to qualify this remark, by distinguishing what is shameful some things considered from what is shameful all things considered.

37. A comparison between the *EE* and *EN* on this point is especially instructive. I hope to present it elsewhere. There are helpful suggestions in D. A. Rees, "Magnanimity in the *EE* and *NE*," in *Untersuchungen zur Eudemischen Ethik,* ed. P. Moraux and D. Harlfinger (Berlin, 1971).

38. On Ajax see *Fragmenta* 147 (Ross); *Analytica Posteriora* 97b15–26.

2

Aristotle on Virtue and Happiness

Julia Annas

Twice in the *Nicomachean Ethics* Aristotle strongly rejects the idea that virtue is sufficient for happiness. At I, 5, 1095b32–1096a2 he says, "it seems to be possible to be asleep while possessing virtue, or to be inactive all one's life, and also to suffer evils and the greatest misfortunes; and someone with a life like that no-one would call happy, unless they were defending a thesis at all costs."[1] And at VII 13, 1153b14–25 Aristotle says that everyone thinks the happy life must be pleasant, since happiness cannot be hampered or impeded. "Hence the happy person needs the goods of the body and the external goods and fortune, so as not to be hampered in these ways. Those who assert that the person broken on the wheel and falling into great misfortunes is happy, provided that he is virtuous are, willingly or unwillingly, talking nonsense."

Aristotle makes clear just what his objection is: the thesis that virtue suffices for happiness is, as we would put it, grossly counter-intuitive.

We may find these passages unremarkable, both because we are not likely, ourselves, to think that virtue suffices for happiness, and because Aristotle here is just employing his familiar method: ethical philosophy ought to start from and clarify our considered and thoughtful judgements. It does not have to accept all our intuitions, but it should be careful about rejecting broadly accepted views. A theory which does that will simply be implausible. (Cf. 1172b35–1173a2)

Nonetheless, Aristotle's attitude here is actually problematic when we consider his theory of happiness as a whole. This is perhaps a surprising thing to say, and this paper is devoted to making a case for it.

Aristotle's ethical theory does not start just from our intuitions as to what happiness is. It starts rather from the notion of our having a final good, an inclusive and unifying aim that structures what we do.[2] In *NE* 17 Aristotle argues that happiness is the final good, on the grounds that it meets three formal conditions for something's being a *final* good. A final good is complete, that is, pursued for its own sake while everything else is pursued for the sake of it; self-sufficient, that is, lacking nothing and making a life choiceworthy on its own; and most choiceworthy, not just one good among others but such that no addition could make it better.[3] Happiness, claims Aristotle, meets these conditions. (1097a25–1097b21)

These three conditions are technical: Aristotle has to explain them. Happiness, he thinks, clearly meets them; but that it does, that these are the conditions on a good's being final, indeed that we have a final good, are all conclusions reached by argument and philosophical reflection. By the time Aristotle gets to considering what the candidates for happiness could be—pleasure, honour and so on—he is measuring them against a notion of happiness which is not just what he, or contemporary Greeks, were inclined to believe, but has already been formalized in a systematic way by reflection.

It has been held, most influentially by Richard Kraut,[4] that Aristotle's ethics deals with an "objective" concept of happiness, while our intuitions incline mainly to a "subjective" one. The contrast could be misleading if it suggested that Aristotle is importing into the discussion before we start a more substantial sense of happiness than we are inclined to accept. Rather, Aristotle is clarifying and making systematic everyday beliefs about happiness, not on the grounds that they are subjective or likely to be wrong, but on the grounds that they are not very clear. The argument that happiness meets the formal conditions on a good's being final makes our vague notion of happiness more precise and formal. It does not import a different sense of "happiness," but it does go beyond what we would be inclined to accept before philosophical reflection.[5]

When Aristotle gives us his candidate for happiness, then, it is not to be tested directly against our inclinations to apply or withhold "happiness" (or those of the Greeks with *eudaimonia*). The question is rather, Is the life of moneymaking (etc.) complete and self-sufficient?[6] Aristotle's own candidate for specifying happiness is a life of virtuous activity, along with adequate external goods. "What then prevents us from saying that someone is happy who is active in accordance with complete virtue and is adequately equipped with the external goods, not for just any length of time but for a complete lifetime?" (*NE* I 10, 1101a14–16). As Cooper has stressed, it is only in the *NE,* not the *EE* or the *MM,* that the external goods come into Aristotle's considered account of what happiness is.[7] However, since the passage 1153b14–25 (discussed above) is in a book common to the *NE* and the *EE,* it is not only in the *NE* that he strongly rejects the thesis that virtue alone suffices for happiness. It is in fact clear in all the Ethics that Aristotle's conception of the life of virtuous activity has external goods in the picture.

External goods, of course, are of many kinds. There are goods of the body, like health, strength, beauty; goods like money and power; the help of others; good external circumstances like a peaceful and flourishing environment. These will impinge on the good life in different ways, and I ignore their differences only because in this paper I focus on the contribution that *any* of them can make, compared with the contribution that virtuous activity does.[8]

In insisting, then, that the external goods are needed, Aristotle is committing himself to the life of virtuous activity's not being on its own complete and self-sufficient. Why not? This may seem a surprising question. We in the twentieth century, with our impoverished concept of virtue, may find it just obvious that virtue alone cannot suffice and that external goods and good fortune are needed for happiness. But Aristotle's notion of virtue is considerably deeper and richer than ours, and there are aspects of his account of virtuous activity which *prima facie* make it a very serious contender for specifying the content of happiness.[9] Aristotelian virtues are not just disposition to do the right thing, or to come to the right moral conclusion. As is familiar, they are settled states of character. They have an affective side: to have a virtue is to have one's relevant motivation habituated and trained in the right direction. It is crucial to Aristotle that there is a difference between the merely self-controlled or encratic person and the fully virtuous.[10] The encratic will make the right judgement, and even do the right thing, but will not *feel* fully motivated to do it. He will only restrain himself by dint of willpower, and will feel the force of desires and other sources of motivation countering the decision to do the right thing. These motivational forces do not win, but they still make their presence felt. Hence there is no guarantee that the encratic will always judge and act this way; he does so, but not reliably. The fully virtuous person, by contrast, does not have to fight down strong desires countering right action; his resolution to act rightly has nothing to oppose it, since opposing desires have not developed or have been habituated to go in the direction of virtue, not against it. The fully virtuous, then, is reliably virtuous; he has no reason not to be, of the kind that the encratic has.[11] Supporting this point, and most important, is Aristotle's connection of virtue and pleasure. The fully virtuous person takes pleasure in being virtuous.[12] Indeed, failure to get the appropriate kind of pleasure is an indication that the agent is not fully virtuous, merely encratic.

In the context of the present issue the main point of interests is that the fully virtuous person not only judges and does the right thing, but has no motivation not to do it. He is not, of course, so habituated as to have tunnel vision when he considers the situation: he is aware of the factors that can and do tempt other people to wrong action. But he is not himself tempted by them—otherwise he would be merely encratic. And this is not asceticism—he *enjoys* what he does, feels positive about it.

Aristotle himself points out that this will have results that may sound very odd in the case of particular virtues, notably courage. The brave person going to certain death will not only judge that he ought to do this, and do it; it will not occur to him not to do it. He will be aware that he will lose his life, and care about this, and realize that he should care. And he will, when it comes to it, feel the fear that would be normal in such circumstances. Yet this coexists with his taking pleasure— the appropriate pleasure—in acting bravely, and with his not being so much tempted to act otherwise; he is aware of the factors that would tempt the vicious or the encratic, but they have for him no motivating force.

The dispositional and affective side of Aristotelian virtue, and its connection with pleasure, have been widely hailed in the twentieth century as attractive features: virtue is not seen as a Kantian strength of will to do one's duty, as a grim battle of reason against the feelings and emotions, but as the positive and enjoyed expression of a unified personality. It is less often remarked that these features make Aristotelian virtue as uncompromising, in its own way, as Kant's. The more unified the moral personality and the more positive the agent is about acting morally, the more the agent can share neither the motivations nor the pleasures of the vicious or encratic; he lives in a different psychological world. And so, when the agent acts virtuously, it is a real question what, from the agent's perspective, could be said to be lost or given up. The temperate person loses the pleasures of unrestrained indulgence—but he does not share these pleasures, finding them disgusting rather than pleasant, and does not see unrestrained indulgence as tempting. And when we apply this model to virtues like courage and justice we see that the virtuous person will give up external goods like money, health, even life—and, if he is fully virtuous, do so in the same spirit: he will not see the possession of these things as tempting, or enjoyable, if it conflicts with virtuous activity, and he will enjoy the virtuous activity that involves their sacrifice. As John McDowell has put it, in the fully virtuous person the claims of everything but virtue are "silenced" by virtue—a Kantian notion, indeed arguably more demanding than Kant in requiring that the virtuous person still *enjoy* the exercise of virtue.[13]

The cognitive side of virtue makes this uncompromising side even more evident. The fully virtuous person will have developed practical reason or *phronēsis;* though much about this is disputed, it is clear at least that the fully virtuous person (unlike us) will not have to work out, on a given occasion, what the features of that occasion are which determine what the right thing to do is. He will, rather, grasp this; he will just see what in the situation is morally relevant. He also, of course, has and employs what we would call moral rules or principles; I will not go into the role of these here, except to say that for Aristotle's fully virtuous person these do not serve, as they do in some modern theories, as a way of discovering or working out what is the right thing to do. Aristotle's fully virtuous person does not calculate and weight up factors in the same way as the encratic or the non-virtuous person, for he is affectively different from them. It is because he is not even tempted by factors that do weigh with them that he has a clear view of what virtue requires; faced by a situation he can perceive, as Aristotle puts it, the factors that are relevant to right action, without having to weigh up other factors, just because these provide no counter-motivation to him. He acts, then, rightly and because it is right—"for the sake of the noble," simply because virtue requires it.[14] For if someone acts for the sake of the noble, but has an ulterior motive in so doing, he would not be fully virtuous; he would have the motivation of the encratic, for whom the course that virtue requires is not motivationally sufficient. Hence Aristotle stresses that the virtuous person does what virtue requires for its own sake.[15]

Here again we find an uncompromising position: to act virtuously is to do what is noble—what virtue requires—for its own sake and for no other reason. Although Aristotle stresses, as Kant does not, that this is an achievement both of the judgement and of the emotions, and requires something like a total affective transformation of the virtuous person, there are affinities between Aristotle and Kant. For both of them the virtuous agent's virtuous activity is in an important way single-minded; he sees what virtue requires, and does it, undistracted by considerations that might counter virtue and unaffected by the losses of whatever external goods acting virtuously might require—not, that is, failing to notice them, but not regarding them as a loss that matters, not being affected in a way that interferes with the enjoyment of the virtuous active, or makes one think of them as a reason not to do it.

For the fully virtuous person, then, the external goods have no power to motivate against virtue, and when virtuous activity requires their loss this does not detract from the agent's full and unified enjoyment of virtuous activity. This is, of course, what happens in the *fully* virtuous person, not in us, with our histories of conflicts and uncertainties; but it is an ideal that we are to have. It is a notion of virtue that is richer and deeper than the twentieth-century kind. It is also more demanding, and has more extreme consequences.

But now the question arises: when we fully bear in mind all that the life of virtuous activity involves for Aristotle, why does he not consider such a life to be complete and self-sufficient? A life is complete if it is chosen only for its own sake, while other things are chosen for the sake of it. And we have seen that Aristotle's fully virtuous person does seek the life of virtuous activity for its own sake; that is what it is, from both the cognitive and the affective side, to be fully virtuous: to be someone who does what virtue requires just for that reason and for no ulterior motives, without having to battle down counter-motivation. Anything less shows that one is not virtuous, but merely encratic. And, if we bear in mind the features of the life of virtue which I have stressed, how can the fully virtuous person have any aims independent of the life of virtue? He will, of course, seek health rather than sickness, wealth rather than poverty, other things being equal. But since these have no weight, and the loss of them causes no regret, in any potential conflict with virtue, it is hard to see how they could be independent aims that the agent has. A life is self-sufficient, again, if it is not made better by the addition of any good. And, again, when we reflect on just what is involved in the life of the Aristotelian fully virtuous person, we have trouble seeing how the external goods could add any further good to them. The virtuous person will relinquish them in the cause of virtue with no loss of enjoyment in being virtuous; he is not losing anything, then, whose loss matters, or makes the life of virtuous activity worse. Since Aristotle stresses that the fully virtuous achieve *eudai-*

monia by their virtuous activity, far from losing by it, the loss of external goods does not seem to worsen the life of virtue; how then can their presence improve it?

The life of virtuous activity, once we take seriously just how much it involves, seems disconcertingly to meet the formal conditions for happiness. Further, it meets other more intuitive conditions also. Happiness is stable, and the virtues, being dispositions of character trained by habituation, are stable, while the external goods unreliably come and go. They are also the province of fortune; they are not up to us to have or not, whereas, Aristotle thinks, we do feel that happiness should be up to us. And it is up to us whether or not we live according to virtue.[16]

Why, then, does Aristotle not take the life of virtuous activity to be sufficient for happiness? We have seen that he rejects this as grossly counter-intuitive, focusing on our attitude to the *loss* of external goods. If it is absurd to consider someone happy who has been deprived of external goods, then there must be something about their presence required for us to be happy. Aristotle uses melodramatic examples, but this need only be a striking way of making a point which is more general. Certainly it is true that we would find it odd to call the virtuous person on the wheel happy, and doubtless Aristotle's contemporaries would feel the same about *eudaimonia*. But by now it should be clear that it is odd for Aristotle to be so impressed by this point just on its own. His account of virtue and happiness (which I have only, of course, just sketched) is extensive and theoretical; it reflects on, formalizes and to some extent revises, the everyday notions of virtue and happiness. Why should Aristotle be so worried by one of our intuitions on its own?

The Stoics at this point, having been led by pretty much the kind of consideration which I have sketched, make the step that Aristotle refuses to do. Virtue, they say, *is* sufficient for happiness—and, while *on its own* this sounds odd and paradoxical[17] it is not so in the context of their theory *as a whole*. The *whole* theory, claim the Stoics, accords with our "common conceptions"—our ethical intuitions and general notions of what is acceptable. One intuition, or group of intuitions, cannot bring down a theory; we must work harder, by facing the theory as a whole with what we think about a range of issues in ethics. The Stoic claims is that if we do this, the price of saying *in a larger context* that virtue is sufficient for happiness is not so terrible.

Aristotle's analyses in the *Physics,* which clarify and formalize our conceptions of the natural world on the basis of our reflected intuitions, are prepared to throw over some basic-seeming beliefs—that time exists independently of us, that there is a void—for these rejections make sense, and are accounted for, within the revised Aristotelian theory on the topic. But in ethics Aristotle is less bold. He feels himself committed to saving, rather than explaining away, the intuition that virtue does not suffice for happiness, that the external goods are also required. But this puts him in an awkward position; for his full account of virtue makes this difficult to sustain: the life of virtuous activity, when fully understood, seems to meet all the conditions for happiness on its own.

Since Aristotle does not take the step that the Stoics do, he is faced at once with a problem. What kind of contribution *do* the external goods make to happiness? Having rejected what seems the obvious corollary of his account of virtue. Aristotle owes us a clear account of this. In fact he says little about the external goods, and the question is broached only in *NE* I18–10. And what he says is curiously ambivalent, and, far from being clear, is susceptible of differing interpretations.

Aristotle distinguishes two ways in which the external goods could contribute to happiness. Firstly, they are clearly instrumental to the production of virtuous activity. One cannot be generous about money, effective in helping others without power and friends, and so on. It is impossible to do what is noble if one has no resources, Aristotle says, since many actions are performed by means of friends and money and political power, as though by means of tools.[18] But this is a wholly expected and uninteresting role for the external goods, and makes no impact on the claims of the life of virtuous activity, since it does not involve ascribing to these goods any value other than this strictly instrumental one, viz., what they contribute to the living of the *virtuous* life.

But Aristotle also ascribes to them a more interesting role: "when deprived of some things people ruin[19] their happiness, such as good birth, good children, beauty. Someone is not exactly a happy kind of person[20] if he is utterly repulsive to look at or of low birth, solitary and childless, and perhaps even less if his children and friends are utterly evil, or are good but die. So, as we said, happiness seems to need this kind of prosperity too; which is why some people identify it with prosperity, while others identify it with virtue" (*NE* 1099b2–8). Aristotle suggests here that he is hewing a middle way between the unreflective view that happiness is just success and the philosophical view (which as we have seen has considerable pull on him) that it is the life of virtue. But in fact what he says comes down heavily towards the former view; his words here clearly indicate that external goods have value in themselves; when deprived of them your happiness is ruined, even if you are virtuous.

But just what kind of contribution is at stake? Talk of ruining happiness is left vague here, and equally vague in other passages, where he says that the external goods must be present (1099b27) or that they add "adornment" to life, while loss of them "cramps and spoils" happiness (1100b22–30). When Aristotle retreats into vagueness, brevity and metaphor, this indicates that he has not fully worked out the terms for answering the problem. (Think of the discussion of the Active Intellect, and pleasure supervening like "bloom" on those in their prime.) In the present case his studiedly vague remarks on the role of the external goods in happiness have led to two quite different lines of interpretation, both of which have support in the texts, and both of which have recently found defenders.

The first I shall call the "proto-Stoic" view, and has been vigorously defended by John Cooper.[21] On this view, the external goods do not just in themselves have any intrinsic value, or add anything to the good life. Hence the fully virtuous person has no reason to aim at getting them just for what they unaided can contribute. Rather their value is never independent of their contribution to the agent's virtuous activity—but this can happen in two ways. Sometimes they are necessary for the performance of the virtuous activity in the first place. Sometimes they are necessary for its performance in "preferred" or "superior" circumstances.[22] Without them, that is, one may still have the virtue, but its exercise will be in a limited and cramping sphere, and one has reason to prefer a life in which one not only acts virtuously, but does so in favourable circumstances, in which the virtue in question can be developed in a wide and varied range of activities. On this view the virtuous, and so happy person will aim at, and so get, the external goods only in the course of, and as a way of achieving, virtuous activities. He has no distinct motivation to pursue health, wealth, and so on.

I do not myself think that this interpretation does justice to the way that Aristotle characterizes the distinct roles for the external goods, but this objection is hard to press in view of the brief and metaphorical character of Aristotle's discussion. More to the point, the proto-Stoic interpretation involves Aristotle in counter-intuitive positions as regards both the possession of external goods and their loss. When we have them, they make no intrinsic contribution of their own to happiness; what we should aim at is virtuous activity, not the results it may bring. But then what does virtuous activity itself aim at?[23] Virtuous activity does not take place in a void; it will typically take the form of attaining some external goods or avoiding some external evils—in a certain way, of course, viz. from a certain disposition, using a certain form of reasoning, and so on. But how does the virtuous person aim at these goods *at all,* if they have no intrinsic value for the good life? How does virtuous activity so much as get started?

The Stoics meet this problem by distinguishing one's *telos* or overall end, the life of virtue, from one's immediate *skopos* or target, obtaining some non-virtuous good, such as health (or avoiding some non-virtuous evil, like sickness). Virtue, then, is *one kind of* end, the external goods a *different* kind. This distinction underlies much of what they say about the development of virtuous dispositions. Aristotle, however, seems simply to be left with the problem.

Worse follows for the loss of the external goods. For the proto-Stoic Aristotle, the loss of external goods will affect one's happiness only because of the way it prevents one from exercising the virtues. As Cooper points out (p. 189) failing to have good children, or losing them, will affect the virtuous person's happiness only "insofar as it prevents the subsequent activities he might have engaged in together with them," not because sterility is itself frustrating or losing one's children distressing. On this view, indeed, the virtuous person broken on the wheel fails to be happy only because his prospects for future virtuous activity are dim, not because of any intrinsic badness about being broken on the wheel. Further, since loss of external goods does not deprive us of anything that contributes intrinsically to happiness, we would appear to have no rational basis for preferring one loss to another, if the upshot for virtuous activity is the same. (We would have a rational basis only if a difference were made to the prospect for virtuous activity.) Why prefer a painless death, or irreversible coma, to being broken on the wheel? All are on a par as far as contributing to one's future virtuous activity goes.

It is perhaps ironical that Aristotle should end up with these counterintuitive results as a consequence of avoiding the counter–intuitiveness of saying that virtue suffices for happiness. Again, the Stoics face these same consequences of accepting the thesis, and meet them by making further moves which are themselves not counter-intuitive. They distinguish two kinds of value: only virtue is good, and everything else is indifferent—that is, virtuous activity and the external goods have value in ineliminably different ways. There is now no problem in finding differences of value among things which are all equally of no value from a different standpoint, that of virtue. We can rank the external goods as being "preferred" or "dispreferred" indifferents; we have reason to choose some and avoid others, while the difference in terminology makes it clear that they are all on a par from one point of view, that of virtue, or as we might be tempted to call it, the moral point of view. Aristotle, however, does not make this distinction and lacks even the means of doing so. Although he is perfectly prepared to introduce technical terms elsewhere, he shrinks from using them as the Stoics do, to distinguish two kinds of value. On this interpretation the proto-Stoic Aristotle is simply left with the problem, as the Stoics themselves are not.

These problems may make more attractive the other, different interpretation, one which accords better with Aristotle's expressed desire to avoid the counter-intuitive conclusion that virtue is sufficient for happiness. On this view the external goods do have intrinsic value for happiness as well as instrumental value for the practice of virtue; happiness thus requires both virtuous activity and, separately, some at least of the external goods.

I shall call this the "Peripatetic" interpretation, since in later Greek philosophy it was taken to be the position of Aristotle and the Peripatetics, and to be distinctively different from that of the Stoics. Later authors, Cicero especially, regard Stoic and Peripatetic views on our final good as having just this contrast, that the Stoics think that virtue is sufficient for happiness, whereas Aristotle also requires some external goods—and this is interpreted as allowing the external goods themselves intrinsic value as contributing to happiness.[24] It is a good question, why Aristotle was interpreted this way, since it is part of what I am arguing that his actual text is vague enough to be indeterminate between this interpretation and the "proto-Stoic" one. Historically, the answer must lie in Theophrastus' book *On Happiness*. For in this book he seems to have come pretty near to saying explicitly that virtue does not suffice for happiness, since one also needs the distinct intrinsic contribution of the external goods; he seems to have claimed this in the way one would expect, namely by following Aristotle in pointing to the absurdity of calling someone happy who is grossly deprived of the external goods. Later writers read Aristotle's more ambivalent pronouncements in the light of Theophrastus' more forthright statements, and interpreted both of them in the "Peripatetic" way; though it is

noteworthy that when they want to attack the view it is usually Theophrastus' more incautious claims that they pick on.[25]

The Peripatetic interpretation, which has recently been defended by
Terence Irwin and by Martha Nussbaum,[26] may seem the natural and
attractive one, because it puts Aristotle in a less awkward position as
regards the further moves he has to make, and because it is nearer
to our common sense. But problems lurk here also, in this case with
Aristotle's formal conditions for happiness. On this view, I am happy if
I am living a life of virtuous activity and have adequate external goods.
(Let us suppose that we can come to a rough but satisfactory estimate
of what "adequate" is in each case here.) But if having some of these
things is needed to make me happy, surely having more of them will
make me happier? If, for example, good health is required to make me
happy, surely excellent health will make me happier, since it will give
me more of what good health gives me—the enjoyable condition of
well-being, absence of worry about illness and so on. This is certainly a
natural assumption, and it is of course compatible with realizing that
there are limits to what health can do for you; and similarly with the
other external goods.

Strain is created, however, with the idea that happiness is complete
and self-sufficient. If it has these properties it cannot be made better
by the addition of any other good. Aristotle thus has an awkward
choice. Either he has to say that external goods are required to make a
virtuous person happy, *but* cannot make him happier by increase. Or
he has to say that happiness is not complete, since it can be increased
by the addition of further goods. Both alternatives are deeply unattrac-
tive. Again, Aristotle seems to have avoided offending our intuitions
only at the cost of worse problems.

Irwin offers Aristotle an escape by showing how the completeness of
happiness can be so understood that it will not conflict with the claim
that increase in external goods can make the agent happier. The idea
is ingenious and I shall merely indicate it briefly here. Since the completeness of happiness is threatened if increase of external goods
makes what you have a better good, the contribution of external goods
is so understood that they do not give me a better good than I have
when I am happy, but merely increase the extent to which I possess
happiness, by increasing the scope and variety of my activities. Thus it
is reasonable for me to want more rather than less of them, though
they do not give me any kind of good that I lacked before. In Irwin's
terms, they do not add any further determinate good to what I had;

they merely add scope for further determinate tokens of these determinable types.

This is an ingenious and attractive solution; I simply do not see any indication in Aristotle's text that he could help himself to any such interpretation of completeness; and so as far as giving us what is clearly Aristotle's position this interpretation is no better off than its rival—what we find in Aristotle here is a series of problems, rather than solutions to them.[27] Aristotle wants to say both that happiness is complete and that external goods can make an agent happier, and has no obvious way of reconciling these.

The problems are, again, arguably worse where *loss* of the external goods is concerned. For on the Peripatetic interpretation, loss of external goods makes you less happy, to the point of making you lose your happiness. But Aristotle denies that the virtuous person could ever become unhappy in misfortune. At 1100b22–35 he says that though loss of the external goods, if important ones, "cramps and spoils" happiness, still "the noble shines through," and since it is activities which are crucial for life *(kuriai tēs zōies)* no happy person could become unhappy. This is a puzzling claim. We can see how it might be read, as Antiochus probably read it, as indicating that Aristotle's real view is that virtue is sufficient for happiness, while the addition of external goods makes you happier, and their loss unhappier, than you might have been. There are, however, too many other passages running against this for this to be Aristotle's own view. But if the passage is to be taken in a way consistent with the Peripatetic interpretation it is hard to see how we can avoid ascribing to Aristotle two kinds or levels of happiness, one that can be increased and reduced and one that cannot. Loss of external goods would then make someone lose their happiness, but never be, as we might say, *really* unhappy. But again Aristotle shows no signs of wanting such a distinction, nor does his vocabulary suggest that he is working with two senses or uses of "happy" or "unhappy."[28]

Thus the Peripatetic interpretation creates problems over the formal conditions for happiness. Either the completeness of happiness is threatened, or Aristotle should make some moves which he does not—for example, distinguishing complete happiness from happiness capable of increase and diminution, or working out explicitly how happiness could be increased or diminished and still remain complete. What Aristotle says is in fact indeterminate and capable of being read either way; he makes the moves necessary to support neither interpretation. We should read Aristotle, then, not as putting forward either interpretation, but rather as putting forward a view capable of being developed into either interpretation. Because of Theophrastus, Aristotle was read in the Hellenistic period in the Peripatetic way; but there are indications in the way that Cicero at least refers to Aristotle that the matter was not entirely clear-cut; and at the end of a long period of Stoic-Peripatetic debate there was still the room, and the need, for an interpretation like that of Antiochus to settle a continuing problem.[29]

It is obvious that as I have presented Aristotle's view of the relation of virtue and happiness, and the resulting problem of the role of the external goods, it seems that Aristotle is trying to do justice to too many things. Pressed, he should either take a line like the Stoics—but he does not have their more elaborate theory and willingness to sharpen conceptual lines with unfamiliar terminology. Or he should stay with a view which is nearer to common sense on the sufficiency of virtue for happiness—but this harbours deep internal problems when made precise. As I have presented it, Aristotle should choose between two alternatives, but never really does; he give the matter amazingly little attention, in fact, in view of its importance, and what he says is indeterminate to a surprising degree.

Is Aristotle then just evading the problem of the relation of virtue and happiness, the problem which was to become *the* major issue in Hellenistic ethics? It is fairer, I think, to say that he reflects the fact that there is a problem, and that he does not solve it not because he consciously evades it but because he does not see the task of his ethical theory as being that of solving it.

Let us ask ourselves the question, "Aristotle apart, *does* virtue suffice for happiness?" We are, of course, more likely to ask ourselves such a question about morality than about virtue, but it seems idle to deny that we do make sense of the question, and we incline to think that it must have an answer. But our thoughts are likely to go both ways. We are easily led to the thought that of course it is absurd that the virtuous person on the wheel is happy; and in so doing we are respecting the well-entrenched idea that happiness has some essential connection with external success (even if it involves more than just that). But we can also see easily why Aristotle insists that if happiness is to be our final end it must be complete and self-sufficient; and if we reflect on the life of the virtuous person we may be led to think that his life was not aimed at any good other than the one he achieved—acting virtuously—and that in living the life of virtue he missed out on no good that could have improved his life: for he had everything he aimed at, everything that mattered. And this may lead us to the thought that it is not so absurd to call the person whose life ends in torture and ignominy[30] happy, if we think that he achieved the life of virtuous activity that he aimed at. To the extent that we do, we are thinking that happiness really, or fundamentally, consists in achieving one's virtuous aim and securing what matters, and if we think *that* we may allow it to come adrift from the notion of worldly success.

I have stressed very heavily Aristotle's account of what the virtuous life involves, since such an account of virtue greatly facilitates the idea that virtue could amount to happiness, for the fully virtuous person has achieved his aim and secured everything that matters. But the thought does not entirely depend on having such an understanding of virtue; even today, lacking such an understanding, we can sensibly raise the question whether, taken as wholes, the life of Jean Moulin was more happy than that of Klaus Barbie. We recognize that it sounds initially paradoxical that someone could be said to have had not just a noble but a happy life when it ended in failure and painful death; we are respecting the intuitions that so trouble Aristotle and Theophrastus. But if we are led to further reflection on what the people concerned were like, and how they regarded their own lives, we may go on to think that outward failure even of an extreme kind does not settle the question of whether a life which had in it the virtuous basis for respect and self-respect was unhappy. The question is rather whether the person did achieve the overall aim of living virtuously; to the extent that they did, they had secured what matters, which painful and ignominious death cannot take away.

The problem could be solved if we thought consistently that any account of happiness *must* answer to intuitions of worldly success, or at least of absence of worldly failure. We would then be consistent Peripatetics—though we would follow Theophrastus rather than Aristotle, allowing that happiness is in the end a matter of fortune, and not up to us even if we do our virtuous best. The problem would also be solved if we thought consistently that happiness just is whatever turns out on reflection to answer best to the formal conditions, and that we should simply live with whatever adjustments turn out to be necessary to our intuitive beliefs about success. We would then be consistent Stoics. But unfortunately our pre-philosophical beliefs contain both tendencies. We feel naturally inclined both to take our everyday intuitions about success as basic, as determining what happiness can be, and also to reject the judgements that this would lead us to make as to the unhappiness of the virtuous who end up in misfortune.

We can see in Cicero a particularly vivid example of an intelligent and philosophically educated person who is aware of these conflicting tendencies in himself without being able to resolve the tension. In his philosophical works he constantly pits the Stoic against the Peripatetic view of happiness, in a way going beyond interest in mere argument; for him *the* problem in ethics is whether virtue suffices for happiness or not, and he feels urgently the situation of finding utterly compelling considerations on both sides. For every passage where he argues passionately for the Stoic view we can find one where he argues with equal force for the Peripatetic view.[31] This is not frivolity, or indecision; rather Cicero is reflecting the fact that in the ancient world what we would call the ordinary moral consciousness contained contradictory tendencies on this issue, and that arguments on each side sharpened the issues without resolving them decisively.

We are used to the idea that twentieth-century common-sense morality might contain contradictory tendencies—towards both consequentialism and deontology, for example. So it should not be too surprising to find the same phenomenon in ancient thought about virtue and happiness. As Aristotle says, some identify happiness with success and prosperity, others with virtue; the hard task is to do justice to the tendencies that exist in us to come to both of these conclusions. But if we do, we come up not with a nice mediating theory which clarifies our thought and produces a consistent compromise; we come up with two very different and conflicting theories, both of which we cannot accept (at the same time; one can self-consciously switch around, like Cicero).

What Aristotle says about virtue and happiness, I suggest, reflects common-sense Greek ethical thought, which is tempted, for good reasons, in both of two conflicting directions. Aristotle is not evading the issue, but leaving the issue where he finds it. If we find what he says unsatisfactory, it is because we think that ethical theory, even of Aristotle's kind, must take sides in a way that Aristotle does not. It is not surprising that we naturally feel an urge to tidy up what Aristotle says, and to understand it in terms of one of the two competing interpretations I have sketched. But if we consider the texts thoroughly, we will admit that not only does each interpretation have indications against it as well as for it in the text, each lands Aristotle with a batch of serious problems and no visible way of solving them.

Cicero, writing after much further thought on this issue, sees his problem as that of having to choose rationally between two clear and opposed theories. Once one has started to reflect on common sense, one is forced to this position, however uncomfortable. The modern analogue is that of a thoughtful person trying to decide whether consequentialism or deontology is correctly seen as the basis for our common-sense moral thinking. They can't both be right, and yet both are developments of something undoubtedly there in common-sense thinking; and each has powerful arguments against the other. Aristotle's account of virtue and happiness takes ordinary thought on the matter and develops it just far enough so that we can see the opposing tendencies, can see what the Stoics and Peripatetics are going to have to say on the matter. But he does not say these things himself; he does us the rather different service of showing us just what the state of the subject is. In the process he has reminded us that ancient as well as modern moral thinking is a difficult matter, in which we have no reason to think that the ancients were less complex than we are.[32]

Notes

1. Cf. 1100a5–9. Note that in this passage *diaphulattōn* has the implication of more than just defending—J. Barnes' revised Oxford translation reads "maintaining a thesis at all costs," T. Irwin's translation of the *NE* (Hackett 1985) reads "defend a philosopher's paradox." I shall not discuss further the inactivity objection, which I take to be obvious.

2. As is rightly stressed by J. Cooper, *Reason and Human Good in Aristotle* (Harvard, 1975) pp. 91ff. In the *NE* this is the order of argument: we have a final good; this must be *eudaimonia;* but this leaves open what *eudaimonia* might consist in. Although the *EE* starts out by focussing on *eudaimonia,* the notion of a final good is fundamental to its argument also: we should have a unifying aim in life (1214b6–14) and this must be *eudaimonia.* See Cooper p. 94.

3. The third condition is partly a linguistic indicator of the other two, and partly marks an insistence that the final good is importantly different in kind from the agent's other goods. Aristotle does not make extensive use of this condition, and in what follows I shall drop separate reference to it.

4. R. Kraut, "Two Conceptions of Happiness," pp. 167–197 of *Philosophical Review* 88 (1979). Kraut takes Aristotle to import an 'objective' sense of *eudaimonia* which we (but not he) cannot accept because we (but not he) see that it requires "philosophical foundations" in a "detailed and plausible theory" explaining "why people prefer the kind of life which he says is best for them." "[T]he objectivist will have to say what the best attainable life is for

each of us, and he must provide some reasonable way of measuring our distance from this reachable ideal." Aristotle does not provide this; but that is because he does not think that our concept of happiness must be worked out in detail by a theory and imposed on us from without. Rather, we clarify and modify our notion of happiness from within, by reflecting on what it is for us to have certain goals, desires, etc. Kraut's unrealistic standards display an inappropriately scientific notion of the kind of theory needed to found ethics.

5. Hence arguments whether "happiness" is the best translation for *eudaimonia* are likely to be unhelpful in advance of studying its use in particular theories. Aristotle's arguments do for "happiness," in translation, what they do for *eudaimonia* in Greek—they partly revise the application. Any English equivalent is thus likely to sound right in some contexts and strained in others. Kraut makes a convincing case for retaining the traditional "happiness"; though Cooper's "flourishing" at least avoids the suggestions of agreeable mental state which have dogged "happiness" in English since Mill and Sidgwick. See Kraut pp. 167–170, Cooper pp. 89–90.

6. There are other conditions on happiness, which we will consider below—that it be stable, for example—but the formal conditions of *NE* 17 are basic; something failing these will just not be happiness.

7. J. Cooper, "Aristotle on the goods of fortune," pp. 173–196 of *Philosophical Review* 94 (1985). On p. 175 n.5 Cooper lists the occurrences of external goods in the *EE* and *MM* (apart from the common book passage 1153b14–25). I am grateful to Larry Jost for emphasizing the significance of the fact that this passage is in a common book, and for letting me read a draft of his paper on "Moral Luck and External Goods in the *Eudemian Ethics.*"

It is significant, I think, that Aristotle does not see that there is an obvious *problem* here; see below, p. 16. In both works Aristotle discusses *eutuchia,* on the grounds that this is thought by some to be necessary for happiness, and then instead of focussing on its role in anyone's happiness turns to the not clearly relevant question of the person for whom things happen to turn out well, asking if this is due to nature or to fortune. (*EE* 1246b37–1248b7. *MM* 1206b30–1207b18).

8. S. White, in "Sovereign Virtue," Berkeley Ph.D. thesis 1987, examines the roles of the different kinds of external goods in detail.

9. The material I present here is inevitably selective and sketchy; I take it to be familiar enough not to need detailed documentation.

10. *NE* 1146a9-12.

11. Cf. the articles by M. Burnyeat, "Aristotle on Learning to Be Good," pp. 69–92 of A. Rorty (ed.) *Essays on Aristotle's Ethics* (Berkeley, Los Angeles, London, 1980) and L.A. Kosman, 'Being Properly Affected,' pp. 103–116, ibid.

12. *NE* 1099a7–21, 1104b3–1105a16. Cf. J. Annas, "Aristotle on Pleasure and Goodness," pp. 285–299 of Rorty, ibid.

13. J. McDowell, "The Role of *Eudaimonia* in Aristotle's Ethics," pp. 359–376 of Rorty, ibid., esp. pp. 368–371. "[T]he thesis is not that the missed chance of pleasure is an admitted loss, compensated for, however, by a counterbalancing gain, but, rather, that in the circumstances (viz. circumstances in which the missed pleasure would involve flouting a requirement of excellence)

missing the pleasure is no loss at all. . . . [E]ven though the attractiveness of the missed pleasure would have been a reason to pursue it if one could have done so without flouting a requirement of excellence, nevertheless in the circumstances that reason is silenced. And if one misses something which one had no reason to pursue, that is no loss." Kant himself does not stress the metaphor of silencing, though it appears in a model "moral catechism" at the end of the *Metaphysical Principles of Virtue* (under "The Didactics of Ethics"). *Student:* I should not lie . . . Here is an unconditional constraint by a command of reason, which I must obey. In the face of this, all my inclinations must be silent."

14. See T. Irwin, "Aristotle's Conception of Morality," pp. 115–143 of *Proceedings of the Boston Area Colloquium in Ancient Philosophy* I (1986), ed. J.J. Cleary (University Press of America). Irwin emphasises the role of "the fine" (or "the noble") *(to kalon)* in Aristotle's thought, and the way in which it is reasonable to consider this a *moral* concern in our terms. Aristotle in the ethical works proper somewhat takes for granted the connection of the fine or noble with the good of others, a connection which Irwin persuasively traces in the *Rhetoric*.

15. "For its own sake" is, however, compatible with its being done "for the sake of" *eudaimonia*, since this is not a further goal separable from virtuous activity; virtuous activity constitutes what *eudaimonia* is. (But for the claim that there is a tension between these two elements of Aristotle's theory, see R. Kraut, "Aristotle on Choosing Virtue for Itself," pp. 223–239 of *Archiv fuer Geschichte der Philosophie* 1976.)

16. Stability: *NE* 1100a10–1101a21; fortune: *NE* 1099b9–1100a9. I do not go further here into the notion of "being up to us," since it is a Protean notion and demands more lengthy treatment. In some theories happiness' being up to us implies subjectivism: if we feel a certain way, which is up to us to feel, then we just are happy. But in all ancient theories, I think, there is no such implication: happiness is up to us in the sense that if we make the right effort, acquire and internalize the right beliefs, we shall be happy, and this no more implies subjectivism as to what happiness is than the claim that it is up to us whether or not we acquire the right scientific beliefs about the world (make the right effort, and so on) implies subjectivism as to what science is.

17. It figures as the second of Cicero's "Stoic paradoxes," for example.

18. *NE* 1099a31–b2. Cf. 1099b27–28 and 1100b22–30. T. Irwin gives a convincing analysis of the two roles of the external goods in "Permanent Happiness: Aristotle and Solon," pp. 89–124 of *Oxford Studies in Ancient Philosophy* III (1985).

19. White, ibid., p. 83 n. 12 points out that *rhupainousi* is usually undertranslated; it is a strong word implying ruination or destruction.

20. The word is not *eudaimōn*, "happy," but *eudaimonikos*. It is not clear exactly what resonance this has, but Anaxarchus (as A.A. Long has pointed out) was called not, "the happy man" but "the happiness man *(eudaimonikos)*" (D.L. IX, 60, Sextus, *M* VII 48).

21. Cooper, above, n. 7. It seems also to be the view of A.A. Long in "Aristotle's Legacy to Stoic Ethics," *Bulletin of the Institute of Classical Studies,* University of London, 15 (1968) pp. 72–85.

22. Cooper cites the use in this connection of *proēgoumenē* (of the use of virtue) in Arius Didymus' account of Peripatetic ethics in Stobaeus, *Ecl.* II. Cooper rightly rejects Wachsmuth's emendation to *chorēgoumenē.*

23. The objection is noted by Irwin, "Permanent Happiness," p. 96 n. 12.

24. See especially Cicero, *Fin.* II 19, 34; *de Off.* III 35; *Lucullus* 13; *T.D.* V 75–76, 82. (*T.D.* V is, however, a special case, since Cicero is there himself trying to force the Peripatetics to a more Stoic view.) Aristotle is consistently said to make virtue not sufficient for happiness, but the most important factor in it. That Cicero takes this in what I have called the "Peripatetic" way is clear from the fact that he characterizes Aristotle's final good as composite. In *Fin.* II 19 "Aristoteles virtutis usum cum vitae perfectae prosperitate coniunxit;" this is listed among those who "haec ultima bonorum luncta fecerunt;" as often, he compared Callipho, who made the final good virtue *plus* pleasure, and Diodorus, who made it virtue *plus* freedom from pain. These comparisons make it clear that for Cicero Aristotle's external goods add a distinct value of their own on top of virtuous activity; they do not just expedite it or extend its range.

25. On Theophrastus Cicero's presentation of various ethical arguments are again the most illuminating source. See *Fin.* V 77, 85–86: "Nam illud vehementer repugnat, eundem beatum esse et multis malis oppressum." The content of this does not go beyond Aristotle's remarks in the *NE,* which are also fairly pointed; Theophrastus must have been even more insistent in tone. Cicero regards Theophrastus as more extreme than the *NE* (*Fin.* V 12, *Off.* III 56), though he is explicit that they hold basically the same position. Cf. *Varro* 33, *T.D.* V 85 for Theophrastus' position. Theophrastus, however, cannot have been all *that* explicit, as appears from *Lucullus* 134 and notably *T.D.* V 24–25 where Cicero says that it is clearly his view that the virtuous person on the wheel cannot be happy—"non usquam id quidem dicit omnino, sed quae dicit idem valent." However, it is also in *T.D.* V that Cicero regards Theophrastus as the only hopeless case among the Peripatetics, while the rest, he thinks, can be urged towards a Stoic view. It seems that Theophrastus reproduced some of the ambivalences of Aristotle on this issue, but went further towards allowing intrinsic value for happiness to the external goods, and that both were generally thought opposed to the Stoics on this point.

26. Irwin, "Permanent Happiness"; Nussbaum, *The Fragility of Goodness,* Cambridge (1986) chs. 11 and 12. Nussbaum focusses especially on the role in the good life of relations with others, personal and political, which I have not been able to consider in this paper.

27. I am indebted to Sandra Sparkman for very helpful discussion of her objections to Irwin's interpretation.

28. Antiochean interpretations have been encouraged by finding different senses for *eudaimōn* and *makarios*; but Aristotle marks no distinction between these. See Irwin's translation of the *NE* (Hackett, 1985), p. 388 (Glossary, s.v. "blessed"); Nussbaum pp. 330–334. Arius Didymus (ap. Stobaeus, *Eclogae* II, 48.6–11) later denies that it makes any difference which word you use.

29. The generally negative attitude to Antiochus' solution to the problems of the final end is arguably unfair. Antiochus argued that virtue is sufficient for

the *vita beata,* but that external goods were required for the *vita beatissima.* He is sometimes taken to be denying the completeness of happiness; but he can retain this if he allows that there are two measures of happiness, one allowing of increase and diminution and the other not. Even if we do not agree with this as an account of happiness (and it is not Aristotle's) it is an intelligent attempt at a solution to a real problem.

30. I take it that the ancient commonplace of the virtuous person ending on the wheel or the rack indicates not just pain, but a whole series of disasters: capture by a cruel enemy in war or political revolution (since Greeks did not usually practice torture on fellow citizens). Twentieth-century analogues are not hard to find; torture is not a legal part of state machinery in many countries, but the chances of a politically active life in the service of noble ideals ending on the equivalent of the wheel are quite high in many parts of the world.

31. See *Fin.* II 68, *Lucullus* 134. *Off.* III 11, 35. Most stroking is *T.D.* V, where Cicero argues passionately for the Stoic view. On being explicitly reminded that he argued against it, and for the Peripatetic view, in *Fin.* IV, he replies that as a good Academic he argues what seems to him most convincing at the time. An Academic will argue on both sides of a question where there are in fact equally compelling considerations on both sides. In the *Lucullus* passage he describes himself as being torn apart on the question. (As a good Academic he is also prepared sometimes to use arguments to the effect that the positions are merely verbally different, e.g. at *Leg.* I38, 53–54. This does not solve the problem, however—for *what* is the position that Stoics and peripatetics have mere verbal variants on?)

32. I am grateful for clarification to the excellent discussion at the Dayton conference, and in particular to Larry Jost and Stephen White.

3

Aristotle on *Eudaimonia*

J. L. Ackrill

I

Like most great philosophical works Aristotle's *Nicomachean Ethics*
raises more questions than it answers. Two central issues as to which
it is not even quite clear what Aristotle's view really is are, first, what is
the criterion of right action and of moral virtue? and, second, what is
the best life for a man to lead? The first question is raised very explicitly
by Aristotle himself at the beginning of book VI, where he recalls that
moral virtue (or excellence of character) was defined as a mean determined by the rule or standard that the wise man would employ, and
now says that this statement though true was not clear: we need also
to discover what *is* the right rule and what *is* the standard that fixes it.
Unfortunately he does not subsequently take up this question in any
direct way. The difficulty about the second question is not that he fails
to discuss it—it is after all the center of his target—or that he fails to
answer it, but that he seems to give two answers. Most of the *Ethics*
implies that good action is—or is a major element in—man's best life,
but eventually in book X purely contemplative activity is said to be
perfect *eudaimonia;* and Aristotle does not tell us how to combine or
relate these two ideas.

One way of answering the two questions brings them into close connection. For if Aristotle really holds, in the end, that it is contemplation
(theoria) that is *eudaimonia,* a possible or even inevitable answer to
the first question is that right actions are right precisely in virtue of
their making possible or in some way promoting *theoria,* and that the
states of character commendable as virtues or excellences are so com-

mendable because they are states that favour the one ultimately worthwhile state and activity, the state of theoretical wisdom *(sophia)* and
the activity of *theoria*. Professors Gauthier and Jolif, in their admirable
commentary,[1] take some such view; and since they recognize that Aristotle sometimes stresses the "immanent character" of moral action
they find here a major incoherence in this thought. They themselves
seek to explain why he falls into this incoherence (recognizing the
moral value of virtuous actions and yet treating them as "means to
arrive at happiness") by suggesting that in his account of action he
brings into play ideas that properly apply not to actions but to productive activities—he fails to free himself from an inappropriate way of
speaking and from the associated way of thinking.

Professor Hintikka too has argued recently[2] that Aristotle remained
enslaved to a certain traditional Greek way of thought ("conceptual
teleology") and that this is why his analysis of human action uses the
ends-and-means schema though this "does not sit very happily with
some of the kinds of human action which he considered most important." According to Hintikka, since Aristotle could not "accommodate
within his conceptual system" an activity that did not have an end
(telos), he had to provide a *telos* even for activities he wanted precisely
to distinguish from productive activities, and so he fell into the absurdity of speaking of an activity of the former kind as *its own end.*

Mr. Hardie,[3] also believing that Aristotle fails in book I of the *Nicomachean Ethics* to think clearly about means and ends, claims that this
fact helps to explain why he confuses the idea of an "inclusive" end
and the idea of a "dominant" end. Hardie attributes to Aristotle as an
"occasional insight" the thought that the best life will involve a variety
of aims and interests, but finds that the other doctrine—that *eudaimonia* must be identified with one supremely desired activity—is Aristotle's standard view, and not merely something to which he moves in
book X. Dr. Kenny[4] agrees in interpreting book I as treating the pursuit
of *eudaimonia* as the pursuit of a single dominant aim: "Aristotle considers happiness only in the dominant sense."

II

In this essay I should like to question some of the views about the
Nicomachean Ethics that I have been outlining. In particular I shall
contend that in book I (and generally until book X) Aristotle is ex-

pounding an "inclusive" doctrine of *eudaimonia,* and that there is no need to suppose that he was led into confusion on this matter by some inadequacy in his understanding of means and ends.

<h1 style="text-align:center">III</h1>

It may be useful before turning to the text, to make two preliminary points. First, the terms "inclusive" and "dominant," which have been prominent in recent discussion, need to be used with some care. The term "inclusive" suggests the contrast between a single aim or "good" and a plurality, while the term "dominant" suggests the contrast between a group whose members are roughly equal and a group one of whose members is much superior to the rest. When used as a contrasting pair of terms how are they to be understood? By "an inclusive end" might be meant any end combining or including two or more values or activities or goods; or there might be meant an end in which different components have roughly equal value (or at least are such that no one component is incommensurably more valuable than another). By "a dominant end" might be meant a *monolithic* end, an end consisting of just one valued activity or good, or there might be meant that element in an end combining two or more independently valued goods that has a dominant or preponderating or paramount importance. The former (strong) sense of "dominant end" is being used when Hardie claims that in book I (apart from his occasional insight) Aristotle "makes the supreme end not inclusive but dominant, the object of one prime desire, philosophy"; the latter (weak) sense when he says that "some inclusive ends will include a dominant end." It is clearly in the strong sense of "dominant" (and the contrasting weak sense of "inclusive") that Hardie and Kenny claim that book I expounds *eudaimonia* as a dominant and not an inclusive end.

The second point concerns the nature of Aristotle's inquiries about *eudaimonia* in book I. It is not always easy to decide what kind of question he is answering—for example, a linguistic, a conceptual, or an evaluative question. At one end of the scale there is the observation that all agree in using the *word eudaimonia* to stand for that which is "the highest of all practicable goods," and that all take the expressions "living well" and "doing well" to be equivalent to it. At the other end there is the substantial question "what *is eudaimonia?*", a question that invites alternative candidates and to which Aristotle offers, with his own arguments, his own answer (or two answers). In between there are remarks about *eudaimonia*, and about what we all think about it, which could be construed as helping to elucidate the very concept of *eudaimonia* or as moves towards answering the question "what is *eudaimonia*? what form of life satisfies the concept?" It will not be necessary to attempt exact demarcations. But it is important to bear in mind that two things might be meant by the assertion that Aristotle makes *eudaimonia* a dominant end: first, that, according to him, consideration of the logical force of the term *eudaimonia*, and of its place in a network of concepts ("good," "end," etc.), shows that *eudaimonia* is necessarily a dominant end; or (secondly) that, according to him, although it is not part of the very *concept* of *eudaimonia* that it should be a single activity, yet it is in fact so—the life that fills the bill proves on inquiry to be "monolithic" although this is not directly deducible from the terms of the bill itself. In claiming that Aristotle expounds in book I an "inclusive" and not a monolithic doctrine of *eudaimonia* I was referring both to his account of the concept itself—or what one might call in a broad sense the meaning of the word—and to his view about the life that satisfies the concept and deserves the name.

IV

At the very start of the *Nicomachean Ethics* (I. I) we find Aristotle expounding and using the notion of an end, and connecting it with terms like "good" and "for the sake of." He distinguishes between activities that have ends apart from themselves (e.g. products like bridles or outcomes like victory), and others that are their own ends. After remarking that where an activity has a separate end that end is better than the activity, he says that one activity or skill, *A*, may be subordinate to another, *B*, and he gives some examples, cases in fact where what *A* produces is used or exploited by *B*. He then makes a statement that is often neglected and never (I think) given its full weight: "it makes no difference whether the activities themselves are the ends of the actions or something else apart from these, as in the case of the above-mentioned crafts" (1094a16–18). He is clearly saying here that his point about the subordination of one activity to another has application not only where (as in his examples) the subordinate activity produces a product or outcome which the superior activity uses, but also where the subordinate activity has no such end apart from itself but is its own end. Commentators have not been sufficiently puzzled as to what Aristotle has in mind. It is after all not obvious what is meant by saying that one action or activity is for the sake of another, in cases where the first does not terminate in a product or outcome which the second can then use or exploit. It is no doubt true, as Stewart remarks, that a builder may walk to his work. But it is not clear that walking to get to the building site is properly to be regarded as an activity that is its own end. Walking to get somewhere is more like fighting for victory: its success or failure depends on the outcome, and that is its point.

It would be natural to expect that corresponding to the initial distinction between activities there would be a fundamental distinction between the ways in which activities of the two different types could be subordinate to another activity. The idea of the use or exploitation of a product or outcome being inappropriate where the subordinate activity is not directed to a product or outcome, what immediately suggests itself instead is a relation like that of part to whole, the relation an activity or end may have to an activity or end that includes or embraces it. Many different types of case could be distinguished. But, to seek no more precision than immediate needs require, one may think of the relation of putting to playing golf or of playing golf to having a good holiday. One does not putt *in order to* play golf as one buys a club in order to play golf; and this distinction matches that between activities that do not and those that do produce a product. It will be "because" you wanted to play golf that you are putting, and "for the sake" of a good holiday that you are playing golf; but this is because putting and golfing are *constituents of* or *ingredients in* golfing and having a good holiday respectively, not because they are necessary preliminaries. Putting *is* playing golf (though not all that playing golf is), and golfing (in a somewhat different way) *is* having a good holiday (though not all that having a good holiday is).

Now the idea that some things are done for their own sake and may yet be done for the sake of something else is precisely the idea Aristotle will need and use in talking of good actions and *eudaimonia*. For *eudaimonia*—what all men want—is not, he insists, the result or outcome of a lifetime's effort; it is not something to look forward to (like a contented retirement), it is a life, enjoyable and worth while all through. Various bits of it must themselves be enjoyable and worth while, not just means for bringing about subsequent bits. That the primary ingredients of *eudaimonia* are for the sake of *eudaimonia* is not incompatible with their being ends in themselves; or *eudaimonia* is constituted by activities that are ends in themselves. More of this in a moment. The main point I want to make about *Nicomachean Ethics* I. i is that it is unreasonable to suggest that Aristotle is slipping into an inherited usage when in fact he is very obviously introducing and expounding distinctions vital for what follows. Hintikka, in the paper from which I have quoted, seems to assume that the word *telos* ("end") must mean an end produced by (instrumental) means, and that "for the sake of" necessarily brings in the idea of an end separate from the action. But the word *telos* is by no means so narrowly confined, and it is absurd to rely on the implications (or supposed implications) of a translation rather than on the substance of what the philosopher is evidently saying. Why should Hintikka, in any case, identify having a "well-defined end or aim" with doing something as a means to producing an outcome? If I play chess because I want to enjoy myself, is not that a well-defined aim? And can we ourselves not speak of "doing something for its own sake"? Of course an action cannot be "a means to performing itself"—but Aristotle's words are not, like these, nonsensical; and his meaning seems clear enough.

Unlike Hintikka, Gauthier and Jolif have no trouble over action being its own end. They recognize the importance of "l'affirmation par Aristote, dès les premières lignes de l'*Éthique,* du caractère immanent de l'action morale," though they add regretfully that its force is "limitée par les lignes 1094a16–18 et par la contradiction qu'elles incluent." In their note on this last sentence they say: "on ne voit pas . . . comment les actions morales, dont c'est la nature d'être à elles-mêmes leur propre fin, pourront ultérieurement être ordonnées à autre chose pour former une série hiérrarchisée." They call this one of Aristotle's "incohérences foncières." "Au lieu d'être sa fin à elle-même, l'action morale devient un moyen de *faire* autre chose qu'elle-même, le bonheur." I have tried to suggest that this offending sentence may in fact invite us to think of a kind of subordination which makes it perfectly possible to say that moral action is for the sake of *eudaimonia* without implying that it is a means of producing ("faire") something other than itself.

V

Aristotle's thought on this matter is more fully developed in the first part of chapter 7 (1097a15–21), where he starts from points about "good" and "end" and "for the sake of" which come from chapter I and concludes with the statement that *eudaimonia* is something final and self-sufficient, and the end of action. In asking what we aim at in action, what its "good" is, Aristotle says that if there is just one end *(telos)* of all action this will be its good; if more, they will be its good. Now, he goes on, there evidently *are* more ends than one, but some are chosen for something else, and so they are not all *teleia* ("final"). But the best, the highest good, will be something *teleia.* So if only one end is *teleion,* that will be what we are looking for; if more than one are *teleia,* it will be the one that is most *teleion (Teleiotaton).*

No reader or listener could be at all clear at this point as to what is meant by "most *teleion.*" The word *teleion* has been introduced to separate off ends desired in themselves from ends desired as means to other ends. What is meant by the suggestion that there may be degrees of finality among ends all of which are desired for themselves? Aristotle goes on at once to explain how, among ends all of which are final, one end can be more final than another: *A* is more final than *B* if though *B* is sought for its own sake (and hence is indeed a final and not merely intermediate goal) it is also sought for the sake of *A.* And that end is more final than any other, final without qualification *(Teleion haplōs)* which is always sought for its own sake and never for the sake of anything else. Such, he continues, is *eudaimonia*: there may be plenty of things (such as pleasure and virtue) that we value for themselves, but yet we say too that we value them for the sake of *eudaimonia*, whereas nobody ever aims at *eudaimonia* for the sake of one of them (or, in general, for anything other than itself).

Surely Aristotle is here making a clear conceptual point, not a rash and probably false empirical claim. To put it at its crudest: one can answer such a question as "Why do you seek pleasure?" by saying that you see it and seek it as an element in the most desirable sort of life; but one cannot answer or be expected to answer the question "Why do you seek the most desirable sort of life?" The answer to the question about pleasure does not imply that pleasure is not intrinsically worth while but only a means to an end. It implies rather that pleasure *is* intrinsically worth while, being an element in *eudaimonia*. *Eudaimonia* is the most desirable sort of life, the life that contains all intrinsically worthwhile activities.

This idea, that takes up the thought suggested in the last sentence of chapter I, is expressed again in the following lines, where the term "self-sufficient" is introduced. That is self-sufficient *(autarkes)* in the relevant sense which, taken along *(monoumenon),* makes life desirable and lacking in nothing *(mēdenos endea). Eudaimonia* does just that. For, Aristotle says, we regard it as the most worth while of all things, *not* being counted as one good thing among others *(pantōn hairetōtatēn mē sunarithmoumenēn)*—for *then* (if it *were* simply the most worth while of a *number* of candidates) the addition of any of the other things would make it better, more worth while—and it would *not* have been lacking in nothing. He is saying, then, that *eudaimonia,* being absolutely final and genuinely self-sufficient, is more desirable than anything else in that it *includes* everything desirable in itself. It is best, and better than everything else, not in the way that bacon is better than eggs and tomatoes (and therefore the best *of the three* to choose), but in the way that bacon, eggs, and tomatoes is a better breakfast than either bacon or eggs or tomatoes—and is indeed the best breakfast without qualification.

It is impossible to exaggerate the importance of this emphatic part of chapter 7 in connection with Aristotle's elucidation of the concept of *eudaimonia.* He is not here running over rival popular views about what is desirable, nor is he yet working out his own account of the best life. He is explaining the logical force of the word *eudaimonia* and its relation to terms like "end," and "good." This is all a matter of report and analysis, containing nothing capable of provoking moral or practical dispute. Aristotle's two points are: (i) you cannot say of *eudaimonia* that you seek it for the sake of anything else, you can say of anything else that you seek it for the sake of *eudaimonia*; (ii) you cannot say you would prefer *eudaimonia* plus something extra to *eudaimonia.* These points are of course connected. For if you could say that you would prefer *eudaimonia* plus something extra to *eudaimonia,* you could say that you sought *eudaimonia* for the sake of something else, namely the greater end consisting of *eudaimonia* plus something extra. The first point is that *eudaimonia* is inclusive of all intrinsic goods; and if that is so by definition it is unintelligible to suggest that *eudaimonia* might be improved by addition. This ends and clinches one part of Aristotle's discussion, and he marks quite clearly the transition to the different and more contentious question to be dealt with in what follows: "*eudaimonia,* then, is something final and self-sufficient, and is the end of action. However, while the statement that *eudaimonia* is the chief good probably seems indisputable *(homologoumenon ti)* what is still wanted is a clearer account of *what it is.*"

It is not necessary to claim that Aristotle has made quite clear how there may be "components" in the best life or how they may be interrelated. The very idea of constructing a compound end out of two or more independent ends may rouse suspicion. Is the compound to be thought of as a mere aggregate or as an organized system? If the former, the move to *eudaimonia* seems trivial—nor is it obvious that goods can be just added together. If the latter, if there is supposed to be a unifying plan, what is it? For present purposes it is enough to claim that Aristotle understands the concept of *eudaimonia* in such a way the *eudaimonia* necessarily includes all activities that are valuable, that he applies the notion of *A's* being for the sake of *B* to the relation between any such activity and *eudaimonia*, and that it is in this sense that he holds that good actions are for the sake of *eudaimonia*.

Commentators have not, I think, given due weight to these interlocking passages about the finality and self-sufficiency of *eudaimonia*. Gauthier and Jolif follow Burnet in giving a correct account of the latter passage, and they say: "le bonheur ne saurait *s'additioner* à quoi que ce soit our faire une *somme* qui vaudrait mieux que lui; il est en effet lui-même la somme qui inclut tous les biens." Unfortunately they fail to connect this with the earlier passage in which Aristotle speaks of ends that are indeed final yet subordinate to one supreme end, *eudaimonia*. Nor do they refer to this text when considering (and rejecting) the suggestion that Aristotle's general idea of *eudaimonia* is of a whole composed of parts.

Mr. Hardie also recognizes that the self-sufficiency passage suggests an inclusive end, yet he offers the previous sections as part of the evidence that Aristotle's main view is different. Aristotle's explicit view, he says, "as opposed to his occasional insight, makes the supreme end not inclusive but dominant, the object of one prime desire, philosophy. This is so even when, as in E.N. I. 7, he has in mind that, *prima facie,* there is not only one final end"; and Hardie then quotes: "if there are more than one, the most final of these will be what we are seeking." I do not think that *"prima facie"* does justice to "if more than one, then the most final." It seems to imply that Aristotle is saying that though there may seem at first sight to be several final ends there can really be only means to it. But there is, of course, no "seems." The hypothesis is that there *are* several final ends. When Aristotle says that if so we are seeking the most final he is surely not laying down that only one of them *(theoria)* is *really* a final end. What he has in mind with this use of "most final" must be discovered by considering the explanation he immediately gives (an explanation which Hardie, very remarkably, does not quote). For certainly the idea of degrees of finality calls for elucidation. The explanation he gives introduces the idea of an objective that is indeed a final end, sought for its own sake, but is nevertheless also sought for the sake of something else. So the *most* final end is that never sought for the sake of anything else because it includes all final ends. That there *is* such an end whenever there are several final ends is not then a piece of unargued dogma; it follows naturally from the very idea of an "inclusive" end. Such, Aristotle immediately continues, is *eudaimonia* (not, we note, *theoria* or *nous*)—and he then passes to the self-sufficiency point which, as Hardie himself recognizes, implies the inclusive approach.

Dr. Kenny, on the other hand, in his paper "Happiness," actually reverses the sense of the passage about self-sufficiency. He attributes to Aristotle the remark that "other goods added to happiness will add up to something more choiceworthy," and he says that this "makes it clear that Aristotle did not consider happiness an inclusive state made up of independent goods." This interpretation will not, I am convinced, survive a careful consideration of the immediate context (especially Aristotle's description of the "self-sufficient" as "lacking nothing" and his statement that *eudaimonia* is best "not being counted as one good thing among others"). Nor are other passages in which the quite special character of the concept *eudaimonia* is dwelt upon compatible with this interpretation of *eudaimonia* as happiness. It is indeed only if one is willing, with Kenny, to treat "happiness" as a fair translation of the word *eudaimonia* that one can feel the slightest temptation to take the self-sufficiency passage as he goes. This willingness to the fatal flaw in his paper considered as a contribution to the understanding of Aristotle. The pint is important enough to deserve a brief digression.

It may be true, as Kenny says, that happiness is not everything, that not everyone seeks it, and that it can be renounced in favour of other goals. What Aristotle says, however, is that *eudaimonia* is the one final good that all men seek; and he would not find intelligible the suggestion that a man might renounce it in favour of some other goal. Nor is Aristotle here expressing a personal view about what is worth while or about human nature. It is in elucidation of the very *concept* that he asserts and emphasizes the unique and supreme value of *eudaimonia* (especially in I. 4, I. 7, I. 12). The word *eudaimonia* has a force not at all like "happiness," "comfort," or "pleasure," but more like "the best possible life" (where "best" has not a narrowly moral sense). This is why there can be plenty of disagreement as to what form of life *is* *eudaimonia*, but no disagreement that *eudaimonia* is what we all want.

Kenny points out that someone might renounce happiness because the only possible way to achieve his own happiness would involve doing wrong. He writes: "In such a case, we might say, the agent must have the long-term goal of acting virtuously: but this would be a goal in a different way from happiness, a goal identified with a certain kind of action, and not a gold to be secured by action." How would the situation envisaged be described by Aristotle? If I find it necessary to undergo privation or suffering in order to do my duty I shall have to recognize that my life will fall short of *eudaimonia*. But what I *renounce* is comfort in favour of right action, not *eudaimonia* in favour of right action. Nor could Aristotle possibly contrast *eudaimonia* with acting virtuously on the ground that *eudaimonia* is "a goal to be secured by action" while acting virtuously is "a goal identified with a certain kind of action." Comfort and prosperity may be goals to be secured by action, but *eudaimonia* is precisely *not* such a goal. It is doing well *(eupraxia)*, not the result of doing well; a life, not the reward of life. Nearly everything Kenny says about happiness goes to show that the word "happiness" is not a proper translation of the word *eudaimonia*.

VI

On what other grounds, then, may it be contended that Aristotle's idea of *eudaimonia* in book I is the idea of a "dominant" end, a "single object of desire"? Hardie takes the notorious first sentence of chapter 2 as expressing this idea—not indeed as asserting it, but as introducing it hypothetically. The sentence and following section run as follows in Ross's translation:

> If, then, there is some end of the things we do, which we desire for its own sake (everything else being desired for the sake of this), and if we do not choose everything for the sake of something else (for at that rate the process would go on to infinity, so that our desire would be empty and vain), clearly this must be the good and the chief good. Will not the knowledge of it, then, have a great influence on life? Shall we not, like archers who have a mark to aim at, be more likely to hit upon what is right?

It is commonly supposed that Aristotle is guilty of a fallacy in the first sentence, the fallacy of arguing that since every purposive activity aims at some end desired for itself there must be some end desired for itself at which every purposively activity aims. Hardie acquits Aristotle. He writes:

> Aristotle does not here prove, nor need we understand him as claiming to prove, that there is only *one* end which is desired for itself. He points out correctly that, if there are objects which are desired but not desired for themselves, there must be *some* object which is desired for itself. The passage further suggests that, if there were *one* such object and one only, this fact would be important and helpful for the conduct of life.

It is, however, not so easy to acquit Aristotle. For what would be the point of the second part of the protasis—the clause "if we do not choose everything for the sake of something else" together with the proof that we do not—unless it were intended to establish as true the first part of the protasis—"there is some end of the things we do, which we desire for its own sake (everything else being desired for the sake of this)"? If the second part were simply a correct remark—irrelevant to, or a mere consequence of, the first part—it would be absurdly placed and serve no purpose.

The outline structure of the sentence is "if p and not q, then r." Nobody will suggest that the not-q is here a condition additional to p. The one natural way to read the sentence as a coherent whole is to suppose that q is mentioned as the only alternative to p. In that case a proof of not-q would be a proof of p. So when Aristotle gives his admirable proof of not-q he is purporting to prove p; and the sentence as a whole therefore amounts to the assertion that r.

This interpretation is confirmed by the fact that in what follows Aristotle does assume that r is true. Hardie attributes to him the suggestion that if there *were* only one object desired for itself, this fact *would* be important. But what Aristotle says is that knowledge of it "*has (echei)* a great influence"; and he says we must try "to determine what it *is (ti pot'esti),* and of which of the sciences or capacities it *is* the object"; and he proceeds to try to do so.

There is, then, a fallacious argument embedded in the first sentence of chapter 2. But further consideration of the context and Aristotle's general approach may help to explain and excuse. What, after all, is the conclusion to which Aristotle's argument is directed? That there is some end desired for itself, everything else being desired for it. This need not be taken to mean that there is a "single object of desire," in the sense of a monolithic as opposed to "inclusive" end. Indeed the immediately following references to the political art as *architectonic* and as having an end that *embraces* the ends of other arts are themselves (as Hardie allows) indicative of an inclusive conception. If, however, the idea is admitted of an end that includes every independently desired end, the possibility presents itself of constructing one (inclusive) end from any plurality of separate ends and of speaking of the one compound or inclusive end as the highest good for the sake of which we seek each of the ingredient ends.

Enough has been said about other passages to suggest that this notion is indeed central to Aristotle's account of *eudaimonia* in book I. The sentence at the beginning of chapter 2 precedes a passage that points to the inclusive conception. It immediately follows (and is connected by an inferential particle with) the remark I discussed earlier to the effect that activities that have no separate product can nevertheless be subordinate to and for the sake of higher activities—a remark which itself invites interpretation in terms of "inclusive" or "embracing" ends. This being the context and the drift of Aristotle's thought it is perhaps not so surprising that he should commit the fallacy we have found it impossible to acquit him of. For the fallacy would disappear if an extra premiss were introduced—namely, that where there are two or more separate ends each desired for itself we can say that there is just one (compound) end such that each of those separate ends is desired not only for itself but also for *it*.

VII

Up to the middle of I. 7, then, Aristotle has explained that the concept of *eudaimonia* is that of the complete and perfectly satisfying life. He has also mentioned various popular ideas as to what sort of life would fulfil that requirement, and he has accepted without discussion some fairly obvious views about certain goods that presumably deserve a place in the best life. Next, in the second part of chapter 7, he develops the *ergon* argument, thus beginning to work out his own account. Something must now be said about the way in which this argument terminates.

Consideration of man's *ergon* (specific function or characteristic

work) leads Aristotle to the thesis that *eudaimonia*, man's highest
good, is an active life of "the element that has a rational principle." This
would of course cover practical as well as theoretical rational activity.
However, Aristotle's final conclusion adds what is usually taken to be a
restriction to theoretical or contemplative thought, *theoria*, and to express therefore a narrow as opposed to an inclusive view of *eudaimonia*. For he says: "the good for man turns out to be the activity of
soul in accordance with virtue, and if there are more than one virtue,
in accordance with the best and most complete" (or "most final" *teleiotaton*); and it is supposed that this last must refer to *sophia*, the virtue
of *theoria*. However, there is absolutely nothing in what precedes that
would justify any such restriction. Aristotle has clearly stated that the
principle of the *ergon* argument is that one must ask what powers and
activities are peculiar to and distinctive of man. He has answered by
referring to man's power of thought; and that this is what distinguishes
man from lower animals is standard doctrine. But no argument has
been adduced to suggest that one type of thought is any more distinctive of man than another. In fact practical reason, so far from being in
any way less distinctive of man than theoretical, is really more so; for
man shares with Aristotle's god the activity of *theoria*.

Aristotle does have his arguments, of course, for regarding *theoria*
as a higher form of activity than practical thought and action guided by
reason. He will even come to say that though it is not *qua* man (but
qua possessing something divine) that a man can engage in *theoria*,
yet a man (like any other system) is most properly to be identified with
what is best and noblest in him. But it is clear that these arguments and
ideas are not stated in the *ergon* argument and involve quite different
considerations. The only proper conclusion of the *ergon* argument
would be: "if there are more than one virtue, then in accordance with
all of them." This is precisely how the conclusion is drawn in the *Eudemian Ethics* (1219a35–9): "Since we saw that *eudaimonia* is something complete [*teleion,*] and life is either complete or incomplete, and
so also virtue—one being whole virtue, another a part—and the activity
of what is incomplete is itself incomplete, *eudaimonia* must be the
activity of a complete life in accordance with complete virtue *(kat'are-
tēn teleian)*." The reference to whole and part makes clear that by
"complete virtue" here is meant all virtues.

If, then, the *Nicomachean Ethics* addition—"if there are more than
one virtue, in accordance with the best and most complete"—is a reference by Aristotle to a "monolithic" doctrine, the doctrine that *eudai-*

monia is really to be found in just one activity, *theoria*, it is entirely unsupported by the previous argument, part of whose conclusion it purports to be. Moreover, it is not called for—and has not been prepared for—by the conceptual clarification of the notion of *eudaimonia* earlier in the book and chapter; for it has not there been said that the end for man must be "monolithic" (or even contain a dominant component). Thus such a restriction will be an ill-fitting and at first unintelligible intrusion of a view only to be explained and expounded much later. Now this is certainly a possibility, but not, in the circumstances, a very strong one. For we are not dealing with a work that in general shows obvious signs that marginal notes and later additions or revisions have got incorporated but not properly integrated into the text. Nor is the case like that of the *De Anima*, in which there are several anticipatory references to "separable reason" before that difficult doctrine is explicitly stated. For there the remarks do not appear as part of conclusions of arguments; they are the lecturer's reminders of a possibility later to be explored, they keep the door open for a new character's later arrival. Here, however, in the *Nicomachean Ethics*, something is being affirmed categorically, and at a critical stage of the work, and as a crucial part of the conclusion of a carefully constructed argument.

Is there not any alternative to construing "the best and most complete virtue" as an allusion to *sophia?* After all it must be allowed that the meaning of the expression "most complete virtue" or "most final virtue" is not perfectly obvious. An alternative may suggest itself if we recall that earlier passage in the same chapter, concerning ends and final ends. For there too there was a sudden baffling use of the term "most final"—and there it was explained. "Most final" meant "final without qualification" and referred to the comprehensive end that includes all partial ends. One who has just been told how to understand "if there are more than one end, we seek the most final" will surely interpret in a similar or parallel way the words "if there are more than one virtue, then the best and most final." So he will interpret it as referring to total virtue, the combination of all virtues. And he will find that this interpretation gives a sense to the conclusion of the *ergon* argument that is exactly what the argument itself requires.

This suggestion is confirmed by two later passages in book I, where Aristotle uses the term *"teleia arete"* and clearly is not referring to *sophia* (or any one particular virtue) but rather to comprehensive or complete virtue. The first of these passages (I. 9. 10) is explicitly taking up the conclusion of the *ergon* argument—"there is required, *as we said,* both complete virtue *(aretes teleias)* and a complete life." The second (I. 13. 1) equally obviously relies upon it: "since *eudaimonia* is an activity of soul in accordance with complete virtue *(areten teleian),* we must investigate virtue." And the whole further development of the work, with its detailed discussion of moral virutes and its stress upon the intrinsic value of good action, follows naturally if (but only if) the conclusion of the *ergon* argument is understood to refer to *complete* and not to some one *particular* virtue.

VIII

It is evidently not possible here to survey all the evidence and arguments for and against the thesis that Aristotle's account of *eudaimonia* in book I is decidedly "inclusive"; but one question should be touched on briefly. If such is indeed Aristotle's account it may well be asked why he does not state it more plainly and unambiguously, using the terminology of parts and whole as in the *Eudemian Ethics.* One possibility worth considering is that he realizes in the *Nicomachean Ethics* that the notion of *parts* is really much too crude. To say that *eudaimonia* is a whole made up of parts does indeed make it quite clear that you are expounding an "inclusive" and not a "dominant" or "monolithic" end. But it leaves quite unclear what kind of partition can be meant and how such "parts" are put together. Plato already brings out in the *Protagoras* the difficulty of understanding the suggestion that there are different virtues which are "parts" of complete virtue. Aristotle is particularly conscious of the variety of ways in which different factors contribute to a good life, and also of the fact that the distinguishable is not necessarily separable. So it may be that the reason why he does not speak of parts of a whole in *Nicomachean Ethics* I is not that he now sees *eudaimonia* as other than inclusive, but that he now has a greater awareness of how difficult it is to say exactly how the notion of 'inclusion' is to be understood. It may have seemed less misleading to speak (rather vaguely) of "contributing to a final end" than to use an expression like "parts of a whole" which sounds entirely straightforward but is not really so.

IX

I have argued with respect to *Nicomachean Ethics* I that when Aristotle says that *A* is for the sake of *B,* he need not mean that *A* is a means to

subsequent *B* but may mean that *A* contributes as a constituent to *B;*
that this is what he does mean when he says that good actions are for
the sake of *eudaimonia*; and that he does not argue or imply that
eudaimonia consists in a single type of activity, *theoria*. This is a defence of Aristotle against the charge that in book I a confusion about
means and ends leads him to hold that action has value only as a means
to *theoria*. But the original questions are now, of course, reopened:
what, according to Aristotle, does make virtuous actions virtuous? and
how are action and *theoria* related in his final account of the best life
for man? I shall conclude with some exceedingly brief remarks on these
questions.

It might be suggested that Aristotle's answer to the first question is
that actions are virtuous in so far as they promote *theoria,* even if that
answer is not argued for or implied in the first book. But although
book X, using new arguments, certainly ranks *theoria* above the life of
action as a higher *eudaimonia* it does not assert roundly—let alone
seek to show in any detail—that what makes any good and admirable
action good and admirable is its tendency to promote *theoria*. Nor
can this thesis be properly read into Aristotle's statement in book VI
(1145a6–9) that practical wisdom does not use or issue orders to *sophia* but sees that it comes into being and issues orders for its sake.
He is here concerned to deal with a problem someone might raise
(1143b33–5): is it not paradoxical if practical wisdom, though inferior
to *sophia,* "is to be put in authority over it, as seems to be implied by
the fact that the art which produces anything rules and issues commands about that thing"? Aristotle's reply does not amount to the un-
necessarily strong claim that *every* decision of practical wisdom, *every*
correct judgement what to do, is determined by the single objective of
promoting *theoria*. It is sufficient, to meet the difficulty proposed, for
him to insist that since *theoria* is an activity valuable in itself the man
of practical wisdom will seek to promote it and its virtue *sophia,* and
that *that* is the relation between practical wisdom and *sophia*. To say
this, that practical wisdom does not control *sophia* but makes it possible, is not to say that making it possible is the only thing that practical
wisdom has to do.

It has sometimes been thought that the last chapter of the *Eudemian Ethics* offers an explicit answer to our question. Aristotle says
here that whatever choice or acquisition of natural goods most produces "the contemplation of god" is best; and any that prevents "the
service and contemplation of god" is bad. However, Aristotle is not

addressing himself at this point to the question what makes good and virtuous actions good and virtuous. Such actions he has described earlier in the chapter as praiseworthy and as done for their own sake by truly good men. It is when he passes from good actions to things like money, honour, and friends—things which are indeed naturally good but which are nevertheless capable of being misused and harmful, and which are not objects of praise—that he raises the question of a criterion or test *(horos)*. The test is only to determine when and within what limits natural goods should be chosen or acquired, and it is to provide this test that the promotion of contemplation is mentioned. So while here, as in *Nicomachean Ethics* X, the value of contemplation is emphasized, it is clearly not put forward as the foundation of morality or as providing the ultimate criterion for the rightness of right actions.

Aristotle does not then commit himself to the thesis that actions are valuable only in so far as they promote *theoria*. But no alternative answer to our first question seems to present itself. He holds no doubt that good actions spring from and appeal to good states of character, and that good states of character are good because they are the healthy and balanced condition of a man. But it will be obvious sooner or later that this is a circle or a blind alley. Again, it is no doubt true and important that the good man does what he does "because it is noble" and that the right thing to do is what the good man would do. But such remarks do not begin to reveal any principle or test whereby the man of practical wisdom can decide what *is* the noble or the right thing to do. Perhaps indeed he can "see," without having to work out, what to do; and that will make him an admirable adviser if we want to know what to do. But if we are inquiring about the "why?" rather than the "what?" references to the good man's settled character and reliable judgement are not helpful.

The other question—what is the best life for a man to lead—also remains without a satisfactory answer. A life of *theoria* would certainly be the best of all lives—and such indeed is the life Aristotle attributes to his god. But, as he himself allows, *theoria* by itself does not constitute a possible life for a man. A man is a sort of compound *(syntheton),* an animal who lives and moves in time but has the ability occasionally to engage in an activity that somehow escapes time and touches the eternal. So you do not give a man a complete rule or recipe for life by telling him to engage in *theoria*. Any human life must include action, and in the best life practical wisdom and moral virtue will therefore be displayed as well as *sophia*. But then the question is unavoidable: if *theoria* and virtuous action are both valuable forms of activity—independently though not equally valuable—how should they be combined in the best possible human life? What really is, in full, the recipe?

Aristotle's failure to tackle this question may be due in part to the fact that he often considers a philosopher's life and a statesman's life as alternatives, following here a traditional pattern of thought, the "comparison of lives." They are indeed alternatives, if (as is presumably the case) concentration on *theoria* is incompatible with concentration on great public issues. But the philosopher's life here in question as one alternative is not a life simply of *theoria,* any more than the statesman's is a life of continuous public action. To contrast the philosopher with the statesman is to leave out of account the innumerable activities common to both. But it is precisely the relation, in the best life, between *theoria* and such activities—the ordinary actions of daily life—that requires elucidation. In so far then as he is concerned to pick out the philosopher's life and the statesman's life as the two worthiest ideals and to rank the former higher than the latter, Aristotle is not obliged to ask how in the philosopher's life the distinctive activity of *theoria* is to be combined with humbler practical activities—any more than to ask how in the statesman's life domestic claims are to weigh against public ones.

However, there must surely be some deeper explanation why Aristotle so signally fails to attempt an answer to the question how *theoria* and virtuous action would combine in the best human life. The question is theoretically crucial for his project in the *Ethics,* and must also have been of practical importance for him. The truth is, I suggest, that the question is incapable of even an outline answer that Aristotle could accept. For he does not wish to claim that actions have value only in so far as they (directly or indirectly) promote *theoria;* and it would have been desperately difficult for him to maintain such a claim while adhering reasonably closely to ordinary moral views. But if actions can be virtuous and valuable not only in so far as they are promoting *theoria,* the need for Aristotle to give a rule for combining *theoria* with virtuous action in the best life is matched by the impossibility of his doing so, given that *theoria* is the incommensurably more valuable activity.

It may seem that one could say: maximize *theoria,* and for the rest act well; and Aristotle's own famous injunction "to make ourselves immortal as far as we can" *(eph'hoson endechetai athanatizein)* might be understood in this way. Such a rule, giving absolute priority to *theoria,* would certainly avoid conflicting claims: it will only be if and when *theoria* cannot be engaged in and nothing can be done to promote *theoria* in any way that the other value will enter into consideration. However, the consequence of such a rule would be no less paradoxical than the consequences of the outright denial of any independent value to action. For the implication of the denial is that one should do anything however seemingly monstrous if doing it has the slightest tendency to promote *theoria*—and such an act would on this view actually be good and virtuous. The implication of the absolute priority rule is also that one should do anything however monstrous if doing it has the slightest tendency to promote *theoria*—though such an act would on this view actually still be monstrous.

The only way to avoid such paradoxical and inhuman consequences would be to allow a certain amount of compromise and trading between *theoria* and virtuous action, treating the one as more important but not incomparably more important than the other. But how can there be a trading relation between the divine and the merely human? Aristotle's theology and anthropology make it inevitable that his answer to the question about *eudaimonia* should be broken-backed. Just as he cannot in the *De Anima* fit his account of separable reason—which is not the form of a body—into his general theory that the soul is the form of the body, so he cannot make intelligible in the *Ethics* the nature of man as a compound of "something divine" and much that is not divine. How can there be coalition between such parties? But if the nature of man is thus unintelligible the best life for man must remain incapable of clear specification even in principle. Nor can it now seem surprising that Aristotle fails also to answer the other question, the question about morality. For the *kind* of answer we should expect of him would be one based on a thesis about the *nature* of man, and no satisfactory account of that kind *can* be given while the nature of man remains obscure and mysterious.

Aristotle is, of course, in good company—in the company of all philosophers who hold that one element in man is supremely valuable, but are unwilling to embrace the paradoxical and extremist conclusions about life that that view implies. And a parallel difficulty is felt in many religions by the enthusiastic. How can the true believer justify taking any thought for the future or devoting any attention to the problems and pleasures of this mortal life? *Sub specie aeternitatis* are not such daily concerns of infinitely little importance? In fact compromises are made, and theologians explain that nobody need feel guilty at making them. But the suspicion remains that a man who really believed in the supreme importance of some absolute could not continue to live in much the same way as others.

Notes

1. R. A. Gauthier and J. Y. Jolif (1958), *Le'Éthique à Nicomaque,* Paris-Louvain. Quotations are from volume ii, pp. 5–7, 199, 574, 886.

2. J. Hintikka (1973), "Remarks on Praxis, Poiesis, and Ergon in Plato and in Aristotle," in *Annales Universitatis Turkuensis* Sarja—Series B Osa–Tom. 126 *(Studia philosophica in honorem Sven Krohn),* Turku. Quotations are from pp. 54, 55, 58.

3. W. F. R. Hardie (1965), "The Final Good in Aristotle's Ethics," in *Philosophy,* xl. Quotations are from pp. 277 and 279. (See also Hardie's *Aristotle's Ethical Theory,* Oxford, 1968, especially chapter II.)

4. A. Kenny (1965–6). "Happiness," in *Proceedings of the Aristotelian Society,* 66. Quotations are from pp. 99 and 101.

4

Aristotle on the Human Good: An Overview

Richard Kraut

1. Is Happiness All-Inclusive?

How broad is Aristotle's conception of happiness in the *Nicomachean Ethics*? Does he take *eudaimonia*[1] to consist in one good alone, or does he instead equate it with a composite of all intrinsic goods? Or does he perhaps waver between a broad and narrow view? In this paper, I argue that he consistently adheres to the thesis that happiness consists in just one type of good—virtuous activity—though I also hope to show that calling this account of the human good "narrow" is misleading. Aristotle thinks that a well-lived human life will be endowed with a rich variety of goods, but that nonetheless it will have a single focus. But before we enter the details of this debate, let us review some familiar and incontestable points.

When Aristotle asks what the human good is, he is seeking something that we desire (and rightly desire) for its own sake and not for the sake of anything else. Furthermore, such a good is that for the sake of which all other goods are desired. It is, in other words, at the top of a hierarchy of ends; lesser goods are sought for its sake, but it is desirable solely for itself and not for the sake of anything else. Aristotle's goal in Book I of the *NE* is to determine whether anything properly occupies this position in human life, and if so, what it is.

He notes (I.4 1095a17–20) that there is general agreement about what to call such a good: it is living well, or doing well, or *eudaimonia*. No one seeks to live well for the sake of some further goal; rather it is by itself the intrinsically desired end for the sake of which we do everything else. But although Aristotle expects there to be general agreement about the ultimate value of *eudaimonia*, he realizes that there is deep disagreement about what happiness or living well consists in. Some say it is pleasure; others wealth, or honor, or virtue. But he thinks that these proposed conceptions of happiness are superficial, and quickly rejects each in turn. What answer does he propose in their place?

According to one interpretation of the *NE*, Aristotle's chief insight into human well-being is that we must not make any single kind of good our ultimate end, because *eudaimonia* is a composite of many different kinds of goods.[2] The underlying idea that this interpretation attributes to Aristotle is quite simple, at least on the surface: the more goods one has, the better off one is—assuming those goods are worth having in themselves. Someone who attains only one intrinsically desirable goal is not as well off as someone else who has attained not only that same goal but another besides.[3] And therefore the best possible life must be the one in which we possess the greatest number of goods. The ultimate end, then, is an all-inclusive aggregate. Noncomposite goods of which such a whole consists are individually inferior to the whole, and are to be sought for its sake. Pleasure, for example, is desirable not only for itself but also for the sake of living well, because living well is a whole of which pleasure is a part.[4]

It is easy to see why this strikes some as an attractive interpretation. To begin with, the idea that more goods are better than fewer seems unassailable. Why should one settle for a smaller number of goods, when one can have those same goods and more?[5] Another appealing and closely related idea is that we should partake of all that human life has to offer. If one's life entirely lacks something that is intrinsically desirable, one is not living as well as one might.[6] Furthermore—and here we turn to a textual point—it is undeniable that according to Aristotle any human being who is living well must enjoy a wide variety of goods: He must, for example, experience pleasure, have friends, practice virtue, receive honor, and so on. So, for both philosophical and textual reasons, it is difficult to resist the temptation to take him to believe that *eudaimonia* consists in the collection of all of the different kinds of goods that make up a well-lived life.

But the most important evidence for such a reading is a passage in which Aristotle seems to be arriving at this simple and appealing conception of happiness as an all-inclusive whole. The passage deserves careful attention because it is found precisely in the chapter (I.7) where Aristotle seeks to improve upon the defective conceptions of happiness that he has criticized earlier. It seems to be no mere aside or after-thought, but can with some plausibility be regarded as central to his whole argument. The crucial part of this passage reads as follows:

> The self-sufficient we posit as that which when taken by itself makes life choiceworthy and in need of nothing. Such we think happiness to be. Furthermore, it is the most choiceworthy of all, without being counted in addition—being counted in addition, it is obviously more choiceworthy [when taken] with the least of goods. For what is added on is an increase of goods, and of goods the greater is always more choiceworthy. (1097b14–20)[7]

Aristotle's thought is not entirely clear, but if we begin with his final words—"of goods the greater is always more choiceworthy"—a plausible reading suggests itself. Here Aristotle formulates the simple thought described in the preceding paragraph: It is always better to have more goods than fewer, and so the composite good that consists of A plus B is always better than either A or B alone. Accordingly, when he defines self-sufficiency in the first sentence, he must mean that the composite of all goods (or, more precisely, all intrinsic goods) must be something that cannot be improved upon. That all-inclusive aggregate makes life "in need of nothing" precisely because it consists of everything that is intrinsically desirable.

Moving to the next portion of the passage, we can now make sense of the idea that happiness is most choiceworthy "without being counted in addition." The good that *is* most choiceworthy "being counted in addition" is the single noncomposite good that happens to be better than any other such noncomposite good. When complex goods are disaggregated into their components, the single atomic part that is better than all other such parts is the one that is most desirable "being counted in addition." And Aristotle's point in this passage seems to be that the superiority of happiness to all other goods should not be looked upon in this way. For if it were merely the single best non-composite good, it could be improved upon by being combined "with the least of goods." It must therefore be most choiceworthy in a different way: its superiority must result from the fact it already contains all intrinsic goods, so that nothing outside it can be combined with it to make it more desirable.

2. The Unity of the Highest Good

But if we interpret Aristotle in this way, we immediately encounter a severe textual difficulty. For soon after the passage cited above, he begins to present his well-known argument that we can discover the good for human beings by determining whether they have an *ergon* ("function," "task"), and if they do, what it is. Our task, he claims, cannot be something we share with plants or other animals—it cannot, for example, be nourishment, or growth, or perception. Aristotle soon arrives at the idea that the human *ergon*, and therefore the human good, consists in activity of the rational soul in accordance with virtue (1098a16–18). This formula seems to be saying that happiness consists not in a composite of goods—not in an aggregate composed of virtue, honor, friends, pleasure, and so on—but in just one type of good, namely, virtuous activity. Perhaps excellent activity is a good that can be analyzed into a number of different components (for example: acts of justice, courage, and the like). But surely such activity is not an all-inclusive whole; it is just one type of good, not an aggregate of honor, pleasure, and the rest. And this conflicts with our reading of the earlier passage (1097b14–20), which we tentatively took to mean that happiness is a composite of all the intrinsic goods.

When we look at Aristotle's attempt to confirm his conception of happiness, in the chapters immediately following I.7, we find further indications that he is not equating the ultimate end with a composite of all intrinsic goods, but with virtuous activity alone. For example, he notes in I.8 that his theory identifies the end with activities of the soul rather than with goods of the body or external goods (1098b12–20). Were he treating happiness as a composite of health, physical pleasure, friends, honors, virtuous activities, and the like, then surely he ought to say that happiness, as he conceives it, is not only a good of the soul *but also* an external good as well as a good of the body. Similarly, were he treating happiness as a composite that includes both virtue and virtuous activity, he would not have said that his theory identifies happiness with an activity *rather than* a state.[8] We should have expected him to say that happiness is both an activity *and* a state, because it is a composite that embraces all intrinsic goods, including virtue and virtuous activity. The fact that he consistently says that happiness, properly understood, consists in activity rather than a state suggests that he does not regard it as a composite of all intrinsic goods.

In order to avoid confusion, it is important to emphasize at this point that of course Aristotle believes that the happy person must have many different types of goods, and cannot live well in the absence of external resources. But we must be careful not to infer that since a happy person must have all sorts of goods, including external and bodily goods, happiness itself consists in all of these different types of goods. "What is happiness?" is a question about what lies at the top of the hierarchy of goods. If we take Aristotle to place virtuous activity alone at the top of that hierarchy, it remains open to him to say that in order to become and remain active as a virtuous person, one must possess many resources.[9] Some of those resources may be desirable in themselves, but they are nonetheless subordinate rather than ultimate ends, because they are also desirable for the sake of virtuous activity. So even though a happy person must possess many intrinsic goods, that does not by itself show that happiness itself—the ultimate end—includes them all.

We should therefore be on guard not to misinterpret one of the fullest and clearest statements Aristotle makes in *NE* Book I about his conception of happiness. At I.10 1101a14–16, he says, "What then prevents us from saying that a happy person is someone who is active in accordance with perfect virtue and who is sufficiently equipped with external good, not for some chance period of time, but for a complete life?" Here and elsewhere Aristotle unequivocally affirms that a life cannot be happy if it lacks external resources.[10] But it is crucial to realize that this passage and others like it do not show that those external resources are themselves components of the ultimate end of a happy life. Rather, our passage is compatible with saying—indeed it implies— that such external goods are desirable for the sake of virtuous activity, and that they therefore lack one of the characteristics of the highest good. They are subordinate goods because of their status as resources: they are desirable in part for the sake of something else.

If we go outside the *Nicomachean Ethics*, and look at Aristotle's other writings, we do not find any passage that expresses or commits him to the view that happiness is a composite of all intrinsic goods.[11] What we find instead—in the *Politics*—is a clear indication that happiness consists in goods of the soul alone. At VII.1 1323b21–6, he says: "Let us agree, then, that each person has just as much happiness as he has virtue and wisdom and action in accordance with them. We use the god as evidence: He is happy and blessed not because of the external goods but because of himself." The quantity of external goods one has is not to be counted in any reckoning of how well-off one is, because happiness does not consist in such goods, but in goods of the soul alone. And as we have seen, we find this identification of happiness with a restricted set of goods in the *NE* as well.

Nonetheless, it might be wondered whether Aristotle sometimes wavers. After all, wc earlier looked at a passage in *NE* I.7 (1097b14–20) that tells us that more goods are better than fewer; and we were tempted to say that Aristotle uses this premise to infer that the best good is the one that results from the aggregation of all intrinsic goods. If we let that interpretation stand, we must conclude that Aristotle contradicts himself in *NE* I.7. So now we must ask: Is there an alternative way to read that passage? Recall what it says:

> The self-sufficient we posit as that which when taken by itself makes life choiceworthy and in need of nothing. Such we think happiness to be. Furthermore, it is the most choiceworthy of all, without being counted in addition—being counted in addition, it is obviously more choiceworthy [when taken] with the least of goods. For what is added on is an increase of goods, and of goods the greater is always more choiceworthy. (1097b14–20)

Another way to put Aristotle's point, when he says "of goods the greater is always most choiceworthy," would be this: If A is a good and B is a different good, then it is better to have A and B than to have either alone. But notice that in putting the point in this way, we have to be careful to make a distinction between something being *a* good and its being *the* good. (Recall that this is a distinction Aristotle makes at the beginning of the *NE*; see I.1 1094a1–3.) If A is desirable for the sake of something else, then it cannot be *the* good, although it may be a good, and it may even be good in itself. So, if virtuous activity is just a good but not the good, then we can arrive at a more desirable good by combining it with something else that also counts as a good. If virtuous activity is just a good and honor is just a good, then the combination of the two of them is more desirable than either alone.

When we put Aristotle's point in this way, we leave room for the fact that he does not treat virtuous activity as just one good alongside many others. As we have seen, he takes the good to consist in virtuous activity alone; it is *the* good, not just a good, because everything else is to be sought for its sake. Were we to say that virtuous activity is better than every other type of good and therefore the single best good, we would not have said enough to elucidate its great importance. It is not just a good that happens to be better than every other, taken in pairwise comparisons. It should occupy a more special place in our lives than that. For if it were just the single best good in such comparisons, then no matter how virtuous we are, our lives would be improved by adding even the smallest of goods. No matter how just and courageous someone is, no matter how much he devotes himself to the well-being of his community by performing virtuous acts, his life would not be as good as that of someone who did all of that and in addition enjoyed the taste of a rare delicacy. The point Aristotle is making in the passage we are examining is simply that anyone who thinks of virtue (or any other good) as being susceptible to this kind of improvement is not identifying it with happiness, but is merely naming one component of happiness that can be improved upon by being supplemented by other goods. If one were to take this view of virtuous activity, then one would not say of it, "taken by itself [it] makes life choiceworthy and in need of nothing."

So read, our passage (1097b14–20) leaves it entirely open whether happiness consists in one good or many. Its purpose is not to decide this question, but rather to make a conceptual point that does not by itself yield a substantive view about which good or goods are included in happiness. Its central point is that there is a special way in which happiness (whatever it turns out to be) is the most desirable good there is. It is not merely better than every other good; rather, it is so good that it cannot be improved upon. Accordingly, whatever the correct conception of happiness turns out to be, it must equate happiness with a good that is beyond improvement. Should it turn out that happiness is a composite of all intrinsic goods, then that would mean that no single component of that composite passes Aristotle's test for happiness; the only thing that passes the test would in that case be the whole aggregate.

But as it happens, that is not the conception of happiness that Aristotle chooses to defend. As we have seen, he thinks that we *should* equate happiness with a single type of good—virtuous activity of the rational soul—because he is prepared to defend the view that such activity is beyond improvement. Someone who is perfectly virtuous and who fully engages in virtuous activity over the whole course of his life thereby has something that is as desirable as can be. In order to lead his life at this high level, he must of course have many other goods that are subordinate to virtue. He must have health, strength, honor, friends, and the like; otherwise his virtuous activity would be diminished to some extent. But his possession of these other goods is not to be thought of as making his life even more desirable than it is already made by his virtuous activity. These resources sustain his virtuous activity but do not increase its value. They do not make his life any more desirable than it already is by virtue of his excellent rational activity.

3. The Philosophical Life

Now that we have rejected the idea that Aristotle treats happiness as a composite of all intrinsic goods, we are in a position to take a fresh look at a question that has sometimes troubled readers of the *Nicomachean Ethics*. The problem is whether his defense of the philosophical life in X.7–8 radically departs from the whole framework of his ethical theory.[12] The main thesis of those late chapters is one that Aristotle states several times: Perfect happiness consists in just one good—*theoria* (contemplation), the actualization of theoretical wisdom.[13] It has seemed to some students of his ethical theory that this is a bizarre repudiation of all that he has said before. And the appearance of contradiction is certainly strong—if we make the assumption that according to Book I of the *NE* (and the remainder of the treatise prior to X.7–8), happiness is an all-inclusive composite. For how can perfect happiness consist in just one good, when happiness includes all intrinsic goods?

One might try to save Aristotle from self-contradiction by taking *teleia eudaimonia* ("perfect happiness") to be the phrase he uses for the best single component of the all-inclusive composite that he identifies with happiness.[14] There is no decisive way to show that this is not what he means, although this interpretation commits him to saying, quite oddly, that happiness (the composite of all goods) is more desirable than perfect happiness (the best single element of this composite). But in any case, we have rejected the thesis that he conceives of happiness as an all-inclusive composite, and this makes it far easier for us to see how his defense of the philosophical life in X.7–8 is substantially in accord with the rest of his theory. Aristotle never deviates from the idea that happiness consists solely in one type of good: virtuous activity of the rational soul. That is a doctrine he puts forward both in Book I and in Book X. It is true that in Book X he defends a new thesis, one for which he had not argued in Book I: namely, that *perfect* happiness consists in *theoria*. But it is hardly a surprise that when he returns to the topic of *eudaimonia* in Book X, he should want to say something he had not said before. The important question is what he means by calling contemplation *perfect* happiness, and how this thesis is connected with his earlier treatment of *eudaimonia*.

It is important to recall, at this point, that in Book I Aristotle leaves unresolved a question faced by the educated elite of fourth century Greek cities: Which kind of life is more desirable—one devoted to public service, or one devoted to study and understanding?[15] The issue receives Aristotle's attention in Book VII of the *Politics*, and in the *NE* he first turns to it in I.5, where we are told that there are three types of life "stand out most of all" (1095b18): one given to physical pleasure, a second devoted to politics, and a third spent in study. The first of these is dismissed as vulgar; the second receives only the briefest discussion; and the third is postponed for later investigation. It is only in Book X that Aristotle tells his audience in unmistakable terms that the contemplative life is best and provides a full defense of that thesis. But in these late chapters he also make it clear that the political life is very much worth living. Although such a life has deficiencies (it is for example unleisurely and aims at a goal external to itself: X.7 1177a27–b15), it would be wrong to characterize it as unhappy. Contemplation is perfect happiness, as he insists, but at the same time a life "in accordance with the other kind of virtue" is happy "in a secondary degree" (1178a7–9). That statement can reasonably be taken to mean that both philosophical and political lives are happy and well lived, but that of these the philosophical life is happiest.

Aristotle is saying, in other words, that the best life that a human being can live is one that has contemplation as its ultimate end. And when we look back at Book I, after having read his defense of the philosophical life in Book X, we can see how he has left room for this denouement. The final lines of the *ergon* argument of I.7 suggest that eventually Aristotle will single out a kind of virtuous activity as preeminent over all the others. As he says, "human good is activity of soul in accordance with virtue, and if the virtues are many, in accordance with the best and most perfect" (1098a16–18).[16] We are not told here in I.7 what the most perfect virtue is, but that after all is not surprising, since Aristotle needs to describe and analyze the virtues before he can pronounce one of them best. He makes it clear in I.13 that this is his program; his task in the remainder of the treatise will be to discuss *both* the virtues of character *and* those of reason (1103a1–10). Part of that program is carried out in Books II–V, which take up ethical virtue; the rest is carried forward in Book VI, which analyzes the various virtues of the reasoning part of the soul. In the concluding lines of Book

VI (1145a6–11), he briefly remarks that theoretical wisdom is superior to practical wisdom, and that the latter issues orders for the sake of the former. But he fully defends this view only when he returns, in X.7–8, to his investigation of the ultimate end. It is noteworthy that when he comes back to this topic in X.7, he picks up the thread of the argument that had been left hanging in the final lines of the *ergon* argument. That argument had told us that happiness consists in activity in accordance with the best single virtue (1098a17–18). And the opening sentence of X.7 returns to this theme: "If happiness is activity in accordance with virtue, it is reasonable that it should be in accordance with the best [virtue]; and this is the virtue of the best [part of us]" (1177a12–13).

Such a life is "in accordance with the highest virtue" in the sense that it has as its ultimate goal the exercise of theoretical wisdom. Contemplation is its highest good, but that hardly means that it is the only good such a life will possess. Aristotle makes it quite clear that the philosopher remains a human being and cannot escape the universal features of the human situation. The highest goal is not to engage in one act of contemplation and then to die, but to lead a complete life devoted to this activity (X.7 1177b25). The philosopher will therefore need the ordinary necessities of life (X.8 1178a25, b33–5), and since such a life depends on leisure (X.7 1177b4) those necessities must be present in sufficient quantities to sustain philosophical work. More important, Aristotle tells us that "in so far as he is a man and lives with many others, he chooses to do what accords with virtue" (X.8 1178b5–6). We are not to think of the philosopher leading the best life as an isolated figure who has completely cut his ties with others and lives a life without friends. As a student in the Academy and the founder of the Lyceum, Aristotle must have assumed that teaching and discussion are central components of the philosophical life—even though such activity can, if need be, be carried out even when one is by oneself (X.7 1177a32–4). We must not be misled by the connotation of our term "contemplation" into thinking that when one is teaching and talking with others, one is not at the same time contemplating. For contemplation is simply the activation of the wisdom one has acquired, and this can be carried out in social interactions as well as in moments of solitude.

This way of reading Aristotle can best be expressed by saying that he takes the highest human life to be constituted by a threefold hierarchy of ends. Contemplation stands by itself at the highest level; it alone is identified with perfect happiness. Just below that level lies the exercise of the practical virtues. Desirable as those activities are in themselves, they are also valuable because they sustain the theoretical activities of the philosopher. The people who are best equipped to engage in *theoria* over a long period of time are those who live in political communities and maintain good relations with family, friends, and citizens. Such character traits as intemperance, cowardice, injustice would ill serve a philosophical life, for reasons Aristotle takes to be too obvious to require mentioning. Impetuous desires for physical pleasures would undermine study; great fear on the battlefield would endanger the city whose existence is necessary to the practice of philosophy; greed and other desires for superfluous resources are distractions and impediments.

Of course, if philosophers are to develop and exercise the ethical virtues, then they will also need the usual resources of ethical life—the external and bodily goods that occupy a still lower level in the hierarchy of ends. Such goods—wealth, honor, power, and the like—are not capable of constituting the highest end of a happy life. They are not components of happiness, but are desirable as means to happiness. Other goods—the practical virtues—do have the capacity to constitute the aim of a well-lived life, but nonetheless they are not the highest goal a human being can attain. They are components of happiness but are not perfect happiness. Someone who reached *only* those ends would be entirely cut off from the best thing available to human beings: an understanding of the highest causes of the cosmos and a life devoted to activating that state of mind. The life of the philosopher, by contrast, exhibits every type of good possessed by the politician—and more. The philosopher chooses to engage in ethical activity (though he may do so less often and fully as a political leader), and he has the external resources any other virtuous person needs (though he needs them to a smaller degree: X.8 1178a28–b5, 1179a3–8). But in addition to these goods, he also enjoys the one good that by itself should constitute the aim of a human life.

When we read the conclusion Aristotle comes to at the end of *ergon* argument, and in particular to the phrase that tells us that the good consists in activity in accordance with "the best and most perfect" virtue, we are not as yet in a position to know what he has in mind. And so it is reasonable, at that stage in our reading, to ask: Does he mean that if one exercises virtues that are less than perfect, then one is not living a happy life? But if we wait patiently for Aristotle to return to the topic of *eudaimonia*, then, as we have seen, he does answer our question. If *eudaimonia* is thought of as perfect happiness—the ultimate end of the best possible life—then one must exercise the highest virtue, theoretical wisdom, in order to be *eudaimon*. But it is reasonable to hold that happiness admits of degrees, and that one can live well even though one could do better. In this sense, someone who lacks "the best and most perfect" virtue can still be happy.

Although I have been emphasizing the difference between the philosophical and political lives—each is devoted to a different end—it is equally important not to lose sight of the fact that they have a great deal in common. It is not as though Aristotle thinks that what makes one life well lived is A, B, and C, whereas what makes the other well lived is X, Y and Z. It is an idea congenial to many contemporary thinkers that good lives exhibit as much diversity as that, but Aristotle cannot be counted as a pluralist of this sort. He thinks that the ultimate goal of the philosophical life—contemplation—has a good deal in common with the highest end of the political life—ethical activity. And that is because he thinks of the political leader as someone who exhibits a high degree of intellectual virtue: He has reflected about the ends of human life, he exhibits sound judgment when difficult decisions must be made, and his reason controls and is thoroughly integrated with his emotions. He is excellent at practical reasoning, just as the philosopher is excellent at theoretical reasoning. Happiness consists in just one thing—virtuous activity of the rational soul—although this one type of good can be further analyzed into two species, and one of them is even more worthwhile than the other.

4. The Mean

Once we see that in the *NE* Aristotle proposes that human beings should devote themselves to one or the other of two ultimate ends, we can make better sense of one of his most familiar ideas, namely that quantitative questions loom large in practical life and that both excess and deficiency must be avoided. The ideal ethical agent has an integrated set of skills that enables him to find the mean in many areas of life. He sees how much money he needs for his household and how much can be suitably spent on worthwhile social projects. His anger and other passions are neither stronger nor weaker than they need be, but are appropriate to the occasion. He has neither too few nor too

many friends. He is not indifferent to such goods as honor and pleasure, but neither does he love them more than they are worth. These
are ideas that Aristotle treats at length in Books II and IV of the *NE*, but
it should be noticed that quantitative questions are not far from his
mind both when he initiates the search for the ultimate end in Book I
and when he returns to the topic of happiness at the close of Book X.
We are told in I.2 that politics is the subject that studies the ultimate
end, because it belongs to this discipline to "determine which of the
sciences should be studied in cities, and which ones each class should
learn, and *to what extent*" (1094a28–b2).[17] And when Aristotle compares the theoretical and political lives in X.7–8, he counts it an advantage of the former that it needs fewer external resources than does
the latter (1178a25–b7, 1178b33–1179a16). Having chosen this or that
ultimate goal allows an individual to make long-term plans about how
many resources he will need, just as the whole polis makes quantitative
judgments about resources by focusing on the ultimate goal of the
political community.

Even though Aristotle frequently calls attention to these quantitative
questions in his practical writings, his readers sometimes have difficulty
understanding a point he makes in *NE* VI.1 about the inadequacy of
vague formulas like "do not go to excess" or "do not do too little."
Referring to the doctrine of the mean that he has defended in Books
II–V, he remarks: "To say this is true, but not precise. . . . If one had
only this, one would be none the wiser. For example, [one would be
none the wiser about] what sorts of things must be applied to the body
if someone were to say: whatever medical science prescribes, and as
the one who has this [science applies them]. Therefore, this also holds
for the states of the soul: one must not only say this thing truly, but
one must also determine what the right reason is and what is its *horos*
[limit, standard, boundary, definition]." The question that these statements naturally raise in our minds is whether anything he says in the
remainder of Book VI—or anywhere else—contributes to a greater degree of precision. Aristotle seems never to return to this topic. The
rest of Book VI presents a detailed discussion of the various kinds of
intellectual virtue, but it is not easy to discern in this material a way of
going beyond such precise formulas as "find the intermediate between
excess and deficiency."

If we think that what Aristotle is looking for, when he raises this
issue in Book VI, is an algorithm for decision-making—some formula
or procedure that can be unthinkingly used to find a solution for every

practical problem—then of course we will be disappointed. There is no such formula in Aristotle's writings—or, for that matter, in the whole literature of moral philosophy. But if this is not what he is seeking in Book VI, then what *is* he looking for, when he writes the passage cited in the previous paragraph? And how does the rest of Book VI give us a more precise standard for answering quantitative questions?

My suggestion is that Aristotle thinks of Book VI as providing a tool for more precise decision-making because he takes exercising two of the intellectual virtues described in Book VI—practical wisdom and theoretical wisdom—to be the ultimate goals of well-lived lives. Book VI gives us a more precise vision of the ultimate goal of life in that the two kinds of happy lives—one philosophical, the other political—are centered around the exercise of intellectual virtues. To live a philo-sophical life well, one needs to know what theoretical wisdom is, and understanding this goal puts one into a better position to determine what one needs and how much one needs in the way of resources. Alternatively, if one decides to make practical activity one's highest goal, then one will need a larger number of external goods, since the politician needs more power and other resources than does a philoso-pher. The purpose of Book VI is not to decide between these two ultimate ends—that question is postponed to Book X—but to provide a better understanding of what the two ultimate ends are. Aristotle seeks a fuller description of the intellectual virtues not for its own sake but because a clearer vision of our highest goal allows us to answer quantitative questions with greater precision.

5. Egoism

The ultimate goal, we have seen, is just one thing: virtuous activity. But now we must raise a further question about what this means. Does Aristotle presuppose that my ultimate goal should simply be *my* good and nothing else? Even if I choose to lead a political life, am I to aim ultimately at my own happiness, and is the good of others to play a subordinate role in my plans?

It is sometimes thought that Aristotle tacitly presupposes the truth of egoism throughout his practical writings. He assumes, in other words, that whatever happiness turns out to be, each person ought to have as his highest goal the maximization of his own happiness. As we discover, happiness consists in virtuous activity, and therefore, if Aristotle is an egoist, he holds that the goal of any agent should be to exercise, as fully as he can, his own virtues. Had it turned out that happiness consists in power, then Aristotle's egoism would have committed him to saying that I should try to maximize my power, that you should try to maximize your power, and so on. His commitment to egoism, in other words, has the potential to set people at odds with each other. But he avoids this result, because when each person takes his ultimate end to be the fullest possible exercise of his own virtues, no one need try to undermine the well-being of others. On the contrary, virtuous activity often benefits many others besides the agent. And so, it might be thought, Aristotle's egoism—still assuming, for the moment that he is an egoist—is not a point on which he can be criticized. Egoism, according to this way of thinking, should not be evaluated in isolation from a conception of the good. For it is not a doctrine that undermines community, friendship, and the like, when the good is properly understood. It is not egoism itself that deserves criticism, but rather a combination of egoism and a conception of the good that counsels us to pursue power or wealth or pleasure as our ultimate end.

But surely this way of defending Aristotle's alleged egoism is open to question. Why should it simply be assumed without question that each person is to place his own well-being above that of every other human being? This is not an unassailable or unavoidable starting point for ethical theory or practical deliberation. And even if it could be shown that the results of making this assumption are not always objectionable—namely, when a formally egoistic premise is combined with virtue-centered theory of the good—that would not show that an agent whose decisions are derived from these starting points is beyond moral criticism. Even if he always chooses the right act, does he act from the best of motives, when his starting point is that it is ultimately his own good and that alone that provides reasons for action?

Furthermore, we are now in a position to recognize that interpreting Aristotle as an egoist would, in light of his conception of perfect happiness, create an immense difficulty for his whole ethical system. He says, as we have seen, that the best choice for an ultimate end is not ethically virtuous activity or some composite of ethical and theoretical activity, but contemplation alone. Accordingly, were he to say that one should make one's ultimate end the fullest attainment of one's own good, he would have to admit that any interruption of one's contemplative activity would be unjustified unless it somehow produced even more such activity over the long run. Setting philosophy aside for few hours, days, or weeks in order to help an ailing parent, for example, would be justified only if that were the best way to maximize one's involvement in such activity over the long run. Surely it would be unreasonable to expect that one's own maximal well-being on the one hand and the requirements of justice and decency on the other are bound to coincide on each and every occasion. If Aristotle really is an egoist, then his conception of perfect happiness as contemplation is very likely to recommend occasional and perhaps frequent departures from ordinary moral standards. And it is hard to believe that he wanted his ethical theory to be revisionary in this way. He never expresses doubts about the choiceworthiness of acting as a virtuous person must, although he realizes that others have such doubts. The defense he gives of the philosophical life in X.7–8 is meant to show that we should make theoretical activity our ultimate goal, but he gives no hint that we should act unethically in order to maximize contemplation.

This objection to combining an egoist reading of Aristotle with his equation of perfect happiness and contemplation should lead us to wonder whether there really is good support for the assumption that he is an egoist in the sense defined. Does he really say or imply that whatever the good is, it is only one's own good that should be one's ultimate end? When we look for evidence for this interpretation, we find none. Consider the way the *NE* begins, for example. Aristotle observes that every craft and decision aims at some good (1094a1–2), but he does not claim that ever craft and decision aims at the good of the craftsman or the decision maker. On the contrary, it is obvious from the examples he uses that crafts typically aim at the good of someone other than the craftsman. Medicine aims at health (a8); this does not mean that the doctor's task is to promote his own health, and that he ministers to others as a means to an ultimate end that is self-interested. Aristotle's point in I.1 is that ends can be arranged in a hierarchy—not that the hierarchy always terminates in one's own good.

In I.2 he goes on to say that he is undertaking a political study, that its goal is to discover the good for man—not merely one's own good—and that it is finer to achieve what is good for a whole community than for oneself alone (1094a27–b10). Nothing in these words suggests that each of us has or ought to have our own good alone as our ultimate end. And we should recall that according to one of the major themes of Aristotle's political theory, a correct constitution is one in which the rulers govern for the good of the whole city, whereas in corrupt constitutions the rulers have only their own interest in mind (*Pol.* III.6

1279a17–20). This strong endorsement of impartiality cannot be combined with a form of egoism that singles out one's own good as having priority over the good of others.

What Aristotle endorses is not egoism but rather the thesis that when we virtuously restrict our pursuit of such external resources as power, honor, and wealth, we are not sacrificing our good but in fact promoting it. In these cases, self-interest and virtuous activity coincide because it is far more advantageous to be a just, courageous, and generous person, and to express these virtues in action, than to acquire a greater stock of external goods (IX.8 1168b23–1169b2). Contrary to what many people think, the virtuous agent is not in these circumstances a noble but naive fellow whose service to others brings him a net loss. But in denying this common view, Aristotle is not committing himself to the formal thesis that, whatever the good is, one's ultimate end should consist solely in one's own good, and that the well-being of others should receive one's attention only to the extent that doing so can be shown to promote one's happiness. He applauds self-love only when and to the extent that it takes a form that directs it at the well-being of others and not only at one's own good. That is an endorsement of a specific kind of self-love, not of the more general thesis of egoism, which elevates oneself above others quite apart from any investigation of what one's good is. It is especially important to realize that Aristotle endorses self-love because he thinks this trait, properly understood, benefits not only the self but the entire community (IX.8 1169a8–11). There is no place in his practical writings where he makes the claims of the self more fundamental than those of the larger whole of which we are a part.[18]

The conclusion we should draw is that we should not look within Aristotle's writings for an abstract and exceptionless thesis about how much weight we are to assign to our own good and how much to the good of others. Egoism and utilitarianism endorse such abstract principles, but we must not assume that every ethical theory takes a stand on this issue once and for all. Aristotle has a theory about how goods stand in relation to each other—which of them are for the sake of others, and which are ultimate ends—but such an ordering of goods does not by itself determine how we are to act in particular circumstances. Since contemplation is the ultimate end, the best one can do for oneself or another is to promote this end. But there are many people who are incapable of achieving this good, and so when one acts for their sake, one ought instead to promote their ability to engage in ethical activity. And what is one to do when there is a conflict between doing what is best for one person and what is best for another, and one must choose between these alternatives? To this common problem, Aristotle has no general solution, because circumstances vary too much to admit of theoretical treatment. The important point is that the status of contemplation as an ultimate end is not meant to serve as a solution to this problem. The superiority of theoretical activity is a thesis about what makes an individual life go best. It tells us how to arrange goods optimally within a single life, but does not address the question of how much weight to attach to one person's life as opposed to another's.

6. Universal and Particular

Now that we have grasped the general outlines of Aristotle's conception of *eudaimonia*, we are in a better position to discuss some broader issues about his approach to ethical theory. To begin with, we can now see that as a treatise the *NE* exhibits a greater degree of organizational structure and unity than is sometimes thought. The defense of the theoretical life in Book X does not deviate significantly from the main outlines of his ethical theory as presented in the earlier portions of the treatise. On the contrary, it is only in those final chapters that Aristotle ties together the strings he has left hanging in the body of his work. As we have seen, the conclusion of the *ergon* argument—and in particular its reference to the virtue that is "best and most perfect"—cannot be understood until Aristotle returns to the topic of happiness at the end of the work. His intention in Book I is not to settle the question of human happiness, but to advance our understanding to the point where we see why a discussion of virtue— both intellectual and practical—is needed. The issue left hanging by the phrase "best and most perfect" cannot be resolved until the different kinds of virtues are discussed. The search for an adequate conception of our ultimate end is still left unresolved as Aristotle opens Book VI with his complaint about the doctrine of the mean, and the purpose of that Book is to improve our understanding of the two intellectual virtues (practical and theoretical) that are at the heart of the two most appealing kinds of lives—one political the other philosophical. And it is only in X.7–8 that we are told which kind of virtuous activity is the ultimate end of the best life. So X.7–8 is not an addendum tacked on to the rest of the work; it is precisely here that Aristotle finally answers the question he first raised.

The *NE* is not only a more systematic and unified treatise than we might have suspected, but it is also a work that presents the reader with a systematic and unified vision of how life should be lived—a vision that is applicable to every decision we make and every activity we undertake. In this respect, Aristotle's moral philosophy may be usefully compared with utilitarianism. One remarkable feature of the philosophy of Bentham, Mill and Sidgwick is that, in equating rightness with the maximization of pleasure, it presents a single formula that is applicable to all practical questions. We are not to make decisions in an *ad hoc* or unsystematic way, but to bring a single rule, standard, or goal to bear on every situation. That is the respect in which utilitarianism and Aristotelianism are of a piece.

Undeniably, there are profound differences as well. The utilitarian looks to some standard that can be understood independently of virtue—pleasure or happiness—and reduces all decision-making to the maximization of that state of mind. Aristotle's standard is virtuous activity, not something beyond it. Furthermore, the utilitarian is indifferent to how the good is distributed among persons: what counts is maximizing it, not giving each a due amount of it. By contrast, Aristotle, as we have seen, does not propose a single answer to the question of how to distribute the good over persons. But in spite of these deep differences, we should not lose sight of one significant similarity: Both are trying to bring order to practical life by proposing a substantive formula about our highest end. Aristotle does not think that each decision should be made merely by responding appropriately to the case at hand, with no reference to some larger goal that links together the various projects we undertake. To think of him in that way is to miss the obvious: as he tells us at the very beginning of the *NE*, he is trying to discover the ultimate end because he thinks that knowing what it is will make us better able to hit our target (I.2 1094a22–4). As we have seen, he eventually proposes two targets. But the point to be emphasized now is that each of these ultimate ends has sufficient content to help answer questions about which resources and how many of them we need in order to lead our lives well. Both the utilitarian and Aristotle think that philosophy discovers a goal which should guide us at every point in our lives.

Since good deliberation requires knowledge of both universals and particulars, an understanding of our ultimate ends is only part of what we need. Aristotle's person of practical wisdom is a successful decision-maker in part because he is able to perceive the salient details of any situation.[19] That he has virtuous activity as his ultimate end does not by itself solve his deliberative problems, because he must use his ethically trained intelligence to decide between competing alternative courses of action. But at the same time, it must be emphasized that Aristotle's ethical agent does not simply happen to find himself in this or that situation. He does not passively wait for problems to present themselves, but has a comprehensive plan that propels his agency. Though unforeseen circumstances arise in anyone's life, Aristotle's skilled moral agent takes control of his circumstances, as best as he can, by developing and acting on a long-term plan. That comprehensive plan is not a hodgepodge of goods, but a structured hierarchy of ends by reference to which he determines roughly how much wealth, power, and other resources he needs. To be sensitive to relevant facts in particular situations, we must know what to look for; and to know this, we must think through highly general questions about the ultimate end of human life.[20]

7. Beyond the Human and the Ethical

Some students of Aristotle's ethics hold that one of its most significant features lies in his rejection of Plato's whole approach to the subject. That there are *some* important differences between them is beyond question, because Plato's ethics is in some way bound up with his theory of forms, and Aristotle rejects the existence of that separate realm of abstract objects. He himself alerts us to his distance from Plato in I.6 of the *NE*, where he considers and rejects the form of the good as an answer to his question, "What is *eudaimonia*?" One of the arguments he gives against Plato is that the goods aimed at by the crafts and sciences are irreducibly different. Weavers and carpenters both produce something good, but each does so by studying a different kind of good, and there is no form or universal, goodness in itself, that they need to study in order to produce good cloaks or houses (1096b35–1097a13).

Such passages as these make it tempting to attribute to Aristotle the idea that the most general species of goodness we can talk about is human goodness, and that any attempt to base ethical theory on a conception of the good more universal than that is fundamentally misguided. The only goods we human beings can know about or should care about are the ones we can acquire, and such goods as these are embedded in the kinds of lives we have—the lives of beings who have human bodies, experience human emotions, require human resources, and live in human communities. Plato's mistake, according to this reading of Aristotle, was to suppose that there are non-human objects—objects that are not themselves human or created by humans—that set our goals for us and serve as paradigms for the kind of life we should live. When Aristotle's rejection of Platonism is read in this way, his ethical theory embraces a kind of perspectivalism; ethical theory and ethical persons have no alternative but to look at the world from the human point of view. If there are other kinds of beings besides humans who are guided by norms, values, goods, or obligations, they would form a moral universe that bears no relation to our own.[21]

Appealing as this approach to ethics may be to some contemporary philosophers, it should not attribute to Aristotle. One of the lengthiest arguments he gives in X.7–8 for his conception of happiness turns on the idea that there is something better in the universe than human beings, and that we should lead our lives by imitating this higher being (1178b7–32). If Aristotle is a perspectivalist—if he thinks that we are confined to looking at our lives from a human point of view—then he is at war with himself, because there are passages in which he derives practical conclusions from the existence and nature of divine beings. But this way of bifurcating Aristotle can be sustained only if the conception of the good he defends in X.7–8 is radically at odds with everything that has preceded it, and we have learned that this is not so. So it must be conceded that there is more in common between Plato and Aristotle than might at first meet the eye. They both look to something non-human and see in it something that is both better than human and a guide to the proper living of a human life. We must be careful not to misunderstand the complaint Aristotle is making against Plato in *NE* I.6. His point is that there is no reason to posit a form of the good or a universal goodness to serve as a paradigm or a highest end. But he is not making the further claim that our lives must be lived from a perspective restricted to the merely human. Like Plato, he looks beyond the human to a divine standard, but his divine standard is a particular thing—a living god—not a form or universal.

The same point can be made from the reverse direction: Just as Aristotle thinks that there is something higher than human life that sets a standard toward which we should strive, so he takes it for granted that there is something less than human and that we should not lower ourselves to that subhuman level. He thinks it makes sense to compare our lives with those of mere animals and plants, and to say that ours can be vastly superior, if we make use of what is uniquely human. In order to systematize our thoughts about our lives and arrive at an appropriate goal for making decisions, we have to find something that explains why human life can be superior to that of any animal and, at its best, an approximation of divine life. Excellence in reasoning, both practical and theoretical, occupies a central place in Aristotle's ethics in part because it explains why we occupy this intermediate position in the cosmic hierarchy. A life devoted to physical pleasure as its ultimate goal could not pass this test, according to Aristotle; the defender of such a life would have to admit that mere animals could live as well or better than human beings, and that a bodiless god would be miserable.

The fact that Aristotle tries to locate human life in a hierarchy of living forms should help us to see just how ambitious his ethical theory is. It is an attempt to find a universally valid standard for the evaluation of human communities, and is not intended as a mere expression of the "Common Sense Morality of Greece," in Sidgwick's phrase.[22] Of course, Aristotle would defend his belief that temperance, justice, courage, and the like are virtues by pointing out that such a view is shared by the many and the wise. He often appeals to consensus as *evidence* of the truth. But he never treats it as an unfailing guarantee of truth; nor does he identify truth with what is universally believed. In fact, he realizes that a whole community can be fundamentally misguided. For example, he frequently criticizes the Spartans for making martial valor the chief virtue and domination the ultimate end.[23] He takes no existing community as a faultless model to be imitated. How we are to live is not a matter that is to be determined by some already existing community or some future consensus towards which we are progressing. Rather, the model community is one we invent through reflection on the nature of happiness.

What grounds Aristotle's belief that courage, temperance, and the like are virtues is not primarily the fact that these qualities are widely admired in many communities, but the more fundamental point that they express the proper ordering of rational and non-rational elements in human life. Temperance is a genuine excellence and not merely a respected skill because physical pleasure has a modest but significant role to play in a well-lived human life; justice is a virtue because the items it distributes are resources needed for a life devoted to excellent reasoning; courage is also a component of happiness because defending such a life requires noble action on the battlefield and therefore control over one's fear of death. What makes these qualities excellent is not the approval they receive from the many or the wise, but rather the way they enhance, protect, and express good reasoning as an end in itself. Aristotle's moral philosophy must be recognized as an attempt, no less ambitious than Plato's, to organize human life into a systematic unity, and to locate human beings within a larger metaphysical framework. It goes well beyond a mere listing of goods as they present themselves to our community.

Perhaps this point has not been sufficiently appreciated because of Aristotle's well-known warning to his readers (I.4 1095b4–6) that his lectures are intended for an audience that has already been brought up well and has acquired, through proper habituation, the starting points of the subject. We might take this to mean that according to Aristotle there is no way to justify an ethical way of life by using premises drawn from areas external to ethics.[24] The study of politics, in other words, is entirely autonomous, and can draw no support from an examination of the soul and its relation to the body, or the relation between human beings and other animals, or god's relation to the cosmos.

But that cannot be Aristotle's point, because his defense of the philosophical life shows how willing he is to help himself to metaphysical and theological ideas. What he must mean, when he restricts his audience to those who have acquired good habits, is that *some* of the points he takes for granted are not recognized by those who have had a deficient upbringing. And we can easily guess what those points are: Aristotle claims without argument that the virtues are desirable in themselves, and it is hard to see how such a thesis could be established to the satisfaction of those whose experience has made temperance, courage, justice and other virtues distasteful and burdensome. These are the people Aristotle characterizes in the closing chapter of the *NE* as lacking "a conception of what is noble and truly pleasant, since they have never tasted it" (X.9 1179b15–16).

Since happiness consists in something that is good in itself, people who take the virtues to be at best desirable as mere means to other ends lack the richness of experience one needs in order to arrive at a proper conception of the final end. Exposure to ethical phenomena and the proper emotional receptivity to such phenomena are among the wherewithal one needs in order to make progress in ethical theory. But that should not be taken to mean that ethical theory is *entirely* autonomous, that it need not draw on anything that lies outside the childhood experience of well-trained listeners. Ethical experience brings us to the realization that the virtues are desirable in themselves; but there are other things that are also intrinsically worthwhile— friendship, honor, pleasure, and so on—and therefore much work remains for an inquiry that seeks to discover the highest among these ends. A young person who begins a study of ethical theory does not yet know which of the many things that are desirable in themselves should be elevated to the role of ultimate end. And so he must undertake a systematic investigation of the different kinds of goods and their relationship to each other. If finding the nature of happiness were simply a matter of listing all the intrinsic goods, there would be no need to make comparisons among them and to determine which should serve the rest. But Aristotle holds that practical wisdom cannot do without such comparisons.[25] To arrive at this systematic understanding, there is no reason why the student should not look beyond ethical experience and beyond the merely human. To elevate one goal above all others, one must go beyond childhood habituation, social customs, and the simple device of aggregation: One must locate human nature in a comprehensive picture of the world.

Notes

This paper presents a brief version of the interpretation I put forward in my book, *Aristotle on the Human Good* (Princeton: Princeton University Press, 1989). I will refer to this work hereafter as *AHG*. For some thoughts and references that go beyond the book, see sections 6 and 7 below.

1. I will sometimes use Aristotle's Greek word (conventionally translated "happiness") to remind the reader not to be misled by the connotations of our own term. For discussion of this issue, see *AHG* p. 1, n. 1; and Richard Kraut, "Two Conceptions of Happiness," *Philosophical Review* 88 (1979): 467–78.

2. According to W. F. R. Hardie, "The Final Good in Aristotle's *Ethics*," in *Aristotle: A Collection of Critical Essays*, ed. J. M. E. Moravcsik (Garden City, N.Y.: Doubleday), pp. 297–322, this is only an occasional insight of the *NE*; by contrast, J. L. Ackrill, "Aristotle on *Eudaimonia*," in *Essays on Aristotle's Ethics*, ed. Amelie Rorty (Berkeley: University of California Press, 1980), pp. 15–33, argues that Aristotle manages to hold onto this thought through almost the whole of his treatise, giving it up only in X.7–8. Both Hardie and Ackrill believe that a contradiction is to be found in the *NE*. For further reading on this issue, see *AHG*, pp. 4–5, n. 7.

3. There is an ambiguity here, but it will not matter for our purposes. The idea that more goods are better than less might mean: (A) it is always better to add another good, provided that in doing so one does not give up, to any

degree, any good that one already has; or (B) it is always better to add another good, *even if* in doing so one gives up, to some degree, a good one already has. The first principle tells us to opt for variety, provided doing so is costless; the second principle tells us to accept smaller quantities of goods in order to increase the number of different types we have. (A) seems hard to resist, whereas (B) is open to question. My claim will be that Aristotle's conception of the ultimate end does not make use of either (A) or (B).

4. It is common ground among all students of Aristotle not only that he recognizes a variety of goods, but that he takes many of them to be desirable in themselves. Among them are honor, pleasure, virtue, and friends (see I.7 1097b2–4, VI.12 1144a1–3, VIII.8 1159a25–7).

5. Here I am appealing to reading (A), described in note 3.

6. Here I make use of reading (B), described in note 3. Admittedly, this thesis is more vulnerable to challenge than is (A).

7. Here and throughout I use my own translations.

8. See I.5 1095b30–1096a2, I.7 1098a5–7, I.8 1098b30–1099a7, I.10 1100a13–14, I.10 1100b33.

9. Here it is important to keep in mind that happiness consists in excellent activity not for a brief moment but for a "complete life" (I.7 1098a18; see too X.7 1177b25).

10. See I.8 1099a31–b7, VII. 13 1153b17–19; *Pol.* VII.1 1323a24–7.

11. *Rhetoric* I.5 1360b14–23 is not an exception, for here Aristotle says he is not presenting his own theory but merely listing a number of widely held views. Nor is *Magna Moralia* I.2 1184a18–19 ("we put together happiness out of many goods"), since this is compatible with the thesis that happiness consists in the many kinds of virtuous activity.

12. For references to some of the secondary literature on this problem, see *AHG*, pp. 4–5, n. 7.

13. See X.7 1177a15–17, X.7 1177b24–5, X.8 1178b7–8. Some translators render this "complete" rather than "perfect" happiness.

14. For a defense of this reading, see David Keyt, "Intellectualism in Aristotle," in *Essays in Ancient Greek Philosophy*, ed. John P. Anton and Anthony Preus (Albany: State University of New York Press, 1983), vol. 2, pp. 364–87.

15. This is of course one of the major themes of Plato's *Gorgias*.

16. An alternative translation would be: "best and most *complete*," the emphasized term implying that the best virtue is the composite of them all. But that interpretation is one I oppose, since I think Aristotle wrote these words in order to anticipate his conclusion that one virtue—theoretical wisdom—is best.

17. See for example *Politics* VIII.2 1337b15–17: there are certain studies that befit a free person but that should be learned only to a limited degree.

18. On the priority of the community to any of its parts, see *Politics* I.2 1253a18–20 and VIII.1 1337a27–32. Aristotle's thesis is that when a community is reasonably designed to achieve the good of all, then its decision-making authority is greater than that of any individual. An egoist can counsel giving the state such authority—but in that case civic authority is derived and transferred from individuals; this is a modern doctrine and cannot be fit into Aristotle's

system. For discussion, see my commentary on Aristotle's *Politics Books VII and VIII* (Oxford: Clarendon Press, 1997), pp. 172–73.

19. For Aristotle's view that practical wisdom requires an understanding of both universal and particulars, see VI.7 1141b14–15. For his view that good decision-making requires ethical perception, see VI.8 1142a25–30, VI.12 1144a29–30.

20. For the view that general goals, standards or rules are at best a rough guide, but should be set aside whenever ethical perception, taking in the full complexity of particular situations, reveals the inadequacy of our general blueprint, see Lawrence Blum, *Moral Perception and Particularity* (Cambridge: Cambridge University Press, 1994), pp. 30–61; Jonathan Dancy, *Moral Reasons* (Oxford: Blackwell, 1993), pp. 60–108; John McDowell, "Virtue and Reason," *Monist* 62 (1979): 331–50; and Martha C. Nussbaum, "The Discernment of Perception," in *Love's Knowledge* (New York: Oxford University Press, 1990). Such a view is attributed to Aristotle by Nussbaum in the chapter just cited as well as in *The Fragility of Goodness* (Cambridge: Cambridge University Press, 1986), pp. 298–306; see too Nancy Sherman, *The Fabric of Character* (Oxford: Clarendon Press, 1989), pp. 13–55. McDowell also denies that Aristotle proposes a "blueprint for doing well." See "Deliberation and Moral Development in Aristotle's Ethics," in *Aristotle, Kant, and the Stoics*, ed. Stephen Engstrom and Jennifer Whiting (Cambridge: Cambridge University Press, 1996), pp. 19–35, esp. p. 21. Sarah Broadie also denies that Aristotle posits a "Grand End" (her term). See *Ethics with Aristotle* (New York: Oxford University Press, 1991), pp. 234–48. For my doubts about her interpretation, see "In Defense of the Grand End," *Ethics* 103 (1993): 361–74.

21. For a defense of this reading, see Nussbaum, *The Fragility of Goodness*, pp. 292, 373–74. For criticism, see *AHG*, pp. 60–1, n. 43.

22. Henry Sidgwick, *The Methods of Ethics*, 7th ed. (New York: Dover, 1966), p. xix.

23. See *Politics* VII.2 1324b7–9, VII.14 1333b12–35, VII.15 1334a40–b5, and VIII.4 1338b24–38.

24. For such a interpretation, see Jonathan Lear, *Aristotle: The Desire to Understand* (Cambridge: Cambridge University Press, 1988); pp. 157, 159, 166, 170, 193–96. For similar ideas, see Christine M. Korsgaard, *The Sources of Normativity* (Cambridge: Cambridge University Press, 1996), p. 77; John McDowell, *Mind and World* (Cambridge: Harvard University Press, 1994), p. 84; Bernard Williams, *Ethics and the Limits of Philosophy* (Cambridge: Harvard University Press, 1985), p. 51. I discuss this issue more fully in "Aristotle on Method and Moral Education," in *Method in Ancient Philosophy*, ed. Jyl Gentzler (Oxford: Clarendon Press, 1998), pp. 271–90.

25. Several prominent philosophers have recently argued that values cannot be meaningfully compared. It is sometimes thought that such comparisons would require a common unit of measure, but that there is no such measure. Aristotle, by contrast, holds that goods can be compared—indeed, that wisdom requires this—even though they are not measurable on a common scale. For discussion, see *Incommensurability, Incomparability, and Practical Reason*, ed. Ruth Chang (Cambridge: Harvard University Press, 1997). Chang argues persuasively (pp. 1–34) against those who hold that values are not comparable.

5

A False Doctrine of the Mean

Rosalind Hursthouse

Introduction

Aristotle says that *ethikē aretē*, excellence of character, is a disposition in virtue of which we are well disposed in respect of feelings (*pathé*). Feelings are said to be such things as appetites, emotions such as anger and fear, and, in general, all conditions that are attended by pleasure or pain (1105b19ff). Taken in isolation, this might sound as though Aristotle makes excellence of character a merely inner matter, but this is not so. Most feelings involve a desire to perform certain actions, so being well disposed in respect of feelings involves being well disposed in respect of actions too. The occasions on which the two come apart are not relevant to anything I say in this paper so let us concentrate on feelings for the moment.

What it is to be *well* disposed in respect of feelings is, apparently, specified by saying that excellence of character is a disposition (concerned with feelings) which is in a *mean*. The thesis that virtue (excellence of character) is a disposition in a mean is Aristotle's doctrine of the mean.

Whether you think of the doctrine as empty, or interesting, bold, and (roughly) true, is partly determined by what you think it is, J. O. Urmson[1] has defended it as the latter, and it is his account of what the doctrine is that provides the main stalking-horse in this paper.

When Urmson gives a summary of Aristotle's account of excellence of character, he begins it like this. (Note that he is using "emotion" as his translation of *pathos*.)

(1) For each specific excellence of character that we recognise there
     will be some specific emotion whose field it is.
(2) In the case of each such emotion it is possible to be disposed to
     exhibit it to the right amount, which is excellence.[2]

We should note one objection here, which is that Aristotle nowhere
commits himself to the thesis that to each specific excellence of character or virtue there corresponds just *one* emotion (*pathos*) whose field
it is. Indeed, much of his discussion shows that he denies this. I shall
return to this point later.

So far, we have some account of virtue, and it is already quite strong.
It is at least strong enough to be falsified. The virtue of *megalopsuchia*
(magnanimity), although it no doubt involves exhibiting a variety of
feelings "to the right amount" consists, according to what Aristotle
himself says, in correct *judgement*. To be magnanimous is to be well-
disposed in respect of *judgements* of one's own worth, neither over-
nor under-estimating it. Only consequentially is it a matter of being
well-disposed in respect of feelings, but it is a disposition in respect of
feelings that virtue is supposed to be.[3]

Similarly, the virtue of *megalopropeia*, magnificence, which is contrasted with vulgarity and pettiness, is a virtue which consists in correct
judgement. The magnificent man judges correctly that the expense is
worthy of the result and the result of the expense; the vulgar and the
petty constantly get this judgement wrong.

So the account even so far is not true of all the virtues. For all that, it
might be true of most of them, and, if it were, it would be an interesting
account. But it is not yet an account that could be called a doctrine of
a *mean*. For we could add to (1) and (2) no more than

(3a) In the case or each such emotion (feeling) it is possible to be
      disposed to exhibit or feel it to a wrong extent, as one should
      not, which is a vice, a defect

and claim no more than that to each virtue there corresponds at least
one vice.

This claim itself is a strong one and we should pause to consider it.
Suppose that it is true—isn't it a surprising truth that calls for some
explanation? Why *should* there be at least one vice corresponding to
each virtue? If we found that, as a matter of fact, when we drew up a
list of virtue words, we could draw up a list of corresponding vice

words, that itself would be a sufficiently striking fact to call for explanation. If, in line with Aristotle's own procedure, we maintained that vices do not necessarily have names, and sometimes said that there *is* a certain vice even if there is no word for it and no one (or no one sane) ever has the vice, the call for an explanation seems even more pressing. What makes us so sure?

A sketch of the explanation of the fact (for I think it is a fact) that to each virtue there corresponds at least one vice, has recently been given, in a different context, by Philippa Foot. She has argued that "the virtues are *corrective*, each one standing at a point at which there is some temptation to be resisted or deficiency to be made good."[4] Courage and temperance, she says, exist as virtues because human nature happens to be such that fear, and the desire for pleasure, often operate as temptations. Justice and charity exist as virtues because there is a deficiency of motivation in most of us to be made good. We happen not to be as much attached to the good of others, or their rights, as we are to our own.

Mrs. Foot's thesis is not restricted to those vices that clearly consist in being disposed to exhibit or feel an emotion to the wrong extent, as one should not, but it clearly applies to them. The thesis is still tentative and sketchy but I think it is very promising and just the sort of thesis one needs to explain why to each virtue there corresponds at least one vice. The explanation is located in exactly the right place—in facts about human nature, about how we go on. A particularly attractive aspect of the thesis is that it suggests an explanation of why, in some cases, several vices might correspond to one virtue. One virtue, upheld as an ideal, might serve to correct several dangerous tendencies all at once.

I have spent a little time on this point in order to make the next point clearer. I said that (3a) does not yield anything that deserves to be called a doctrine of a *mean*. *This* comes in only when we add something like

(3b) One's character may err in *two opposed* ways

as Urmson does.[5] Now this is, I think, definitely false, but the point I want to make here is that, if it *were* true, its truth would be a deeply mysterious fact. That to each virtue there corresponds at least one vice is an odd fact, but one for which we can imagine an explanation. But that to each virtue there should correspond precisely two vices, neither more nor less—what kind of explanation could there be of this extraordinary mathematical symmetry? What could there be about our lives and the way we conduct them, about our feelings and our dispositions to have those feelings, that necessitated such a symmetry?

The problem is made even worse by the idea that each pair of vices is a pair of *opposed* vices. I haven't yet said in what way they are meant to be opposed, and to complete the Urmsonian view of Aristotle's doctrine of the mean, (3b) should be replaced by something which specifies the opposition (and also preserves the connexion with emotion or feeling). Hence

(3c) In the case of each such emotion it is possible to have an excessive or deficient disposition with respect to it: (or perhaps—in the case of each such emotion it is possible to be disposed to exhibit or feel it either too much, excessively, or too little, deficiently).

I am not sure whether Aristotle does maintain the thesis of (3b) and (3c). Much of Book 2 suggests that he does; but there he disarmingly says that he is talking in outline only, and much of the *detailed* discussion of the particular virtues in Books 3 and 4 shows that he is aware that both (3b) and (3c) are, in fact, false. However, there are more elaborate versions of the doctrine of the mean which are not merely false but extremely silly, and I am sure that Aristotle did not always hold *them*.

More elaborate versions arise from filling out "excess" and "deficiency," "too much" and "too little." It is worth noting that we cannot find any detailed specification of how to fill them out in Aristotle. To get such a specification we must leave him and turn to, for example, Urmson, who unhesitatingly commits himself to the following:

(4) "Too much" includes "on too many occasions" and similar possibilities as well as "too violently"; "too little" includes "on too few occasions" and similar possibilities as well as "too weakly."[6]

The "similar possibilities" are given earlier. "One may exhibit an emotion too often or too rarely; about too many or too few things; toward too many or too few people; for too many or too few reasons."[7] I take it that, given that he holds (4), Urmson would specify what it is to have a disposition in a mean in the following way:

(5) To have a disposition regarding a certain emotion in a mean is to be disposed to exhibit or feel that emotion neither too often nor too rarely; about or toward neither too many nor too few objects or people, for neither too many nor too few reasons, neither too strongly nor too weakly

and that he would regard that as being *equivalent* to Aristotle's statement of what it is to have a disposition in a mean, namely

(5a) To have a disposition regarding a certain emotion in a mean is to be disposed to exhibit or feel that emotion on the right occasions, about or towards the right objects or people, for the right reasons, in the right manner.

It may be that Urmson's way is the only way to fill out "too much" and "too little"; about that I am not sure. If it *is* the only way then in so far as Aristotle committed himself to (3c) he committed himself to nonsense. His saving grace will then be inconsistency, for he very rarely lapses into the nonsensical (4) and (5), and, even when he does, does not do so wholeheartedly. What he usually does is operate straightforwardly within the terms of (5a), using the concept *dei—right* object, *right* occasion, *right* reason, or the very general *hōs dei*, as one should, without any suggestion that this concept can either be captured by, or can necessarily generate, concepts of too much or too little.

The idea that the concept of the *right reason* could be captured by specifying it as a mean between too many and too few reasons has only to be stated to be seen as absurd. What I want to illustrate in what follows is that *right object* and *right occasion* similarly cannot be specified as means, and that, more generally, some vices that correspond to the virtues of temperance, courage, and what is usually translated as "patience" or "gentleness"—the right disposition with respect to anger—cannot be understood as dispositions to exhibit or feel an emotion (a *pathos*) too much or too little.

Temperance

There is a fairly obvious quibble to be made about there being *a* specific emotion or feeling to be the field of temperance, namely that *the* appetite for physical pleasure need not be an appetite for food *and* drink *and* sex. Some people are temperate with respect to sex but not with respect to food and drink and *vice versa*: some people are intemperate only with respect to drink and so on.

Though I think this is an unimportant quibble in this context, I want to discuss temperance with respect to food and drink by itself first because it raises problems that become especially acute when we turn to temperance with respect to sex.

Temperance with Respect to Food and Drink

"In the case of natural desires, few people go wrong, and only in one way, in the direction of too much" (1118b16–17). "The licentious display excess in every form" (1118b24–5). How literal is the talk of "excess" and "too much" here? Aristotle says licentious people go wrong "in enjoying the wrong objects" (1118b23–4), that "they enjoy things it is wrong to enjoy" (1118b25–6). Are we to understand this as saying that they enjoy too many objects?

Some things are naturally wrong objects for appetite, for example foetuses, raw meat, human flesh, charcoal and earth. (Book 7, chap. v.) But the licentious man does not err in virtue of enjoying these sorts of things; only the brutish and the mad eat them. What else could wrong objects be?

It is initially very plausible to say that "wrong objects" just are "too many objects." The licentious man enjoys too many courses, too many pints; he eats and drinks until he is full to bursting, thus *exceeding* his natural limit (1118b17–18), that is, he eats the right amount and then some. Moreover, he does not do this only on the rare occasions when it is necessary (as it might be if one wasn't going to eat again for forty-eight hours) but on all those occasions and then some—on too many occasions. And whenever he does it he enjoys it more than he should—too much. Moreover, all these excesses seem to be the natural outcome of not desiring physical pleasure to the right extent but too much.

So far, so good. "Wrong objects," "wrong occasions," "wrong manner" are all captured by "too . . ." and the Urmsonian doctrine of the mean applies.

But so far temperance seems important for preserving health and not particularly important otherwise. A licentious person, one who desires physical pleasure too much, will simply be a greedy person who, if not forced to be sensible, will make himself fat and alcoholic. But it is clear that Aristotle thinks licentiousness leads, not merely to ill health but to other vices. *Sophrosune*, thought which saves, saves one not merely from the defect of ill health but from vice in general (1140b12). Why is this so?

The significant difference between the temperate and the licentious seems to be this. The temperate man not only avoids pleasures which are incompatible with health, but also pleasures which are dishonourable (contrary to what is *kalos*, 1119a15–18). The licentious man disregards these limitations (1119a19) and enjoys not only unhealthy excessive guzzling but also things which are odious (*miseta*) (1118b26).

Odious things are presumably contrary to what is *kalos*, and are things it is wrong to enjoy. But what can these wrong objects be, given that they are something other than unhealthily excessive extra helpings, and presumably not unnatural objects such as foetuses and earth? Aristotle does not tell us but I think we can easily imagine examples. The best way to recognise this particular sort of wrong object is to distinguish, as Aristotle does not, two quite different ways in which someone might become and be licentious. Let us imagine the likely effects of two different sorts of upbringing.

Suppose we have one person who was brought up by greedy, gourmand parents who encouraged their child to eat too much, but who also brought him up to be polite, considerate, unselfish and fair. That is, they brought him up to delight in food and drink (though not in health) but also to delight in acting fairly, generously and considerately. Now I imagine that someone brought up this way is likely to turn out to be one of those fat, jovial, generous, scrupulously fair people who are indeed the despair of their doctors, but the delight of their friends.

Now let us think of another person, brought up, say, by a dietician and a doctor, who believe in the law of the jungle and arming their child to fight in it. They taught him how to preserve his health, but nothing about being fair, generous or considerate. I imagine that he is likely to turn out to be slim, healthy and wicked. He will not scruple to take my food if he has a (healthily moderate) desire for it, even if I am starving; he will happily cheat fellow soldiers out of their rations on campaign. He does such things in pursuit of physical pleasure, having been taught to delight in nothing but health and satisfying his own desires where these are not incompatible with it.

Both these people are licentious according to what Aristotle says about licentiousness, but it is clear that they are licentious in very different ways. The fat jovial person does indeed have an "excessive disposition"; he eats and drinks too much, too often, enjoys it too much. His "wrong objects" are "too many objects." But he is not disposed to pursue pleasures that are dishonourable or odious. The slim wicked person, on the other hand, does *not* have an excessive disposition but nevertheless he is licentious and enjoys things it is wrong to enjoy—not wrong because they are excessive and unhealthy, but just plain wrong, dishonourable, what one should not enjoy.[8]

I think Aristotle overlooked the possibility of being brought up to the healthily moderate but wicked. Moreover, I think he assumes that anyone who has been brought up greedy must inevitably become greedier and greedier until, almost maddened by the desire for physical pleasure, he will cease to care about the limitations imposed by the other virtues and get out of the habit of being generous, fair and so on. (cf. 1119b8–12) But even if this assumption were true, it would guarantee that licentiousness was an excess, and that "a wrong object" was "at least one object too many" only by fortuitous overlap. Some of the wrong objects which the greedy and wicked person enjoyed would still be wrong simply in so far as they were contrary to what is honourable; if they were cases of excess this would be accidental.

It might be thought that there is something perverse, or at least very un-Aristotelian about calling "the food someone else needs" or "other people's rations" wrong objects which the licentious man goes wrong in enjoying. But it seems to me they are exactly the sorts of examples we need in order to capture the idea that the licentious man disregards the limits set by what is honourable. Moreover, we find that this sort of idea of a wrong object becomes essential when we turn to temperance with respect to sex.

Temperance with Respect to Sex

When Aristotle actually specifies the wrong actions that licentiousness disposes one to commit, he specifies (unhealthy) excessive guzzling with respect to food and drink, and adultery with respect to sex. This is mentioned four times (1117a2, 1129b21, 1130a24f, 1130a29f) and I used to find this odd—I mean, why *adultery* in particular? But then I found that "It was *moikheia*, 'adultery' to seduce the wife, widowed mother, unmarried daughter, sister or niece of a citizen";[9] and then it made more sense.

One might plausibly say that any man who seduced the wives and widowed mothers and unmarried daughters etc. of citizens must be a man greedy for sexual pleasures, and, as in the case of greed with respect to food and drink, we can maintain that such a man will be disposed to enjoy too many women, too often, too intensely—more than the temperate man—and all because he desires sexual pleasure too much. (There is probably the same connexion with health; it seems likely that Aristotle would believe that there is an excess of sexual activity which is unhealthy.)

Some people are greedy for sexual pleasure, and in such cases we can make good sense of licentiousness being a form of excess. There is a corresponding deficiency, for we may speak of people as being unnaturally or unhealthily indifferent to sexual pleasure. But cases of excess may well be rare though licentiousness with respect to sex be common. A man who commits "adultery" just *once* has done an act which "connotes depravity" and is "simply wrong" (1107a10ff). He goes wrong in enjoying something it is wrong to enjoy, and this wrong object is not "unhealthily excessive sexual activity" or one woman over the eight, but intercourse with someone it is "adulterous," and hence dishonourable, to have intercourse with. (Of course, someone might commit adultery for gain not for pleasure; but *if* he does it for pleasure [however minimal] rather than for gain, he counts as licentious [1130a25–30].)

No doubt it is often the case that excessively lustful people are impelled by their excessive desire to commit "adultery." And then, perhaps, by fortuitous overlap, each "wrong object" will happen to be "at least one object too many." But it is certain that excessive lust is not necessary. It might be that one had moderate, or even unnaturally low, sexual drive. But if one has any sexual drive at all *and* cares naught for what is honourable, then one will be disposed to commit licentious acts of "adultery." So having a licentious disposition is not necessarily a matter of having excessive sexual desire; someone could have his disposition with respect to sexual desire in a mean, or deficient, and *still* be licentious. He will be licentious just in so far as, for example, he sees sex solely in terms of satisfying his own healthy desires, or in terms of fun, as if it were not connected to anything else in life. And when he enjoys something it is wrong to enjoy, this wrong object will not be one object too many, nor (assuming he *is* licentious, not brutish) an unnatural object, but an object which the temperate man would not pursue in similar circumstances because the pleasure would be dishonourable.

Courage

As with temperance, there is a fairly obvious quibble to be made about there being *one* specific emotion or feeling which is the field of courage, namely that Aristotle himself specifies two—fear and confidence. One can attempt to preserve the thesis by maintaining that Aristotle has confused two distinct virtues, courage and caution, and Urmson, in support of his own position, and in line with several other commentators[10] does just this. For reasons too lengthy to go into here (but see David Pears, "Aristotle's Analysis of Courage," *Midwest Studies in Philosophy*, III 1978), I think this is a mistake. But I can make the points I want to make without begging this question, so I shall follow Urmson in discussing only fear, in relation to courage.

The cowardly err on the side of "excess"; they are disposed to exhibit fear "too much." Once again, how literal is this talk of "excess" and "too much" here? Is fearing the wrong objects on the wrong occasions a matter of fearing too many too often?

It is noteworthy that Aristotle begins his discussion of courage by stating baldly that fearing the *right* objects as part of being upright and decent is a matter of fearing e.g. disgrace. He goes on to specify the other things it is *right* to fear which are the concern of the courageous man, and these right objects are picked out without any reference or covert appeal to any notion of the mean. There are some things it is natural for men to fear and a kind of thing that we describe as being beyond human endurance; these things are the ones it is right to fear and they are these three—death, great pain and fairly extensive physical damage.

So fearing the right objects is fearing just those three things and fearing the wrong objects is fearing anything else. It is true that most cowards will fear those three things and then some; that is, they will fear some wrongs things just in so far as they fear *more* things than the courageous man does, i.e. too many. But, as in the case of temperance, this is a matter of fortuitous overlap. Just suppose that although I fear the dark, enclosed spaces and mice, I do not fear death, pain or physical damage. (This is not an entirely silly supposition given the phobias people genuinely have.) Then, given that it is death and so on, rather than mice and so on, that create the problem on the battlefield, it seems that whatever defect or vice I have, it is not cowardice. On the contrary, despite my fear of mice and so on, my defect is more like fearlessness—not because I fear too few objects (I fear as many as the courageous man), but because I do not fear the *right* ones.

Fearing the right objects is not a matter of fearing, say, three, some figure in a mean between two or less and four or more; it is a matter of fearing death, pain and physical damage. Hence, a corresponding vice is not a matter of fearing too many or too few objects, but simply a matter of fearing anything other than the right ones, or not fearing the right ones. The imaginary "fearless phobic" certainly fails to fear the right objects, but he is neither excessive nor deficient. (Or, if you like, he is both.)

What about fearing things "on the wrong occasions"? Is this a matter of fearing things too often or too seldom? Only accidentally. *Any* time you fear a wrong object you have felt fear on a wrong occasion. By fortuitous overlap, a coward who fears the three right things and then some (the dark, mice) will indeed feel fear more often than the courageous man, i.e. too often. But without the fortuitous overlap, this is not guaranteed. If I spend my life safely in the well-lit, mouse-free battlefield I may, if I do *not* fear the three right things, hardly ever feel fear at all. But I shall still do so "on the wrong occasion" if I do.

Mutatis mutandis, the same can be said for "wrong amount." Any time I feel *any* fear towards a wrong object I have felt a wrong amount; this is not because there is a right amount of fear to feel which I overshoot, but simply because wrong object guarantees both wrong occasion and wrong amount.

What about fearing the *right* things the right or wrong amount? I submit that we cannot maintain that fearing death etc. "the right amount" is fearing them somewhere between too much and too little. What fearing death "the right amount" comes to is fearing death the right way, and what *that* comes to is fearing an ignoble dishonourable death but not fearing an honourable one. And the same, I think, applies to fearing great pain or damage "the right amount."

The Background Assumptions

Why does Aristotle talk in terms of excess and deficiency, too . . . and too . . . at all? Why should he not rest content with saying that men may go wrong in *countless* ways, but hit the target and achieve excellence in only one (1106b30ff) rather than even suggesting that, for each virtue, there are just two opposed ways of going wrong?

I think the explanation of this lies in the fact that, in some cases, he is making certain background assumptions about how we are.

The assumption in the case of courage is, roughly, that all (sane) human beings fall somewhere on a range that goes from fearing almost everything, to fearing almost nothing, and passes through sensibly fearing death, pain and damage. Now, as a matter of fact, this assumption is generally true—the sorts of phobias I mentioned are rare and even more rarely, if ever, combined with a lack of fear of death etc. This rather general fact about us provides the explanation I said earlier was needed of why, to the virtue of courage, there correspond just two vices. The explanation is—that's just the way we happen to be; we just do go wrong in these two ways. Similarly, the explanation of why the two vices should be opposed, as excess to deficiency is—that's just the way things happen to turn out; fear works that way with us. The possibility of the "fearless phobic" shows that things might have been otherwise. If he were as common as the cowardly and the fearless, there would be three vices not two; if the and the cowardly were common and no-one was fearless, there would be two vices but they would not be *opposed* ones.

Since the assumption is roughly true, it is roughly true that to have the virtue of courage is to have one's disposition regarding fear in a mean. But courage is not a virtue *because* it is a disposition in a mean; and cowardice and fearlessness are not vices because they are excessive or deficient dispositions. This is to bet the order of explanation the wrong way round. Courage is a virtue because it is having the right disposition with respect to fear; cowardice and fearlessness are vices because they are both wrong dispositions with respect to fear. And it so happens that they can be called excessive or deficient; it so happens that they involve exhibiting fear too. . . .

Aristotle's assumption in the case of temperance is roughly, that all sane human beings fall on a range that goes (in theory) from being utterly indifferent to the pleasures of food, drink and sex, to being utterly consumed by the desire for them, and conveniently passes through being healthily interested *and* sensible about the relative importance of satisfying our own physical desires and other considerations.

If we *were* like that, then indeed temperance would have exactly two corresponding opposed vices, and that we were this way would explain why. But, as I have suggested, this assumption is manifestly false. The way we are guarantees that to the virtue of temperance there correspond at least the following vices—ordinary gluttony, drunkenness, lasciviousness, and a particular lack of scruple. The former may be called excesses: the latter is neither an excess nor a deficiency.

Patience

Now although Aristotle makes this sort of assumption about human beings in the case of courage and temperance, he does not do so in the case of all the other virtues. Interestingly enough it is Urmson, not Aristotle, who makes the (as it happens) false assumption about human beings which is required to guarantee that the right disposition with respect to anger is a disposition in a mean. Urmson says:

> The man whose character is such that he feels only mild annoyance at a trivial slight and is enraged by torture (of his wife?) has a character which is in a mean between one which exhibits rage on trivial *as well as important occasions* and one which can coolly contemplate the greatest outrages.[11] (My italics)

Note that here we must assume that the man who can coolly contemplate the greatest outrages is also someone who coolly contemplates trivial slights, in order to make sense of the first man's character as being in a mean. But there is the rub—why should we assume any such thing?

If we assume that human beings mostly fall on a range that goes from being angered by nearly everything (the trivial *and* the important) to being angered by hardly anything (neither the trivial nor the important) and conveniently passes through being angered by the important but not by the trivial, then we could indeed say that *praotes*, patience, like courage, is a disposition that lies in a mean between excess and deficiency. But the assumption is false. The defect many of us have is to be angered by the trivial and *not* by the important, or by the trivial and just those few important things that touch us very nearly.

As Urmson's own use of "trivial" and "important" implicitly recognises, Aristotle's talk about getting angry at the right (or wrong) objects is quite independent of any notion of excess and deficiency. Someone who gets angry about the wrong objects can *easily* be someone who fails to get angry about the right ones. Someone who is bad tempered might well be angry less often with fewer objects than someone who is constantly enraged by say injustices, but because these objects are wrong objects, such as tin openers and people disagreeing with him, we call him bad tempered. A person who hasn't grasped the idea of the *right* objects of anger, will, like the "fearless phobic," be neither excessive nor deficient, or, if you like, both.

As in the case of fear, getting angry about a wrong object will automatically guarantee that one is angry on a wrong occasion, to a wrong extent, and only fortuitous overlap will guarantee that each wrong occasion is a case of at least once too often. Similarly, failing to get angry about a wrong object will be not getting angry on a right occasion, and only fortuitous overlap will guarantee that this is a case of once too seldom.

Conclusion

Urmson says that "Aristotle . . . fails to notice that it is possible, if unlikely, that one's character should exhibit deficiency in some respect, the mean in others, and excess in others, even with regard to a single specific excellence,"[12] and I find this an odd remark for two reasons.

One is that it is so clearly false. Regarding anger, Aristotle says "the excess occurs in respect of all the circumstances, with the wrong people, for the wrong reasons, more than is right . . . ; but *of course these conditions do not all attach to the same subject*" (1126a9ff) and he explicitly contrasts the irascible, who stop quickly, with the bitter, who keep up their anger too long. He also acknowledges the same complexity when he discusses liberality (which Urmson does not mention); the prodigal, he says, go too far in giving and fall short in receiving . . . thus the faults of prodigality are hardly ever found together (1121a12ff).[13]

The other thing I find odd about Urmson's remark is that he does not seem to realise that, according to him, it must amount to "Aristotle fails to notice that the doctrine of the mean is false." For according to him, the doctrine of the mean requires at least the mysterious 3b, that one's character may err in two, exactly two, opposed ways, and this is admitted to be false as soon as one admits more than two vices corresponding to a virtue.

Of course it is true that, even if, like Aristotle, one does recognise more than two vices corresponding to a virtue, one could try to describe them all in terms of "too . . .". The irascible are too violent; the bitter are angry for too long; the irritable are angered too often (by too many objects?). Perhaps it is the apparent possibility of doing this that continues to entice people into believing that there is some truth in some quasi-Urmsonian doctrine of the mean. But this is an illusion. To many of the virtues there correspond vices which consist simply in being disposed to feelings about wrong objects, as I have illustrated. The objects are not "too many" or "too few," but just plain wrong; the vices are not excesses or deficiencies but just ways of going wrong. The fact that many vices can be characterised in terms of "too . . ." is a fact that has its own interest, but it does not serve to support the doctrine of the mean.

Notes

1. J. O. Urmson, "Aristotle's Doctrine of the Mean," *American Philosophical Quarterly* (1973).

2. Urmson, p. 226.

3. Compare W. F. R. Hardie, " 'Magnanimity' in Aristotle's Ethics," *Phronesis* (1978).

4. Philippa Foot, *Virtues and Vices* (Berkeley: University of California Press, 1978), p. 8.

5. Urmson, p. 225.

6. Urmson, p. 226.

7. Urmson, p. 225.

8. And it is clearly this second sort of licentiousness that inevitably brings the other vices in its train.

9. K. J. Dover, *Greek Popular Morality* (1974), p. 209.

10. E.g. David Ross.

11. Urmson, p. 225.

12. Urmson, p. 225.

13. And see also the *Eudemian Ethics*, 1232a10–15, where Aristotle goes even further and rightly distinguishes the man who has strong feelings about small amounts as a special case of meanness, thus admitting at least three sorts of illiberality.

6

Virtue and Reason

John McDowell

1. Presumably the point of, say, inculcating a moral outlook lies in a concern with how people live. It may seem that the very idea of a moral outlook makes room for, and requires, the existence of moral theory, conceived as a discipline which seeks to formulate acceptable principles of conduct. It is then natural to think of ethics as a branch of philosophy related to moral theory, so conceived, rather as the philosophy of science is related to science. On this view, the primary topic of ethics is the concept of right conduct, and the nature and justification of principles of behaviour. If there is a place for an interest in the concept of virtue, it is a secondary place. Virtue is a disposition (perhaps of a specially rational and self-conscious kind) to behave rightly; the nature of virtuc is cxplained, as it were, from the outside in.

My aim is to sketch the outlines of a different view, to be found in the philosophical tradition which flowers in Aristotle's ethics. According to this different view, although the point of engaging in ethical reflection still lies in the interest of the question "How should one live?",[1] that question is necessarily approached *via* the notion of a virtuous person. A conception of right conduct is grasped, as it were, from the inside out.

2. I shall begin with some considerations which make it attractive to say, with Socrates, that virtue is knowledge.

What is it for someone to possess a virtue? "Knowledge" implies that he gets things right; if we are to go any distance towards finding plausibility in the Socratic thesis, it is necessary to start with examples whose status as virtues, and hence as states of character whose pos-

121

sessor arrives at right answers to a certain range of questions about how to behave, is not likely to be queried. I shall use the example of kindness; anyone who disputes its claim to be a virtue should substitute a better example of his own. (The objectivity which "knowledge" implies will recur later.)

A kind person can be relied on to behave kindly when that is what the situation requires. Moreover, his reliably kind behaviour is not the outcome of a blind, non-rational habit or instinct, like the courageous behaviour—so called only by courtesy—of a lioness defending her cubs.[2] Rather, that the situation requires a certain sort of behaviour is (one way of formulating) his reason for behaving in that way, on each of the relevant occasions. So it must be something of which, on each of the relevant occasions, he is aware. A kind person has a reliable sensitivity to a certain sort of requirement which situations impose on behaviour. The deliverances of a reliable sensitivity are cases of knowledge; and there are idioms according to which the sensitivity itself can appropriately be described as knowledge: a kind person knows what it is like to be confronted with a requirement of kindness. The sensitivity is, we might say, a sort of perceptual capacity.[3]

(Of course a kind person need not himself classify the behaviour he sees to be called for, on one of the relevant occasions, as kind. He need not be articulate enough to possess concepts of the particular virtues; and even if he does, the concepts need not enter his reasons for the actions which manifest those particular virtues. It is enough if he thinks of what he does, when—as we put it—he shows himself to be kind, under some such description as "the thing to do." The description need not differ from that under which he thinks of other actions of his, which we regard as manifesting different virtues; the division into actions which manifest kindness and actions which manifest other virtues can be imposed, not by the agent himself, but by a possibly more articulate, and more theoretically oriented, observer.)

The considerations adduced so far suggest that the knowledge constituted by the reliable sensitivity is a necessary condition for possession of the virtue. But they do not show that the knowledge is, as in the Socratic thesis, to be identified with the virtue. A preliminary case for the identification might go as follows. On each of the relevant occasions, the requirement imposed by the situation, and detected by the agent's sensitivity to such requirements, must exhaust his reason for acting as he does. It would disqualify an action from counting as a manifestation of kindness if its agent needed some extraneous incentive to compliance with the requirement—say, the rewards of a good reputation. So the deliverances of his sensitivity constitute, one by one, complete explanations of the actions which manifest the virtue. Hence, since the sensitivity fully accounts for its deliverances, the sensitivity fully accounts for the actions. But the concept of the virtue is the concept of a state whose possession accounts for the actions which manifest it. Since that explanatory role is filled by the sensitivity, the sensitivity turns out to be what the virtue is.[4]

That is a preliminary case for the identification of particular virtues with, as it were, specialized sensitivities to requirements. *Mutatis mutandis*, a similar argument applies to virtue in general. Indeed, in the context of another Socratic thesis, that of the unity of virtue, virtue in general is what the argument for identification with knowledge really concerns; the specialized sensitivities which are to be equated with particular virtues, according to the argument considered so far, are actually not available one by one for a series of separate identifications.

What makes this plausible is the attractive idea that a virtue issues in nothing but right conduct. Suppose the relevant range of behaviour, in the case of kindness, is marked out by the notion of proper attentiveness to others' feelings. Now sometimes acting in such a way as to indulge someone's feelings is not acting rightly: the morally important fact about the situation is not that A will be upset by a projected action (though he will), but, say, that B has a right—a consideration of a sort sensitivity to which might be thought of as constituting fairness. In such a case, a straightforward propensity to be gentle to others' feelings would not lead to right conduct. If a genuine virtue is to produce nothing but right conduct, a simple propensity to be gentle cannot be identified with the virtue of kindness. Possession of the virtue must involve not only sensitivity to facts about others' feelings as reasons for acting in certain ways, but also sensitivity to facts about rights as reasons for acting in certain ways; and when circumstances of both sorts obtain, and a circumstance of the second sort is the one that should be acted on, a possessor of the virtue of kindness must be able to tell that that is so.[5] So we cannot disentangle genuine possession of kindness from the sensitivity which constitutes fairness. And since there are obviously no limits on the possibilities for compresence, in the same situation, of circumstances of the sorts proper sensitivities to which constitute all the virtues, the argument can be generalized: no one virtue can be fully possessed except by a possessor of all of them, that is, a possessor of virtue in general. Thus the particular virtues are not a batch of independent sensitivities. Rather, we use the concepts of the particular virtues to mark similarities and dissimilarities among the manifestations of a single sensitivity which is what virtue, in general, is: an ability to recognize requirements which situations impose on one's behaviour. It is a single complex sensitivity of this sort which we are aiming to instil when we aim to inculcate a moral outlook.

3. There is an apparent obstacle to the identification of virtue with knowledge. The argument for the identification requires that the deliverances of the sensitivity—the particular pieces of knowledge with which it equips its possessor—should fully explain the actions which manifest virtue. But it is plausible that appropriate action need not be elicited by a consideration apprehended as a reason—even a conclusive reason—for acting in a certain way. That may seem to open the following possibility: a person's perception of a situation may precisely match what a virtuous person's perception of it would be, although he does not act as the virtuous person would. But if a perception which corresponds to the virtuous person's does not call forth a virtuous action from this non-virtuous person, then the virtuous person's matching perception—the deliverance of his sensitivity—cannot, after all, fully account for the virtuous action which it does elicit from him. Whatever is missing, in the case of the person who does not act virtuously, must be present as an extra component, over and above the deliverance of the sensitivity, in a complete specification of the reason why the virtuous person acts as he does.[6] That destroys the identification of virtue with the sensitivity. According to this line of argument, the sensitivity can be at most an ingredient in a composite state which is what virtue really is.

If we are to retain the identification of virtue with knowledge, then, by contraposition, we are committed to denying that a virtuous person's perception of a situation can be precisely matched in someone who, in that situation, acts otherwise than virtuously. Socrates seems to have supposed that the only way to embrace this commitment is in terms of ignorance, so that, paradoxically, failure to act as a virtuous person would cannot be voluntary, at least under that description. But there is a less extreme possibility, sketched by Aristotle.[7] This is to allow that someone who fails to act virtuously may, in a way, perceive what a virtuous person would, so that his failure to do the right thing is not inadvertent; but to insist that his failure occurs only because his appreciation of what he perceives is clouded, or unfocused, by the impact of a desire to do otherwise. This preserves the identification of virtue with a sensitivity; contrary to the counter-argument, nothing over and above the unclouded deliverances of the sensitivity is needed to explain the actions which manifest virtue. It is not that some extra explanatory factor, over and above the deliverances of the sensitivity, conspires with them to elicit action from the virtuous person, but rather that the other person's failure to act in that way is accounted for by a defectiveness in the approximations to those deliverances which he has.

It would be a mistake to protest that one can fail to act on a reason, and even on a reason judged by oneself to be better than any reason which one has for acting otherwise, without there needing to be any clouding or distortion in one's appreciation of the reason which one flouts.[8] That is true; but to suppose it constitutes an objection to Aristotle is to fail to understand the special nature of the conception of virtue which generates Aristotle's interest in incontinence.

One way to bring out the special nature of the conception is to note that, for Aristotle, continence is distinct from virtue, and just as problematic as incontinence. If someone needs to overcome an inclination to act otherwise, in getting himself to act as, say, temperance or courage demand, then he shows not virtue but (mere) continence. Suppose we take it that a virtuous person's judgment as to what he should do is arrived at by weighing, on the one side, some reason for acting in a way that will in fact manifest, say, courage, and, on the other side, a reason for doing something else (say a risk to life and limb, as a reason for running away), and deciding that on balance the former reason is the better. In that case, the distinction between virtue and continence will seem unintelligible. If the virtuous person allows himself to weigh the present danger, as a reason for running away, why should we not picture the weighing as his allowing himself to feel an inclination to run away, of a strength proportional to the weight which he allows to the reason? So long as he keeps the strength of his inclinations in line with the weight which he assigns to the reasons, his actions will conform to his judgment as to where, on balance, the better reason lies; what more can we require for virtue? (Perhaps that the genuinely courageous person simply does not care about his own survival? But Aristotle is rightly anxious to avert this misconception.[9]) The distinction becomes intelligible if we stop assuming that the virtuous person's judgment is a balancing of reasons for and against. The view of a situation which he arrives at by exercising his sensitivity is one in which some aspect of the situation is seen as constituting a reason for acting in some way; this reason is apprehended, not as outweighing or over-riding any reasons for acting in other ways which would otherwise be constituted by other aspects of the situation (the present danger, say), but as silencing them. Here and now the risk to life and limb is not seen as any reason for removing himself. Aristotle's problem about in-continence is not "How can one weigh considerations in favour of ac-tions X and Y, decide that on balance the better reasons are in favour of X, but nevertheless perform Y?" (a question which, no doubt, does not require the idea of clouded judgment for its answer); but rather (a problem equally about continence) "How can one have a view of a situation in which considerations which would otherwise appeal to one's will are silenced, but nevertheless allow those considerations to make themselves heard by one's will?"—a question which clearly is answerable, if at all, only by supposing that the incontinent or conti-nent person does not fully share the virtuous person's perception of the situation.[10]

A more pressing objection is directed against the special conception of virtue: in particular, the use of cognitive notions in characterizing it. According to this objection, it must be a misuse of the notion of per-ception to suppose that an unclouded perception might suffice, on its own, to constitute a reason for acting in a certain way. An exercise of a genuinely cognitive capacity can yield at most part of a reason for act-ing; something appetitive is needed as well. To talk of virtue—a pro-pensity to act in certain ways for certain reasons—as consisting in a sensitivity, a perceptual capacity, is to amalgamate the required appeti-tive component into the putative sensitivity. But all that is achieved thereby is a projection of human purposes into the world. (Here it becomes apparent how the objection touches on the issue of objectiv-ity.) How one's will is disposed is a fact about oneself; whereas a genu-inely cognitive faculty discloses to one how the world is independently of oneself, and in particular independently of one's will. Cognition and volition are distinct: the world—the proper sphere of cognitive capaci-ties—is in itself an object of purely theoretical contemplation, capable of moving one to action only in conjunction with an extra factor—a state of will—contributed by oneself. I shall return to this objection.

4. Presented with an identification of virtue with knowledge, it is natu-ral to ask for a formulation of the knowledge which virtue is. We tend to assume that the knowledge must have a stateable propositional con-

tent (perhaps not capable of immediate expression by the knower). Then the virtuous person's reliably right judgments as to what he should do, occasion by occasion, can be explained in terms of interaction between this universal knowledge and some appropriate piece of particular knowledge about the situation at hand; and the explanation can take the form of a "practical syllogism," with the content of the universal knowledge, or some suitable part of it, as major premiss, the relevant particular knowledge as minor premiss, and the judgment about what is to be done as deductive conclusion.

This picture is congenial to the objection mentioned at the end of §3. According to this picture, the problematic concept of a requirement figures only in the major premiss, and the conclusion, of the syllogism which reconstructs the virtuous person's reason for acting. Knowledge of the major premiss, the objector might say, is none other than the disposition of the will which is required, according to the objection, as a further component in the relevant reasons for acting, and hence as a further component in virtue, over and above any strictly cognitive state. (We call it "knowledge" to endorse it, not to indicate that it is genuinely cognitive.) What a virtuous person really perceives is only what is stated in the minor premiss of the syllogism: that is, a straightforward fact about the situation at hand, which—as the objection requires— would be incapable of eliciting action on its own.

This picture fits only if the virtuous person's views about how, in general, one should behave are susceptible of codification, in principles apt for serving as major premisses in syllogisms of the sort envisaged. But to an unprejudiced eye it should seem quite implausible that any reasonably adult moral outlook admits of any such codification. As Aristotle consistently says, the best generalizations about how one should behave hold only for the most part.[11] If one attempted to reduce one's conception of what virtue requires to a set of rules, then, however subtle and thoughtful one was in drawing up the code, cases would inevitably turn up in which a mechanical application of the rules would strike one as wrong—and not necessarily because one had changed one's mind; rather, one's mind on the matter was not susceptible of capture in any universal formula.[12]

A deep-rooted prejudice about rationality blocks ready acceptance of this. A moral outlook is a specific determination of one's practical rationality: it shapes one's views about what reasons one has for acting. Rationality requires consistency; a specific conception of rationality in a particular area imposes a specific form on the abstract requirement of consistency—a specific view of what counts as going on doing the same thing here. The prejudice is the idea that acting in the light of a specific conception of rationality must be explicable in terms of being guided by a formulable universal principle. This prejudice comes under radical attack in Wittgenstein's discussion, in the *Philosophical Investigations*, of the concept of following a rule.

Consider an exercise of rationality in which there *is* a formulable rule, of which each successive action can be regarded as an application, appropriate in the circumstances arrived at: say (Wittgenstein's example) the extending of a series of numbers. We tend to picture the understanding of the instruction "Add 2"—command of the rule for extending the series 2, 4, 6, 8, . . .—as a psychological mechanism which, aside from lapses of attention and so forth, churns out the appropriate behaviour with the sort of reliability which a physical mechanism, say a piece of clockwork, might have. If someone is extending the series correctly, and one takes his behaviour to be compliance with the understood instruction, then, according to this picture, one has postulated such a psychological mechanism, underlying his behaviour, by an inference analogous to that whereby one might hypothesize a physical structure underlying the observable motions of some inanimate object. But this picture is profoundly suspect.

What manifests the pictured state of understanding? Suppose the person says, when asked what he is doing, "Look, I'm adding 2 each time." This apparent manifestation of understanding (or any other) will have been accompanied, at any point, by at most a finite fragment of the potentially infinite range of behaviour which we want to say the rule dictates. Thus the evidence for the presence of the pictured state is always compatible with the supposition that, on some future occasion for its exercise, the behaviour elicited by the occasion will diverge from what we would count as correct. Wittgenstein dramatizes this with the example of the man who continues the series, after 1000, with 1004, 1008, . . .[13] If a possibility of the 1004, 1008, . . . type were to be realized (and we could not bring the person to concede that he had simply made a mistake), that would show that the behaviour hitherto was not guided by the psychological conformation which we were picturing as guiding it. The pictured state, then, always transcends the grounds on which it is allegedly postulated.

There may be an inclination to protest: "This is merely inductive scepticism about other minds. After all, one knows in one's own case that one's behaviour will not come adrift like that." But this misses the point of the argument.

First, if what it is for one's behaviour to come adrift is for it suddenly to seem that everyone else is out of step, then clearly the argument bears on one's own case just as much as on the case of others. (Imagine that the person who goes on with 1004, 1008, . . . had said, in advance, "I know in my own case that my behaviour will not come adrift.")

Second, it is a mistake to interpret the argument as making a sceptical point: that one does not know, in the case of another person (or in one's own case either, once we have made the first correction), that the behaviour will not come adrift. The argument is not meant to suggest that we should be in a state of constant trepidation lest possibilities of the 1004, 1008, . . . type be realized.[14] We are confident that they will not: the argument aims, not at all to undermine this confidence, but to change our conception of its ground and nature. We tend to picture our transition to this confident expectation, from such grounds as we have, as being mediated by the postulated psychological mechanism. But we can no more find the putatively mediating state manifested in the grounds for our expectation than we can find manifested there the very future occurrences we expect. Postulation of the mediating state is an idle intervening step; it does nothing to underwrite the confidence of the expectation.

(The content of the expectation is not purely behavioural. We might have a good scientific argument, mediated by postulation of a physiological mechanism, for not expecting any particular train of behaviour, of the 1004, 1008, . . . type, which we might contemplate. Here postulation of the mediating physiological state would not be an idle intervening step. But the parallel is misleading. We can bring this out by considering a variant of Wittgenstein's example, in which, on reaching 1000, the person goes on as we expect, with 1002, 1004, . . . , but with a sense of dissociation from what he is doing. What he does no longer strikes him as going on in the same way; it feels as if a sheer habit has usurped his reason in controlling his behaviour. We confidently expect that this sort of thing will not happen; once again, postulation of a psychological mechanism does nothing to underwrite this confidence.)

What *is* the ground and nature of our confidence? About the competent use of words, Stanley Cavell writes:

We learn and teach words in certain contexts, and then we are expected, and expect others, to be able to project them into further contexts. Noth-

ing insures that this projection will take place (in particular, not the grasping of universals nor the grasping of books of rules), just as nothing
insures that we will make, and understand, the same projections. That on
the whole we do is a matter of our sharing routes of interest and feeling,
modes of response, senses of humour and of significance and fulfilment,
of what is outrageous, of what is similar to what else, what a rebuke, what
forgiveness, of when an utterance is an assertion, when an appeal, when
an explanation—all the whirl of organism Wittgenstein calls "forms of
life." Human speech and activity, sanity and community, rest upon nothing more, but nothing less, than this. It is a vision as simple as it is difficult,
and as difficult as it is (and because it is) terrifying.[15]

The terror of which Cavell speaks at the end of this marvellous passage is a sort of vertigo, induced by the thought that there is nothing
but shared forms of life to keep us, as it were, on the rails. We are
inclined to think that that is an insufficient foundation for a conviction
that when we, say, extend a number series, we really are, at each stage,
doing the same thing as before. In this mood, it seems to us that what
Cavell describes cannot be a shared conceptual framework within
which something is, given the circumstances, objectively the correct
move;[16] it looks, rather, like a congruence of subjectivities, with the
congruence not grounded as it would need to be to amount to an
objectivity. So we feel we have lost the objectivity of (in our case) mathematics (and similarly in other cases). We recoil from this vertigo into
the idea that we are kept on the rails by our grasp of rules. This idea
has a pair of twin components: first, the idea (as above) that grasp of
the rules is a psychological mechanism which (apart from mechanical
failure, which is how we picture mistakes and so forth) guarantees that
we stay in the straight and narrow; and, second, the idea that the rails—
what we engage our mental wheels with when we come to grasp the
rules—are objectively there, in a way which transcends the "mere"
sharing of forms of life (hence, for instance, platonism about numbers).
This composite idea is not the perception of some truth, but a consol-
ing myth, elicited from us by our inability to endure the vertigo.

Of course, this casts no doubt on the possibility of putting explanations of particular moves, in the extending of a number series, in a
syllogistic form: universal knowledge of how to extend the series interacts with particular knowledge of where one is in it, to produce a non-
accidentally correct judgment as to what the next number is. In this
case we can formulate the explanation so as to confer on the judgment

explained the compellingness possessed by the conclusion of a proof. What is wrong is to take that fact to indicate that the explanation lays bare the inexorable workings of a machine: something whose operations, with our understanding of them, would not depend on the deliverances, in particular cases, of (for instance, and centrally) that shared sense of what is similar to what else which Cavell mentions. The truth is that it is only because of our own involvement in our "whirl of organism" that we can understand the words we produce as conferring that special compellingness on the judgment explained.

Now it is only this misconception of the deductive paradigm which leads us to suppose that the operations of any specific conception of rationality in a particular area—any specific conception of what counts as doing the same thing—must be deductively explicable; that is, that there must be a formulable universal principle suited to serve as major premiss in syllogistic explanations of the sort considered above.

Consider, for instance, a concept whose application gives rise to hard cases, in this sense: there are disagreements which resist resolution by argument, as to whether or not the concept applies. Convinced that one is in the right on a hard case, one will find oneself saying, as one's arguments tail off without securing assent, "You simply aren't seeing it," or "But don't you see?" In such cases the prejudice takes the form of a dilemma. One horn is that the inconclusiveness of one's arguments stems merely from an inability, in principle remediable, to articulate what one knows. It is possible, in principle, to spell out a universal formula which specifies the conditions under which the concept, in that use of it which one has mastered, is correctly applied. That would elevate one's argument to deductiveness. (If one's opponent refused to accept the deductive argument's major premiss, that would show that he had not mastered the same use of the concept, so that there would be, after all, no substantive disagreement.) If this assimilation to the deductive paradigm is not possible, then—this is the other horn of the dilemma—one's conviction that one is genuinely making a correct application of a concept (genuinely going on in the same way as before) must be an illusion. The case is revealed as one which calls, not for finding (seeing) the right answer to a question about how things are, but (perhaps) for a creative decision as to what to say.[17] Thus: either the case is not really a hard case, since sufficient ingenuity in the construction of arguments will resolve it; or, if its hardness is ineliminable, that shows that the issue cannot, after all, be one about whether an application of a concept is correct.

In a hard case, the issue turns on that appreciation of the particular instance whose absence is deplored, in "You simply aren't seeing it," or which is unsuccessfully appealed to, in "But don't you see?" The dilemma reflects the view that a putative judgment which is grounded in nothing firmer than that cannot really be going on in the same way as before. This is an avoidance of vertigo. The thought is: there is not enough there to constitute the rails on which a genuine series of consistent applications of a concept must run. But in fact it is an illusion to suppose that the first horn of the dilemma yields a way of preserving from risk of vertigo the conviction that we are dealing with genuine concept-application. The illusion is the misconception of the deductive paradigm: the idea that deductive explicability characterizes an exercise of reason in which it is, as it were, automatically compelling, without dependence on our partially shared "whirl of organism." The dilemma registers a refusal to accept that when the dependence which induces vertigo is out in the open, in the appeal to appreciation, we can genuinely be going on in the same way; but the paradigm of a genuine case, that with which the rejected case is unfavourably compared, has the same dependence, only less obviously.[18]

Contemplating the dependence should not induce vertigo at all. We cannot be whole-heartedly engaged in the relevant parts of the "whirl of organism," and at the same time achieve the detachment necessary in order to query whether our unreflective view of what we are doing is illusory. The cure for the vertigo, then, is to give up the idea that philosophical thought, about the sorts of practice in question, should be undertaken at some external standpoint, outside our immersion in our familiar forms of life.[19] If this cure works where explanations of exercises of rationality conform to the deductive paradigm, it should be no less efficacious where we explicitly appeal to appreciation of the particular instance in inviting acceptance of our judgments. And its efficacy in cases of the second kind is direct. Only the illusion that the deductive cases are immune can make it seem that, in order to effect the cure in cases of the second kind, we must first eliminate explicit dependence on appreciation, by assimilating them, as the prejudice requires, to the deductive paradigm.

If we make the assimilation, we adopt a position in which it is especially clear that our picture of a psychological mechanism, underlying a series of exercises of rationality, is a picture of something which transcends the grounds on which it is ascribed to anyone. In the cases in question, no one can express the envisaged universal formula. This transcendence poses difficulties about the acquisition of the pictured state. We are inclined to be impressed by the sparseness of the teaching which leaves someone capable of autonomously going on in the same way. All that happens is that the pupil is told, or shown, what to do in a few instances, with some surrounding talk about why that is the thing to do; the surrounding talk, *ex hypothesi* given that we are dealing with a case of the second kind, falls short of including actual enunciation of a universal principle, mechanical application of which would constitute correct behaviour in the practice in question. Yet pupils do acquire a capacity to go on, without further advice, to novel instances. Impressed by the sparseness of the teaching, we find this remarkable. But assimilation to the deductive paradigm leaves it no less remarkable. The assimilation replaces the question "How is it that the pupil, given that sparse instruction, goes on to new instances in the right way?" with the question "How is it that the pupil, given that sparse instruction, divines from it a universal formula with the right deductive powers?" The second question is, if anything, less tractable. Addressing the first, we can say: it is a fact (no doubt a remarkable fact) that, against a background of common human nature and shared forms of life, one's sensitivities to kinds of similarities between situations can be altered and enriched by just this sort of instruction. This attributes no guesswork to the learner; whereas no amount of appealing to common human nature and shared forms of life will free the second question from its presupposition—inevitably imported by assimilation to the deductive—that the learner is required to make a leap of divination.[20]

It is not to be supposed that the appreciation of the particular instance, explicitly appealed to in the second kind of case, is a straightforward or easy attainment on the part of those who have it; that either, on casual contemplation of an instance, one sees it in the right light, or else one does not, and is then unreachable by argument. First, "Don't you see?" can often be supplemented with words aimed at persuasion. A skilfully presented characterization of an instance will sometimes bring someone to see it as one wants; or one can adduce general considerations, for instance about the point of the concept a particular application of which is in dispute. Given that the case is one of the second kind, any such arguments will fall short of rationally necessitating acceptance of their conclusion in the way a proof does.[21] But it is only the prejudice I am attacking which makes this seem to cast doubt on their status as arguments: that is, appeals to reason. Second, if effort can induce the needed appreciation in someone else, it can also take effort to acquire it oneself. Admitting the dependence on appreciation does not imply that, if someone has the sort of specific determination of rationality we are considering, the right way to handle a given situation will always be clear to him on unreflective inspection of it.

5. If we resist the prejudice, and respect Aristotle's belief that a view of how one should live is not codifiable, what happens to our explanations of a virtuous person's reliably right judgments as to what he should do on particular occasions? Aristotle's notion of the practical syllogism is obviously meant to apply here; we need to consider how.

The explanations, so far treated as explanations of judgments about what to do, are equally explanations of actions. The point of analogy which motivates the quasi-logical label "practical syllogism" is this. If something might serve as an argument for a theoretical conclusion, then it can equally figure in an account of someone's reasons for believing that conclusion, with the premisses of the argument giving the content of the psychological states—beliefs, in the theoretical case—which we cite in the reason-giving explanation. Now actions too are explained by reasons; that is, by citing psychological states in the light of which we can see how acting in the way explained would have struck the agent as in some way rational. The idea of a practical syllogism is the idea of an argument-like schema for explanations of actions, with the "premisses," as in the theoretical case, giving the content of the psychological states cited in the explanation.[22]

David Wiggins has given this account of the general shape of a practical syllogism:

> The first or major premiss mentions something of which there could be a desire, *orexis*, transmissible to some practical conclusion (i.e., a desire convertible *via* some available minor premiss into an action). The second premiss pertains to the feasibility in the particular situation to which the syllogism is applied of what must be done if the claim of the major premiss is to be heeded.[23]

This schema fits most straightforwardly when reasons are (in a broad sense) technical: the major premiss specifies a determinate goal, and the minor premiss marks out some action as a means to it.[24]

The role played by the major premiss, in these straightforward applications of the schema, is to give the content of an orectic psychological state: something we might conceive as providing the motivating energy for the actions explained. Aristotle's idea seems to be that what fills an analogous role in the explanation of virtuous actions is the virtuous person's conception of the sort of life a human being should lead.[25] If that conception were codifiable in universal principles, the explanations would take the deductive shape insisted on by the prejudice discussed in §4. But the thesis of uncodifiability means that the envisaged major premiss, in a virtue syllogism, cannot be definitively written down.[26] Any attempt to capture it in words will recapitulate the character of the teaching whereby it might be instilled: generalizations will be approximate at best, and examples will need to be taken with the sort of "and so on" which appeals to the cooperation of a hearer who has cottoned on.[27]

If someone guides his life by a certain conception of how to live, then he acts, on particular occasions, so as to fulfil suitable concerns.[28] A concern can mesh with a noticed fact about a situation, so as to account for an action: as, for instance, a concern for the welfare of one's friends, together with awareness that a friend is in trouble and open to being comforted, can explain missing a pleasant party in order to talk to the friend. On a suitable occasion, that pair of psychological states might constitute the core of a satisfying explanation of an action which is in fact virtuous. Nothing more need be mentioned for the action to have been given a completely intelligible motivation. In Aristotle's view, the orectic state cited in an explanation of a virtuous action is the agent's entire conception of how to live, rather than just whatever concern it happened to be; and this may now seem mysterious. But the core explanation, as so far envisaged, lacks any indication that the action explained conformed to the agent's conception of how to live. The core explanation would apply equally to a case of helping one's friend because one thought it was, in the circumstances, the thing to do, and to a case of helping one's friend in spite of thinking it was not, in the circumstances, the thing to do.

A conception of how one should live is not simply an unorganized collection of propensities to act, on this or that occasion, in pursuit of this or that concern. Sometimes there are several concerns, fulfilment of any one of which might, on a suitable occasion, constitute acting as a certain conception of how to live would dictate, and each of which, on the occasion at hand, is capable of engaging with a known fact about the situation and issuing in action. Acting in the light of a conception of how to live requires selecting and acting on the right concern. (Compare the end of §1, on the unity of virtue.) So if an action whose motivation is spelled out in our core explanation is a manifestation of virtue, more must be true of its agent than just that on this occasion he acted with that motivation. The core explanation must at least be seen against the background of the agent's conception of how to live; and if the situation is one of those on which any of several concerns might impinge the conception of how to live must be capable of actually entering our understanding of the action, explaining why it was this concern rather than any other which was drawn into operation.

How does it enter? If the conception of how to live involved a ranking of concerns, or perhaps a set of rankings each relativized to some type of situation, the explanation of why one concern was operative rather than another would be straightforward. But uncodifiability rules out laying down such general rankings in advance of all the predicaments with which life may confront one.

What I have described as selecting the right concern might equally be described in terms of the minor premiss of the core explanation. If there is more than one concern which might impinge on the situation, there is more than one fact about the situation which the agent might, say, dwell on, in such a way as to summon an appropriate concern into operation. It is by virtue of his seeing this particular fact rather than that one as the salient fact about the situation that he is moved to act by this concern rather than that one.[29] This perception of saliences is the shape taken here by the appreciation of particular cases which I discussed in §5: something to which the uncodifiability of an exercise of rationality sometimes compels explicit appeal when we aim to represent actions as instances of it. A conception of how to live shows itself, when more than one concern might issue in action, in one's seeing, or being able to be brought to see, one fact rather than another as salient. And our understanding of such a conception enters into our understanding of actions—the supplementation which the core explanation needs—by enabling us to share, or at least comprehend, the agent's perception of saliences.[30]

It is not wrong to think of the virtuous person's judgments about what to do, or his actions, as explicable by interaction between knowledge of how to live and particular knowledge about the situation at hand. (Compare the beginning of §4.) But the thought needs a more subtle construal than the deductive paradigm allows. With the core explanations and their supplementations, I have in effect been treating the complete explanations as coming in two stages. It is at the first stage—hitherto the supplementation—that knowledge of how to live interacts with particular knowledge: knowledge, namely, of all the particular facts capable of engaging with concerns whose fulfilment would, on occasion, be virtuous. This interaction yields, in a way essentially dependent on appreciation of the particular case, a view of the situation with one such fact, as it were, in the foreground. Seen as salient, that fact serves, at the second stage, as minor premiss in a core explanation.[31]

6. We can go back now to the non-cognitivist objection outlined at the end of §3. Awareness that one's friend is in trouble and open to being comforted—the psychological state whose content is the minor premiss of our core explanation—can perhaps, for the sake of argument, be conceded to be the sort of thing which the objection insists cognitive states must be: something capable of eliciting action only in conjunction with a non-cognitive state, namely, in our example, a concern for one's friends.[32] But if someone takes that fact to be the salient fact about the situation, he is in a psychological state which is essentially practical. The relevant notion of salience cannot be understood except in terms of seeing something as a reason for acting which silences all others (compare §3). So classifying that state as a cognitive state is just the sort of thing which the objection attacks.

The most natural way to press the objection is to insist on purifying the content of what is genuinely known down to something which is, in itself, motivationally inert (namely, given the concession above, that one's friend is in trouble and open to being comforted); and then to represent the "perception" of a salience as an amalgam of the purified awareness with an additional appetitive state. But what appetitive state? Concern for one's friends yields only the core explanation, not the explanation in which the "perception" of salience was to figure. Perhaps the conception of how to live? That is certainly an orectic state. But, given the thesis of uncodifiability, it is not intelligible independently of just such appreciation of particular situations as is involved in the present "perception" of a salience; so it is not suitable to serve as an element into which, together with some genuine awareness, the "perception" could be regarded as analysable. (This non-cognitivist strategy is reflected in assimilation to the deductive paradigm: that the assimilation is congenial to the non-cognitivist objection was noted early in §4. The failure of the strategy is reflected in the failure of the assimilation, given the thesis of uncodifiability.)

If we feel the vertigo discussed in §4, it is out of distaste for the idea that a manifestation of reason might be recognizable as such only from within the practice whose status is in question. We are inclined to think there ought to be a neutral external standpoint from which the rationality of any genuine exercise of reason could be demonstrated. Now we might understand the objection to be demanding a non-cognitive extra which would be analogous to hunger: an appetitive state whose possession by anyone is intelligible in its own right, not itself open to assessment as rational or irrational, but conferring an obvious rationality, recognizable from outside, on behaviour engaged in with a view to its gratification. In that case it is clear how the objection is an expression of the craving for a kind of rationality independently demonstrable as such. However, it is highly implausible that all the concerns which motivate virtuous actions are intelligible, one by one, independently of appreciating a virtuous person's distinctive way of seeing situations. And even if they were, the various particular concerns figure only in the core explanations. We do not fully understand a virtuous person's actions—we do not see the consistency in them—unless we can supplement the core explanations with a grasp of his conception of how to live. And though this is to credit him with an orectic state, it is not to credit him with an externally intelligible over-arching desire; for we cannot understand the content of the orectic state from the envisaged external standpoint. It is, rather, to comprehend, essentially from within, the virtuous person's distinctive way of viewing particular situations.[33]

The rationality of virtue, then, is not demonstrable from an external standpoint. But to suppose that it ought to be is only a version of the prejudice discussed in §4. It is only an illusion that our paradigm of reason, deductive argument, has its rationality discernible from a standpoint not necessarily located within the practice itself.

7. Although perceptions of saliences resist decomposition into "pure" awareness together with appetitive states, there is an inclination to insist, nevertheless, that they cannot be genuinely cognitive states. We can be got into a cast of mind in which—as it seems to us—we have these problematic perceptions, only because we can be brought to care about certain things; hence, ultimately, only because of certain antecedent facts about our emotional and appetitive make-up. This can seem to justify a more subtle non-cognitivism: one which abandons the claim that the problematic perceptions can be analysed into cognitive and appetitive components, but insists that, because of the anthropo-

centricity of the conceptual apparatus involved, they are not judgments, true or false, as to how things are in an independent reality; and that is what cognitive states are.[34]

I cannot tackle this subtle non-cognitivism properly now. I suspect that its origin is a philistine scientism, probably based on the misleading idea that the right of scientific method to rational acceptance is discernible from a more objective standpoint than that from which we seem to perceive the saliences. A scientistic conception of reality is eminently open to dispute. When we ask the metaphysical question whether reality is what science can find out about, we cannot, without begging the question, restrict the materials for an answer to those which science can countenance. Let the question be an empirical question, by all means; but the empirical data which would be collected by a careful and sensitive moral phenomenology—no doubt not a scientific enterprise—are handled quite unsatisfyingly by non-cognitivism.[35]

It would be a mistake to object that stress on appreciation of the particular, and the absence of a decision procedure, encourages everyone to pontificate about particular cases. In fact resistance to non-cognitivism, about the perception of saliences, recommends humility. If we resist noncognitivism, we can equate the conceptual equipment which forms the framework of anything recognizable as a moral outlook with a capacity to be impressed by certain aspects of reality. But ethical reality is immensely difficult to see clearly. (Compare the end of §4.) If we are aware of how, for instance, selfish fantasy distorts our vision, we shall not be inclined to be confident that we have got things right.[36]

It seems plausible that Plato's ethical Forms are, in part at least, a response to uncodifiability: if one cannot formulate what someone has come to know when he cottons on to a practice, say one of concept-application, it is natural to say that he has seen something. Now in the passage quoted in §4, Cavell mentions two ways of avoiding vertigo: "the grasping of universals" as well as what we have been concerned with so far, "the grasping of books of rules." But though Plato's Forms are a myth, they are not a consolation, a mere avoidance of vertigo; vision of them is portrayed as too difficult an attainment for that to be so. The remoteness of the Form of the Good is a metaphorical version of the thesis that value is not in the world, utterly distinct from the dreary literal version which has obsessed recent moral philosophy. The point of the metaphor is the colossal difficulty of attaining a capacity to cope clear-sightedly with the ethical reality which *is* part of our world. Unlike other philosophical responses to uncodifiability, this one may actually work towards moral improvement; negatively, by inducing humility, and positively, by an inspiring effect akin to that of a religious conversion.[37]

8. If the question "How should one live?" could be given a direct answer in universal terms, the concept of virtue would have only a secondary place in moral philosophy. But the thesis of uncodifiability excludes a head-on approach to the question whose urgency gives ethics its interest. Occasion by occasion, one knows what to do, if one does, not by applying universal principles but by being a certain kind of person: one who sees situations in a certain distinctive way. And there is no dislodging, from the central position they occupy in the ethical reflection of Plato and Aristotle, questions about the nature and (hardly discussed in this paper) the acquisition of virtue.

It is sometimes complained that Aristotle does not attempt to outline a decision procedure for questions about how to behave. But we have good reason to be suspicious of the assumption that there must be something to be found along the route he does not follow.[38] And there is plenty for us to do in the area of philosophy of mind where his different approach locates ethics.

Notes

1. Aristotle, *Nicomachean Ethics* (henceforth cited as *NE*), e.g., 1103b 26–31; cf. Plato, *Republic* 352d 5–6.

2. Cf. *NE* VI. 13 on the distinction between "natural virtue" and "virtue strictly so called."

3. Non-cognitivist objections to this sort of talk will be considered later.

4. There is a gap here. Even if it is conceded that the virtuous person has no further *reason* for what he does than the deliverance of his sensitivity, still, it may be said, two people can have the same reason for acting in a certain way, but only one of them act in that way. There must then be some further *explanation* of this difference between them: if not that the one who acts has a further reason, then perhaps that the one who does not is in some state, standing or temporary, which undermines the efficacy of reasons, or perhaps of reasons of the particular kind in question, in producing action. This suggests that if we are to think of virtue as guaranteeing action, virtue must consist not in the sensitivity alone but in the sensitivity together with freedom from such obstructive states. These issues recur in §3 below.

5. I do not mean to suggest that there is always a way of acting satisfactorily (as opposed to making the best of a bad job); nor that there is always one right

answer to the question what one should do. But when there is a right answer, a virtuous person should be able to tell what it is.

6. If we distinguish the reason why he acts from his reason for acting, this is the objection of n4 above.

7. *NE* VII. 3.

8. Cf. Donald Davidson, "How is Weakness of Will Possible?," in Joel Feinberg, ed., *Moral Concepts* (Oxford: Oxford University Press, 1969), pp. 93–113, at pp. 99–100.

9. *NE* III. 9.

10. On this view, genuine deliverances of the sensitivity involved in virtue would necessitate action. It is not that action requires not only a deliverance of the sensitivity but also, say, freedom from possibly obstructive factors, for instance distracting desires. An obstructive factor would not interfere with the efficacy of a deliverance of the sensitivity, but rather preclude genuine achievement of that view of the situation. This fills the gap mentioned in n4 above. (My discussion of incontinence here is meant to do no more than suggest that the identification of virtue with knowledge should not be dismissed out of hand, on the ground that it poses a problem about incontinence. I have said a little more in §§9, 10 of my "Are Moral Requirements Hypothetical Imperatives?" *Proceedings of the Aristotelian Society Supplementary Volume* 52 [1978], pp. 13–29; but a great deal more would be needed in a full treatment.)

11. See, e.g., *NE* I. 3.

12. See *NE* V. 10, especially 1137b 19–24.

13. *Philosophical Investigations* (Oxford: Basil Blackwell, 1953), §185.

14. Nor even that we really *understand* the supposition that such a thing might happen. See Barry Stroud, "Wittgenstein and Logical Necessity," *Philosophical Review* 74 (1965), pp. 504–518.

15. *Must We Mean What We Say?* (New York: Charles Scribner's Sons, 1969), p. 52.

16. Locating the desired objectivity *within* the conceptual framework is intended to leave open, here, the possibility of querying whether the conceptual framework itself is objectively the right one. If someone wants to reject the question whether this rather than that moral outlook is objectively correct, he will still want it to be an objective matter whether one has, say, succeeded in inculcating a particular moral outlook in someone else; so he will still be susceptible to the vertigo I am describing.

17. Why not abandon the whole practice as fraudulent? In some cases something may need to be said: for instance by a judge, in a lawsuit. Against the view that in legal hard cases judges are free to *make* the law, see Ronald Dworkin, "Hard Cases," in *Taking Rights Seriously* (London: Duckworth, 1977), pp. 81–130.

18. In the rejected case, the dependence is out in the open in an especially perturbing form, in that the occasional failure of the appeal to appreciation brings out how the "whirl of organism" is only partly shared; whereas there are no hard cases in mathematics. This is indeed a significant fact about mathematics. But its significance is not that mathematics is immune from the dependence.

19. I am not suggesting that effecting this cure is a simple matter.

20. See Wittgenstein, *Philosophical Investigations*, e.g., §210.

21. If general considerations recommend a universal formula, it will employ terms which themselves give rise to hard cases.

22. I distinguish practical reason from practical reasoning. From *NE* 1105a 28–33, with 1111a 15–16, it might seem that virtuous action, in Aristotle's view, must be the outcome of reasoning. But this doctrine is both incredible in itself and inconsistent with 1117a 17–22. So I construe Aristotle's discussion of deliberation as aimed at the reconstruction of reasons for action not necessarily thought out in advance; where they were not thought out in advance, the concept of deliberation applies in an "as if" style. See John M. Cooper, *Reason and Human Good in Aristotle* (Cambridge, Mass. and London: Harvard University Press, 1975) pp. 5–10. (It will be apparent that what I say about Aristotle's views on practical reason runs counter to Cooper's interpretation at many points. I am less concerned here with what Aristotle actually thought than with certain philosophical issues; so I have not encumbered this paper with scholarly controversy.)

23. David Wiggins, "Deliberation and Practical Reason," *Proceedings of the Aristotelian Society* 76 (1975–76): 29–51, at p. 40. The quoted passage is an explanation of Aristotle, *De Motu Animalium* 701a 9ff. My debt to Wiggins's paper will be apparent.

24. There is an inclination to insist on the only, or best, means. But this is the outcome of a suspect desire to have instances of the schema which *prove* that the action explained is the thing to do.

25. *NE* 1144a 31–33.

26. This is distinct from the claim that a person may at any stage be prone to change his mind (cf. §3 above). Wiggins (cited in n23 above) appears at some points to run the two claims together, no doubt because he is concerned with practical reason generally, and not, as I am, with the expression in action of a specific conception of how to live. The line between realizing that one's antecedent conception of how to live requires something which one had not previously seen it to require, on the one hand, and modifying one's conception of how to live, on the other, is not a sharp one. But I do not want to exploit cases most happily described in the second way.

27. Cf. Wittgenstein, *Philosophical Investigations* §208.

28. I borrow this excellent term from Wiggins (cited in n23 above), p. 43ff.

29. This use of "salient" follows Wiggins, p. 45.

30. On the importance of the appreciation of the particular case, see *NE* 1142a 23–30, 1143a 25–b5; discussed by Wiggins, cited in n23, pp. 46–49. (For the point of "or at least comprehend," see n33 below.)

31. That the interaction, at the first stage, is with *all* the potentially reason-yielding facts about the situation allows us to register that, in the case of, say, courage, the gravity of the risk, in comparison to the importance of the end to be achieved by facing it, makes a difference to whether virtue really does require facing the risk; even though at the second stage, if the risk is not seen as salient, it is seen as no reason at all for running away. I am indebted here to a version of Wiggin's (f) (cited in n23 above, p. 45), importantly modified for a

revised excerpt from his paper in Joseph Raz, ed., *Practical Reasoning* (Oxford: Oxford University Press, 1978).

32. Actually this is open to question, because of special properties of the concept of a friend.

33. The qualification "essentially" is to allow for the possibility of appreciating what it is like to be inside a way of thinking without actually being inside it, on the basis of a sufficient affinity between it and a way of thinking of one's own. These considerations about externally intelligible desires bear on Philippa Foot's thesis, in "Morality as a System of Hypothetical Imperatives," *Philosophical Review* 81 (1972), pp. 305–16, that morality should be construed, or recast, in terms of hypothetical imperatives, on pain of being fraudulent. Her negative arguments seem to me to be analogous to an exposé of the emptiness of platonism, as affording a foundation for mathematical practice external to the practice itself. In the mathematical case it is not a correct response to look for another external guarantee of the rationality of the practice, but that seems to me just what Mrs Foot's positive suggestion amounts to in the moral case. (If the desires are not externally intelligible the label "hypothetical imperative" loses its point.) See, further, my "Are Moral Requirements Hypothetical Imperatives?" cited in n10 above.

34. On anthropocentricity, see David Wiggins, "Truth, Invention, and the Meaning of Life," *Proceedings of the British Academy* 62 (1976), 331–78, at pp. 348–49, 360–63.

35. See Wiggins, cited in n34, above; and Iris Murdoch, *The Sovereignty of Good* (London: Routledge and Kegan Paul, 1970).

36. Cf. Iris Murdoch, cited n35, above. I am indebted here to Mark Platts.

37. This view of Plato is beautifully elaborated by Iris Murdoch.

38. The idea, for instance, that something like utilitarianism *must* be right looks like a double avoidance of vertigo: first, in the thought that there must be a decision procedure; and second, in the reduction of practical rationality to the pursuit of neutrally intelligible desires.

7

The Discernment of Perception: An Aristotelian Conception of Private and Public Rationality

Martha C. Nussbaum

> What one acquires here is not a technique; one learns to correct judgements. There are also rules, but they do not form a system, and only experienced people can apply them right. Unlike calculating-rules.
>
> What is most difficult here is to put this indefiniteness, correctly and unfalsified, into words.
>
> Ludwig Wittgenstein, *Philosophical Investigations*, II.xi

> Of these States the poet is the equable man . . .
> He bestows on every object or quality its fit proportion, neither
>   more nor less . . .
> He judges not as the judge judges, but as the sun falling round a
>   helpless thing . . .
> He sees eternity in men and women, he does not see men and
>   women as dreams or dots.
>
> Walt Whitman, from *By Blue Ontario's Shore*

Is practical reasoning scientific?[1] If it is not, as it is ordinarily practiced, can it be made to be? And would it be a good thing if it were?[2] Much contemporary writing in moral philosophy and in the social sciences gives a vigorously affirmative answer either to the first question or to the conjunction of the second and third. Aristotle's ethical and political writings present powerful negative arguments. "It is obvious," he writes, "that practical wisdom is not scientific understanding (*epistēmē*)" (*EN* 1142a24). And this is not just an admission of a defect in contemporary theory. For he makes it clear elsewhere that it is in the very nature of truly rational practical choice that it cannot be made more "scientific" without becoming worse. Instead, he tells us, the "discernment" of the correct choice rests with something that he calls "perception."[3] From the context it is evident that this is some sort of complex responsiveness to the salient features of one's concrete situation.

Aristotle's position is subtle and compelling. It seems to me to go further than any other account of practical rationality I know in capturing the sheer complexity and agonizing difficulty of choosing well. But whether we are in the end persuaded by it or not, the need to study it is urgent. Even more in our time than in his, the power of "scientific" pictures of practical rationality affects almost every area of human social life, through the influence of the social sciences and the more science-based parts of ethical theory on the formation of public policy. We should not accept this situation without assessing the merits of such views against those of the most profound alternatives. If we do not finally accept Aristotle's conception, at least we will have found out more about ourselves. . . .

In this essay the word "scientific" will be used as Aristotle used it, to designate a family of characteristics that were usually associated with the claim that a body of knowledge had the status of an *epistēmē*. Since the aspiration to *epistēmē* took different forms in the projects of different opponents, Aristotle's attack on scientific conceptions of rationality is a family of attacks, directed at logically distinct positions—although these positions are in some forms mutually consistent and were combined into a single conception in certain works of Plato. I shall suggest that Aristotle's attack has three distinct dimensions, closely interwoven. These are: an attack on the claim that all valuable things are commensurable; an argument for the priority of particular judgments to universals; and a defense of the emotions and the imagination as essential to rational choice. Each of the three features he attacks was prominent in the ancient ethical debate; and each has been important in contemporary writing on choice. Once we have understood the three features of Aristotle's criticism separately, and understood the corresponding features of his own positive conception, we shall see how the parts of his conception fit together. . . .

I. Plural Values and Noncommensurability

Aristotle knew of the view that a hallmark of rational choice is the measurement of all alternatives by a single quantitative standard of value. Such a "science of measurement,"[4] in his day as in ours, was motivated by the desire to simplify and render tractable the bewildering problem of choice among heterogeneous alternatives. Plato, for example, argues that only through such a science can human beings be rescued from an unendurable confusion in the face of the concrete situation of choice, with its qualitative indefiniteness and its variegated plurality of apparent values. Plato even believed, and argued with power, that many of the most troublesome sorts of human irrationality in action were caused by passions that would be eliminated or rendered innocuous by a thoroughgoing belief in the qualitative homogeneity of all the values. The weak (akratic) agent will be less tempted to deviate from the path of greater known good if he or she understands that the less good, but prima facie alluring, item simply contains a smaller quantity of the very same value that can be found by going toward the better item. The proposed "science" relies on the idea that the some such single standard of value can be found and that all rational choice can be recast as a matter of maximizing our quantities of that value.

We can break the "science of measurement" down into four distinct constituent claims. First, we have the claim that in each situation of choice there is some one value, varying only in quantity, that is common to all the alternatives, and that the rational chooser weighs the alternatives using this single standard. Let us call this claim *Metricity*. Next, there is the claim of *Singleness*: that is, that in all situations of choice there is one and the same metric. Third is a claim about the end of rational choice: that choices and chosen actions have value not in themselves, but only as instrumental means to the good consequences that they produce. We call this *Consequentialism*. If we combine Consequentialism with Metricity, we have the idea of maximization: that the point of rational choice is to produce the greatest amount of the single value at work in each case. Combining both of these with Singleness, we have the idea that there is some one value that it is the point of rational choice, in every case, to maximize.[5] Finally, there are in Aristotle's opponents, as in modern Utilitarian writers, various accounts of the content of the end that is to serve as the metric and the item to be maximized. Pleasure, for Aristotle as for us, is the most familiar candidate.[6] Aristotle rejects all four of these components of the "science measurement," defending a picture of choice as a quality-based selection among goods that are plural and heterogeneous, each being chosen for its own distinctive value.

Arguments against pleasure as a single end and standard of choice occupy considerable space in his ethical works. The other available candidate, the useful or advantageous, is criticized only implicitly, in many passages that treat it as a nonhomogeneous, nonsingle item. Presumably this is because it had no prominent defenders. The popularity of hedonism as a theory of choice called, on the other hand, for detailed criticism. There are numerous well-known difficulties surrounding the interpretation of Aristotle's two accounts of pleasure.[7] What we can confidently say is that both accounts deny that pleasure is a single thing yielded in a qualitatively homogeneous way by many different types of activity. According to *EN* VII, my pleasures just are identical with the activities that I do in a certain way: viz., the unimpeded activations of my natural state. Pleasures, then, are just as distinct and incommensurable as are the different kinds of natural activity: seeing, reasoning, acting justly, and so forth (1153a14–15, b9–12). According to *EN* X, pleasure supervenes upon the activity to which it attaches, like the bloom on the cheek of a healthy young person, completing or perfecting it. Here pleasure is not identical with the activity; but it cannot be identified without reference to the activity to which it attaches. It cannot be pursued on its own without conceptual incoherence,[8] any more than blooming cheeks can be cultivated in isolation from the health and bodily fitness with which they belong.[9] Still less could there be a single item, Pleasure, that is separable from *all* the activities and yielded up by all of them in differing quantities. To these criticisms, Aristotle adds the observation that pleasures "differ in kind" as the associated activities differ (1173b28ff.). Some are choiceworthy and some are not, some are better and some are worse. Some, furthermore, are pleasures only for corrupt people, while some are pleasures for good people (1173b20ff.). Thus the *way* in which pleasure is not single provides us with additional reasons not to set it up as the end of practical choice.

Pleasure does not fall short by lack of singleness alone. It fails, as well, in inclusiveness: that is, it does not cover or contain everything that we pursue as choiceworthy. For, Aristotle writes, "there are many things that we would eagerly pursue even if they brought no pleasure, such as seeing, remembering, knowing, having the excellences. And even if pleasures follow upon these of necessity, it makes no difference;

for we *would* choose them even if no pleasure came from them" (*EN* 1174a4–8). Even if in fact pleasure is firmly linked to excellent action as a necessary consequence, it is not the end *for which* we act. We choose the action for its own sake alone. Deliberative imagination can inform us that we would do so even if the link with pleasure were broken. Elsewhere Aristotle shows us cases where the link is in fact broken: for example, a good person will sometimes choose to sacrifice life itself, and therefore all possibility of present and future pleasure, for the sake of helping a friend or acting courageously (1117b10ff.). Aristotle shows us, then, that we do in fact pursue and value ends that are not reducible to pleasure; we shall later see that he makes an implicit argument for the value and goodness of these plural commitments.

Argument against pleasure is strong argument against Singleness, since no other plausible candidate for a homogeneous single standard was being put forward. But it is plain that Aristotle's opposition to Singleness is general. In his attack on the Platonic notion of the single Good,[10] he insists that "the definitions of honor and practical wisdom and pleasure are separate and different *qua* goods" (*EN* 1096b23–25); from this he draws the conclusion that there can be no single common notion of good across these things. What he seems to be saying is that what we pursue or choose when we deem each of these items choiceworthy is something distinct, peculiar to the item in question; there is no single thing that belongs to all of them in such a way as to offer a plausible unitary account of their practical value. In the *Politics* he rejects even more explicitly the view that all goods are commensurable. In this important passage he has been describing a theory about the basis of political claims according to which any and all differences between persons are relevant to political distribution. If A is the same as B in all other respects but excels B in height, A is *eo ipso* entitled to a greater share of political goods than B; if A excels B in height and B excels A at playing the flute, we will have to decide which excels the other by more. And so on. Aristotle's first objection to this scheme is specific: it recognizes as relevant to political claims many features that are totally irrelevant to good political activity. But his second objection is general. The scheme is defective because it involves treating all goods as commensurable with one another: height and musicianship are measured against wealth and freedom. "But since this is impossible, it is obvious that in politics it is reasonable for men not to base their claim upon any and every inequality" (1283a9–11).[11]

Clearly this, like the *EN* argument, is an argument against Singleness: there is no one standard in terms of which all goods are commensurable *qua* goods. It looks like an argument against Metricity as well: for it suggests that there is something absurd in supposing that even in each single pairwise comparison of alternatives we will find a single relevant homogeneous measure. And in fact the *EN* remarks about definition, when linked to other observations about the intrinsic value of activity according to excellence, do yield arguments against Metricity, and Consequentialism as well, in favor of a picture in which the end or good consists of a number of distinct component activities (associated with the several excellences), each of these being an ultimate end pursued for its own sake. The good life for a human being consists, Aristotle argues, in activity according to the excellences; repeatedly he insists that it is these activities, not either their consequences or the states of soul that produce them, which are the ultimate bearers of value, the ends for which we pursue everything else that we pursue. It is actually part of the definition of activity according to excellence that it should be chosen for its own sake and not for the sake of something else (*EN* 1105a28–33), so to choose good activity only for the sake of some further consequences will not only be to misunderstand the relative value of actions and consequences, it will actually be to fail to act well. . . .

At this point, the proponent of Metricity will press questions. First, how can non-metric choice really be rational? If in choosing between A and B I do not choose so as to maximize one single item, and do not even compare the two in terms of a single item, then how on earth *can* I rationally compare the diverse alternatives? Isn't choice without a common measure simply arbitrary, or guesswork? Second, suppose that Aristotle has correctly described the way in which most people do in fact make choices, seeing their values as plural and incommensurable. Why should we think this is a particularly good way to choose? Why shouldn't this messy state of things motivate us to press for the development of Metricity, and even of Singleness, where these currently do not exist?[12] The questions are connected. For if we feel that choice without at least this limited commensurability is not rational, this will be a strong reason to favor the development of a superior technique.

The Aristotelian position does not simply describe the status quo. It also makes a strong implicit case for the preservation of our current ways of deciding, as both genuinely rational and superior in richness of value. We begin to see this if we return to the idea of difference of definition. To value each of the separate types of excellent activity as a constituent of the good life is tantamount, in Aristotle's conception, to saying that a life that lacked this item would be deficient or seriously incomplete, in a way that could not be atoned for by the presence of other items, in however great a supply. To value friendship (for example) in this way is to say (as Aristotle explicitly does) that a life that lacked this one item, even though it had as much as you like of every other item, would fall short of full value or goodness in an important way.[13] Friendship does not supply a commodity that we can get elsewhere; it is that very thing, in its own peculiar nature, that is the bearer of value. This is what it means to judge that something is an end, not simply a means to an end: there are no trade-offs without loss.

To value each separate constituent of the good life for what it is in itself entails, then, recognizing its distinctness and separateness from each of the other constituents, each being an irreplaceable part of a composite whole. A rational Aristotelian adult will have a reasonably good understanding of what courage, justice, friendship, generosity, and many other values are. He or she will understand how, in our beliefs and practices, they differ from and are noninterchangeable with one another. Suppose now that a proponent of ethical progress suggests that things can be made neater by doing away with some or all of this heterogeneity. He or she will reply that to do away with this is to do away with the nature of these values as they are, and hence with their special contribution to the richness and fullness of the good life. The proposal threatens to impoverish our practical world: for we have said that each of these items makes its own distinctive contribution, one that we will not get by trading it in for something else. Can it be rational to deliberate in a way that effaces this distinctness? To purchase neatness at such a price appears irrational rather than rational. Would we want to be, or to have, friends who were able to deliberate efficiently about friendship because they could get themselves to conceive of it as a function of some other value? The really rational way to choose, says Aristotle with great plausibility, is to reflect on and acknowledge the special contribution of each item, and to make the understanding of that heterogeneity a central part of the subject matter of deliberation. Evasiveness is not progress.

As for the first question: The Aristotelian should begin by objecting to the way it is posed; for the opponent suggests that deliberation must be either quantitative or a mere shot in the dark.[14] Why should we believe this? Experience shows us a further alternative: that it is qualitative and not quantitative, and rational just because it is qualitative, and based upon a grasp of the special nature of each of the items in question. We choose this way all the time; and there is no reason for us to let the rhetoric of weighing and measuring bully us into being on the defensive here, or supposing that we must, if we are rational, be proceeding according to some hidden metric.[15]

I mean to speak later on of social reasoning. So I need to do more now to begin bringing out the contrast between the Aristotelian picture and some pictures of deliberation that are used in contemporary social science.[16] We can readily see how Aristotelianism is at odds with the foundations of classical utilitarianism, and indeed any contemporary Utilitarianism that relies on Singleness or even Metricity. But so far it looks perfectly compatible with a decision procedure that makes use of a purely ordinal ranking of preferences, where the alternatives ranked would prominently include situations in which the agent either does or does not perform some excellent action, or some combination of such actions.[17] Why should we not envisage the rational agent as proceeding according to some such ordering, and social rationality as aggregation of such individual orderings?

We shall soon see how Aristotle objects to the idea of any antecedently fixed ordering or ranking of ends; I therefore defer discussion of the implications of these arguments for social choice. I am also unable to discuss at length two other ways in which Aristotle's ethical approach is at odds with models dominant in social science. I mention them briefly. First, as we have begun to see, Aristotle does not make the sharp distinction between means and ends that is taken for granted in much of social science literature, in economics, perhaps, above all (see n.15). Nor does he hold that ultimate ends cannot be objects of rational deliberation. We can ask concerning each ultimate end not only what the instrumental means to its realization are, but also what *counts* as realizing this end. Furthermore, against the background of our (evolving) pattern of ends, we can always ask of some putative constituent, for example friendship, whether or not it really belongs there as a constituent of the end: that is, whether life would be less rich and complete without it. All this is a part of rational deliberation; and by extending the sphere of practical rationality in this way, Aristotelianism certainly diverges from much that economic accounts of rationality either assume or explicitly state. I cannot enter further here into this highly important and complex subject.[18]

Another evident difference between Aristotle and the theorist who proceeds by ordering preferences concerns the relationship between desire and value. Aristotle does not think that the bare fact that someone prefers something gives us any reason at all for ranking it as preferable. It all depends who the someone is and through what procedures the ranking has been effected. The rankings of the person of practical wisdom will be criterial of our norms, both personal and social; what the bad or mad or childish person prefers counts little or nothing. Nor are the judgments of severely deprived people to be trusted: for frequently they will adjust their preferences to what their actual situation makes possible. Value is anthropocentric, not fixed altogether independently of the desires and needs of human beings;[19] but to say this is very far from saying that every preference of every human being counts for evaluative purposes.

Aristotle would be even more strongly opposed, clearly, to any proposal in which alternatives are ranked in terms of a metric of desire strength. If the fact that someone desires something gives us, all by itself, no good reason to value it, a fortiori the strength or quantity of someone's actual desire give us no good reason for valuing it proportionally to that strength. Even if Aristotle should grant that desire strength *can* be measured and numbered in the unitary way required by this theory—as he almost certainly would not—he would surely view it as an even more perverse and less plausible version of commensurability than the one that locates commensurability in the object or alternative chosen. The Platonic thesis errs by making values commensurable; but at least it locates value in the right place, in objects and activities, not in our feelings about these. This proposal, by contrast, says something no more plausible, and locates value in the wrong place.[20]

But instead of pursuing this important subject further, I want to turn now to one of its offshoots, one that will focus the difference between Aristotelianism and some forms of technical social theory in a particularly interesting way. In the theory of ordered preferences, when there is a choice (personal or collective) to be made between A and B, only one question is typically asked and considered salient, namely, which alternative is preferred. (Sometimes, as in the Griffin proposal, questions of the weight or intensity of preference are raised, but this is notoriously difficult and controversial.) The agent works with the picture of a single line or scale, and the aim is simply to get as high up on this line as possible. Although the line does not imply, in this case, the presence of a unitary measure of value in terms of which all alternatives are seen as commensurable, there is still a single line, the ranking of actual preferences from among the available alternatives. All alternatives are arranged along this line, and the agent is to look to nothing else in choosing. Aristotelianism asks about overall preferability. But its rather difficult picture of the choice situation also encourages us to ask and to dwell upon a further question about A and B. We have said that the Aristotelian agent scrutinizes each valuable alternative, seeking out its distinct nature. She is determined to acknowledge the precise sort of value or goodness present in each of the competing alternatives, seeing each value as, so to speak, a separate jewel in the crown, valuable in its own right, which does not cease to be separately valuable just because the contingencies of the situation sever it from other goods and it loses out in an overall rational choice. This emphasis on the recognition of plural incommensurable goods leads directly and naturally to the perception of a possibility of irreconcilable contingent conflicts among them. For once we see that A and B have distinct intrinsically valuable goods to offer, we will also be prepared to see that a situation in which we are forced by contingencies beyond our control to choose between A and B is a situation in which we will be forced to forgo some genuine value. Where both A and B are types of virtuous action, the choice situation is one in which we will have to act in some respect deficiently; perhaps even to act unjustly or wrongly. In such situations, to decide that A is preferable to B is sometimes the least of our worries. Agamemnon saw that between the sacrifice of his daughter Iphigenia and an impiety that would bring in its wake the death of all concerned, there was hardly a question of *how* to choose for a rational agent. But here the further problems have only begun. What can be done, thought, felt, about the deficiency or guilt involved in missing out on B? What actions, emotions, responses, are appropriate to the agent who is trapped in such a situation? What expressions of remorse, what reparative efforts, does morality require here? The individual cannot neglect these concerns without grave moral deficiency. Agamemnon neglected them, in the belief that the problem of preference was the only one to be solved by rationality. The chorus of elders regard this not as wisdom, but as madness. . . .

In R. M. Hare's recent book *Moral Thinking*, two stylized reasoners are introduced. They are called the Archangel and the Prole.[21] The Prole, stuck with ordinary daily intuitive rationality, sees moral dilemmas as real and indissoluble, requiring remorse and reparative efforts.

The Archangel, a Utilitarian philosopher, is able to see that from the critical perspective of this theory (as Hare describes it) such dilemmas vanish. She learns to rise above them, and has disdain for those who continue to recognize them. Hare presents his position, as always, with vigor and subtlety. He qualifies his contrast by arguing that there are many reasons why, in most daily choices, we should behave like proles. And yet the Archangel is a norm for practical reasoning, when it is at its best. And it is clear that the Archangel is Hare's answer to his own urgent motivating questions about how a theory of choice can actually make things better in human life. I believe, with Aristotle, that the Archangel's superior clarity and simplicity does not make things better; that rising above a human problem does not solve it. I believe that we want more proles and fewer Archangels, not only in daily choice, but as leaders and models. Angels, Thomas Aquinas held, cannot perceive what is there for perceiving in this world of contingency. And thus they are, as Aquinas concluded, poor guides indeed for getting around in this world, however well off they might be in heaven. It is, said Aristotle, the human good that we are seeking, and not the good of some other being.

II. Priority of the Particular

"The discernment rests with perception." This phrase, from which my title is taken, is used by Aristotle in connection with his attack on another feature of pseudo-scientific pictures of rationality: the insistence that rational choice can be captured in a system of general rules or principles which can then simply be applied to each new case. Aristotle's defense of the priority of "perception," together with his insistence that practical wisdom cannot be a systematic science concerned throughout with universal and general principles, is evidently a defense of the priority of concrete situational judgments of a more informal and intuitive kind to any such system. Once again he is attacking an item that is generally taken to be criterial of rationality in our day, particularly in the public sphere. His attack on ethical generality is closely linked to the attack on commensurability. For the two notions are closely related, and both are seen by their defenders as progressive stratagems that we can use to extricate ourselves from the ethical vulnerability that arises from the perception of qualitative heterogeneity. Too much heterogeneity leaves the agent who sees it open to the possibility of surprise and perplexity. For a new situation may strike her as unlike any other. A valuable item may seem altogether distinct and new. But if she tells herself either that there is only a single item in terms of which all values are commensurable—or that there is a finite number of general values, repeatedly instantiated, under which all new cases are bound to fall as instances—by either of these routes she will escape from the burden of the intractable and unexpected. She will come to each new situation prepared to see only those items about which she already knows how to deliberate.

The perception of heterogeneity brings another problem with it: vulnerability to loss. To view a beloved person (country, occupation) as not unique but an instance of a homogeneous general concept is to view it as potentially replaceable by another similar instance, should the world take from us the one we now have. Plato's Diotima argues that making the general prior in this way to the particular brings a "relaxing" and "easing" of the strains involved in planning a life. With value-generality, as with commensurability's more radical reduction to a single value, if the world removes something you love there is likely to be a ready supply of other similarly valuable items. Many Greek thinkers believed that a hallmark of a truly rational decision procedure would be that it should remove some of our ethical perplexity and vulnerability, putting us more securely in control of the more important things. This idea still has a powerful appeal.

Here we must begin to distinguish, as Aristotle himself does not, or does not with clarity, the *general* from the *universal*. The *general* is opposed to the *concrete*; a general rule not only covers many cases, it applies to them in virtue of some rather non-concrete characteristics. A *universal* rule, by contrast, applies to all cases that are in the relevant ways similar; but a universal may be highly concrete, citing features that are not very likely to be replicated. Many moral views that base correct choice on universal principles employ principles of broad generality. And this is a natural link, if one is interested in the codifying and action-guiding force of principles. One could not teach a child what to do using rules whose terms were too concrete to prepare the child for new cases as yet unseen; and one epistemological role for rules in morality has traditionally been to simplify and systematize the moral world, a task that highly refined and concrete universals have difficulty performing. But universals may also be concrete; and some philosophers, notably R. M. Hare,[22] who have a deep interest in the universalizability of moral prescriptions have also insisted that principles should often be highly context-specific. Aristotle's claims that the "particular" is "prior" in ethical reasoning are directed, in different ways and with different arguments, at both general principles and universal principles. His attack on the general is more global and more fundamental. Universalizability he accepts up to a point, though I believe that in certain cases he denies its moral role, holding that it is not, in these cases, correct to say that were the same circumstances to occur again, the same choice would again be correct. So to give a clear description of the view and the arguments that support it, we must insist on this distinction more forcefully than does Aristotle, whose primary opponent is a Plato whose universals are also highly general.

Aristotelian arguments against commensurability do not by themselves imply that particular judgments are prior to general rules. His attack on commensurability, as we have described it, relied on the picture of a plurality of distinct values, each generating its own claims, but each having, as well, its own general definition and being instantiable in any number of particular situations and actions. So the bare fact that, for example, courage and justice and friendship are plural and distinct does little to support the priority of particular perceptions to systems of rules or principles. On the contrary, our talk of distinctness in definition suggested that Aristotle might have had a strong interest in such a system. On the other hand, Aristotle does insist, as we have seen, that practical wisdom is not *epistēmē*, that is, systematic scientific understanding. He defends this claim by arguing that it is concerned with ultimate particulars (*ta kath'hekasta*) and that these particulars cannot be subsumed under any *epistēmē* (a system of universal principles) but must be grasped with insight through experience (*EN* 1142a11ff.). In praising perception, he is praising the grasping of particulars contained in this sort of experienced judgment. His statement seems to be an assault on the priority of the *general*, and probably of the *universal* as well. We need, then, to ask how the further moves from plurality to specificity or concreteness, and sometimes also from concreteness to singularity, are defended. And we need to know, as well, what role rules, of various sorts, actually do play in Aristotelian rationality.

We must notice first that rules could play an important role in practical reason without being prior to particular perceptions.[23] For they might be used not as normative for perception, the ultimate authorities against which the correctness of particular choices is assessed, but more as summaries or rules of thumb, highly useful for a variety of purposes, but valid only to the extent to which they correctly describe good concrete judgments, and to be assessed, ultimately, against these. On this second picture, there is still room for recognizing as ethically salient the new or surprising feature of the case before us, features that have not been anticipated in the rule, or even features that could not in principle be captured in any rule. If Aristotle's talk of rules is of this second kind, there need be no tension at all between his evident interest in rules and definitions, and his defense of the priority of perception. I shall now argue that this is, in fact, the situation, and explore his reasons for giving priority to the particular.

We can begin with the two passages in which our title phrase is introduced. In both he explicitly claims that priority in practical choice should be accorded not to principle, but to perception, a faculty of discrimination that is concerned with apprehending concrete particulars:

> The person who diverges only slightly from the correct is not blameworthy, whether he errs in the direction of the more or the less; but the person who diverges *more* is blamed; for this is evident. But to say to what point and how much someone is blameworthy is not easy to determine by a principle: nor in fact is this the case with any other perceptible item. For things of this sort are among the concrete particulars, and the discernment rests with perception. (*EN* 1109b18–23)

Again, in a discussion of one of the specific virtues, mildness of temper, Aristotle writes: "What degree and type of divergence is blameworthy, it is not easy to express in any general principle: for the discernment lies in the particulars and in perception" (1126b2–4). The subtleties of a complex ethical situation must be seized in a confrontation with the situation itself, by a faculty that is suited to address it as a complex whole. Prior general formulations lack both the concreteness and the flexibility that is required. They do not contain the particularizing details of the matter at hand, with which decision must grapple; and they are not responsive to what is there, as good decision must be.

These two related criticisms are pressed repeatedly, as Aristotle argues for the ethical priority of concrete description to general statement, particular judgment to general rule. "Among statements about conduct," he writes in an adjacent passage, "those that are universal (*katholou*) are more general (*koinoteroi*, common to many things),[24] but the particular are more true—for action is concerned with particulars, and statements must harmonize with these" (1107a29–32). Principles are authoritative only insofar as they are correct; but they are correct only insofar as they do not err with regard to the particulars. And it is not possible for a formulation intended to cover many different particulars to achieve a high degree of correctness. Therefore, in his discussion of justice Aristotle insists that the experienced judgments of the agent must both correct and supplement the general and universal formulations of law:

> All law is universal; but about some things it is not possible for a universal statement to be correct. Then in those matters in which it is necessary to speak universally, but not possible to do so correctly, the law takes the usual case, though without ignoring the possibility of missing the mark. . . . When, then, the law speaks universally, and something comes up that is not covered by the universal, then it is correct, insofar as the legislator has been deficient or gone wrong in speaking simply, to correct his omission, saying what he would have said himself had he been present and would have legislated if he had known. (*EN* 1137b13ff.)

The law is authoritative insofar as it is a summary of wise decisions. It is therefore appropriate to supplement it with new wise decisions made on the spot; and it is also appropriate to correct it where it diverges from what a good judge would do in this case. Here again, we find that particular judgment is superior both in correctness and in flexibility.

Aristotle illustrates the idea of ethical flexibility in a vivid and famous metaphor. He tells us that a person who makes each choice by appeal to some antecedent general principle held firm and inflexible for the occasion is like an architect who tries to use a straight ruler on the intricate curves of a fluted column. No real architect does this. Instead, following the lead of the builders of Lesbos, he will measure with a flexible strip of metal, the Lesbian Rule, that "bends to the shape of the stone and is not fixed" (1137b30–32). This device is still in use, as one might expect. I have one. It is invaluable for measuring oddly-shaped parts of an old Victorian house. (The Utilitarian who recently wrote that "we" prefer ethical systems in the style of the Bauhaus[25] had fortunate architectural tastes, given his view of rules.) It is also of use in measuring the parts of the body, few of which are straight. We could anticipate our point, not too oddly, by saying that Aristotle's picture of ethical reality has the form of a human body or bodies rather than that of a mathematical construct. So it requires rules that fit it. Good deliberation, like the Lesbian Rule, accommodates itself to the shape that it finds, responsively and with respect for complexity.

But perhaps Aristotle is speaking here only of the defectiveness of actual systems of rules; perhaps he says nothing against the idea that an ethical science could come into being if its rules were made precise or complicated enough. The image of the Lesbian Rule does not encourage this thought. But we can go further in answering this objection, showing, first, that he believes that correct choice cannot, even in principle, be captured in a system of rules, then going on to point out three features of the "matter of the practical" that show why not.

In this same section of *EN* V, Aristotle tells us that practical matters are in their very nature indeterminate or indefinable (*aorista*)—not just so far insufficiently defined. The universal account fails because no universal can adequately capture this matter. "The error is not in the law or in the legislator, but in the nature of the thing, since the matter of practical affairs is of this kind from the start" (1137b17–19). Again, in Book II, discussing the role of universal definitions and accounts in ethics (and preparing to put forward his own definition of the virtues) he writes:

> Let this be agreed on from the start, that every statement about matters of practice ought to be said in outline and not with precision, as we said in the beginning that statements should be demanded in a way appropriate to the matter at hand. And matters of practice and questions of what is advantageous never stand fixed, any more than do matters of health. If the universal definition is like this, the definition concerning particulars is even more lacking in precision. For such cases do not fall under any science or under any precept, but the agents themselves must in each case look to what suits the occasion, as is also the case in medicine and navigation. (1103b34–1104a10)

The general account *ought*[26] to be put forward as an outline only, and not the precise final word. It is not just that ethics has not yet attained the precision of science; it should not even try for such precision.

Three reasons for this are suggested in this brief passage. First, practical matters are mutable, or lacking in fixity. A system of rules set up in advance can encompass only what has been seen before—as a medical treatise can give only the recognized pattern of a disease. But the world of change confronts us with ever new configurations, ever new situations for the determining of the virtuous course. What is more, since the virtues themselves are individuated and defined with reference to contingent circumstances that may themselves undergo change (for example, Aristotle himself points out that there will be no virtue of generosity in a city with communistic property institutions),[27] the good agent may need not only to locate the virtuous action among strange new events, but also to deal with an evolving and situation-relative list of virtues. Even natural justice for human beings, Aristotle says, is "all mutable," i.e. historically rooted, relative to circumstances of scarcity and also of personal separateness that are relatively stable, but still in the natural world.[28] A doctor whose only resource, confronted with a new configuration of symptoms, was to turn to the textbook would be a poor doctor; a pilot who steered his ship by rule in a storm of unanticipated direction or intensity would be incompetent. Even so, people of practical wisdom must meet the new with responsiveness and imagination, cultivating the sort of flexibility and perceptiveness that will permit them, in the words of Thucydides (articulating an Athenian ideal of which Aristotle is the heir and defender) to "improvise what is required" (I.118). In several contexts, Aristotle speaks of practical wisdom as an ability concerned with *stochazesthai*. This word, which originally means "to take aim at a target," comes to be used of an improvisatory conjectural use of reason. He tells us that "the person who is good at deliberation without qualification is the one who takes aim (*stochastikos*) according to reason at the best for a human being in the sphere of things to be done" (1141b13–14); he associates this ideal closely with the observation that practical wisdom is concerned with particulars and not universals (1141b14–16).

In the *EN* V passage, and implicitly in the one from Book II, Aristotle alludes to a second feature of the practical, its indeterminate or indefinable character (*to aoriston*). It is difficult to interpret this feature; it seems to be connected with the variety of practical contexts and the situation-relatively of appropriate choice. One example is revealing. There is no definition (*horismos*) of good joke-telling, Aristotle writes, but it is *aoristos*, since it is so much a matter of pleasing the particular hearer, and "different things are repugnant and pleasant to different people" (1128a25ff). To extrapolate from this case, excellent choice cannot be captured in general rules, because it is a matter of fitting one's choice to the complex requirements of a concrete situation, taking all of its contextual features into account. A rule, like a manual of humor, would do both too little and too much: too little, because most of what really counts is in the response to the concrete; and this would be omitted. Too much, because the rule would imply that it was itself normative for response (as a joke manual would ask you to tailor your wit to the formulae it contains), and this would impinge too much on the flexibility of good practice. The Lesbian Rule is called *aoristos*, presumably because, unlike such precepts, it varies its own shape according to the shape of what is before it. In speaking of mutability Aristotle stresses change over time and the moral relevance of surprise; in speaking of the *aoriston* he stresses complexity and context. Both features call for responsiveness and yielding flexibility, a rightness of tone and a sureness of touch that no general account could adequately capture.

Finally Aristotle suggests that the concrete ethical case may simply contain some ultimately particular and non-repeatable elements. This is one part of what he means when he says that they simply do not fall under any general science or precept. Complexity and variety already yield a high degree of situational particularity, for the occurrence of properties that are, taken singly, instantiated elsewhere in an endless variety of combinations can make the whole context a unique particular. But Aristotle also recognizes the ethical relevance of non-repeatable components. The moderate diet for Milo the wrestler is not the same as the moderate diet for Aristotle (indeed, for any other human being), because Milo's concrete, and presumably unique combination of size, weight, needs, goals and activity are all relevant to determining the appropriate for him. This is a contingent limitation on the universal; we could try to say that we have here a universal principle with only a single instance, in that if anyone else should turn up with that precise size, weight, etc., the ethical prescription would be the same. Even so, this would not be the sort of universal principle that would satisfy most devotees of principles, since it is rooted in the particulars of Milo's historical context in such a way that it could not have been anticipated with precision in advance; and perhaps (indeed, very likely) will be of no further use in the future. An ethical science with "principles" this context-specific would have to have a vast and infinitely extensible series of principles; and this is not a science that will satisfy those who are looking for science.

But Aristotle goes further still in some cases. The particularity of love and friendship seems to demand nonrepeatability in yet a stronger sense. Good friends will attend to the particular needs and concerns of their friends, benefiting them for the sake of what they are, in and of themselves. Some of this "themselves" consists of repeatable character traits; but features of shared history and of family relationship that are not even in principle repeatable are allowed to bear serious ethical weight. Here the agent's own historical singularity (and/or the historical singularity of the relationship itself) enter into moral deliberation in a way that could not even in principle give rise to a universal principle, since what is ethically important (among other things) is to treat the friend as a unique nonreplaceable being, a being not like anyone else in the world.[29] "Practical wisdom is not concerned with universals only; it must also recognize particulars, for it is practical, and practice concerns particulars" (1141b4–16).[30]

In all of these ways, rules, general and/or universal, seen as normative for correctness of judgment, fail in their very nature to measure up to the challenge of practical choice. And Aristotle's arguments are strong not only against the normative use of a systematic hierarchy of rules, but in general against any general algorithm for correct choice. The defense of the Lesbian rule and the account of the context-relativity of the mean imply not only that the good judge will not decide by subsuming a case under antecedently fixed rules, but also that there is no general procedure or algorithm for computing what to do in every case. The appropriate response is not arrived at mechanically; there is no general procedural description that can be given concerning how to find it. Or if there is, it is about as useful as a joke manual, and as potentially misleading. Here again, Aristotle's picture breaks sharply with contemporary attempts to describe a general formula or technique of choice which can then be applied to each new particular. Aristotle has no objection to the use of general guidelines of this sort for certain purposes. They have a useful role to play so long as they keep their place. Rules and general procedures can be aids in moral development, since people who do not yet have practical wisdom and insight need to follow rules that summarize the wise judgments of others. Then too, if there is not time to formulate a fully concrete decision in the case at hand, it is better to follow a good summary rule or a standardized decision procedure than to make a hasty and inadequate contextual choice. Again, if we are not confident of our judgment in a given case, if there is reason to believe that bias or interest might distort our particular judgment, rules give us a superior constancy and stability. (This is Aristotle's primary argument for preferring the rule of law to rule by decree.) Even for wise adults who are not short of time, the rule has a function, guiding them tentatively in their approach to the new particular, helping them to pick out its salient features. This function we shall later examine in more detail.

But Aristotle's point in all these cases is that the rule or algorithm represents a falling off from full practical rationality, not its flourishing or completion. The existence of a formal choice function is not a condition of rational choice, any more than the existence of a navigation manual is a condition (surely not sufficient and usually not even necessary) of good navigation. Either the choice function is simply the summary of what good judges do or have done in situations so far encountered—in which case it will be true but posterior, and the more posterior the more it simplifies[31]—or it is an attempt to extract from that which they do and have done some more elegant and simple procedure that can from then on be normative for what they do—in which case it will be false and even corrupting.

An important thing to remember, in assessing this claim, is that Aristotelian deliberation does not confine itself to means–end reasoning. It is, as we have insisted, concerned as well with the specification of ultimate ends. But this means that the contextual and nonrepeatable material can enter into the agent's deliberation at a much more basic level than at the level of means calculation and (for example) the reckoning up of probabilities in connection with this. A great part of *rational* deliberation will be concerned with questions about whether a certain course of action here and now really counts as realizing some important value (say, courage or friendship) that is a prima facie part of her idea of the good life; or even whether a certain way of acting (a certain relationship—type or particular) really counts as the sort of thing she wants to include in her conception of a good life at all. Whether this friendship, this love, this courageous risk, really is something without which her life will be less valuable and less complete. For this sort of question, it seems obvious that there is no mathematical answer; and the only procedure to follow is (as we shall see) to imagine all the relevant features as well and fully and concretely as possible, holding them up against whatever intuitions and emotions and plans and imaginings we have brought into the situation or can construct in it. There is really no shortcut at all; or none that is not corrupting. The most we have by way of a theory of correct procedure is the account of good deliberation given by Aristotle himself, which is deliberately thin, referring for its content to the account of character. It not only does not tell us how to compute the mean, it tells us that there is no general true answer to this question. Beyond this, the content of rational choice must be supplied by nothing less messy than experience and stories of experience. Among stories of conduct, the most true and informative will be works of literature, biography, and history; the more abstract the story gets, the less rational it is to use it as one's only guide. Good deliberation is like theatrical or musical improvisation, where what counts is flexibility, responsiveness, and openness to the external; to rely on an algorithm here is not only insufficient, it is a sign of immaturity and weakness. It is possible to play a jazz solo from a score, making minor alterations for the particular nature of one's instrument. The question is, who would do this, and why?

If all this is so, Aristotle must also refrain from giving any formal normative account of the properties of adult deliberative rationality. For, like its subject matter, it is too flexible to be pinned down in a general way. Instead, he stresses the importance of experience in giving content to practical wisdom, developing a contrast between practical insight and scientific or mathematical understanding:

> It is obvious that practical wisdom is not deductive scientific understanding (*epistēmē*). For it is of the ultimate and particular, as has been said—for the matter of action is like this. It is the analogue of theoretical insight (*nous*): for *nous* is of the ultimately first principles, for which there is no external justification; and practical wisdom is of the ultimate and particular, of which there is no scientific understanding, but a kind of perception—not, I mean, ordinary sense-perception of the proper objects of each sense, but the sort of perception by which we grasp that a certain figure is composed in a certain way out of triangles. (1142a23)[32]

Practical insight is like perceiving in the sense that it is noninferential, nondeductive; it is an ability to recognize the salient features of a complex situation. And just as the theoretical *nous* comes only out of a long experience with first principles and a sense, gained gradually in and through experience, of the fundamental role played by these principles in discourse and explanation, so too practical perception, which Aristotle also calls *nous*, is gained only through a long process of living and choosing that develops the agent's resourcefulness and responsiveness:

> Young people can become mathematicians and geometers and wise in things of that sort; but they do not appear to become people of practical wisdom. The reason is that practical wisdom is of the particular, which

becomes graspable through experience, but a young person is not experienced. For a quantity of time is required for experience. (1142a12–16)

and again:

> We credit the same people with possessing judgment and having reached the age of intuitive insight and being people of understanding and practical wisdom. For all of these abilities are concerned with the ultimate and the particular . . . and all practical matters are concerned with the particular and the ultimate. For the person of practical wisdom must recognize these, and understanding and judgment are also concerned with practical matters, i.e. with ultimates. And intuitive insight (*nous*) is concerned with ultimates in both directions . . . [There follows a development of the parallel between grasp of first principles and grasp of ultimate particulars.] . . . This is why we should attend to the undemonstrated sayings of experienced and older people or people of practical wisdom not less than to demonstrations. For since experience has given them an eye they see correctly. (1143a25–b14)

By now we are inclined to ask what experience can possibly contribute, if what practical wisdom sees is the idiosyncratic and the new. Our emphasis on flexibility should not, however, make us imagine that Aristotelian perception is rootless and ad hoc, rejecting all guidance from the past. The good navigator does not go by the rule book; and she is prepared to deal with what she has not seen before. But she knows, too, how to use what she has seen; she does not pretend that she has never been on a boat before. Experience is concrete and not exhaustively summarizable in a system of rules. Unlike mathematical wisdom it cannot be adequately encompassed in a treatise. But it does offer guidance, and it does urge on us the recognition of repeated as well as unique features. Even if rules are not sufficient, they may be highly useful, frequently even necessary. We turn now to the third feature of his conception, which will further illuminate the others.

III. The Rationality of Emotions and Imagination

So far the Aristotelian picture has attacked two items that are commonly alleged to be criterial of rationality. His third target is even more broadly so held: the idea that rational choice is not made under the influence of the emotions and the imagination. The idea that rational deliberation might draw on and even be guided by these elements has sometimes even been taken (in both ancient and modern times) to be a conceptual impossibility, the "rational" being defined by opposition to these "irrational" parts of the soul. (This is especially true of emotion, but important writers in both ancient and modern times have included imagination in their blame of the irrational. This is, surprisingly, true even of some philosophers, like Stuart Hampshire, who are otherwise sympathetic to Aristotle's conception of choice.)[33] Plato repudiated emotion and appetite as corrupting influences, insisting that correct practical judgments are reached only by encouraging the intellect to go off "itself by itself," free from their influence as far as possible. The condition of the person in which they lead or guide intellect is given the pejorative name of "madness," which is definitionally contrasted with rationality or soundness of judgment.[34] The two dominant moral theories of our own time, Kantianism and Utilitarianism, have been no less suspicious of the passions; indeed, this is one of the few things on which they (usually) agree. For Kant, the passions are invariably selfish and aimed at one's own states of satisfaction. Even in the context of love and friendship, he urges us to avoid becoming subject to their influence; for an action will have genuine moral worth only if it is chosen for its own sake; and given his conception of the passions he cannot allow that action chosen only or primarily because of passion could be chosen for its own sake. The Utilitarian believes that a passion like personal love frequently impedes rationality by being too parochial: it leads us to emphasize personal ties and to rank the nearer above the further, obstructing that fully impartial attitude toward the world that is the hallmark of Utilitarian rationality.

Imagination fares no better. Plato's rejection of the influence of sensuous cognition is part and parcel of his general rejection of the influence of the bodily. Without attempting to characterize Kant's own complex view of imagination, we may say that modern Kantians have shown considerable interest in curbing flights of deliberative imagination that they see as potential strong impediments to action in accordance with duty. Imagination is thought to be too often egoistic and self-indulgent, too concerned with particulars and with their relation to the self. One can be correctly motivated by duty without developing imagination; therefore its cultivation is at best a luxury, at worst a danger.

Nor do Utilitarians approve of imagination's vivid portrayal of alternatives in all their color and singularity; again this faculty is suspected of being wedded to particularity and the recognition of incommensurables, therefore of being a threat to the impartial assessment of facts and probabilities. Whatever the faults of Dickens's *Hard Times* as a portrait of Utilitarianism—and they are many—he is surely correct in depicting the Benthamite father as holding the view that "fancy" is a form of dangerous self-indulgence, and that reason (conceived of as that fact-storing and calculative power in virtue of which Mr. Gradgrind is always "ready to weigh and measure each parcel of human nature, and tell you exactly what it comes to") is the only faculty to which education is properly addressed, if we are to build a properly impartial society. (Concerning Louisa, from the cradle starved in fancy, he reflects with moral satisfaction, "would have been self-willed . . . but for her bringing-up.") Contemporary theorists follow these leads, either explicitly repudiating imagination and emotion as irrational or offering a picture of rationality in which they play no positive role.

I have sketched these motivations for the rejection of imagination and emotion in order to indicate that Aristotelian perception may have corresponding motives for their cultivation. If these facilities are indeed closely linked with our ability to grasp particulars in all of their richness and concreteness, then perception will disregard them at its peril. As we pursue this lead, we shall at the same time see how Aristotle answers the charges that these faculties are invariably distorting and self-serving.

Aristotle does not have a single concept that corresponds exactly to our "imagination." His *phantasia*, usually so translated, is a more inclusive human and animal capability, that of focusing on some concrete particular, either present or absent, in such a way as to see (or otherwise perceive) it *as* something, picking out its salient features, discerning its content.[35] In this function it is the active and selective aspect of perception. But *phantasia* also works closely in tandem with memory, enabling the creature to focus on absent experienced items in their concreteness, and even to form new combinations, not yet experienced, from items that have entered sense-experience. So it can do much of the work of our imagination, though it should be stressed that Aristotle's emphasis is upon its selective and discriminatory character rather than upon its capability for free fantasy. Its job is more to focus on reality than to create unreality.

Phantasia appears to be a faculty well suited to the work of deliberation as Aristotle understands it, and it is no surprise to find him invoking it in connection with the minor premise of the "practical syllogism," that is, the creature's perception of an item in the world *as* something that answers to one of his or her practical interests or concerns. Elsewhere he shows imagination working closely with an ethical conception of the good: our imaginative view of a situation "marks off" or "determines" it as presenting elements that correspond to our view of what is to be pursued and avoided.[36] It is also no surprise that he ascribes to human beings the capacity for a special sort of imagining, which is called "deliberative *phantasia*," and which involves the ability to link several imaginings or perceptions together, "making a unity from many." All thought, for Aristotle, is of necessity (in finite creatures) accompanied by an imagining that is concrete, even where the thought itself is abstract. This is just a fact of human psychology. But whereas the mathematician can safely disregard the concrete features of his or her imagined triangle when she is proving a theorem about triangles, the person of practical wisdom will not neglect the concrete deliverances of imagination when thinking about virtue and goodness. Instead of ascending from particular to general, deliberative imagination links particulars without dispensing with their particularity.[37] It would involve, for example, the ability to recall past experience as one with, as relevant to, the case at hand, while still conceiving of both with rich and vivid concreteness. We are now prepared to understand that the Aristotelian will hold this concrete focusing to be not dangerously irrational, but an essential ingredient of responsible rationality, to be cultivated by educators.

As for the emotions, Aristotle notoriously restores them to the central place in morality from which Plato had banished them. He holds that the truly good person will not only act well but also feel the appropriate emotions about what he or she chooses. Not only correct motivation and motivational feelings but also correct reactive or responsive feelings are constitutive of this person's virtue or goodness. If I do the just thing from the wrong motives or desires (not for its own sake but, say, for the sake of gain), that will not count as virtuous action. This much even Kant could grant. More striking, I must do the just thing without reluctance or inner emotional tension. If my right choices always require struggle, if I must all the time be overcoming powerful feelings that go against virtue, then I am less virtuous than the person whose emotions are in harmony with her actions. I am assessible for my passions as well as for my calculations; all are parts of practical rationality.

Lying behind this is a picture of the passions as responsive and selective elements of the personality. Not Platonic urges or pushes, they possess a high degree of educability and discrimination. Even appetitive desires for Aristotle are intentional and capable of making distinctions; they can inform the agent of the presence of a needed object, working in responsive interaction with perception and imagination.[38] Their intentional object is "the apparent good." Emotions are composites of belief and feeling, shaped by developing thought and highly discriminating in their reactions. They can lead or guide the perceiving agent, "marking off" in a concretely imagined situation the objects to be pursued and avoided. In short, Aristotle does not make a sharp split between the cognitive and the emotive. Emotion can play a cognitive role, and cognition, if it is to be properly informed, must draw on the work of the emotive elements.[39] It is no surprise that choice is defined as an ability that lies on the borderline between the intellectual and the passional, partaking of both natures; it can be described, says Aristotle, either as desiderative deliberation or as deliberative desire (*EN* 1113a10–12, 1139b3–5).

Putting all this together, and allowing ourselves to extrapolate from the text in a way that appears to be consistent with its spirit, we might say that a person of practical insight will cultivate emotional openness and responsiveness in approaching a new situation. Frequently, it will be her passional response, rather than detached thinking, that will guide her to the appropriate recognitions. "Here is a case where a friend needs my help": this will often be "seen" first by the feelings that are constituent parts of friendship, rather than by pure intellect. Intellect will often want to consult these feelings to get information about the true nature of the situation. Without them, its approach to a new situation would be blind and obtuse. And even where correct choice is reached in the absence of feeling and emotional response, Aristotle will insist that it is less virtuous than choice that is emotional. If I help a friend unfeelingly, I am less praiseworthy than if I do so with appropriate love and sympathy. Indeed my choice may not really be virtuous at all; for an action to be virtuous, it must not only have the same content as the virtuously disposed person's action, it must be done "in the same manner" as the manner in which a person whose passions love the good would do it. Without feeling, a part of correct perception is missing.

I believe that such statements imply that perception is not merely aided by emotion but is also in part constituted by appropriate response. Good perception is a full recognition or acknowledgment of the nature of the practical situation; the whole personality sees it for what it is. The agent who discerns intellectually that a friend is in need or that a loved one has died, but who fails to respond to these facts with appropriate sympathy or grief, clearly lacks a part of Aristotelian virtue. It seems right to say, in addition, that a part of discernment or perception is lacking. This person doesn't really, or doesn't fully, *see* what has happened, doesn't recognize it in a full-blooded way or take it in. We want to say that she is merely saying the words. "He needs my help," or "she is dead," but really doesn't yet fully *know* it, because the emotional part of cognition is lacking. And it isn't just that sometimes we need the emotions to *get to* the right (intellectual) view of the situation; this is true, but not the entire story. Neither is it just that the emotions supply extra praiseworthy elements external to cognition but without which virtue is incomplete. The emotions are themselves modes of vision, or recognition. Their responses are part of what knowing, that is truly recognizing or acknowledging, *consists in*. To respond "at the right times with reference to the right objects, toward the right people, with the right aim, and in the right way, is what is appropriate and best, and this is characteristic of excellence" (*EN* 1106b21–3).

To read Aristotle this way offers a surprising exegetical and philosophical dividend, which can be only briefly described here. It has long troubled interpreters that, just after rejecting Socrates' account of *akrasia*, according to which all action against ethical knowledge is produced by intellectual failure, Aristotle goes on to offer an account of his own that itself characterizes *akrasia* as an intellectual failure. The ordinary belief that it is possible to know the better and to do the worse because one is overcome by pleasure or passion was flouted in Socrates' account, which claimed that these failures were really due to ignorance. Aristotle, having set himself to preserve the ordinary belief, does indeed mention the motivating role of the desire for pleasure in *akrasia*, but says that this desire would not overpower knowledge but for a simultaneous intellectual failure, the failure of the agent to grasp the "minor premise" of the practical syllogism. He or she has general ethical knowledge, and uses it, but either lacks or fails to use the concrete perception of the nature of this particular case. How, then, has he escaped his own criticism?

Without becoming too deeply entangled in the interpretative issues surrounding this difficult text, I want to suggest that this frequently scorned position makes far more sense if we take the inclusive view of perception that I have just outlined, according to which it has emotional and imaginative, as well as intellectual, components. The agent who is swayed by pleasure does not have to be dislodged from factual knowledge of his or her situation, that is, that this is a case of infidelity or overeating. There is a sense in which she can be said to know this throughout: for, as Aristotle in the same context says explicitly, she may say all the right things when questioned, and offer factually correct descriptions. She may, he adds, even correctly perform means–end deliberations in connection with her akratic action, which presumably she could not if she did not in a certain sense grasp, by intellect, its character.[40] She is, however, evasive. She is not fully confronting or acknowledging the situation to herself, allowing herself to see vividly its implications for her life and the lives of others, and to have the responses that are appropriate to that vision. Her interest in short-term pleasure causes her to insulate herself from these responses and from the knowledge they help to constitute. So her intellectual grasp doesn't amount to perception, or to a real grasp and use of the minor premise. Even though she has the facts right, there is a perfectly good, though quite non-Socratic, sense in which she doesn't know what she is doing.

This reading offers a new insight into the phenomenon of *akrasia*, one that places the Aristotelian view in an illuminating relation both to its own tradition and to ours. Our Anglo-American tradition tends, like Plato, to think of *akrasia* as a problem of passion, whose solution lies either in some rational modification of the troublesome passions or in some technique of mastery and control. Like Plato again, we tend (influenced, certainly, by the modern moral theories I have mentioned) to think of the passions as dangerously selfish and self-indulgent items that will, given any latitude, swell up and lead us away from the good. On the Socratic view, it is ethical knowledge that stops *akrasia*, by transforming the beliefs on which complex passions are based; on the mature Platonic view, knowledge must be combined with suppression and "starvation." But the cause of the edge must be combined with suppression and "starvation." But the cause of the problem, in all these cases, is found in the so-called irrational part of the soul.

If I am right, the Aristotelian account quietly turns this picture on its head, pointing out that *akrasia* is frequently (though not always) caused by an excess of theory and a deficiency in passional response. The person who acts akratically against his or her knowledge of the good is frequently quite capable of performing correctly in all the intellectual ways; what she lacks is the heart's confrontation with concrete ethical reality. We could express this by saying that knowledge needs responsiveness to be effective in action; we could also say that in the absence of correct response there is no, or no full, practical knowledge. The Aristotelian account, putting things in the second way, urges us to think of real practical insight and understanding as a complex matter involving the whole soul. The opposite of Platonic knowledge is ignorance; the opposite of Aristotelian perception can, in some cases, be ignorance; but it can also, in other cases, be denial or self-deceptive rationalization.

We can go further. Frequently a reliance on the powers of the intellect can actually become an impediment to true ethical perception, by impeding or undermining these responses. It frequently happens that theoretical people, proud of their intellectual abilities and confident in their possession of techniques for the solution of practical problems, are led by their theoretical commitments to become inattentive to the concrete responses of emotion and imagination that would be essential constituents of correct perception. It is a familiar problem. Sophocles' Creon, fascinated by his theoretical effort to define all human concerns in terms of their productivity of civic well-being, does not even perceive what at some level he knows, namely that Haemon is his son. He mouths the words; but he does not really acknowledge the tie—until the pain of loss reveals it to him. Proust's narrator, after a systematic study of his heart using the methods of precise empirical psychology, concludes that he does not love Albertine. This false conclusion (which, again, he soon acknowledges as false in and through responses of suffering) is reached not in spite of the intellect, but in a way because of it; because he was encouraging it to go off "itself by itself," without the necessary companionship of response and feelings. Henry James's *The Sacred Fount* is a fascinating account of what the world looks like to a man who carries this separation all the way, allowing theoretical intellect to determine his relation to all concrete phenomena, refusing himself any other human relation to them, and yet at the same time priding himself on the fineness of his perception. What we discover as we read is that such a person cannot have *any* knowledge of the people and events around him. His sort of incomplete perception can never reach the subject matter or engage with it in a significant way. So the Aristotelian position does not simply inform us that theorizing needs to be completed with intuitive and emotional responses; it warns us of the ways in which theorizing can impede vision. The intellect is not only not all-sufficient, it is a dangerous master. Because of its overreaching, knowledge can be "dragged around like a slave."[41]

All this, once again, has clear implications for the contemporary theory of choice. Many contemporary theories of rationality, as taught and practiced in the academy and in public life, share the goals and the policies of Mr. Gradgrind. That is, they make every attempt to cultivate calculative intellect and none at all to cultivate "fancy" and emotion. They do not concern themselves with the books (especially works of literature) that would cultivate those responses; indeed they implicitly deny their relevance to rationality. Aristotle tells us in no uncertain terms that people of practical wisdom, both in public and in private life, will cultivate emotion and imagination in themselves and in others, and will be very careful not to rely too heavily on a technical or purely intellectual theory that might stifle or impede these responses. They will promote an education that cultivates fancy and feeling through works of literature and history, teaching appropriate occasions for and degrees of response. They will consider it childish and immature *not* to cry or be angry or otherwise to experience and display passion where the situation calls for it. In looking for private models and public leaders, we should desire to be assured of their sensitivity and emotional depth, as well as of their intellectual competence.

IV. The Three Elements Together

We have now identified three different parts of Aristotle's picture of perception and practical knowing. All of them appear to form part of his attack on the notion that practical reason is a form of scientific understanding, a view that is defended prominently by Plato. Plato's conception (at least at some periods) insists on the qualitative homogeneity of the values; it argues that practical knowledge is completely summarized in a system of (timeless) highly general universals; it also insists that intellect is both necessary and sufficient for correct choice. Plato is certainly not the only thinker in history who has linked these three ideas together. In this sense, Aristotle's conception already looks unified, as being directed against different elements of a single coherent position. But it is possible to say more about the internal coherence of this picture of perception; for its various elements support one another in more than a polemical way.

Noncommensurability, as we have said, is not sufficient for the priority of particular to universal. But commensurability in the strong form of Singleness is certainly sufficient for the priority of both the general and the universal to the particular: for the single measure will have to be some sort of highly general universal, that is, one thing that turns up in qualitatively the same way in many different things. Even the limited commensurability of Metricity is sufficient for the rejection of unique nonrepeatable properties from practical salience. And we can see that the general spirit of Aristotle's noncommensurability leads directly to and supports his account of the priority of particulars. For his noncommensurability says, Look and see how rich and diverse the ultimate values in the world are. Do not fail to investigate each valuable item, cherishing it for its own specific nature and not reducing it to something else. These injunctions lead in the direction of a long and open-ended list—for we would not want to rule out beforehand the possibility that some new item will turn up whose own separate nature is irreducibly distinct from those we have previously recognized. In the context of friendship and love, especially, these injunctions are virtually certain to guarantee that the list of ultimate values will include some nonrepeatable particular items: for each friend is to be cherished for his or her own sake, not simply as an instantiation of the universal value, friendship. And it appears that this will include not only character, but also a shared history of mutuality. In this way, although Aristotle does have independent arguments for the priority of particulars (those having to do with indefiniteness and mutability), the first two elements certainly support each other well.

The account of emotion and imagination gives further support to and is supported by both elements. For it is in the nature of imagination, as we have said, to recognize highly concrete and, frequently, uniquely particular objects. And the objects to which we are most strongly attached by our passions are frequently like this as well. In the *Politics*, arguing against Plato, Aristotle says that the two things that above all make people love and care for something are the thought that it is all their own and the thought that it's the only one they have (1262b22–3); so our most intense feelings of love and fear and grief are likely to be directed at objects and persons who are seen as irreducibly particular in their nature and in their relationship to us. To argue that emotion and imagination are essential components of practical knowing and judging is to suggest very strongly that good judging will at least in part be a matter of focusing on the concrete and even the particular, which will be seen as incommensurate with other things. And in *EN* X.9 he indeed explicitly connects the loving relation between parent and child with an ethical knowledge that is superior to that of the public educator in its concrete particularity (1180b7–13). On the other hand, to defend noncommensurability is to reopen the space in which the emotions and imagination operate and have their force. A Platonist ethical position, Aristotle plausibly argues, undermines the strength of the emotions (Pol. 1262b23–4); and Plato himself would concede that belief in commensurability and universality at least cuts away many of the most common emotional reactions, since he, too, grants that these are based on perceptions of specialness. Again, to defend the priority of particulars is to inform us that imagination can play a role in deliberation that cannot be altogether replaced by the functioning of abstract thought. It would be possible to defend a flexible context-oriented perception of particulars without giving a prominent role to emotion and imagination; for one might try to describe a purely intellectual faculty that would by itself be adequate for seizing the relevant features. There is some precedent for this in some pre-Aristotelian Greek accounts of practical wisdom, which defend an improvisatory contextual use of reason that looks very cool, wily, and self-controlled.[42] Aristotle would feel, I think, that this sort of reason was insufficient for the sensitive task of deliberating about ends, though it might be all right for technical means–end reasoning. Here he is in agreement with an important tradition in Athenian political thought. For although Thucydides, as we have mentioned, praises the resourceful improvisational ability of Themistocles without mention of emotions, the funeral oration of Pericles makes it abundantly clear that full political rationality requires passion, and the sort of judgment that is made with and through love and vision. Athenians are to cultivate the ability to conceive in imagination of their city's greatness and still greater promise; and they are to "fall in love" with her when they see this greatness (II.43.1). He would probably conclude, not implausibly, that a citizen who did not feel this love had in a certain way failed to perceive both Athens and his own place in her.

One final connection between this feature and the other two: if one believes, with Plato, that the strong emotions are sources of unbearable tension and strain in a human life, one will have good reason to cultivate a way of seeing and judging that limits and reduces their power. Both commensurability and universality do this, as Plato argues. Because the Aristotelian position accepts emotional attachment as an intrinsically valuable source of richness and goodness in human life, it lacks one of Plato's most prominent motivations for the transformations involved in the first two features.

The three elements fit together, then, to form a coherent picture of practical choice. I see no significant tensions among them, and numerous reasons why the defender of one will wish to defend the others as well. They seem to articulate different aspects of a single idea. We might characterize this central idea, borrowing a phrase from Henry James, as one of becoming "finely aware and richly responsible"; of being a person on whom nothing is lost."[43] Being responsibly committed to the world of value before her, the perceiving agent can be counted on to investigate and scrutinize the nature of each item and each situation, to respond to what is there before her with full sensitivity and imaginative vigor, not to fall short of what is there to be seen and felt because of evasiveness, scientific abstractness, or a love of simplification. The Aristotelian agent is a person whom we could trust to describe a complex situation with full concreteness of detail and emotional shading, missing nothing of practical relevance. As James writes, "The person capable of feeling in the given case more than another of what is to be felt for it, and so serving in the highest degree to record it dramatically and objectively, is the only sort of person on whom we can count not to betray, to cheapen, or, as we say, give away the value and beauty of the thing."[44]

Notes

1. This topic was first addressed in my *Aristotle's De Motu Animalium* (Princeton, N.J., 1978) Essay 4; it was developed further in *The Fragility of Goodness* (New York: Cambridge University Press, 1986), chap. 10.

2. On "scientific," see further below; and, for a discussion of ancient conceptions of science, see *Fragility* chap. 4.

3. *EN* 1109b18–23, 1126b2–4—on which see below.

4. This phrase is taken from Plato, *Protagoras*, 356. For a full discussion of the claims made in this paragraph, see *Fragility*, chap. 4, and also, in this collection, "Plato on Commensurability." I do not believe that Plato is the only proponent of the "science" that Aristotle has in view; on some of the other relevant background, see my "Consequences and Character in Sophocles' *Philoctetes*," *Philosophy and Literature* 1 (1976–7) 25–53.

5. It is, of course, not necessary to accept or reject all of these as a single package. We could have Metricity without any of the others; Metricity and Singleness without Consequentialism (if a metric could be found, for example, in the actions themselves); Consequentialism without either Metricity or Singleness.

6. On the role of hedonism in Plato and its relationship to the historical

context, see *Fragility*, chap. 4, which includes full references to the secondary literature.

7. These difficulties include: the question whether the two accounts are answers to a single or to two different questions; the question whether the two accounts are compatible or incompatible; the question whether *EN* VII (= *EE* VI) belongs with the *Nicomachean* or the *Eudemian* work, and what difference this makes to our analysis. Some important items in the vast literature on these questions are discussed in *Fragility*, chap. 10.

8. For one account of the relationship between the conceptual and the empirical in Aristotle, see *Fragility*, chap. 8.

9. The interpretation given here is the most common one; a recent reinterpretation is discussed in *Fragility*, chap. 10, n. 12.

10. See further discussion of this passage in *Fragility*, chap. 10, with notes. I argue there that several other interesting and profound arguments in this chapter of the *EN* are not really pertinent to the criticism of Plato with reference to the notion of a single good in a human life: this is the argument that seems to do the important work on that topic.

11. For further discussion of this passage, and of Aristotle's arguments that the goal of political distribution should be capability to function, see my "Nature, Function, and Capability: Aristotle on Political Distribution," *Oxford Studies in Ancient Philosophy*, Supplementary Volume 1988. On the need to recognize qualitatively heterogeneous ends in political planning, see Robert Erikson, "Descriptions of Inequality: the Swedish Approach to Welfare Research," paper for the Quality of Life Conference arranged by the World Institute for Development Economics Research in Helsinki, in *The Quality of Life*, ed. M. Nussbaum and A. Sen (New York: Oxford University Press, 1993).

12. On this ambition as a theme in early Greek ethics, see *Fragility*, chaps. 3 and 4.

13. In Book I of the *EN*, in discussing the criterion of "sufficiency," Aristotle suggests that we ask, concerning a candidate for component membership in *eudaimonia*, whether a life that was complete with respect to every other item, but lacked this one alone, was truly complete without it. The argument in *EN* IX for the role of friendship in *eudaimonia* works the same way: see *Fragility*, chap. 12.

14. This is a deep and pervasive thought, from ancient Greek times until the present. For a critical discussion, see Amartya Sen, "Plural Utility," *Proceedings of the Aristotelian Society* 83 (1982–3). Sen argues plausibly that utility cannot adequately be understood as a single metric, since not all qualitative distinctions can be reduced to quantitative distinctions. Then, however, he comes to the conclusion that utility must be understood as a plurality of vectors, along each of which there is full quantitative commensurability, and between which there is total non-comparability. This view is still, then, in the grip of the picture that Aristotle attacks. In more recent work, Sen has defended a more thoroughly Aristotelian conception. See especially *Commodities and Capabilities*, a Hennipman Lecture (Amsterdam, 1985), in which the valuation function is an incomplete partial ordering based on qualitative comparison and not on reduction to any single metric.

15. I do not discuss here the apparent difficulties caused by the presence in most translations of the phrase, 'We deliberate not about the end, but about the means to the end." The mistranslation is discussed in *Fragility*, chap. 10, with references, especially to David Wiggins, "Deliberation and Practical Reason," *Proc. Arist. Soc.* 76 (1975–6) 29–51, to which my understanding of Aristotle on these issues is much indebted. Deliberation about "what pertains to the end" (the correct translation of the Greek) includes, as well, the further specification of what is to count as the end. Starting, for example, from the valued end of love and friendship, I can go on to ask for a further specification of what, more precisely, love and friendship *are* and for an enumeration of their types, without implying that I regard these different relationships as commensurable on a single quantitative scale, either with one another or with other major values. And if I should ask of justice or of love whether both are constituent parts of *eudaimonia*, I surely do not imply that we can hold these two things up to a single measuring standard, regarding them as productive of some one further thing. The question whether something is or is not to count as part of *eudaimonia* is just the question whether that thing is a valuable component in the best human life. Since Aristotle holds that the best life is inclusive of all those things that are choiceworthy for their own sake, this is equivalent to asking whether that item has intrinsic value. But in his discussion of Plato on the good, Aristotle has argued that valuing a virtue for its own sake not only does not require, but is incompatible with viewing it as qualitatively commensurable with other valuable items. To view it in that way would not be to have the proper regard for the distinctions of *its* nature.

16. On the relevance of Aristotelian conceptions to contemporary social thinking, see "Perception and Revolution," this volume. See also "Non-Relative Virtues: an Aristotelian Approach," *Midwest Studies in Philosophy*, 1988.

17. So far, too, it appears compatible with a single-valued ranking in terms of the strength of agents' desires, the view defended by James Griffin in "Are There Incommensurable Values?" *Philosophy and Public Affairs* 7 (1977) 34–59, and discussed by Dan Brock in his commentary on the original version of this paper in *Proceedings of the Boston Area Colloquium for Ancient Philosophy* 1 (1985); for an Aristotelian criticism of that view, see below.

18. For the bare beginnings of a discussion, see n. 15, *Fragility*, chap. 10, and *De Motu*, Essay 5. On this subject, in addition to the Wiggins article cited in n. 15, see also his "Claims of Need," in *Morality and Objectivity*, ed. T. Honderich (London, 1985) 149–202. An excellent discussion of this whole topic is in Henry Richardson, *Deliberation Is of Ends*, Harvard Ph.D. dissertation, 1986.

19. On this anthropocentricity, see *Fragility*, chaps. 10 and 11, and "Aristotle on Human Nature and the Foundations of Ethics," in *World, Mind, and Ethics: Essays on the Ethical Philosophy of Bernard Williams*, ed. by J. Altlam and R. Harrison (New York: Cambridge University Press, 1995).

20. Nor would the Griffin view solve the difficulties that Plato wishes to solve by the introduction of metricity and singleness. On these see "Plato on Commensurability," this volume. Sen's *Commodities and Capabilities* (see n. 14) contains a very illuminating discussion of this issue.

21. R. M. Hare, *Moral Thinking* (Oxford, 1981).

22. See *Moral Thinking*.

23. For a longer account of this point, see *Fragility*, chap. 10.

24. Note here the slide from universal to general: but the point is that the moment it covers many particulars it gets too unspecific to be the best way of approaching a concrete context. A universal need not abstract from contextual features (see below); but the sort of universal principle that can be fixed in advance and applied to many cases will have to do this too much for Aristotle. I translate *katholou*, for consistency, as "universal" throughout, though in my interpretive remarks I try to make clear exactly which issue Aristotle has in mind.

25. J. Glover, quoted in D. Wiggins, "Deliberation and Practical Reason" (see n. 18).

26. This "ought to" is sometimes mistranslated as "will have to." On this, see *De Motu*, Essay 4, *Fragility*, chap. 10.

27. *Pol.* 1263b7–14. Here, however, Aristotle actually concludes that the Platonic scheme should be blamed for eliminating the virtue, a response that appears to run counter to his overall position (on which see *Fragility*, chap. 10, 11). The remark is probably best understood as saying that Plato has not eliminated property itself, he has just eliminated individuals' control over property; thus, there is still the conceptual space for the virtue, but there is no sphere of choice in which individuals can exercise the virtue. See also "Non-Relative Virtues."

28. *EN* 1134b28–33; on Aristotle's arguments as to why laws should be made difficult to change, see *Fragility*, chap. 10.

29. On the types of individuality recognized as relevant to love and friendship, see *Fragility*, chaps. 6, 7, 12. For some doubts as to whether the Aristotelian position really satisfies all our intuitions about this individuality, see *Love's Knowledge*, "Love and the Individual." Further remarks are in the Introduction in the section entitled "The Aristotelian Ethical View," and in the endnote to "'Finely Aware.'"

30. For a list of passages in which Aristotle speaks this way, see *Fragility*, chap. 10, n. 29. Compare the illuminating discussion of these issues in Andrew Harrison, *Making and Thinking: A Study of Intelligent Activities* (Hassocks, Sussex, 1978), esp. chap. 3.

31. See *Aristotle's De Motu*, Essay 4.

32. See the excellent discussion of this passage in Wiggins, "Deliberation." I am to some extent indebted to his translation-cum-explication here, as in 1143a25–b14 below.

33. See, for example, Hampshire, *Morality and Conflict*, pp. 130–135—where imagination is contrasted with the "rational" and said to be a faculty inappropriate for judgments about justice. (Here I should say, "sympathetic to the picture of choice that I have ascribed to Aristotle"—since Hampshire and I do not have altogether the same interpretation of Aristotle.)

34. See *Fragility*, chaps. 5, 7. The *Phaedrus*, I argue, modifies this picture.

35. See *De Motu*, Essay 5, where I discuss all the relevant texts, and the secondary literature.

36. See *De Anima*, 431b2ff, discussed in greater length in *Fragility*, chap. 10. In "Changing Aristotle's Mind" (in M. Nussbaum and A. Rorty, eds., *Essays on Aristotle's "De Anima"* [New York: Oxford University Press, 1991], Hilary Putnam and I bring forward evidence that Aristotle regards emotion, as well as imagination, as a selective form of cognitive awareness.

37. This view of deliberative *phantasia* is not certain, but it has a long and venerable history; see, for example, Aquinas's fascinating discussions of why God equipped humans with *phantasia* for life in this world, and why an angel who lacked it would be confused and at a loss in a world of particulars. (The numerous references in the *Summa Theologica* to this topic are brought together and discussed in Putnam and Nussbaum, *ibid.*)

38. See *Fragility*, chap. 9.

39. See my "The Stoics on the Extirpation of the Passions," *Apeiron* (1987) 20: 129–78.

40. *EN*, 1142b18,20; see also 1147a18–24, where Aristotle compares the intellectual grasp of the akratic agent to the grasp of a principle that a student has when he or she is first learning it: "That they [sc. akratics] make the statements of a knowing person is no sign of anything. For people affected in this way can also recite demonstrations and quote the verses of Empedocles. And students who are learning something for the first time string statements together, but they don't yet understand; for the statements have to grow to be a part of them (*sumphuēnai*), and this requires time. So we should suppose that akratics speak in about the way that actors do." Both the student and the actor comparison bear out my point. What the akratic has is factual (intellectual) knowledge; what she lacks is real recognition or understanding, the kind of grasp of what is really at stake that comes from somewhere deep within her, from something that is part of her. The comparison to the actor makes it especially likely that deficiency of genuine feeling is in question, at least some of the time.

41. On all these issues, see *Fragility*, especially chap. 3, Interlude 2.

42. See M. Detienne and J. P. Vernant, *Les ruses de l'intelligence: la mètis des grecs* (Paris, 1974), discussed in *Fragility*, esp. chaps. 1, 7.

43. H. James, *The Princess Casamassima* (New York, 1907–9) I. 169.

44. Ibid., preface, I. xiii.

8

Aristotle on *Akrasia, Eudaimonia,* and the Psychology of Action

Alfred R. Mele

Although Aristotle's work on *akrasia* has prompted numerous competing interpretations, at least one point seems clear: incontinent action is, for him, dependent upon some deficiency in the agent's cognitive condition at the time of action.[1] But why, exactly, did he take this view? This question, my central concern in the present paper, is not *just* a query about Aristotle's understanding of incontinent action. It leads us at once into a tangled web of questions about his conception of human action and its psychological antecedents, questions which careful attention to the issue at hand promises to illuminate. Moreover, though this line cannot be fully developed here, I think that Aristotle's largely ignored attempt (examined in Section II below) to bring certain traits of character into the explanation of incontinent and continent action is remarkably insightful and that philosophers who continue to be intrigued by the theoretical questions raised by incontinent action will share my interest in it.

In the "formal" discussion of *akrasia* in NE, VII.3, the cognitive deficiency in the absence of which akratic action cannot occur is located specifically in the agent's relation to a "particular" or "minor" practical-syllogistic premise (1146b35–1147a10).[2] Although Aristotle does not make it clear why he takes this position, it is often thought that his doctrine of the so-called practical syllogism commits him to denying that there can be akratic actions against practical-syllogistic conclusions, in which case it is natural to suppose that he imports the idea of cognitive or epistemic deficiency in order to explain why "right" conclusions are not reached in cases of akratic action. This interpretation of the practical syllogism and its bearing upon the epistemic deficiency of the akratic agent is the focus of the present paper.

My primary purpose here is to show that Aristotle's conception of practical inference does not preclude there being akratic actions against practical-syllogistic conclusions (including conclusions concerning something to be done here and now) and that there are good textual reasons for maintaining that he did not mistakenly think that it did. This project is undertaken in the first two sections below. Section III addresses a related matter. *Something* must account for Aristotle's making epistemic deficiency of the sort in question a necessary condition of akratic action; and, as I see it, it is incumbent upon me to propose an alternative to the explanation to be rejected here. In Section III, I suggest that the key to Aristotle's attribution of epistemic deficiency to the *arkatēs* lies in the idea of a motivationally indefeasible reason for action. I shall propose that akratic action against a practical conclusion is possible, in Aristotle's view, provided that the conclusion is not grounded in an occurrent desire for happiness (*eudaimonia*), and that, for Aristotle, a practical conclusion (concerning present action) which *is* so grounded is indefeasible, in the sense that it cannot be motivationally overridden by a competing desire or set of desires. Epistemic deficiency with respect to a premise of the particular may, as we shall see, take many forms; but I shall suggest that it *must*, for Aristotle, involve the agent's failing to see how the "particular facts" of his present situation bear upon his happiness—i.e., it must preclude the agent's reaching a right conclusion grounded in an occurrent desire of his for happiness. I hasten to add that I shall not, in Section III, be asking what Aristotle's *explicit* reasons were for holding the epistemic deficiency thesis. This would be pointless, since, as I mentioned, Aristotle does not make his reasons explicit. Rather I shall ask what theoretical commitments motivated him to make epistemic deficiency concerning a "particular" premise a necessary condition of akratic action.

I

In this section, I shall consider two seemingly plausible explanations of Aristotle's holding that akratic action depends upon the agent's being epistemically deficient. I shall argue that the first explanation is unsuccessful, and I shall set the stage for the rejection of the second, which explanation is attacked in Section II.

Explanation 1. If the *akratēs* were not epistemically deficient, he would complete a relevant "right" practical syllogism; for he would fully or non-deficiently now both the relevant "right" universal premise and the relevant particular premise, in which case he could not fail to reach the right conclusion. But the conclusion of a practical syllogism *is* an action. Therefore, if the *akratēs* had full knowledge of the right premises, he would act in accordance with the right syllogism—i.e., continently.[3]

Explanation 2. For the reasons just cited, full knowledge of the right premises implies completion of the right syllogism. The conclusion of a practical syllogism concerning present action, rather than being an (external) action, is a choice, decision, or intention to do A here and now, or a judgment that one ought to do A straightaway. But the relationship between conclusions of practical syllogisms and actions is such that if the *akratēs* were to draw a conclusion concerning immediate action he would act accordingly. "[W]hen a single opinion results" from one's practical premises, "the man who can act (*dunamenon*) and is not prevented (*mē koluomenon*) must immediately act accordingly" (NE, VII.3 1147a26–31); and to suppose that akratic action depends in any way on the agent's being unable to act on his conclusion or on his being prevented from doing so, is to construe ability or prevention so broadly as to make Aristotle's position on the connection between practical reasoning and action vacuous. Therefore, Aristotle cannot allow the *akratēs* to reach a right conclusion (about an action to be performed at once) in cases of akratic action; and, consequently, he must insist that the *akratēs* is epistemically deficient with respect to one or more of his premises.

The element of the first answer on which I shall concentrate is the claim that the conclusion of a practical syllogism is an action. Aristotle does, to be sure, say of one of the syllogisms discussed in *De Motu Animalium* 7 that its conclusion "is an action" (701a20), and he asserts two lines later that "the action is the conclusion."[4] But these claims should be interpreted in the light of the following points. (i) The example in question reads as follows:

> I need a covering, a coat is a covering; I need a coat. What I need I ought to make, I need a coat: I make a coat. And the conclusion I must make a coat is an action. (701a18–20)

Here we see that there are propositional conclusions of practical syllogisms (e.g., "I must make a coat") which, precisely because they are
propositional, are distinguishable from the ensuing (external) action
(cf. [7], p. 230). (ii) There are two syllogisms and two conclusions in
the preceding example, and the first conclusion, "I need a coat," does
not specify an action to be done nor an action-type to be instantiated.[5]
(iii) Given Aristotle's definition of a *protasis* (proposition or premise)
in the *Prior Analytics* as "a sentence affirming or denying one thing or
another" (24a16–17), it is difficult to believe that he could think that a
proposition *is* an action. (iv) As we have already seen, Aristotle asserts
in NE, VII.3 that "when a single opinion results" from the premises of
a practical syllogism, an appropriate action must be performed at once
(if the agent "can act and is not prevented"). But if the immediate
result of one's practical premises is an *opinion*, then the appropriate
action is preceded by a conclusion (or result). (v) Similarly, we are told
in *De Motu An.*, 8 that "thinking that one ought to go and going are
virtually simultaneous (*hama hōs eipein*), unless there be something
else to hinder" (702a15–17). Here, only sixty some lines after our initial
example, Aristotle clearly distinguishes between an opinion of the sort
which could be the conclusion of a practical syllogism and a corresponding action.[6] (vi) Furthermore, if the proximate conclusions
"reached" from practical premises *are* opinions, and an agent's forming a "concluding" opinion is virtually simultaneous with his performing the relevant action, then there is an extended sense of
"conclusion" in which an (external) action *is* characteristically a conclusion of a practical syllogism. It is not an immediate conclusion; for it is
mediated by a concluding opinion. But it is "virtually simultaneous"
with the formation of such an opinion; and, of course, the primary
purpose of practical reasoning is, not to arrive at opinions, but to generate action. This, I think, is the intended meaning of Aristotle's claim
that the conclusion of the second coat syllogism is an action—not that
the making of a coat is the immediate result of assent to the premises,
but that it, or at least its initial stage, follows immediately upon the
formation of a concluding propositional attitude.[7]

If this is right, explanation 1 is undercut: practical-syllogistic conclusions are not actions for Aristotle. This certainly is a point in his favor.
Suppose, e.g., that a person decides, on the basis of his practical premises, to leave his easy chair for a stroll but is shot dead before he has
time to make a move. Surely, it is false that his practical syllogism had
no conclusion. We should also notice, to return to *akrasia*, that the

weak *akratēs*[8] is said to fail to act in accordance with deliberative conclusions (1150b19–21; 1152a18f., 28f.; cf. 1151a1–3).

The texts just cited bear importantly on explanation 2. In the first, a
well-known passage from NE, VII.7, Aristotle says that "some men [*viz.*,
weak *akrateis*] after deliberating fail . . . to stand by the conclusions of
their deliberation" (1150b19–21). Since we are told in NE III that we
deliberate until we "come to the first cause" of the desired end
(1112b11–19)—i.e., an action, believed to be conducive to the desired
end, which it is in the deliberator's power to perform straightaway (cf.
Met. 1032b8–9, 20–21)—it is natural to understand the deliberative
conclusions which weak *akrateis* fail to stand by as conclusions to be
executed at once. (Cf. *De Anima*, 433a1–3: "even when the mind does
command and thought bids us pursue or avoid something, sometimes
no movement is produced; we act in accordance with *epithumia*, as in
the case of *ho akratēs.*") A proponent of explanation 2 may attempt to
save his interpretation in either of two ways: (i) he may deny that the
deliberative conclusions against which *akrateis* act are *practical-syllogistic* conclusions;[9] (ii) he may insist that although these conclusions
are practical-syllogistic, they are concerned only with something to be
done in the (non-immediate) future.[10] Since I have argued at length in
[15] that all deliberative conclusions are conclusions of practical syllogisms and since, as we shall see, 2 suffers from problems to which (i)
is irrelevant, I shall not mount a direct attack against (i). Concerning
(ii), it should be observed that there is no direct evidence for this contention and that to defend it one must appeal to the very ground on
which explanation 2 rests—*viz.*, that if Aristotle does allow for akratic
action against the agent's practical conclusions about something to be
done here and now, he trivializes (or perhaps contradicts) his position
on the connection between practical syllogisms and action—or to an
independently developed interpretation which excludes the possibility
of incontinent behavior of the sort in question. Moreover, the context
of the claim from VII.7 quoted earlier in this paragraph makes (ii) exceedingly implausible. In VII.7, after observing that some incontinent
agents act against their deliberative conclusions and contrasting the
former with impetuous agents who "because they have not deliberated
are led by their emotion," Aristotle asserts that "It is keen and excitable
people that suffer especially from the impetuous form of incontinence;
for the former by reason of their quickness and the latter by reason of
the violence of their passions do not await the argument, because they
are apt to follow their imagination" (1150b25–28). His point here, I

should think, is not that keen and excitable people *never* deliberate, but rather, at least in the case of the latter, that there is a kind of akratic agent who, due to his character and the strength of certain of his desires, does not "await the argument" that he would be in a position to construct or rehearse at the time if he resisted the temptation to act on impulse.[11] This kind of *akratēs* is properly contrasted with a kind who, upon being faced with temptation, does "await the argument"—an argument concerning what is to be done here and now—but acts against its conclusions.

Even if the passages on the defeated deliberative conclusions of akratic agents were set aside, we should still ask whether the psychological antecedents of action mentioned in explanation 2 do preclude akratic action and whether there is good reason to believe that Aristotle thought so. The second issue will be addressed in the following section. The first is more pressing.

Suppose that Mrs. S has asked her husband to put his favorite dog, a large German shepherd, out of its misery. The dog, as she pointed out, is very old, is often in pain, and has become quite irritable—indeed, on several occasions in recent weeks it has tried to bite the children. Mrs. S has purchased a fast-acting, painless poison which she has urged her husband to administer to the dog. And Mr. S, with the poison, the dog, and the dog's dinner before him, is attempting to come to a decision. After careful reflection, he judges that it would be best, all things considered, to kill the dog, and to do it there and then by pouring the poison into the dog's dinner. He intends to act accordingly; but as he begins to tilt the raised bottle of poison toward the dog's meal, he stops. The task is more difficult for him than he expected. He is not yet prepared to abandon his decision, however. It occurs to him that things might be made easier if the dog were not there, and he has his wife take the dog from the room. He raises the bottle of poison over the food again; but again he stops short of pouring it in.

There is no need to suppose that Mr. S was psychologically unable to poison his dog. He made one unsuccessful attempt to alter his environment in such a way as to reduce his motivation to refrain from poisoning his dog. But he may well have been able to bring about the favored balance of motivation in other ways—e.g., by refusing to entertain fond memories of his dog and focusing his attention exclusively on the intended task and the reasons for executing it, or by generating a vivid image of the dog mauling his young daughter. It is clear, moreover, that Mr. S is physically able to act as he judged best. And, of course, no external force prevented him from dumping the poison into the dog's meal. So if explanation 2 is correct, we have here a case which falsifies Aristotle's position on the relationship between practical conclusions and action.[12] But *do* we?

If there are actual cases of the preceding sort, then some intentional behavior is not successfully explained solely in terms of practical conclusions or judgments, physical and psychological ability, and absence of external prevention (or compulsion). Since these elements plainly do have a role to play in explaining intentional behavior, it is natural to think that if cases of akratic action of the type just described are explicable, the explanation is to be achieved, not by abandoning the above-mentioned explanatory elements, but by importing additional ones. And if these difficult cases can be explained in this way, then there must be some way of adding to the original set of explanatory elements without generating a vacuous account of the connection between practical conclusions and intentional behavior; for, of course, vacuous accounts explain nothing. Furthermore, on their most natural reading, Aristotle's claims that weak *akrateis* sometimes fail to stand by the conclusions of their deliberation indicate that he is sensitive to the inadequacy of the set of explanatory conditions in question to account for intentional behavior of the sort just described. (We shall see further evidence of this sensitivity later.) And if there is a significant chance that he is sensitive to this point, one must surely ask what additional explanatory elements he has at his disposal before one can confidently assert that he takes his theory of action (or of the practical syllogism) to exclude akratic action of the type at issue. It is to this question that I now turn.

II

Weak *akrateis* "after deliberating fail, owing to their emotion (*pathos*), to stand by the conclusions of their deliberation" (1150b20–21). But, of course, it is not due *solely* to emotion or desire that they act against their deliberative conclusions. Other people are quite successful in resisting evil passions and pleasures of the sort which "defeat" the *akratēs*. Continent people, for example, have bad appetites and "feel pleasure contrary to the rule," but they are such as not to be led (*agesthai*) by their evil appetites and pleasures (1151b34–1152a3). The dif-

ference between the *akratēs* and the *enkratēs* (continent man) is not
that they are subject to different types of passion, nor to passions of
different strengths or intensities, but that the former has a weak character and the latter has a strong one. The *akratēs* is "in such a state as to
be defeated even by" those passions and pleasures "which most people master," whereas the *enkratēs* is in such a state as "to master even
those by which most people are defeated" (1150a11–13). ("The state
[*hexis*] of most people is intermediate, even if they lean more towards
the worse states" [1150a15–16].)

The account here of *akrasia* and *enkrateia* is plainly dispositional.
But one wants to ask in virtue of what the *akratēs* and *enkratēs* are
respectively more and less disposed than most people to be defeated
by evil or excessive appetites and passions. A possible answer is that
they have respectively weaker and stronger "good" and "moderate"
desires than most people, so that although their evil and excessive desires do not differ in respect of strength, the *balance* of the *akratēs'*
motivations or wants (*orexeis*) is weighted toward incontinent action
more often, and that of the *enkratēs* less often, than is the balance of
the wants of most people. This, however, is not Aristotle's answer. And
he characterizes the *enkratēs*, not as a person whose "good" desires
outweigh his "bad" ones with a commendable frequency, but rather as
one whose "desiring element" (*orektikon*) is obedient to his "rational
principle," though less obedient than the virtuous person's (1102b26–
28).

The metaphor of obedience is an important one for our purposes.
Having a desire in accordance with what one's reason commands is not
sufficient for obedience; for one might have, at the same time, a
stronger competing desire, or the former desire, though unopposed,
may not have been formed in response to the command. Obedience
of the desiring faculty to reason involves responsiveness to reason and,
if not an unopposed desire in accordance with the command (as in the
case of the virtuous agent [1151b33ff.]), at least an appropriate balance
of desire. (Cf.: A general commands his army to enter the plain. (1)
The army enters the plain, but not because of the general's command—indeed, the soldiers were unaware of the order. (2) Most of the
army remains immobile.)

We have come again to the idea that the *enkratēs* and *akratēs* may
be contrasted in respect of balance of motivation; but this time it is
evident that there is a more fundamental difference. The tendency of
their motivations (*orexeis*) to stack up as they do is due to an impor-

tant psychic dissimilarity. The desiring element of the *enkratēs'* soul is characteristically obedient to reason whereas that of the *akratēs* is not. Given Aristotle's view that "reason more than anything else is man" (1178a7; cf. 1166a17, 22–23; 1168b27ff.), the difference between the *enkratēs* and the *akratēs* is well-captured by saying that the former, but not the latter, is *self*-controlled (cf. 1168b34–35). And self-control, rather than being identical with a certain condition or balance of one's wants, is *manifested* in that condition if the condition comes about as an appropriate response to reason. (This is consistent with Aristotle's claim that "Intellect itself . . . moves nothing, but only intellect which aims at an end and is practical" [1139a35–36]. Reason's commands are presumably issued with an end in view.)

One point that this metaphor of obedience makes clear is that Aristotle is sensitive to the fact that the balance of an agent's motivation (*orexis*) may not be in line with his practical judgments, or at least with practical judgments of a certain type or types (cf. 1110a29–31). One's desiring element (*orektikon*) disobeys one's reason in a particular case precisely by failing to align itself with what reason commands. But how is such disobedience possible? How can the balance of one's motivations fail to be in line with one's judgments? Talk of upbringing and habituation is appropriate (cf. [20], p. 182); but a deeper conceptual issue is involved. We cannot understand how someone can *come to have* a disobedient orectic faculty until we understand how it is possible for the faculty to fail to obey reason. If Aristotle has an answer to our present question, one might hope to find it in his most detailed discussion of akratic action, i.e., in NE, VII.3.

According to VII.3, in all cases of akratic action the agent is epistemically deficient with respect to the "particular" premise of a relevant right practical syllogism. However, the weak *akratēs* acts against deliberative conclusions; and if they are practical-syllogistic conclusions, his epistemic deficiency must be such that he not only has some awareness of what is expressed or represented by the particular premise of a practical syllogism, but "combines" his particular and universal premises in such a way as to arrive at the right conclusion.[13] But, one wants to ask, if he draws the right conclusion, how is his epistemic deficiency relevant to his failing to act continently. The *impetuous akratēs* does not see what he ought, specifically, to be doing. But the weak *akratēs* apparently does see this, so how can his epistemic deficiency help to explain what he does and fails to do? Or to return to the metaphor of obedience, how can his epistemic deficiency explain the failure of his reason to be "authoritative," i.e., his being more motivated to do A than B, when B is what he judges best?

Brief attention to some ways in which the *enkratēs* may exercise his powers of self-control will prove instructive. Suppose that Sam, an amorous bachelor, finds himself seated next to a sensuous woman (Cindy) at a local tavern. In conversation, Sam discovers both that Cindy is married and that she is quite attracted to him. He has a strong desire to seduce her, yet he believes that adultery ought always to be avoided. Furthermore, Sam is a continent man, a man who characteristically "conquers" his evil or excessive desires. How might he do so in this case? One thing that Sam might attempt to do is to avoid thinking about the pleasures of seduction. Such thoughts might both strengthen his sexual appetites and decrease his attention to his attitude toward adultery, thus decreasing attendant motivation. He might also attempt to make vivid for himself not only his beliefs that adultery ought always to be avoided and that Cindy is married, but his reasons for holding the former belief, e.g., that adultery, by his own standards, is morally wrong, and that doing what is morally wrong is detrimental to one's moral character and therefore to one's happiness. If he succeeds in all this, the balance of his motivations may well be such that he is able to enjoy the remainder of his pleasant conversation and be content to part company when it is over.

Let us now substitute for Sam an agent, Sid, who is significantly different from Sam only in being akratic. When Sid discovers that Cindy is married he has the premises for the following syllogism:

1. A man ought never to seduce another man's wife.
2. This woman is another man's wife (and I am a man).
So 3. I ought not to seduce this woman.

Let us suppose, if we can, that he completes this syllogism and even reasons that, since he is weak, the best way to avoid running the risk of committing adultery is to take immediate steps toward terminating the conversation in a quick yet graceful manner, but that he takes no such steps and leaves much later with Cindy for a passionate evening.

If Aristotle is correct, Sid's akratic behavior is partially explicable in terms of deficiency in his epistemic relation to some premise "of the particular." Both Sam and Sid know the central particular fact, that the woman is married; both combine it with a universal premise forbidding adultery; and both conclude that seduction is to be avoided. Nevertheless, there may be a significant difference between their respective epistemic relations to the "particular" premise in question. Sam occurrently knows the particular premise in its connections with those values which constitute his reasons for assenting to the universal premise forbidding adultery, i.e., he sees how the particular fact is relevant to his moral character and his happiness; but Sid, we may suppose, does not. Although Sid makes the connection between the particular and the right universal, we may suppose that he does not relate the former to higher relevant ends of his and so does not have the additional motivation to eschew seducing the woman which we might expect his recognition of these further connections to bring.

I have argued in [16] that, for Aristotle, to know fully (i.e., wholly non-deficiently) a "particular" practical premise is not only to be aware of the fact which the premise expresses—e.g., that the thing before one is sweet—but to appreciate its practical import as well. The practical import of a particular premise is not in general defined or limited by the universal premise with which it is conjoined. E.g., the practical import of the fact that the thing before me is sweet is not just that, because it is sweet, it is the sort of thing which my universal premise, "Everyone in my condition should avoid eating anything sweet," forbids me to eat. If I should avoid eating sweets because, say, I am diabetic, then the fact that the thing before me is sweet has practical import *vis-à-vis* my health. And if ill health stands in the way of happiness, then the fact in question is practically important *vis-à-vis* my happiness. Thus, even though the epistemic condition of the weak *akratēs* (in cases of akratic action) is such that he sees that A is to be done, it may also be such that he is less motivated to do A than he might have been; for an agent whose practical conclusion is explicitly supported by his desires for health and happiness will, *ceteris paribus*, be more motivated to act in accordance with his conclusion than he would otherwise be. Furthermore, if an agent's attention, rather than being directed toward the bearing of his present situation upon higher ends of his, is largely occupied by thoughts of "evil or excessive" pleasures, his appetites and passions would seem naturally to have a greater chance of being efficacious.

One might object that the present suggestion locates a deficiency in the *akratēs* grasp of a "*major*" premise, which possibility Aristotle does not consider. But this is not the case. On the suggestion at issue, the *akratēs* fails to grasp the "*minor*" in its connections with one or more of his higher ends—he fails to see how his present situation is related to those ends. This is quite consistent with his having the "right major" premise clearly in mind and seeing its connections with any pertinent higher goals which he may have; for a person might apprehend a "minor" premise only in its connections with the *content* of a major, without relating the particular fact to the higher goals which he believes to support the major. E.g., Sol may occurrently believe that adultery ought always to be avoided, and that it ought to be avoided because it is destructive of moral character and *eudaimonia*, and he may occurrently know that Wilma is married and that to have sexual relations with her would consequently be adulterous; but he may fail to consider, or occurrently believe, that having sexual relations with *Wilma* would be destructive of moral character and happiness. What is crucial, motivationally speaking, is the bringing of higher goals to bear upon the *particular fact*.

If all deliberation began with an occurrent desire for happiness, the line which I am attempting to develop would be fundamentally misguided. But, for Aristotle, deliberation typically begins with occurrent desires for lower-level ends. Just agents deliberate with a view to the end of doing what is just,[14] while physicians and statesmen aim in their professional deliberation at health and social order (*Met.*, 1032b6–7, 15–19; NE, 1112b11–16). These agents might appeal to happiness if asked to *justify* their desires for these lower-level ends; but considerations of happiness typically do not explicitly enter into their deliberations (though they may when ends conflict).[15]

This section has thus far been devoted to locating in Aristotle an explanatory element other than practical-syllogistic conclusions, physical and psychological ability, and absence of external prevention (or compulsion) which might be used in accounting for certain pieces of intentional behavior. My suggestion is that this element is to be found in a proper understand of Aristotle's dispositional conception of *akrasia* itself. The simple answer to the question why the weak *akratēs* acts incontinently is that he suffers from *akrasia*—his character is weak, he is uncommonly deficient in respect of self-control. But this simple answer is filled in by an explanation of how, due to a person's *akrasia*, his evil and excessive appetites and passions may have the result both that he fails to take cognitive steps which might well have resulted in his having sufficient motivation to behave continently and that he in fact increases his "incontinent" motivation by focusing his attention on the evil or excessive pleasures available to him in his present situation.

What I have argued, in effect, is that the concept of prevention or of ability at work in Aristotle's claim that when "a single opinion results" from one's practical premises, "the man who can act and is not prevented must at the same time actually act accordingly" is such that one might properly be said to have been made unable to act accordingly, or to have been prevented from so acting, by one's *akrasia* in conjunction with one's occurrent evil or excessive desires. On this account, Aristotle is neither ruling out akratic action against the "single opinion" in question nor advancing the seemingly trivial claim that a person who reaches such an opinion (about present action) must immediately act accordingly provided that he can do so, is not prevented from doing so by some external force, *and* is not more motivated to do something else. Rather, he is noticing that *an agent's character has a bearing upon the effectiveness of his practical conclusions*. The conclusions of a perfectly self-controlled agent, since he is perfectly *self*-controlled, cannot be defeated by opposing desires. But if an agent is deficient in self-control, it is possible for his appetites, rather than his "self," to "move each of [his] bodily parts" (NE, VII.3 1147a35). When a person acts in this way he is not, in the strictest sense, a *self*-mover (though the moving principle of his action is, of course, *in* him). Thus it is that although the *akratēs* may "reach as a result of his calculation" an evil end which he sets before himself (1142b18–20), his akratic practical conclusions do not count as choices (1111b13–14, 1148a4–17, 1151a5–7, 1152a15–17); for an agent's choice is reflective of a conception of the good or good living with which he identifies,[16] and an akratic agent does not regard his akratic ends as goods (NE, 1136b6–9; cf. EE, 1223b7–8). Akratic action therefore exhibits, in a sense, not only a failure of rationality, but a failure of agency. There is a sense in which, rather than moving himself, the *akratēs* is *being moved by* his appetites or passions. Nevertheless, insofar as the *akratēs* is responsible for the condition of his desiring faculty, the faculty which moves him, he is responsible for what he does.[17]

If we think that an account of the bearing of practical syllogistic conclusions upon action is empty or trivial unless it includes a statement of the weakest set of sufficient conditions of any person's executing his conclusion, then Aristotle's account is seriously flawed. He is in a position to provide *a* statement of sufficient conditions: e.g., that any person who is physically and psychologically able to act in accordance with a practical conclusion of his about present action, who is not prevented by an external force from doing so, and who is perfectly self-controlled, "must at the same time actually act accordingly." But this is a statement only about persons who are agents in the fullest sense, persons who are self-movers in the strictest sense of the term. The fact that some people are less self-controlled than others complicates the picture. Although Aristotle deals admirably with the complications, he does not provide us with the weakest conditions sufficient for a less than fully self-controlled person's execution of a practical conclusion. Ability, absence of external prevention, and not being more motivated to do something else fit the bill in a sense; but the third condition has an empty ring. What is needed is some weakest statement of sufficient conditions of an agent's not being more motivated to do something other than what is specified by his practical conclusion. And providing this is no mean task; for such a statement must take into account, among other things, various *degrees* both of self-control and of the initial motivating force of appetites or passions.

Aristotle is not in a position to offer an account of the relationship between practical conclusions and actions which will enable us, in all cases in which we know what a person's practical conclusion is, to predict what he will do. But this hardly shows that what he says about this relationship is false or unhelpful. If there were no akratic actions against practical conclusions (about present action), Aristotle's task in linking beliefs, wants, and practical inference to action would have been much easier. But, as we have seen, he does not take the easy route around this problem. He does not deny that there are such actions. Rather, he provides us with an illuminating explanation of the bearing of *akrasia*, qua disposition, upon an agent's cognitive and conative condition, an explanation which leaves room for defeated practical conclusions, including conclusions concerning present action.

III

We are still left with the question why Aristotle insisted that all cases of akratic action involve an epistemic deficiency in the agent's relationship to a relevant "particular" premise. If the answer is not that he thought that in the absence of epistemic deficiency one must draw a practical conclusion which is either itself an action or at least conceptually related to action in such a way that akratic action against it is impossible, then what is it?

The main argument of the present section is as follows: (1) If, as

Aristotle claims, the occurrence of an akratic action implies the presence of a deficiency in the agent's epistemic relation to a "particular" premise—let us call this a "P-deficiency"—then (by contraposition) the absence of this deficiency implies the non-occurrence of akratic action. Therefore, if the Aristotelian claim in question is correct, there is some epistemic condition, concerning a "particular" premise, which precludes akratic action. (This is not to ignore the "major" premise: the description of the epistemic condition in question may, e.g., involve the "minor's" being known in its connections with the "major.") (2) On a standard interpretation (discussed shortly) of NE, VII.3, Aristotle commits himself to the view that akratic action always involves a failure to draw a "right" conclusion. But even if this is correct (which I strongly doubt), it can hardly account for Aristotle's holding that all cases of akratic action are to be explained (in part) by a P-deficiency. For the view on P-deficiency occurs again in VII.10 (1150a14–15), where Aristotle explicitly states that some *akrateis* deliberate and act against their deliberative conclusions (a18–19, 28–29). (If he did think the position on P-deficiency to depend on the view about the non-formation of practical conclusions, it would be extremely difficult to understand how the former could be embraced in a passage in which he affirms, almost in the same breath, the *denial* of the latter.) (3) If Aristotle's general conception of practical inference is compatible with akratic action against a conclusion of such inference, and if, moreover, he is sensitive to this fact (both of which points I have defended above), then if all akratic action is, for him, to be explained in part by P-deficiency, the deficiency must be such as to allow the "right" conclusion to be drawn in some cases. (4) Whatever the epistemic condition is which precludes akratic action, it must preclude the final balance of the agent's motivation falling on the side of incontinent action. (5) Given that an agent's apprehending a relevant "minor" premise in conjunction with a lower-level end or principle of his may result in his drawing the right conclusion without having sufficient motivation to act accordingly, it is natural to look to higher-level ends or principles of the agent for additional motivation, and to an epistemic condition which brings this added motivation to bear on the present situation. And the strongest rational motivator, for Aristotle, is an *orexis* for *eudaimonia*. (We might also, or instead, look for an epistemic condition which would decrease or dissolve the "incontinent" motivation. *Phronēsis* [practical wisdom] may seem to be an ideal candidate, since one cannot be *phronimos* without having the moral virtues [1144b31–32,

1145a1–2], and one of these virtues, temperance, involves the absence of all evil and excessive desires of the sort with which *akrasia* and *enkrateia* are, for Aristotle, concerned [1152a1–3]. However, *phronē-sis* is not a purely epistemic condition [see, esp., 1140b28–30]; and even if it were, what frees a person from temptation may well be an *orectic* commitment to a conception of the good or happiness which conditions both one's perception of particular situations and the desires that arise therein.)[18]

In NE, VII.3, Aristotle contends that two epistemic deficiencies are to be found in all cases of akratic action: the *akratēs*, when he acts incontinently, does not "exercise" or "use" his knowledge of a relevant "particular" premise (1146b31–1147a24); what is more, he has this knowledge only "in a sense (*pōs*)" whereas, in another sense, he lacks it (1147a10–24). According to a traditional interpretation of VII.3, to fail to use or exercise knowledge that *p* is to be unaware of it being the case that *p*, and the second deficiency involves the agent's being yet another step removed from occurrent or conscious knowledge—his knowledge is like the geometrical knowledge of the sleeping geometer, as opposed to that of the geometer who is awake but occupied with other matters.[19] This interpretation is plainly radically at odds with the one(s) suggested by argument (1)–(5) above; for by making the agent unaware of the pertinent "minor," it precludes his drawing a conclusion on the basis, in part, of this premise. I have argued in [16] that there is good reason to reject the traditional interpretation in favor of one according to which the first deficiency is, minimally, a failure to focus one's attention on the relevant "minor," a failure to hold it vividly before one's mind (cf. *theōrounta, theōrōn*: 1146b33–35), and the second is a failure (again minimally) to notice the bearing of the "minor" upon one or more ends of the agent which support his "right major," especially his highest end. (Some *akrateis may* be unaware of the particular fact in question, but they must be impetuous *akrateis* as opposed to *weak* ones.) But, for present purposes, there is no need to reject standard interpretations of the epistemic points made in VII.3. (See point 2 above.)

On the line which I am suggesting, Aristotle believes that anyone who both attends to the particular facts of his situation and judges, in light of those facts, that doing *A* is more conductive to his happiness than any imagined alternative, will, given "the facts of human nature" (1147a24), be more motivated to do *A* than any alternative. Aristotle rightly leaves room for irrational action; but, if I am right, he believes that no one is so irrational as to act against what he judges to be most in line with the achievement of his "complete," "self-sufficient," and "highest" end. I have nowhere claimed that Aristotle explicitly affirms this view. Rather, my argument has the form of an inference to the best explanation. Two further points: First, I do not insist that there is for Aristotle, no end "lower" than *eudaimonia* such that any agent who brings a desire for it to bear upon a particular situation thereby avails himself of indefeasible motivation. But if there is such an end, Aristotle does not say what it is; and any selection on a commentator's part must be largely arbitrary. Second, part of the reason that VII.3 has generated so much controversy and so many competing interpretations is, I think, that Aristotle was not himself sure precisely where the absurdity lay in akratic actions performed in the presence of full or non-deficient "knowledge." In any case, he does not tell us why akratic action of this sort is impossible; so the fact that he does not appeal to the motivational force of a desire for *eudaimonia* to explain this is no impediment to my argument in this section. If he *had* told us why full-blown akratic action is impossible, there would have been no need for the present section.

If I am right about what lies behind Aristotle's rejection of full-blown akratic action, there is still a question to be answered. Why should he have thought that the above-mentioned, or any other, epistemic condition is sufficient to preclude incontinent action? David Wiggins has suggested that Aristotle draws the line where he does because he fears that his "notions of practical reason and *eudaimonia* are subverted . . . if anything qualifies with men as they actually are as a counterattraction to the attractions of *eudaimonia*" ([22], p. 266). But this (sensible) suggestion is far from compelling. Suppose that someone who understands what *eudaimonia* is is more attracted to X-ing than to promoting *eudaimonia* on a particular occasion (cf. [22], p. 265). Would this, as Wiggins contends (ibid), "impugn the title of *eudaimonia* to satisfy the criteria of adequacy announced by Aristotle himself in Book I" (Wiggins specifies completeness and self-sufficiency)? Surely not, unless there is reason to believe that whatever satisfies these criteria must be such that no "men as they actually are" will both recognize that it satisfies them and be more attracted to a competing goal. Only someone who has a conception of "men as they actually are," however, has a reason to hold this belief. And once this is noticed it is clear that Aristotle's rejection of full-blown akratic action may be motivated, not by a concern to defend his conception of *eudaimonia*, but rather by his understanding of "men as they actually are." That is, Aristotle's position on *akrasia*, rather than being a defensive maneuver, may be a manifestation of his optimism about human nature and human rationality.

It is worth noting that there are conceptions of "men as they actually are"—reasonable conceptions, I think—on which it is possible for a person to judge that, all things considered, his doing A here and now is most conducive to his achieving his complete, self-sufficient end and yet akratically do B.[20] If Aristotle wanted to defend his conception of *eudaimonia* against alleged instances of full-blown akratic action, it was open to him to argue for an understanding of human nature according to which irrationality of this sort is possible. He does not take this route; for he does not believe that human beings "as they actually are" are capable of this type of irrationality. His conception of the human person constitutes at least part of his reason for ruling akratic action of the type at issue out of court. And it may, indeed, be his only reason.

This is not to say, of course, that Aristotle has no reason for conceiving of human nature as he does. I suspect that his optimism derives at least in part from his natural teleology. If all natural things naturally strive to achieve the type of perfection open to them (see, e.g., *De Anima* 415a29 ff.), it is more plausible than it would otherwise be (other things being equal) to suppose that a person who saw what most contributed to his perfection or *eudaimonia* in a particular case could not akratically act against a practical conclusion reflective of that recognition. An investigation of this suggestion is, however, beyond the scope of this paper. I shall be satisfied if I have made a convincing case for the answer offered here to the question why Aristotle's *akratēs* must be epistemically deficient (in cases of akratic action)—*viz., not* because of some special relationship which is supposed to hold between practical-syllogistic conclusions and actions, but rather because the absence of such deficiency implies a grasp of the bearing of one's present situation upon one's *eudaimonia*, which grasp, for Aristotle, precludes akratic action (i.e., provides one with a motivationally indefeasible reason for action).

IV

On the interpretation which I have defended, Aristotle moves much further from the Socratic position on akratic action than some commentators have thought (e.g.[22], p. 262). For Socrates, everyone judges and acts with reference to a single standard (the good), so that if someone fails to do what is best it can only be because he was *ignorant* of the best course of action.[21] For Aristotle too there is, in a sense, a single practical standard (*viz., eudaimonia*); but it is a standard to which agents often do not refer when judging and acting, and when the connection between one's happiness and one's present situation is not made it is possible for one who forms correct judgment of the best to act akratically against it. Akratic action, for Aristotle as for Socrates, depends upon ignorance or epistemic deficiency; but for Aristotle the "ignorance" is not always of the best course of action.[22]

The difference between the Aristotelian and Socratic position represents, in my opinion, a significant advance. Perhaps the advance is due in part to Aristotle's greater concern with *ta phainomena*. But I believe that it is largely a consequence of his paying close attention to the bearing of wants, beliefs, practical inference, and character on action. There is in Aristotle a powerful theory of action, the beauty of which can only be obscured by a misunderstanding of his "formal" discussion of *akrasia* in NE, VII.3.[23]

Notes

1. Burnet and others have suggested that, of the four analyses of *akrasia* in NE, VII.3, only the final one (1147a24–b5), in which there is no explicit reference to epistemic deficiency, is Aristotle's "real *lusis*" (John Burnet, *The Ethics of Aristotle* [London: Methuen, 1900], 299 ff; cf., e.g., W. H. Fairbrother, "Aristotle's Theory of Incontinence—A Contribution to Practical Ethics," *Mind* 6 [1897], pp. 359–370; R. A. Gauthier and J. Y. Jolif, *Aristote, L'Éthique à Nicomaque*, 2nd ed. [Louvain: Publications Universitaires, 1970], vol. II, p. 609). This suggestion is unacceptable. First, the central question of NE, VII.3 is "whether incontinent people act knowingly or not and in what sense knowingly" (1146b8–9); and the question of knowledge is explicitly addressed only in the first three *luseis*. Second, as D. G. Ritchie has noted, in the final "summary or repetition of the argument [1147b9–15] . . . more obvious use is made of" the first three analyses than the fourth ("Aristotle's Explanation of *Akrasia*," *Mind* 6 [1897], p. 536). Moreover, later in book VII, Aristotle, appealing to the epistemic distinctions developed in the earlier analyses, asserts that the *akratēs* is not "like the man who knows and is contemplating a truth, but like the man who is asleep or drunk" (1152a14–15; cf. 1147a10–24, b6–12, and 1152a20–21). (James J. Walsh, *Aristotle's Conception of Moral Weakness* [New York: Columbia University Press, 1963] provides a useful survey of many competing interpretations.)

2. Cf. VII.3 1147b9–10: "Now, *hē teleutaia protasis* being an opinion about a perceptible object, and being what determines our actions, this man either has not when he is in the state of passion, or has it only in the sense in which having knowledge did not mean knowing but only talking, as a drunken man may mutter the verses of Empedocles." Some commentators (see, e.g., James Bogen and Julius Moravcsik, "Aristotle's Forbidden Sweets," *Journal of the History of Philosophy* 20 [1982], pp. 123–126; Anthony Kenny, *The Anatomy of the Soul* [Bristol: Basil Blackwell, 1973], p. 49; Gerasimos Santas, "Aristotle on Practical Inference, the Explanation of Action, and Akrasia," *Phronesis* 14 [1969], pp. 183–184; David Charles, *Aristotle's Philosophy of Action* [Ithaca: Cornell University Press, 1984], pp. 120ff.) have argued that "*hē teleutaia protasis*" here means, not "the last premise," as Ross has it, but "the conclusion." However, I doubt that in a context in which syllogistic terminology is as prevalent as it is in VII.3, "*protasis*" could mean anything but "premise" (cf. William F. R. Hardie, *Aristotle's Ethical Theory*, 2nd ed. [Oxford: Clarendon Press, 1980], p. 287; and notice that the terminology includes "*sumperanthen*" [conclusion, 1147a27]). And even if "*teleutaia protasis*" did mean "conclusion," there would be no need to suppose that Aristotle has retracted his claim at 1146b35 ff.; for if, when the *akratēs* acts against a practical-syllogistic conclusion, that conclusion is only deficiently known, this deficiency may be traceable to a flaw in the agent's epistemic relation to the "particular" premise from which it was in part derived.

3. Cf. Alexander Grant, *The Ethics of Aristotle* [London: Longmans, Green, and Co., 1885], Vol. 1, pp. 267–268; Hardie, pp. 269–270; David Wiggins, "Weakness of Will, Commensurability, and the Objects of Deliberation and Desire," *Proceedings of the Aristotelian Society* 79 [1978/79], p. 262.

4. 701a13 (*ek tōn duo protaseōn to sumperasma ginetai hē praxis*) is ambiguous. "*Ginetai*" many mean either "is" or "becomes" (a thing which *has become X is X*). And the assertion consequently may be either that "the two premisses result in a conclusion which is an action" (Oxford translation) or that "the conclusion drawn form the two premisses becomes the action" (Loeb translation). Notice that a conclusion may *become* an action (in a sense) by generating it.

5. John Cooper, partly for the reason mentioned, sets this example aside as aberrant and inappropriate (John M. Cooper, *Reason and Human Good in Aristotle* [Cambridge: Harvard University Press, 1975], p. 25 n. 26). For a reply to Cooper, see my "The Practical Syllogism and Deliberation in Aristotle's Causal Theory of Action," *The New Scholasticism* 55 (1981), Section 4.

6. Nussbaum (*Aristotle's De Motu Animalium* (Princeton: Princeton University Press, 1978), p. 358) contends that *noei hoti poreuteon* ("thinking that one ought to go") "need not refer to an explicit propositional conclusion to the syllogism" and that "it is more likely to designate the major premise." However, there is nothing in the immediate context of the assertion to suggest this reading; and in the very similar claim at 1147a26–31, it is "when a single opinion results" from one's practical premises that one who "can act and is not prevented must immediately act accordingly."

7. I develop the points outlined in this paragraph in greater detail in "Aris-

totle on the Proximate Efficient Cause of Action," *Canadian Journal of Philosophy*, Sup., 10 (1984), pp. 133–155. See also Charles, pp. 91–95.

8. Aristotle contrasts weak and impetuous *akrateis*. The latter "do not await the argument" (e.g., 1150b25–28), i.e., they do not deliberate in cases of akratic action.

9. Cooper (pp. 28–51 *passim*) argues that the practical syllogism is not part of deliberation but is rather the link between deliberation and action, in which case *no* deliberative conclusion is a practical-syllogistic conclusion.

10. Richard Robinson commits himself to this view in "Aristotle on Akrasia," in J. Barnes, M. Schofield, R. Sorabji (eds.), *Articles on Aristotle*; vol. 2 (New York: St. Martin's Press, 1977), see esp. p. 87. Cf. Walsh, p. 121.

11. VII.10 1152a18–19, pp. 28–29 should be read accordingly (cf. a19–21). For further discussion of these passages and Aristotle's related contention that the *akratēs* has a good *prohairesis*, see my "Choice and Virtue in the *Nicomachean Ethics*," *Journal of the History of Philosophy* 19 (1981), pp. 417–418.

12. For a more detailed (non-historical) discussion of the possibility of akratic action against an intention to do something "here and now," see my "*Akrasia*, Reasons, and Causes," *Philosophical Studies* 44 (1983), pp. 345–368.

13. As NE, VII.3 is commonly understood, Aristotle does not there allow the *akratēs* to reach the conclusion of a "right" practical syllogism when he acts incontinently. For references to the secondary literature and a detailed criticism of this common understanding, see my "Aristotle on *Akrasia* and Knowledge," *Modern Schoolman* 58 (1981), pp. 137–157. (The present paper takes up roughly where that article ends.)

14. Cf. 1129a7–9. On the nature of the ends with a view to which virtuous agents typically deliberate, see my "Choice and Virtue," Section 1.

15. On the possibility of conflicting ends, see Cooper, pp. 16–18. Cf. my "Aristotle on the Roles of Reason in Motivation and Justification," *Archiv für Geschichte der Philosophie* (1984), pp. 124–47.

16. See my "Aristotle's Wish," *Journal of the History of Philosophy* 22 (1984), pp. 139–156. Some supporting references are: NE, 1110b31, 1111b5, 1117a5, 1144a18–20 (cf. 1105a28–33), 1163a22, 1164b1, 1114b22–24, 1139a33–34; EE, 1227b34 ff.

17. Aristotle insists that the *akratēs* act "willingly (*hekōn*)," "for he acts in a sense with knowledge both of what he does and of the end to which he does it" (1152a15–16). The moving principles of his akratic actions are, in Aristotle's terminology, *in* him (see, e.g., 1113b21), and these actions must therefore be said to be in the akratic agent's power and voluntary (1113b19–21). We are told in another connection that "if each man is somehow responsible for his state of mind, he will also be himself somehow responsible" for what appears to him to be good (1114b1–3). A comparable claim may plausibly be made concerning a person's being responsible for the condition of his desiring faculty and his being responsible for actions of his to which his desires lead.

18. John McDowell, "The Role of *Eudaimonia* in Aristotle's Ethics," in A. O. Rorty (ed.), *Essays on Aristotle's Ethics* (Berkeley: University of California Press, 1980) is interesting and useful in this connection, though McDowell is there contending only for a related view.

19. See my "Aristotle on *Akrasia*" for references to the secondary literature and criticism.

20. Wiggins recognizes this. He argues that we can "drop Aristotle's doctrine of the *akratēs'* ignorance of the minor premise" and advance a "neo-Aristotelian doctrine of incontinence" according to which no form of ignorance is required (p. 270; cf. pp. 255–258).

21. *Protagoras*, 352a–258d; cf. *Republic*, 439a–441a.

22. Aristotle does, of course, assert toward the end of VII.3 that "the position that Socrates sought to establish actually seems to result" (1147b14–15). But this is simply to say that there is a kind of knowledge (or epistemic condition) which precludes akratic action.

23. David Charles's important book *Aristotle's Philosophy of Action* was published after this paper was submitted for publication. I have added only brief citations of it in endnotes.

9

Aristotle on Learning to Be Good

M. F. Burnyeat

The question "Can virtue be taught?" is perhaps the oldest question in moral philosophy. Recall the opening of Plato's *Meno* (70a): "Can you tell me, Socrates—can virtue be taught, or is it rather to be acquired by practice? Or is it neither to be practiced nor to be learned but something that comes to men by nature or in some other way?" This is a simple version of what was evidently a well-worn topic of discussion. Socrates' characteristic but still simple reply is that until one knows what virtue is, one cannot know how it is (to be) acquired (*Meno* 71ab). I want to reverse the order, asking how, according to Aristotle, virtue is acquired, so as to bring to light certain features in his conception of what virtue is which are not ordinarily much attended to. Aristotle came to these questions after they had been transformed by the pioneering work in moral psychology which the mature Plato undertook in the *Republic* and later dialogues; by his time the simplicities of the debate in the *Meno* lay far behind. Nevertheless, about one thing Socrates was right: any tolerably explicit view of the process of moral development depends decisively on a conception of virtue. This dependence makes it possible to read a philosopher's account of moral development as evidence for what he thinks virtue is. In some ways, indeed, it is especially revealing evidence, since in problems of moral education the philosopher has to confront the complex reality of ordinary imperfect human beings.

My aim, then, is to reconstruct Aristotle's picture of the good man's development over time, concentrating on the earlier stages. Materials for the construction are abundant in the *Nicomachean Ethics*, but scattered; the construction will be gradual, its sense emerging progressively as the pieces come together from their separate contexts. I shall have to forgo extended exegesis of the various discussions from which Aristotle's remarks are extracted, but I trust that it is not necessary to apologize for the undefended interpretative decisions this will involve; such decisions are an inescapable responsibility of the synoptic enterprise.

Aristotle's good man, however, is not the only character I have in view. I am also interested in the conflicted akratic, the weak-willed (incontinent) man who knows the good but does not always achieve it in action. I want to place his problem too in the perspective of his development through time. And while I am not going to attempt anything like a full treatment of Aristotle's account of *akrasia* (incontinence, weakness of will), my hope is that the temporal perspective I shall sketch will remove one major source, at any rate, of the dissatisfaction which is often, and understandably, felt with Aristotle's account of the phenomenon.

In both cases, the good man and the akratic, we shall be concerned with the primitive materials from which character and a mature morality must grow. A wide range of desires and feelings are shaping patterns of motivation and response in a person well before he comes to a reasoned outlook on his life as a whole, and certainly before he integrates this reflective consciousness with his actual behavior. It is this focus of interest that constitutes the chief philosophical benefit, as I conceive it, of what is a predominantly historical inquiry. Intellectualism, a one-sided preoccupation with reason and reasoning, is a perennial failing in moral philosophy. The very subject of moral philosophy is sometimes defined or delimited as the study of moral reasoning, thereby excluding the greater part of what is important in the initial—and, I think, continuing—moral development of a person. Aristotle knew intellectualism in the form of Socrates' doctrine that virtue is knowledge. He reacted by emphasizing the importance of beginnings and the gradual development of good habits of feeling. The twentieth century, which has its own intellectualisms to combat, also has several full-scale developmental psychologies to draw upon. But they have not been much drawn upon in the moral philosophy of our time, which has been little interested in questions of education and development.[1] In this respect Aristotle's example has gone sadly unstudied and ignored.

No doubt Aristotle's developmental picture is still much too simple, by comparison with what could be available to us. Let that be conceded at once—to anyone who can do better. What is exemplary in Aristotle is his grasp of the truth that morality comes in a sequence of stages with both cognitive and emotional dimensions. This basic insight is already sufficient, as we shall see, to bring new light on akrasia.

So let us begin at the beginning, which Aristotle says is "the *that*." This somewhat cryptic phrase occurs in an admitted digression (cf. 1095b14) toward the end of 1.4. Aristotle has just begun the search for a satisfactory specification of happiness and the good for man when he pauses to reflect, with acknowledgments to Plato, on the methodological importance of being clear whether one is on the way to first principles or starting points or on the way from them (1095a14–b1). The answer to Plato's question is that at this stage Aristotle is traveling dialectically toward a first principle or starting point, namely, the specification of happiness, but in another sense his inquiry must have its own stating points to proceed from. As he explains (1095b2–13),

> For while one must begin from what is familiar, this may be taken in two ways: some things are familiar to us, others familiar without qualification. Presumably, then, what *we* should begin from is things familiar to *us*. This is the reason why one should have been well brought up in good habits if one is going to listen adequately to lectures about things noble and just, and in general about political (social) affairs. For the beginning (starting point) is "the *that*," and if this is sufficiently apparent to a person, he will not in addition have a need for "the *because*." Such a person has, or can easily get hold of, beginnings (starting points), whereas he who has neither [sc. neither "the *that*" nor "the *because*"],[2] let him hearken to the words of Hesiod:

> > The best man of all is he who knows everything himself,
> > Good also the man who accepts another's sound advice;
> > But the man who neither knows himself nor takes to heart
> > What another says, he is no good at all.

The contrast here, between having only "the *that*" and having both "the *that*" and "the *because*" as well, is a contrast between knowing or believing that something is so and understanding why it is so, and I would suppose that Aristotle quotes the Hesiodic verses in all seriousness. The man who knows for himself is someone with "the *because*"—in Aristotle's terms he is a man of practical wisdom equipped with the understanding to work out for himself what to do in the varied circumstances of life—while the one who takes to heart sound advice learns "the *that*" and becomes the sort of person who can profit from

Aristotle's lectures. These lectures are no doubt designed to give him a reasoned understanding of "the *because*" which explains and justifies "the *that*" which he already has or can easily get hold of. What, then, is "the *that*"?

The ancient commentators are agreed that Aristotle has in mind knowledge about actions in accordance with the virtues; these actions are the things familiar to us from which we must start, and what we know about them is that they are noble or just.[3] This fits an earlier statement (1.3. 1095a2–4, quoted below) that the lectures assume on the part of their audience a certain experience in the actions of life, because they are concerned with these actions and *start from them*. It also conforms to what 1.4 says is the subject matter of the lectures for which knowledge of "the *that*" is a prerequisite: things noble and just.

Now the noble and the just do not, in Aristotle's view, admit of neat formulation in rules or traditional precepts (cf. 1.3 1094b14–16; 2.2. 1104a3–10; 5.10. 1137b13–32; 9.2. 1165a12–14). It takes an educated perception, a capacity going beyond the application of general rules, to tell what is required for the practice of the virtues in specific circumstances (2.9. 1109b23; 4.5. 1126b2–4). That being so, if the student is to have "the *that*" for which the doctrines in Aristotle's lectures provide the explanatory "*because*," if he is to be starting out on a path which will lead to his acquiring that educated perception, the emphasis had better be on his knowing of specific actions that they are noble or just in specific circumstances. I put it as a matter of emphasis only, of degree, because often, no doubt, moral advice will come to him in fairly general terms; a spot of dialectic may be needed to bring home to the young man the limitations and imprecision of what he has learned. But even where the advice is general, this need not mean he is taught that there are certain rules of justice, say, which are to be followed as a matter of principle, without regard for the spirit of justice and the ways in which circumstances alter cases. What Aristotle is pointing to is our ability to internalize from a scattered range of particular cases a general evaluative attitude which is not reducible to rules or precepts. It is with this process in view that he emphasizes in 1.4 that the necessary beginnings or starting points, which I have argued to be correct ideas about what actions are noble and just, are not available to anyone who has not had the benefit of an upbringing in good habits.

We can put this together with some further remarks about "the *that*" at the end of 1.7 (1098a33–b4):

> We must not demand explanation [sc. any more than precision] in all matters alike, but it is sufficient in some cases to have "the *that*" shown properly, just as in the case of starting points. "The *that*" is a first thing and a starting point. Of starting points some are seen by induction, some by perception, some by a certain habituation, and others in other ways again.

This time the wider context points to the outline definition of happiness or the good for man as the particular "*that*" which Aristotle has initially in mind. The search for a satisfactory specification of happiness and the good for man has just been completed, and Aristotle is reflecting on the extent to which he should claim precision and proof for his answer: it has the status of "the *that*" merely, and, being general, no more precision than the subject matter allows. Thus it would obviously be wrong to think of the notion of "the *that*" as intrinsically tied to particular low level facts. Nevertheless, in this passage the thesis that we have to start from "the *that*" without an explanation, without "the *because*," is reasserted for starting points quite generally, and is complemented by a brief survey of various ways in which we acquire starting points. We already know that in ethics good habits are a prerequisite for grasping "the *that*." It is now added that habituation is actually a way of grasping it, on a par with, though different from, induction, perception, and other modes of acquisition which Aristotle does not specify (the ancient commentators fill out the list for him by mentioning intellectual intuition and experience).[4] Each kind of starting point comes with a mode of acquisition appropriate to it; to give a couple of examples from the ancient commentators, we learn by induction that all men breathe, by perception that fire is hot. In ethics the appropriate mode for at least some starting points is habituation, and in the light of 1.4 it is not difficult to see which starting points these must be.[5] The thesis is that we first learn (come to see) what is noble and just *not* by experience of or induction from a series of instances, nor by intuition (intellectual or perceptual), but by learning to do noble and just things, by being habituated to noble and just conduct.

In part, this is the well-known doctrine of 2.1 and 4 that we become just or temperate by doing, and becoming habituated to doing, just and temperate things. But the passages we have examined from 1.4 and 7 add to those chapters a cognitive slant. It turns out that Aristotle is not simply giving us a bland reminder that virtue takes practice. Rather, practice has cognitive powers, in that it is the way we learn what is noble or just. And on reflection we can see that this addition is quite in accord with 2.1 and 4, even demanded by them. For according to 2.4 the ultimate goal toward which the beginner's practice is aimed is that he should become the sort of person who does virtuous things in full knowledge of what he is doing, choosing to do them for their own sake, and acting out of a settled state of character (1105a28–33). The beginner would hardly be on the way to this desirable state of affairs if he were not in the process forming (reasonably correct) ideas as to the nobility or justice of the actions he was engaged in; if you like, he must be on his way to acquiring a mature sense of values.

Let me skip here to 7.3, where at 1147a21–22 Aristotle has an interesting remark about learners in general:

> Those who have learned a subject for the first time connect together[6] the propositions in an orderly way, but do not yet know them; for the propositions need to become second nature to them, and that takes time.

We shall come later to the significance of this learner as one of Aristotle's models for the state of mind of the akratic man. At present I want simply to connect the thought in 7.3 of ideas or beliefs becoming second nature to someone with the thought in 2.4 of the learner in morals as someone who is tending toward a firmly established state of character which includes, and therefore must in part have developed out of, convictions about what is noble and just. The fully developed man of virtue and practical wisdom understands "the *because*" of these convictions—in terms of 1.4's contrast between things familiar without qualification and things familiar to us, he has knowledge or familiarity in the unqualified sense—but this state is preceded by the learner's knowledge (in the qualified sense) of "the *that*," acquired by habituation so that it is second nature to him. Although only at the beginning of the road to full virtue, the learner has advanced to a stage where, having internalized "the *that*," he has or can easily get hold of the type of starting point which is seen by habituation.

Thus the picture forms as follows. You need a good upbringing not simply in order that you may have someone around to tell you what is noble and just—you do need that (recall the Hesiodic verses), and in 10.9 and again in the *Politics* 8.1 Aristotle discusses whether the job is best done by one's father or by community arrangements—but you need also to be guided in your conduct so that by doing the things you are told are noble and just you will discover that what you have been told is *true*. What you may begin by taking on trust you can come to know for yourself. This is not yet to know *why* it is true, but it is to have *learned that* it is true in the sense of having made the judgment your own, second nature to you—Hesiod's taking to heart. Nor is it yet to have acquired any of the virtues, for which practical wisdom is required (6.13; 10.8 1178a16–19), that understanding of "the *because*" which alone can accomplish the final correcting and perfecting of your perception of "the *that*." But it is to have made a beginning. You can say, perhaps, "I have learned that it is just to share my belongings with others," and mean it in a way that someone who has merely been told this cannot, even if he believes it—except in the weak sense in which "I have learned such and such" means simply that such and such was the content of the instruction given by parent or teacher.

This is a hard lesson, and not only in the moralist's sense. How can I learn that something is noble or just by becoming habituated to doing it? Is it not one thing to learn *to* do what is just and quite another to learn *that* it is just? Clearly, we need to look further at what Aristotle has to say about learning to do what is noble and just. Let us begin again at the beginning presupposed by Aristotle's lectures. For more is said about good upbringing and its benefits in 10.9, the very last chapter of the *Nicomachean Ethics*, which is specifically devoted to moral education.

In this chapter Aristotle gives an explanation (1179b4–31) of why it is that only someone with a good upbringing can benefit from the kind of argument and discussion contained in his lectures.

Now if arguments were in themselves enough to make men good, they would justly, as Theognis says, have won very great rewards, and such rewards should have been provided; but as things are, while they seem to have power to encourage and stimulate the generous-minded among our youth, and to make a character which is well-bred,[7] and a true lover of what is noble, ready to be possessed by virtue, they are not able to encourage the *many* to nobility and goodness. For these do not by nature obey the sense of shame, but only fear, and do not abstain from bad acts because of their baseness but through fear of punishment; living by passion they pursue the pleasures appropriate to their character and the means to them, and avoid the opposite pains, and have not even a conception of what is noble and truly pleasant, since they have never tasted it. What argument would remould such people? It is hard, if not impossible, to remove by argument the traits that have long since been incorporated in the character; and perhaps we must be content if, when all the influences by which we are thought to become good are present, we get some tincture of virtue.

Now some think that we are made good by nature, others by habituation, others by teaching. Nature's part evidently does not depend on us, but as a result of some divine causes is present in those who are truly fortunate; while argument and teaching, we may suspect, are not powerful with all men, but the soul of the student must first have been cultivated, by means of habits, for noble joy and noble hatred, like earth which is to nourish the seed. For he who lives as passion directs will not hear argument that dissuades him, nor understand it if he does; and how can we persuade one in such a state to change his ways? And in general passion seems to yield not to argument but to force. The character, then, must somehow be there already with a kinship to virtue, loving what is noble and hating what is base.[8]

This important and neglected passage is not rhetoric but precise argument,[9] as I hope eventually to show. My immediate concern is the student Aristotle wants for his lectures. He is someone who already loves what is noble and takes pleasure in it. He has a conception of what is noble and truly pleasant which other, less well brought up people lack because they have not tasted the pleasures of what is noble. This is what gives his character a kinship to virtue and a receptiveness to arguments directed to encouraging virtue.

The noble nature here described—Aristotle's prospective student—we met earlier as the person with a starting point. He is one who has learned what is noble ("the *that*") and, as we now see, thus come to love it. He loves it because it is what is truly or by nature pleasant. Compare 1.8 1099a13–15:

> Lovers of what is noble find pleasant the things that are by nature pleasant; and virtuous actions are such, so that these are pleasant for such men as well in their own nature.

This is from a context which makes clear that the word *love* is not idly used; Aristotle has in mind a disposition of the feelings comparable in intensity, though not of course in every other respect, to the passion of a man who is crazy about horses. And the point he is making is that what you love in this sense is what you enjoy or take pleasure in. But equally he insists (10.9 1179b24–26) that the capacity for "noble joy and noble hatred" grows from habituation. I should now like to suggest that the prominence given to pleasure in these passages is the key to our problem about how practice can lead to knowledge.

There is such a thing as learning to enjoy something (painting, music, skiing, philosophy), and it is not sharply distinct from learning that the thing in question is enjoyable. Once again we need to eliminate the weak sense of *learn*, the sense in which to have learned that skiing is enjoyable is simply to have acquired the information, regardless of personal experience. In the strong sense I learn that skiing is enjoyable only by trying it myself and coming to enjoy it. The growth of enjoyment goes hand in hand with the internalization of knowledge.

There is also such a thing as learning to enjoy something properly, where this contrasts with merely taking pleasure in it. This is a hard subject, but I can indicate roughly what I mean by a few examples of not enjoying something properly: enjoying philosophy for the sense of power it can give, enjoying a trip abroad because of the splendid photographs you are taking on the way, enjoying a party because you are meeting important people, letting a symphony trigger a release of sentimental emotion. Aristotle's virtue of temperance is about the proper enjoyment of certain bodily pleasures having to do with taste and touch. These are things that any man or beast can take pleasure in, but not necessarily in the right way. Take the example of the gourmand who prayed that his throat might become longer than a crane's, so that he could prolong his enjoyment of the feel of the food going down (3.10 1118a26–b1): this illustrates the perversion of a man who takes more pleasure in brute contact with the food than in the flavors which are the proper object of taste. Aristotelian temperance is also concerned with sexual relations:

> All men enjoy in some way or other good food and wines and sexual intercourse, but not all men do so as they ought. [7.14 1154a17–18]

And this again is a thought we can understand, however difficult it might be to elaborate.

Now Aristotle holds that to learn to do what is virtuous, to make it a habit or second nature to one, is among other things to learn to enjoy doing it, to come to take pleasure—the appropriate pleasure—in doing it. It is in the light of whether a man enjoys or fails to enjoy virtuous actions that we tell whether he has formed the right disposition toward them. Thus 2.3 1104b3–13 (but the whole chapter is relevant):

We must take as a sign of states of character the pleasure or pain that ensues on acts; for the man who abstains from bodily pleasures and delights in this very fact is temperate, while the man who is annoyed at it is self-indulgent, and he who stands his ground against things that are terrible and delights in this or at least is not pained is brave, while the man who is pained is a coward.[10] For moral excellence is concerned with pleasures and pains; it is on account of the pleasure that we do bad things, and on account of the pain that we abstain from noble ones. Hence we ought to have been brought up in a particular way from our very youth, as Plato says, so as both to delight in and to be pained by the things that we ought;[11] this is the right education. [Cf. 1.8 1099a17–21; 2.9 1109b1–5; 3.4 1113a31–33; 4.1 1120a26–27; 10.1 1172a20–23]

Such passages need to be received in the light of Aristotle's own analysis of pleasure in Books 7 and 10 (cf. esp. 10.3 1173b28–31): the delight of the temperate man who is pleased to be abstaining from overindulgence, or that of the brave man who is pleased to be standing up to a frightful situation, is not the same or the same in kind as the pleasure of indulgence or the relief of safety. The character of one's pleasure depends on what is enjoyed, and what the virtuous man enjoys is quite different from what the nonvirtuous enjoy; which is not to say that the enjoyment is not as intense, only that it is as different as the things enjoyed. Specifically, what the virtuous man enjoys, as the passage quoted makes very clear, is the practice of the virtues undertaken for its own sake. And in cases such as the facing of danger, cited here, and others, the actions which the practice of the virtues requires *could* only be enjoyed if they are seen as noble and virtuous and the agent delights in his achievement of something fine and noble (cf. 3.9 1117a33–b16). That is why his enjoyment or lack of it is the test of whether he really has the virtues.

Next, recall once more the statement in 2.4 that virtue involves choosing virtuous actions for their own sake, for what they are. If we are asked what virtuous actions are, an important part of the answer must be that they are just, courageous, temperate, and so forth, and in all cases noble. (It is common to all virtuous actions that they are chosen because they are noble: 3.7. 1115b12–13; 4.1. 1120a23–24; 4.2 1122b6–7;[12] *EE* 1230a27–29.) Accordingly, of learning to do and to take (proper) enjoyment in doing just actions is learning to do and to enjoy them for their own sake, for what they are, namely, just, and this is not to be distinguished from learning that they are enjoyable for themselves and their intrinsic value, namely, their justice and nobility, then perhaps we can give intelligible sense to the thesis that practice leads to knowledge, as follows. I may be told, and may believe, that such and such actions are just and noble, but I have not really learned for myself (taken to heart, made second nature to me) that they have this intrinsic value until I have learned to value (love) them for it, with the consequence that I take pleasure in doing them. To understand and appreciate the value that makes them enjoyable in themselves I must learn for myself to enjoy them, and that does take time and practice—in short, habituation.

Back now to 10.9. We have come to see that the young person there spoken of as a true lover of what is noble is not simply someone with a generalized desire to do whatever should turn out to be noble, but someone who has acquired a taste for, a capacity to enjoy for their own sake, things that are in fact noble and enjoyable for their own sake. He has learned, really learned, that they are noble and enjoyable, but as yet he does not understand why they are so. He does not have the good man's unqualified knowledge or practical wisdom, although he does have "the *that*" which is the necessary starting point for acquiring practical wisdom and full virtue. He is thus educable. According to 10.9, argument and discussion will encourage him toward virtue because he obeys a sense of shame (*aidōs*) as opposed to fear. What does this mean?

Aristotle discusses shame in 4.9:

> Shame should not be described as a virtue; for it is more like a feeling than a state of character. It is defined, at any rate, as a kind of fear of disgrace. . . .
>
> The feeling is not becoming to every age, but only to youth. For we think young people should be prone to the feeling of shame because they live by feeling and therefore commit many errors, but are restrained by shame; and we praise young people who are prone to this feeling, but an older person no one would praise for being prone to the sense of disgrace, since we think he should not do anything that need cause this sense. [1128b10–12, 15–21]

Shame is the semivirtue of the learner. The learner is envisaged as a young person who lives by the feelings of the moment and for that reason makes mistakes. He wants to do noble things but sometimes does things that are disgraceful, ignoble, and then he feels ashamed of himself and his conduct.[13] Now Aristotle holds that all young people (and many older ones) live by the feeling of the moment and keep chasing after what at a given time appears pleasant. A sample statement is the following from 8.3. 1156a31–33:

> The friendship of young people seems to aim at pleasure; for they live under the guidance of emotion, and pursue above all what is pleasant to themselves and what is immediately before them. [cf. 1.3 1095a4–8]

The point about those of the young who have been well brought up is that they have acquired a taste for pleasures—namely, the pleasures of noble and just actions—which others have no inkling of. The less fortunate majority also live by the feelings of the moment (10.9. 1179b13, 27–28), but since they find no enjoyment in noble and just actions, the only way to get them to behave properly is through fear of punishment (10.9. 1179b11–13). They will abstain from wrongdoing not because it is disgraceful, not because of what the actions are, unjust, but simply and solely as a means of avoiding the pains of punishment. Whereas the well-brought-up person has an entirely different sort of reason for avoiding them. Insofar as he realizes they are unjust or ignoble, they do not appear to him as pleasant or enjoyable; insofar as he does not realize this and so desires and perhaps does such things, he feels badly about it, ashamed of his failure. The actions pain him internally, not consequentially. He is therefore receptive to the kind of moral education which will set his judgment straight and develop the intellectual capacities (practical wisdom) which will enable him to avoid such errors.

The fundamental insight here is Plato's. For in discussing the development in the young of a set of motives concerned with what is noble and just, we are on the territory which Plato marked out for the middle part of his tripartite soul. The middle, so-called spirited part strives to do what is just and noble (*Rep.* 440cd), and develops in the young before reason (441a; cf. Ar. *Pol.* 1334b22–25). It is also the seat of shame: implicitly so in the story of Leontius and his indignation with himself for desiring to look on the corpses, explicitly in the *Phaedrus* (253d, 254e). The connection with anger, which we shall also find in Aristotle, is that typically anger is this same concern with what is just and noble directed outward toward other people (cf. *NE* 5.8. 1135b28–29). Aristotle owes to Plato, as he himself acknowledges in 2.3, the idea that these motivating evaluative responses are unreasoned—they develop before reason and are not at that stage grounded in a general view of the place of the virtues in the good life—and because they are unreasoned, other kinds of training must be devised to direct them on to the right kinds of object: chiefly, guided practice and habituation, as we have seen, but Aristotle also shares with Plato the characteristically Greek belief that musical appreciation will teach and accustom one to judge rightly and enjoy decent characters and noble actions through their representation in music (*Pol.* 1340a14 ff.). In both cases the underlying idea is that the child's sense of pleasure, which to begin with and for a long while is his only motive, should be hooked up with just and noble things so that his unreasoned evaluative responses may develop in connection with the right objects.

To say that these responses are unreasoned is to make a remark about their source. The contrast is with desires—the reasoned desires to which we shall come shortly—which derive from a reflective scheme of values organized under the heading of the good. But where desires and feelings are concerned, the nature of the response and its source are connected. It is not that the evaluative responses have no thought component (no intentionality): on the contrary, something is desired as noble or just, something inspires shame because it is thought of as disgraceful. The responses are grounded in an evaluation of their object, parallel to the way appetite is oriented to a conception of its object as something pleasant; in this sense both have their "reasons." The point is that such reasons need not invariably or immediately give way or lose efficacy to contrary considerations. There are, as it were, pockets of thought in us which can remain relatively unaffected by our overall view of things. This is a phenomenon which the century of psychoanalysis is well placed to understand, but the Greek philosophers already saw that it must be central to any plausible account of akrasia. It is that insight which backs their interweaving of the topics of akrasia and moral development.[14]

From all this it follows not only that for a long time moral development must be a less than fully rational process but also, what is less often acknowledged, that a mature morality must in large part continue to be what it originally was, a matter of response deriving from sources other than reflective reason. These being the fabric of moral character, in the fully developed man of virtue and practical wisdom they have become integrated with, indeed they are now infused and corrected by, his reasoned scheme of values. To return to temperance:

As the child should live according to the direction of his tutor, so the appetitive element should live according to reason. Hence the appetitive

element in a temperate man should harmonize with reason; for the noble
is the mark at which both aim, and the temperate man desires the things
he ought, as he ought, and when he ought; and this is what reason directs. [3.12. 1119b13–18; cf. 1.13. 1102b28; 9.4 1166a13–14]

This is Aristotle's version of the psychic harmony which Plato sought
to establish in the guardians of his ideal republic.

But Aristotle, as 10.9 makes clear, draws an important conclusion
from the requirement of unreasoned beginnings which is not, perhaps,
so evident in Plato (though we shall come back to Plato in a while). In
Aristotle's view it is no good arguing or discussing with someone who
lacks the appropriate starting points ("the *that*") and has no conception of just or noble actions as worthwhile in themselves, regardless
of contingent rewards and punishments. To such a person you can
recommend the virtues only insofar as they are required in a given
social order for avoiding the pain of punishment—that is, for essentially external, contingent reasons. You cannot guarantee to be able to
show they will contribute to some personal goal the agent already has,
be it power, money, pleasure, or whatever; and even if in given contingent circumstances this connection with some antecedent personal
goal could be made, you would not have given the person reason to
pursue the virtues for their own sake, as a *part* of happiness, but only
as a means to it.

This casts some light on what Aristotle takes himself to be doing in
the *Nicomachean Ethics* and on why he asks for a good upbringing as
a condition for intelligent study of the subject. If he is setting out, "the
because" of virtuous actions, he is explaining what makes them noble,
just, courageous, and so on, and how they fit into a scheme of the
good life, not why they should be pursued at all. He is addressing
someone who already wants and enjoys virtuous action and needs to
see this aspect of his life in a deeper perspective. He is not attempting
the task so many moralists have undertaken of recommending virtue
even to those who despise it: his lectures are not sermons, nor even
protreptic argument, urging the wicked to mend their ways. From 10.9
it is clear that he did not think that sort of thing to be of much use;
some, perhaps most, people's basic desires are already so corrupted
that no amount of argument will bring them to see that virtue is desirable in and for itself (cf. 3.5. 1114a19–21). Rather, he is giving a course
in practical thinking to enable someone who already wants to be virtuous to understand better what he should do and why.[15] Such under-

standing, as Aristotle conceives it, is more than merely cognitive. Since it is the articulation of a mature scheme of values under the heading of the good, it will itself provide new and more reflective motivation for virtuous conduct. That is why Aristotle can claim (1.3. 1095a5–6; 2.2. 1103b26–29; 2.4. 1105b2–5; 10.9. 1179a35–b4) that the goal of the study of ethics is action, not merely knowledge: to become fully virtuous rather than simply to know what virtue requires.[16] Someone with a sense of shame will respond, because he wants to do better at the right sorts of things. Someone with nothing but a fear of punishment will not respond; the only thing to do with him is tell him what he will get into trouble for.

After these rather general remarks about the character of Aristotle's enterprise we can begin to move toward the topic of akrasia. We need first to round out the picture of the motivational resources of the well-brought-up young person. For the unreasoned evaluative responses with which his upbringing has endowed him are not the only impulses that move him to act. Being a human being he has the physiologically based appetites as well. The object of these is, of course, pleasure (3.2. 1111b17; 3.11. 1118b8 ff.; 3.12. 1119b5–8; 7.3. 1147a32–34; 7.6. 1149a34–36; *EE* 1247b20), but they can be modified and trained to become desires for the proper enjoyment of bodily pleasures; this, we saw, is what is involved in acquiring the virtue of temperance. There are also instinctive reactions like fear to be trained into the virtue of courage. In a human being these feelings cannot be eliminated; therefore, they have to be trained. It would also be wrong to omit, though there is not room to discuss, the important fact that Aristotle in Books 8 and 9 takes seriously his dictum that the human being is by nature a social animal: friendship is itself something noble (8.1. 1155a29), and among the tasks of upbringing and education will be to give the right preliminary shape to the feelings and actions bound up with a wide range of relationships with other people.[17]

That said by way of introduction, we can consider a passage that takes us from moral education to akrasia (1.3. 1095a2–11):

> Hence a young man is not a proper hearer of lectures on political science; for he is inexperienced in the actions that occur in life, but its discussions start from these and are about these; and, further, since he tends to follow his passions, his study will be vain and unprofitable, because the end aimed at is not knowledge but action. And it makes no difference whether he is young in years or youthful in character; the defect does not depend

upon time, but on his living, and pursuing each successive object, as passion directs. For to such persons, as to the incontinent, knowledge brings
no profit; but to those who form their desires and act in accordance with
reason knowledge about such matters will be of great benefit.

Reason will appeal and be of use to the well-brought-up student because he is ready to form his desires in the light of reasoning; that we
have already discovered. Other people, the immature of whatever age,
form desires in a different way, and this is what happens in akrasia; or
rather, as we shall see, it is one half of what happens in akrasia. We
have here two kinds of people, distinguished by two ways of forming
desires. What are these two ways of forming desires and how are they
different?

As Aristotle describes what he calls deliberation (cf. esp. 3.2–4), it is
a process whereby practical thought articulates a general good that we
wish for and focuses it on a particular action it is in our power to do,
thereby producing in us a desire to do this thing. A desire is formed by
the realization that the action will fulfill one of the ends endorsed by
our reasoned view of the good life, and this more specific desire—
more specific, that is, than the general wish from which it derived—is
what Aristotle calls choice:

> The object of choice being one of the things in our own power which is
> desired after deliberation, choice will be deliberated desire of things in
> our own power; for when we have decided as a result of deliberation, we
> desire in accordance with our deliberation.[18] [3.3. 1113a9–12]

Or, to paraphrase his remarks in a later book (6.2. 1139a21–33), choice
is desire pursuing what reason asserts to be good.

So much for the forming of desires in the light of reasoning, which
means: reasoning from the good. If a piece of practical reasoning does
not relate to one's conception of the good, Aristotle does not count it
deliberation, nor its outcome choice. But that does not mean he denies
that reasoning and thinking are involved when desires are formed by
the alternative process mentioned in 1.3. On the contrary, he describes
such thinking in some detail, as we shall see if we now turn to his
discussion of akrasia in Book 7.

The akratic (weak-willed) man is one who acts against his knowledge
(judgment) and choice of the good;[19] he has a reasoned desire to do
one thing, but under the influence of a contrary desire he actually does

another. Clearly, however, this contrary desire itself needs to be generated if we are to understand how it fixes upon some particular object and fits into an adequate explanation of the akratic's behavior. Equally clearly, at least one main purpose Aristotle has in 7.3 is to exhibit akratic behavior under a standard pattern of explanation which he schematizes in the practical syllogism. His model case turns on the point that bodily appetite can supply a major premise of its own having to do with the pleasant rather than the good ("Everything sweet is pleasant" or "Sweets are nice"). That is to say, appetite sets an end that is not integrated into the man's life plan or considered scheme of ends, his overall view of the good. Unlike the self-indulgent man, whose (perverted) reason approves of every kind of sensual gratification as good in itself, the akratic is tempted to pursue an end which his reasoned view of life does not approve. But he acts, Aristotle emphasizes (7.3. 1147a35–b1), under the influence of a sort of reason and an opinion. His action is to be explained on the standard pattern by a combination of desire and thought, articulated in the syllogism "Sweets are nice; this is a sweet; so I'll have this." For the akratic this is only half the story—we have explained the action he actually performs but not the conflict behind it—but it is presumably the whole story of the immature people in 1.3. They form desires and undertake actions not in accordance with reason because their ends are simply things that strike them as pleasant at a given moment; they have no steady conception of the good to reason from.[20]

But there are other sources of incontinence than the bodily appetites: most notably, the unreasoned evaluative responses we met before as an important characteristic of the well-brought-up beginner. A parallel procedure to the one we have just followed will give us a picture of the sort of error that makes Aristotle's prospective student ashamed of himself. What in him is a mistake is one half of the conflict involved in nonappetitive akrasia.

The details appear in 7.6. 1149a25–b2:

> Spirit seems to listen to reason to some extent, but to mishear it, as do hasty servants who run out before they have heard the whole of what one says and then mistake the order, or as dogs bark if there is but a knock at the door, before looking to see if it is a friend; so spirit on account of the warmth and hastiness of its nature, no sooner hears—even though it has not heard an order—than it springs to take revenge. For reason or imagination informs us that we have been insulted or slighted, and spirit, rea-

soning as it were that anything like this must be fought against, boils up straightway; while appetite, if reason or perception merely says that an object is pleasant, springs to the enjoyment of it. Therefore spirit follows reason in a sense, but appetite does not.

The description, which owes much to Plato (*Rep.* 440cd again),[21] implies the usual pattern of practical thought and reasoning: "Slights and injustices must be fought against; I have been wronged/slighted; so I should take revenge." Aristotle does not specify in detail the better syllogism which must also be present if this is to be a case of full incontinence, but we can supply the order which spirit does not stop to hear—for example, "It is better to wait and investigate an apparent wrong before taking revenge; this is an apparent wrong; so wait and investigate." As in Plato, the overeager dog in us[22] is concerned with what is noble and just, with honor and self-esteem, without taking thought for the consequences or the wider view.

If, then, these evaluative responses are in us as a result of our upbringing, and the bodily appetites are in us as a part of our natural inheritance as human beings, the seeds of akrasia are going to be with us as we enter Aristotle's lecture room. He will encourage us to think about our life as a whole, to arrive at a reasoned view of the good for man; but to begin with, until our understanding of "the *because*" has had a chance to become second nature with us, this will be superimposed upon well-established, habitual patterns of motivation and response which it will take time and practice to integrate with the wider and more adult perspective that Aristotle will help us achieve.

This seems to me important. I think many readers feel that Aristotle's discussion of akrasia leaves unexplained the point most in need of explanation. What they want to know is why the better syllogism is overcome. Not finding an answer they look for one in what Aristotle says in 7.3 about the akratic's knowledge and the way this is not used, not had, or dragged about. And then they are dissatisfied because no adequate answer is to be found in the discussion of *that* issue, for the good reason, I believe, that none is intended. The treatment of knowledge pinpoints what is to be explained. It is not itself the explanation. Even in the relatively easy case where a man simply fails to bring to bear on the situation (fails to use) some knowledge that he has, the fact of his failure requires explanation: he was distracted, overanxious, in haste, or whatever. For the more difficult cases Aristotle announces his explanation at 1147a24–25:

> Again, we may also view the cause as follows with reference to the facts
> of human nature.

Thus Ross's translation, but I think that the scope of "also" is the whole
sentence,[23] which means this: we may also give an explanation of the
phenomenon we have been endeavoring, with some difficulty, to describe. The explanation that follows is in terms of the two syllogisms,
which together account for the conflict, and one of which explains the
action the akratic man performs. But the outcome of the conflict might
have been different. In the continent man it is; his action is to be explained by the better syllogism. So what determines whether it is appetite or reason that is victorious?

I submit that the question is misguided, at least so far as it looks for
an answer in the immediate circumstances of the conflicted decision.
If there is an answer, it is to be found in the man's earlier history. We
must account for his present conflict in terms of stages in the development of his character which he has not yet completely left behind.
For on Aristotle's picture of moral development, as I have drawn it, an
important fact about the better syllogism is that it represents a later
and less established stage of development. Hence what needs explanation is not so much why some people succumb to temptation as why
others do not. What calls for explanation is how some people acquire
continence or, even better, full virtue, rather than why most of us are
liable to be led astray by our bodily appetites or unreasoned evaluative
responses. It is no accident that Aristotle gives as much space to the
akratic as a type of person as to isolated akratic actions, and it is characteristic of him that he measures the liability to incontinence by comparison with the normal man. Thus 7.10. 1152a25–33:

> Now incontinence and continence are concerned with that which is in
> excess of the state characteristic of most men; for the continent man
> abides by his resolutions more and the incontinent man less than most
> men can.
> Of the forms of incontinence, that of excitable people is more curable
> than that of those who deliberate but do not abide by their decision,[24]
> and those who are incontinent through habituation are more curable than
> those in whom incontinence is innate; for it is easier to change a habit
> than to change one's nature; even habit is hard to change just because it
> is like nature, as Evenus says;

> I say that habit's but long practice, friend,
> And this becomes men's nature in the end.

I trust that this second set of verses will by now reverberate in their full significance.

Given this temporal perspective, then, the real problem is this: How do we grow up to become the fully adult rational animal that is the end toward which the nature of our species tends? How does reason take hold on us so as to form and shape for the best the patterns of motivation and response which represent the child in us (3.12. 1119a33 ff.), that product of birth and upbringing which will live on unless it is brought to maturity by the education of our reason? In a way, the whole of the *Nicomachean Ethics* is Aristotle's reply to this question, so that this paper is nothing but a prolegomenon to a reading of the work. But I would like, in conclusion, to make a few brief comments concerning one important aspect of the process.

Consider 2.3. 1104b30–35:

> There being three objects of pursuit[25] and three of avoidance, the noble, the advantageous, the pleasant, and their contraries, the base, the injurious, the painful, about all of these the good man tends to go right, and especially about pleasure; for this is common to the animals, and also it accompanies all objects of pursuit; for even the noble and the advantageous appear pleasant. Again, it has grown up with us all from infancy; which is why it is difficult to rub off this feeling, dyed as it is into our life.[26]

There are three irreducibly distinct categories of value for the fully virtuous man to get right—the three we have been discussing. Pursuit of pleasure is an inborn part of our animal nature; concern for the noble depends on a good upbringing; while the good, here specified as the advantageous,[27] is the object of mature reflection. We have seen that each of the three categories connects with a distinct set of desires and feelings, which acquire motivating effect at different stages of development. It has also become clear that Aristotle's insistence on keeping these distinctions is a key tactic in his vindication of akrasia against Socratic intellectualism.

Historically, the greatest challenge to the intelligibility of akrasia was the argument mounted by Socrates in Plato's *Protagoras* (351b ff.), which showed that weakness of will is unintelligible on the assumption, precisely, that there is only one "object of pursuit"—one category of value, within which all goods are commensurable, as it were, in terms of a single common coinage. Pleasure was the coinage chosen for the argument, but the important consideration was that if, ultimately, only one factor counts—call it F—and we have measured two actions X and Y in terms of F, and X comes out more F than Y does, there is nothing left to give value to Y to outweigh or compensate for its lesser quantity of F. The supposed akratic cannot possibly find reason to do Y, the less valuable action, rather than the better action X, because Y offers him less of the only thing he is after: pleasure or whatever else the F may happen to be. If what Y offers is less of the only thing the man seeks, pleasure, its offering that pleasure cannot intelligibly function as a reason for doing Y instead of the admittedly more attractive X.[28] The moral is close to hand: Y must offer something different in kind from X if the temptation and the man's succumbing to it are to be intelligible. Plato came to see this, and in the *Republica* it was in part to make akrasia and other forms of psychological conflict intelligible that he distinguished different objects of pursuit for the three parts of the soul. The passage quoted is Aristotle's version of that Platonic insight.[29]

However, the fact that there are three irreducibly distinct categories of value need not mean that one and the same thing cannot fall under two or more of them at once. To vindicate akrasia it is necessary only that this need not happen. The continent and the incontinent man do find the good and the pleasant or, in the anger case, the good and the noble in incompatible actions. Therein lies their conflict. The self-indulgent man, on the other hand, has no use for the noble and identifies present pleasure with his long-term good (cf. 3.11. 1119a1–4; 7.3. 1146b22–23; 7.7. 1150a19–21; 7.8. 1150b29–30; 7.9. 1152a5–6). It would seem to follow that what we need to do to become fully virtuous instead of merely continent or worse is to bring those three categories of value into line with each other. We have already seen how a good upbringing makes the noble a part, perhaps the chief part, of the pleasant for us. Aristotle's lectures are designed to take the next step and make the noble a part, perhaps the chief part, of one's conception of the good (cf. *EE* 1249a11). That is why in 2.4 he makes it a condition of virtue that virtuous actions be chosen for their own sake. Choice, which is reached by deliberation from a conception of the good, includes a desire for them as good in themselves as well as noble and pleasant. But then he adds a further condition, and rightly, since choice by itself is compatible with incontinence and indeed continence. The further condition is that all this must proceed from a firm and unchangeable character. That is, it is second nature to the virtuous man to love and find his greatest enjoyment in the things he knows to be good (cf. 8.3. 1156b22–23). In him the three categories of value are in harmony. They have *become* commensurable in terms of pleasure and pain, but not in the objectionable way which led to Socratic intellectualism, since the virtuous person's conception of what is truly pleasant is now shaped by his independent, reasoned conception of what is good, just as it was earlier shaped by his father's or his teacher's advice about what is noble. Indeed, one definition of the noble given in the *Rhetoric* (1366a34) is to the effect that the noble is that which, being good, is pleasant because it is good (cf. *EE* 1249a18–19). And with all three categories in harmony, then, and then only, nothing will tempt or lure him so much as the temperate or brave action itself. Nothing else will seem as pleasurable. That is how Aristotle can assert (7.10. 1152a6–8) that the fully formed man of virtue and practical wisdom cannot be akratic. Quite simply, he no longer has reason to be.

Notes

For details of the works cited in these notes see the bibliography at the end of this essay. References by name alone, without page number, are to a commentator's note on or a translator's rendering of the passage under discussion.

This paper was one result of the leisure I enjoyed from my tenure of a Radcliffe Fellowship. I am grateful to the Radcliffe Trust for the gift of the Fellowship and to University College, London, for allowing me to take it up. The paper has been improved by discussions at a number of universities (London, Cambridge, Reading, Sussex, Princeton, Berkeley, and the University of Massachusetts at Amherst) and by the comments of David Charles, James Dybikowski, Martha Craven Nussbaum, Amélie O. Rorty, Richard Sorabji, and Susan Khin Zaw. I only regret that to deal adequately with all their criticisms would require the paper to be even longer than it is. But perhaps my greatest debt is to the members of my graduate seminar at Princeton in 1970 (two of them now writing in the present volume), from whom I received my first understanding and appreciation of Aristotle's ethics.

1. One exception is John Rawls, *A Theory of Justice*, chaps. 8–9, but the exception that most completely exemplifies what I am looking for is Richard Wollheim, "The Good Self and the Bad Self: The Moral Psychology of British Idealism and the English School of Psychoanalysis Compared"; it is noteworthy that he too has to go to the history of philosophy—specifically, to F. H. Bradley—to find a serious philosophical involvement with developmental questions.

2. *Contra* Aspasius, Stewart, Burnet, Ross, and Gauthier-Jolif, who take Ar-

istotle to be speaking of a person of whom it is true neither that he has nor that he can get starting points.

3. So Aspasius, Eustratius, Heliodorus ad loc. and on 1098a33–b4. Stewart agrees. Burnet's proposal that "the *that*" is the much more general fact that the definition of happiness is such and such is right for 1.7 (see below), but at the moment the definition of happiness is the first principle or starting point we are working towards. For sane remarks on this and other misunderstandings of 1.4, see W. F. R. Hardie, *Aristotle's Ethical Theory*, pp. 34–36, although Hardie's own suggestion ("the *that*" is "a particular moral rule or perhaps the definition of a particular moral virtue") also errs on the side of generality.

4. Some scholars (Peters, Grant, Stewart, Gauthier-Jolif) keep the modes of acquisition down to the three explicitly mentioned by reading *Kai allai d'allōs* (1098b4) as a summary rather than an open-ended extension of the list: "some in one way, some in another" rather than "others in other ways again." The rendering I have preferred has the support of Ross as well as the ancient tradition.

5. Not, or at least not in the first instance, the definition of happiness, as Burnet thinks: although this is "the *that*" which initiates the passage, it was secured by argument, not habituation, and Aristotle has turned parenthetically to a survey of wider scope (cf. T. H. Irwin, "First Principles in Aristotle's Ethics," p. 269 n. 18). Of course, the starting points in question and the habituation they presuppose will lead further (cf. esp. 7.8. 1151a15–19), but we are still at the beginning of Aristotle's lectures and of the progress they are designed to encourage.

6. Ross translates "string together"; he may not have intended the disparaging note the phrase now sounds. The fact is, the verb (*sunerein*) is not invariably, or even usually, disparaging in Aristotle's vocabulary. It is disparaging at *Met.* 1090b30, *De div.* 464b4, but not at *Soph. El.* 175a30, *Met.* 986a7, 995a10, 1093b27, *De gen. et corr.* 316a8, 336b33, *De gen. anim.* 716a4, 741b9, *Probl.* 905a19.

7. Ross translates "gently born," which has aristocratic overtones irrelevant to the argument, even if Aristotle's sympathies happened to run in that direction. In fact, in the *Rhetoric* (1390b22–25) Aristotle says that most of the products of noble birth are good for nothing, and he makes a sharp distinction between noble birth (*eugeneia*) and noble character (*gennaiotēs*). His view in the *Politics* is that it is likely that good birth will go with moral merit, but no more than that (*Pol.* 1283a36 in its wider context from 1282b14).

8. From here on I quote Ross's translation, corrected in a few places.

9. Strictly, the argument occurs twice, each paragraph being a distinct version, as Rassow saw ("Zu Aristoteles," pp. 594–596). But all that shows is that Aristotle thought the material important enough to have had two goes at expressing it satisfactorily.

10. Strictly, as Grant observes, doing the right thing with reluctance and dislike is rather a sign of continence (self-control) than of vice proper (cf. 3.2. 1111b–14–15, *EE* 1223b13–14, 1224b16–18); the attributions of self-indulgence and cowardice should not be pressed.

11. The reference is to Plato *Laws* 653a; cf. also *Rep.* 395d, featuring the idea that habit becomes second nature.

12. In the first and third of these passages Ross rather misleadingly translates "for honour's sake."

13. The connection between shame and the desire to do what is noble is very clear in the Greek. Shame is felt for having done *aischra* (things disgraceful, ignoble, base), and *aischra* is the standard opposite of *kala* (things noble, fine, honorable). Hence to do something from fear of disgrace is not incompatible with doing it for the nobility of the act itself. This is made clear at 3.8 1116a27–29, on "citizenly" courage: the only thing that is "second best" about this form of courage is that the citizen soldier takes his conception of what is noble from the laws and other people's expectations (1116a17–21) rather than having his own internalized sense of the noble and the disgraceful (cf. 3.7. 1116a11–12).

14. For a twentieth-century philosophical discussion that makes interesting use of Greek ideas to bring out the significance of the different sources of desire, see Gary Watson, "Free Agency." Watson goes so far as to claim (pp. 210–211) that there are desires carrying absolutely no positive favoring of their object, not even an idea that it is pleasurable. But the cases he cites (a mother's sudden urge to drown her bawling child in the bath, a man who regards his sexual inclinations as the work of the devil) cry out for treatment in terms of the thought of pleasure having to be kept unconscious.

15. An example to the point is the celebrated argument in 1.7 which uses considerations about the distinctive activity (*ergon*) of man to show that happiness is activity in accordance with virtue: it is not an argument that would appeal to anyone who really doubted or denied that he should practice the virtues—so much is made clear in the closing pages of Book 1 of Plato's *Republic*, where Thrasymachus remains totally unmoved by an earlier version of the same argument—but it would say something to the reflective understanding of someone with the basic moral concerns which Aristotle presupposes in his audience. (Irwin, pp. 260–262 seems to be more optimistic.)

16. Not that Aristotle ever suggests that attendance at lectures such as his is the only way to get practical wisdom nor that attendance is sufficient by itself for developing the needed intellectual virtues. But he is serious about aiming to help his students in that direction, in a quite practical way. This is the solution to the traditional problem (most sharply formulated by Joachim, pp. 13–16) about why Aristotle failed to recognize that the *Ethics* is not itself practical but a theoretical examination *of* the practical. The real failure here is in the impoverished conception of practical reason which finds it a puzzle to accept the practical orientation of Aristotle's enterprise (see further Irwin, pp. 257–259).

17. Here again Aristotle borrows from the middle part of Plato's tripartite soul: the *Republic* (375a ff.) likened the guardians to noble dogs, with special reference to their warm and spirited nature, and in the *Politics* (1327b38–1328a1) Aristotle expressly alludes to the *Republic* when he suggests that the capacity of the soul in virtue of which we love our familiars is spirit (*thumos*).

18. It might be objected that Aristotle did not need to make choice a new and more specific desire. Given a wish for X and the realization that Y will secure X, explanation is not furthered by adding in another desire; it should

be enough to say that the man wanted X and saw Y as a way of securing it (for intimations of this line of argument see Thomas Nagel, *The Possibility of Altruism*, chaps. 5–6). But a new and specific desire is not explanatorily redundant in Aristotle's scheme if it helps to explain the pleasure taken in a virtuous act, a pleasure that ought to be more specific to the particular action than the pleasure of simply doing *something* to fulfill one's wish to be virtuous.

19. Against knowledge or judgment: 7.1. 1145b12; 7.3. 1146b24 ff. Against choice: 7.3. 1146b22–24; 7.4. 1148a9–10; 7.8. 1151a5–7; 7.10. 1152a17.

20. That this is the point, not a denial that they engage in practical thinking at all, is clear from 10.9. 1179b13–14: "living by passion they pursue the pleasures appropriate to their character and *the means to them*." Cf. 6.9. 1142b18–20; *EE* 1226b30.

21. This is one of the reasons why it seems preferable to translate *thumos* "spirit" throughout, rather than "anger" (Ross).

22. The dog image of 1149a28–29 brings with it an allusive resonance to large tracts of Plato's *Republic*; cf. n. 17 above.

23. Compare W. J. Verdenius, "*Kai* Belonging to a Whole Clause." A good parallel in Aristotle is *An. Post.* 71b20–22, where *kai* emphasizes not the immediately following *tēn apodeiktikēn epistēmēn*, which merely resumes *to epistasthai* and the point that this must be of necessary truths, but rather the subsequent characterization of the premises from which these necessary truths are derived; that is the new point signaled by *kai* (here I am indebted to Jacques Brunschwig).

24. For these two forms of akrasia see 7.7. 1150b19–22.

25. Ross's translation "choice" badly misses the point, since not every pursuit (*hairesis*) is a choice (*prohairesis*) in the technical sense explained earlier. Note that this means that Aristotle does not endorse in every particular the commonplace (*endoxon*) which forms the famous first sentence of *NE*: he does not, strictly, think that every action aims at some good—for one thing, akratic action does not.

26. The dyeing metaphor is yet another allusion to Plato's treatment of these topics: cf. *Rep.* 429d–430b.

27. Perhaps because Aristotle is making argumentative use of a commonplace (endoxon): cf. *Top.* 105a27, 118b27. For the sense in which the advantageous = the good is the object of practical wisdom see 6.5. 1140a25–28, 6.7. 1141b4–8: the man of practical wisdom deliberates correctly about what is good and advantageous to himself with reference to the supreme goal of living the good life; but of course the same equation can be made when the deliberation concerns a more particular end (6.9. 1142b27–33).

28. Here I can only sketch my account of the *Protagoras* argument, but various people have independently been propounding similar accounts for quite a time, and the key idea is beginning to emerge in print: see, for example, David Wiggins, "Weakness of Will, Commensurability, and the Objects of Deliberation and Desire."

29. In a different context (*Pol.* 1283a3–10) Aristotle expressly denies that all goods are commensurable (*sumblēton*); similarly *EE* 1243b22, *NE* 9.1. 1164b2–6. Earlier in life Aristotle may have been tempted to think otherwise.

An. Pr. 68a25–b7 is a sketch toward a calculus of preference relations as envisaged in *Top.* 3.1–3, where 116b31–36 aspires to cardinal measurement, not just
a relative ordering. Yet it is difficult to judge how far Aristotle thought he could
take the project, for *Top.* 118b27–37 seems to be clear that there is no question
of quantitative commensurability across the three categories of the noble, the
pleasant, and the advantageous. Hence when Aristotle at *De an.* 434a8–9 says
that deliberation requires the measurement of alternatives by a single standard,
it is important that in the context he is concerned to mark the difference between rational agents and unreasoning animals, for which purpose the simplest
achievement of deliberative calculation will suffice. *anagkē heni metrein* need
not be generalized to all deliberation.

Bibliography

Aspasius. *In Ethica Nicomachea quae supersunt commentaria*. Edited by G.
    Heylbut. Berlin, 1889.
Burnet, John. *The Ethics of Aristotle*. London, 1900.
Eustratius. *Eustratii et Michaelis et Anonyma in Ethica Nicomachea com-
    mentaria*. Edited by G. Heylbut. Berlin, 1892.
Gauthier, René Antoine, and Jean Yves Jolif. *L'Éthique à Nicomaque*, 2d edi-
    tion. Louvain and Paris, 1970.
Grant, Sir Alexander. *The Ethics of Aristotle*, 4th edition. London, 1885.
Hardie, W. F. R. *Aristole's Ethical Theory*. Oxford, 1968.
Heliodorus. *In Ethica Nicomachea paraphrasis*. Edited by G. Heylbut. Berlin,
    1889.
Irwin, T. H. "First Principles in Aristotle's Ethics," *Midwest Studies in Philoso-
    phy* 3 (1978), 252–272.
Joachim, H. H. *Aristotle: the Nicomachean Ethics*. Oxford, 1951.
Nagel, Thomas. *The Possibility of Altruism*, Oxford, 1970.
Peters, F. H. Translation of *Nicomachean Ethics*. 10th ed. London, 1906.
Rassow, H. "Zu Aristoteles," *Rheinisches Museum*, N.F. 43 (1888), 583–596.
Rawls, John. *A Theory of Justice*. Oxford, 1972.
Ross, Sir David. Translation of *Nicomachean Ethics* in *The Works of Aristotle
    Translated into English*, vol. 9. Oxford, 1925.
Stewart, J. A. *Notes on the Nicomachean Ethics*. Oxford, 1892.
Verdenius, W. J. "*Kai* Belonging to a Whole Clause," *Mnemosyne*, 4th ser. 29
    (1976), 181.
Watson, Gary. "Free Agency," *Journal of Philosophy* 72 (1975), 205–220.
Wiggins, David. "Weakness of Will, Commensurability, and the Objects of De-
    liberation and Desire," *Proceedings of the Aristotelian Society*, n.s. 79
    (1978–79), 251–277 (chap. 14 of this anthology).
Wollheim, Richard. "The Good Self and the Bad Self: The Moral Psychology
    of British Idealism and the English School of Psychoanalysis Compared,"
    Proceedings of the British Academy 61 (1975), 373–398.

10

The Habituation of Character

Nancy Sherman

Aristotle's remarks on the habituation of character have been accepted for the most part as an uncontroversial part of his ethical theory. What seems certain on any reading is that character states are acquired through practice of corresponding actions. Under traditional interpretations, however, practice is seen primarily as a non-rational training of desires towards appropriate objects. Habituation is thus viewed as essentially separate from and antecedent to the development of rational and reflective capacities.

A well-known commentator has made the following remarks about the second book of the *Nicomachean Ethics*:

> We need only compare the theory of virtue in this book with the discussions in the *Meno* of Plato, to see how immensely moral philosophy has gained in definiteness in the meantime. While becoming definite and systematic, however, it had also to some extent become scholastic and mechanical . . . A mechanical theory is here given both of the intellect and the moral character, as if the one could be *acquired* by teaching, the other by a course of habits.[1]

To be sure, the commentator, namely Alexander Grant, is critical of this mechanical theory; but he none the less takes it to be Aristotle's view—Aristotle's alternative to Socratic intellectualism, and the equation of ethical virtue with knowledge (*epistēmē*). Socrates' mistake, Aristotle himself says, is that "he used to inquire what virtue is, but not how and from what sources it arises" (*EE* 1216b10–11; cf. 1216b19–22).

But Aristotle's inquiry into these questions, indeed his transformation of ethical theory into a theory, like Plato's, about *how* to be good, does not issue in a mechanical theory of habituation. . . . Similar claims have been made by others in recent years, most notably by Burnyeat and Sorabji.[2] If my argument is distinctive, it is because it brings to bear a broader range of texts which show just how thoroughgoing Aristotle's conception of critical habituation is. In particular, I hope to show how . . . perceptual, affective, and deliberative capacities are cultivated within such an education.

My motive in taking a serious look at the process of moral education is the belief that the mechanical theory of habituation ultimately makes mysterious the transition between childhood and moral maturity. It leaves unexplained how the child with merely 'habituated' virtue can ever develop the capacities requisite for practical reason and inseparable from full virtue. . . . Full virtue is not simply the excellence of the non-rational part, but itself combines the excellences of character and of practical reason. This is the unmistakable force of the definition of virtue in *NE* 11. 6 as a character state concerning choice as determined by the reasoning of the *phronimos* (person of practical wisdom). It is the point of the claim made in Book VI that one cannot be good without practical wisdom nor wise without virtue (1144b30–3).

Now it is true that no one would seriously hold that rationality emerges in an instant. To say "Now a boy becomes a man" (at whatever age—thirteen, eighteen, or twenty-one) is to create an artifice for law, not to explain when and how.[3] But the mechanical theory does not offer such an explanation, nor allow us plausibly to infer any. It gives us no indication of the way capacities are cultivated for their eventual maturity. A reasonable account need not require that such capacities develop perfectly continuously, nor at an even pace. A more plausible alternative is that there is an uneven rate of growth, with starts and stops in the development of particular capacities. Aristotle might accept something like this picture: there might be an early period in which affective capacities are cultivated, followed by the more active development of rational (and deliberative) capacities, and then eventually the emergence of full rationality.[4] This recognizes the general fact that there are conditions of internal readiness as well as environmental factors that affect the rate of progress. Growth will be marked by spurts and impasses. Thus, the extremely young child, on his view, may not engage in the reasoning process in a very extensive way. It is true, his perceptual and discriminatory capacities will awaken early on, as Aristotle indicates in various places (1161b28, 184b14, 1448b7–10), and he will enjoy the power of discriminating differences. As the child becomes older, the cultivation of these cognitive capacities will become an essential element in the development of the affections. But he will not yet, in a substantive way, cultivate the more deliberative skills that enter into complex choice-making. That comes later.

I shall argue for something like this conception in the pages that follow. My overall claim is that if full virtue is to meet certain conditions, then this must be reflected in the educational process. The child must be seen as being educated towards that end. This will require a developmental conception of cognitive and affective capacities, as well as a conception of habituation in varying degrees reflective and critical.

The chapter, then, will proceed roughly in this way: after introductory remarks about the plausibility of ascribing to Aristotle a developmental model of the child's ethical growth, I shall examine the non-rational part of the soul and consider the sort of rationality it none the less includes. This will lead us to Aristotle's intentional theory of the emotions, and to a broad sketch of how we refine the discriminatory capacities included in the emotions. With this as background, we shall be in a position to assess Aristotle's remarks about the habituation of character and to consider the way in which it allows for the critical practice necessary for developing fine discrimination. Central to the account will be Aristotle's view that practice yields pleasure to the extent to which it exhibits increasingly fine powers of discernment. Finally, I shall argue that the general conception of habituation as reflective and critical coheres with Aristotle's view of experience as training practical reason through trial and error as well as inquiry.

1. The Viability of a Developmental Model

Before proceeding, then, we need to assess the viability of ascribing to Aristotle a developmental conception of the child's ethical growth. Some hesitation about this point seems well grounded, given Aristotle's general tendency to lump the child, together with the animal, as constituting a single contrast case to the ethically mature adult. The single grouping implies that the child's defects are in some way permanent (at least for the duration of childhood), and that the acquisition of certain abilities and states is an all or nothing matter. So Aristotle tells us that along with the animal, the child lacks the deliberative ca-

pacities for choice (*prohairesis*) and action (*praxis*) characteristic of
the adult (1111a25–6, 1111b8–9, 1144b8, *EE* 1224a26–30 and
1240b31–4). Both pursue pleasures which are not unqualifiedly good
(*NE* 1152b19–20, 1153a28–31, 1176b28–30, *EE* 1236a2–7, 1228b19–22,
1238a32–4) and lack the sort of judgement (*hupolēpsis*) that can oppose and control desires (*NE* 1147b5, *EE* 1224a25–7); thus they can be
neither akratic nor enkratic (continent or controlled). Like the slave,
the child requires external reason for guidance (*Pol.* 1260a34, 1260b3–
8). The picture, on the whole, is derogatory and static: "No one would
choose to live through his life with the mind of a child, however much
he were to enjoy the things that children enjoy" (*NE* 1174a1–4). "No
sensible person could endure to go back to it again" (*EE* 1215b22–5).

But we should not be misled by what Aristotle says. First, it is immediately obvious that any grouping of child and animal is undercut by an
argument for species differences of the sort that Aristotle emphasizes
elsewhere, and that form the basis of his doctrine of a peculiar human
function (*ergon*) and excellence.[5] Second, the grouping obscures the
notion of maturation which Aristotle himself deploys in other contexts,
and which is crucial for a more accurate characterization of the child
and of education. Thus, in Book I of the *Politics* Aristotle says that the
child has a deliberative part (*to bouleutikon*), "but in an undeveloped
form" (*atelēs*, 1260a13–14). And he continues: "Since the child is undeveloped [*atelēs*], it is clear that his virtue is not relative to himself,
but relative to the fully developed individual, and the one who is an
authority over him" (1260a32–3). These remarks openly invite a developmental model in which the child is viewed not statically, but as in
progress toward full humanity, on his way towards some end. Deficiencies of reasoning are regarded not as fixed, but as merely temporary phenomena within a complex, and differentially paced, process of
growth. To lack deliberative skills at a certain stage does not imply the
absence of other cognitive capacities specific to ethical response.

An important caveat needs to be made here: this model will apply
primarily to the male child. . . . The female, Aristotle contends, has
rational capacities that are permanently deficient, and that permanently
limit the sort of virtue she can attain (*Pol.* 1260a12–30). In a sense she
is and will remain forever a child, her limited opportunities designed
to reflect her limited abilities. At full maturity, she will still lack rational
authority and will be capable only of a subordinate sort of virtue and
happiness.[6] It can be argued, as I have, that even within her restricted
domestic sphere the woman demonstrates considerably more virtue

than Aristotle's official doctrine allows. But for the time being, the contrast between the male and female child underlines the merely transient nature of the boy's rational defects.

2. The Rationality of the Non-Rational Part

Part of the impetus for viewing the habituation process as essentially non-cognitive comes from Aristotle's remarks at the end of Book I and beginning of Book II of the *Nicomachean Ethics* that virtuous character is acquired through habituation (*ex' ethous*) of the non-rational part (*to alogon echon*) of the soul. This is distinguished from the virtue or excellence of the rational or intellectual part (*to logon echon*), acquired for the most part through systematic teaching and exposition (*ek didaskalias*). But the separation of these parts of the soul (and their training) requires, as Aristotle himself recognizes, considerable qualification. After adopting the Platonic division into rational and non-rational parts "as adequate" for his own purposes (1102a26–8), Aristotle thus proceeds for the rest of *NE* I. 13 to clarify and refine the distinction: the desiderative part of the non-rational soul (*to orektikon*, i.e. appetites, emotions, and in general feelings—*pathē*) does not engage in reasoning but can listen to reason, and thus partake of reason in a certain way (1102b14, 1102b26–1103a3; cf. 1098a4). It can be controlled, persuaded, and shaped by the rational part.

In the *De Anima* Aristotle is openly cautious about the practice of dividing the soul into parts, warning that any division will always be relative to a particular pursuit or inquiry, and that consequently parts can be proliferated or diminished, carved up in this way or that, to suit an inquiry. In certain schemes, particular capacities will thus resist easy pigeon-holing. So the perceptual capacity is not easily classifiable as exclusively desiderative or rational, nor is imagination. In a more custom-tailored scheme, these capacities might be assigned to distinct parts (*DA* 432a30). But equally, Aristotle argues, desire (*orexis*) is considerably more complex than the division of the soul into rational and non-rational parts suggests. There is . . . a kind of desire—rational wish or *boulēsis*—which is distinctive to the rational part and which is intimately connected with the capacities of reflection and revision. Even appetites and emotions, which Aristotle is never tempted to assign to the rational part, will have cognitively specifiable constituents.

We must bear in mind these clarifications as we go on to examine the process of habituation. In particular, we will want to have them in mind in assessing Aristotle's claim that the rationality of desire is a kind of obedience, a way of listening to and obeying (*katēkoon, peitharchi-kon*) the authority of a separate and higher part (*NE* 1102b12–1103a4). The analogy Aristotle adopts in Book I of the *Nicomachean Ethics* is of the child's relation to the parent: desire obeys the reason of the rationally authoritative part as a child listens to his father (*hōsper to patros akoustikon ti*, 1102b31–1103a3). The analogy informs the claim made in the *Eudemian Ethics* that "character [*ēthos*] is a quality of the part of the soul that is non-rational, but capable of following reason [*dunamenē akolouthein*], in accordance with a prescriptive principle" (1220b6–8; cf. 1220a5–13).

The analogy of a child compliant to the exhortations of a rational adult might seem to reinforce the image of desire borrowing reason exclusively from outside, being guided primarily by exogenous con-trols.[7] But as a picture either of the child or of the tutoring of desire it oversimplifies and misrepresents more interesting things Aristotle has to say about both. First, as we shall see, though the child's reasons will be borrowed in varying degrees from outside, they will also be gener-ated internally by the child's own perceptions, beliefs, and feelings. These, in dialogue with the beliefs of an experienced adult, will shape desire and emotion. Second, leaving aside the source of reasons and reasoning, the notion of desire co-operating with reason is at best vague, and needs to be filled in by a more precise account of exactly how cognitive elements inform desires and emotions, and how habitu-ation is involved in this process. Without some answers to these ques-tions, we can hardly begin to understand the process of educating character.

3. The Inappropriateness of Harsh Sanctions

We shall be filling out the picture, but first it is worth making some negative remarks that will delimit the account. The educational process does not seem to be, on Aristotle's account, one that is particularly harsh or coercive. This is not to deny that the threat of punishment will have a place, just as will the use of external rewards and positive reinforcement. These will be present, most obviously in the form of praise and blame, and in the reactive attitudes of parents. Rather, the intention is to distinguish such gentle methods of external sanction from those which are excessively coercive or severe and which bypass altogether the engagement of reason. The latter, too, will have a place in the city, as methods of deterrence and reform for likely and actual offenders. But they will be restricted to those who are insensitive to reason, who because of a life pursuant of brutish pleasures require brutish methods of constraint (1179b27–9, 1179b23, 1180a12). The child is excluded from this camp, not only on the grounds that he is not yet fully responsible and hence fully culpable, but on the grounds that his reason, though undeveloped, is not corrupted or incapable of response. He is educable, and if properly brought up, can be moved by argument:

> And argument and teaching surely do not influence everyone, but rather the soul of the listener must be cultivated beforehand by means of habits for loving and hating finely, juts like earth that is to nourish the seed. For the individual whose life is governed by passion will not even listen to an argument that dissuades him nor even understand it; for how can we ever persuade such an individual to change his ways? And in general, passion seems to yield not to argument, but to force. (1179b24–31; tr. Irwin)

The key is thus early training. As such, the picture is as it should be, forward-looking—of a child who will some day more fully understand and reason; of an education that, as Aristotle says in the *Politics*, is "with a view towards the next stages"[8] and "which allows us to pursue through it many other kinds of learning" (1338a39–41); of a life that can be spoken of as happy, on the expectation (*dia tēn elpida*) that the child will some day have both the intrinsic and the extrinsic goods necessary for happiness (*NE* 1100a1–4).

In this regard, though Aristotle says ethical immaturity can occur at any chronological age (1095a5), he must view as significantly different the way we treat such immaturity in the young and in those in their prime. For those who have already been corrupted by a life of pleasure and immoderate feeling, rational persuasion and dialogue are no longer viable means of effecting reform. For the young, though they naturally veer toward excess and immoderation, the aim of education is to ensure that reason and argument have sway.

4. The Intentionality of Emotions

A comprehensive account of the acquisition of Aristotelian virtue would require going through the full range of virtues implicit in goodness, and saying something about what the subconstituents of each virtue are and how they might be acquired, e.g. for courage, how fear must be felt but confronted, the sorts of circumstances and beliefs appropriate to the right response, exposure to which might cultivate that response. Different emotions will be involved in different virtues, and different circumstances will be appropriate for the exercise of each. The opportunities and resources for cultivating one virtue need not coincide with the opportunities for cultivating another. Some emotions might be more resistant to reform than others, and some vices more blameworthy (1119a22–32). Though Aristotle himself undertakes this sort of extensive accounting of the virtues, I cannot go through it in detail. Rather, what I wish to do is to consider virtue in a general way as a complex of capacities—perceptual, affective, and deliberative—and suggest how these capacities are cultivated.

I shall begin with the training of the emotional or affective capacities. Virtue, on Aristotle's view, is a mode of affect and conduct. To be generous is to choose to give assistance to those who merit it without undue internal noise or resistant inclination. Both correct judgement and correct feeling are required. Though Aristotle does not insist, as some have, that the child's initial stance to the world is egoistic (indeed a child may be endowed with considerable 'natural' virtue, 1144b3–5), he does hold the uncontroversial view that virtue without wisdom can be blind (1144b10), just as unbridled passion can interfere with the pursuit of chosen ends. Kindness towards the wrong persons can be harmful, just as uncontrolled fear can stand in the way of facing the challenges and risks necessary for pursuing desired ends. There is a certain urgency about moderating emotions and directing them towards the right objects: 'Hence we ought to have been brought up, from our very youth, as Plato says, to find pleasure and pain as it is appropriate. For this is right education' (1104b11–13; cf. 1105a6–7).

But to appreciate the urgency shaping emotions is not to say how or in what way to effect the change. I want to argue that Aristotle's explicit theory of emotion as intentional or cognitive provides us with a clue: emotions will be educated, in part, through their constitutive beliefs and perceptions. Cultivating the dispositional capacities to feel fear, anger, goodwill, compassion, or pity appropriately will be bound up with learning how to discern the circumstances that warrant these responses. Non-accidentally hitting the mean in our affective response, i.e. getting right the degree and nuance of the reaction, and in general its inflection, would be inconceivable apart from some constitutive appraisal which informed it, however implicit that appraisal might be.

Granted, appropriately directed emotion may still lack the univocal and unconflicting voice that Aristotle requires of mature virtue. My pity for the homeless may betray a certain arrogance about my own good fortune, and my goodwill may have to fight to conquer less noble desires. To the extent that I struggle against what I view to be recalcitrant desires, my virtue is still only a kind of control or continence (*egkrateia*) and falls short of the more thoroughgoing harmony that the *sōphrōn* or truly temperate person exhibits. This is a reminder of what a tall order Aristotelian virtue may be. But it does not compromise the claim that the training towards that end is none the less a process in which desire is informed through the formation of belief.

We can take as background to this claim Aristotle's insistence, in various key places, on the central human desire to perceive and discriminate difference. This is explicit in the opening remarks of the *Metaphysics*:

> All human beings desire to know [*eidenai*] by nature. And evidence of this is the pleasure that we take in our senses; for even apart from their usefulness they are enjoyed for their own sake, and above all others, the sense of eyesight. . . . For this more than the other senses enables us to know [*gnōrizein*] and brings to light many distinctions. (980a20–7)

These remarks, conjoined with parallel remarks in *Poet.* IV, make it explicit that critical activity and its enjoyment characterize all stages of development. At the early stages,[9] discriminatory activity will often take the form of *mimēsis*. The latter is roughly understood to mean our notions of imitation and representation and implies here a way of coming to identify actual object and events through familiarity with representations and enactments of them:

> It seems in general that the origin of poetry has two causes, and that these have to do with human nature. For imitating is natural to humankind from childhood up and human beings differ from animals in this, that they are the most imitative of creatures and learn first through imitation. And it is also a part of human nature that they all delight in imitative work [of others]. And a sign of this is what happens in actual practice. For though objects themselves may be painful to see, we enjoy seeing the most detailed representations of them, for example, forms of the least distinguished of animals and of corpses. And the reason for this delight

> is that learning [*manthanein*] is the greatest of pleasures, not only for
> philosophers, but also for all others as well, to whatever extent they may
> share in the capacity. And it is for this reason that they delight in seeing
> representations. For it turns out that in seeing they learn and figure out
> [*sullogizesthai*] what each thing is, for example, that this is a that . . .
> (*Poet.* 1448b4–17; cf. *Rh.* 1371b4–10)

Intellectual delight, here, seems to hang on making a discovery, on
coming to understand or actively puzzle out (*sullogizesthai*) what is
not yet familiar in terms of what is. 'This is a that' is, within the mimetic
mode, a classification of actual characters, ways of acting and feeling,
features of circumstances, etc., through familiarity with some represented form. Within the ethical sphere, "to figure out that this is a
that" is again a matter of broadening one's inductive base, of the
learner sizing up situations in terms of past experience plus some imaginative and affective feel for how it is related to what is at hand. It is
significant that Aristotle describes this process as *sullogizesthai*. It is
itself a kind of critical activity which, in the case of action, precedes the
practical inference (*sullogismos* or deliberation) about what to do. As
we have described it in earlier chapters, it involves a discerning of the
particulars, a reading of the situation in terms of salient considerations.
As such it is a reasoning that is non-procedural; it is a "figuring out" by
"improvising" (1106b15), by remaining close to and affected by the
concrete details.

The discrimination of ethical relevance will ground affective responses. By tutoring the child's vision of the world, by instructing him
to attend to these features rather than those, desires become focused
and controlled in specific ways.

These remarks rely heavily on the account of the emotions in the
Rhetoric. As I have hinted, what Aristotle outlines there is an intentional theory in which passions are viewed not as blind promptings and
urgings that merely happen to us, but rather as selective responses to
articulated features of our environment. This same sort of selectivity
characterizes, on Aristotle's view, the appetites of both humans and
animals. The agent moved by thirst or hunger responds cognitively to
those features of the environment which can satisfy that need. Moreover, the need itself comes to be more specific and particular as it
focuses on some apparent good. In this way, then, desires "are prepared" by cognition.[10] They display an intentional character in so far as
they are directed at features of situations which an agent regards in a
certain light.

The intentional theory of emotion in the *Rhetoric* falls within the general aim of that book, which is to familiarize the orator with the sorts of beliefs that typically accompany the different emotions. The claim is that the orator will be effective in arousing emotions if he can bring his listeners to the appropriate beliefs. To this end, he will need to know the dispositions associated with the different emotions (*pōs diakemenoi*), their typical objects (*tisin*), and the sorts of circumstances and occasions in which they are typically manifest (*epi poiois*, 1378a22–4). So, for example, if anger is to be aroused against an opponent in court, the orator must persuade his hearer that his client has suffered gratuitously at the hands of that party. By manipulating belief and perception in this way, the rhetorician hopes to provoke a specific emotional response against a specific individual.

Within Aristotle's analysis, however, beliefs, perceptions, and *phantasiai* or imaginings[11] are not merely causes of emotion, but partial constituents. The definition of anger illustrates this. "Anger is a desire [*orexis*] accompanied by pain towards the revenge of what one regards as a slight [*phainomenēn oligorian*] towards oneself or one's friends that is unwarranted" (*Rh.* 1378a30–2). Here it is clear that while emotions are expressed as feelings involving pleasure or pain,[12] these feelings are not identifiable independent of their relation to specific appraisals, perceptions, or beliefs constitutive of the emotion.

In addition to reactive beliefs, beliefs (and desires) about acting on an emotion will often figure in the definition and may occasion a distinct set of derivative feelings. Anger will thus include a consequent desire for revenge, the prospect (*phantasia*) of which yields pleasure (*Rh.* 1378b1–2; cf. 1370b1, 1370b29). Aristotle suggests that it is often such constitutive beliefs about goals that demarcate otherwise similar emotional responses. Spite and hubris (*epēreasmos, hubris*), for example, are forms of slighting that fall under the general definition of "an actively held belief [*energeia doxēs*] about someone who appears to be of little worth" (1378b11); they become distinguished, however, by their goals: spite aims at thwarting another's wishes without specific advantage to oneself (1378b18–20) while hubris aims at enhancing one's self-image by proving oneself, through such slights, to be superior and more powerful (1378b27 ff.).

5. Learning to See Aright

The above remarks about the cognitive content of emotions have significant consequences for the account of ethical education. Though

Aristotle does not fully elaborate upon these in the text, we can allow ourselves to extrapolate in a way that is consistent with its spirit.

We should begin by asking how the perceptions and appraisals constitutive of emotions, and ultimately of moral responses, become refined. The parent, like the orator, is in the position of persuading. He or she makes prescriptions to the child and the child listens out of a complex set of desires (love of parents, the desire to imitate, fear of punishment, hope of reward, etc.). But the parent aims not simply to affect specific actions or desires; e.g. to thwart greed, to encourage compassion, to temper anger. Rather, part of what the parent tries to do is to bring the child to see the particular circumstances that here and now make certain emotions appropriate. The parent helps the child to compose the scene in the right way. This will involve persuading the child that the situation at hand is to be construed in this way rather than that, that what the child took to be a deliberate assault and cause for anger was really only an accident, that the laughter and smiles which annoy were intended as signs of delight rather than of teasing, that a particular distribution, though painful to endure, is in fact fair— that if one looked at the situation from the point of view of the others involved, one would come to that conclusion.

These examples illustrate that the child is not an empty box in which beliefs are instilled, but an individual who has, to a greater or lesser degree, already formed certain construals and judgements, which become adjusted and revised through interaction with an adult. Education is thus a matter of bringing the child to more critical discriminations. The Aristotelian presupposition is that the ability to discriminate is already there and in evidence, as is an interest and delight in improvement. What is required is a shifting of beliefs and perspectives through the guidance of an outside instructor. Such guidance cannot merely be a matter of bringing the child to see this way now, but of providing some sort of continuous and consistent instruction which will allow for the formation of patterns and trends in what the child notices and sees.

This emphasis on the internal process must be central to education in a way that it remains at best peripheral to rhetoric. Though the educator persuades and exhorts, the goal is not to *manipulate* beliefs and emotions—to influence an outcome here and now—but to prepare the learner for eventually arriving at competent judgements and reactions on his own. Any method which secures rational obedience must at the same time encourage the child's own development. This implies that the child borrows the eyes of wisdom (1144b10–12), 'listens to the words of elders and of the more experienced' (1143b11–13), not passively but in a way that actively engages his own critical capacities. Accordingly, Aristotle would probably object to the practice of the parent who says, "Do this, don't do that" without further descriptions or explanations. The child can legitimately ask "why," and some description and explanation will be in order. What is required is some dialogue and verbal exchange about what one sees (and feels) and should see (and feel); in other words, actual descriptions which articulate a way of perceiving the situation and which put into play the relevant concepts, considerations and emotions (see *Pol.* 1253a12). I take something like this to be a part of the sort of reasoned "admonition" and "exhortation" by which parents guide children (*NE* I. 13, 1102b33–1103a1).[13] It seems to be an essential part of how we train sensitive discernment of the particulars. Within this Aristotle can no doubt say, as we do, that there are many proscriptions that the child cannot understand until later and many partial explanations that will have to suffice until then. Nothing I have said would require a claim to the contrary. The point is the much more modest one: that emotions cannot be shaped without some simultaneous cultivation of discriminatory abilities. This is included as a part of habituation. It is a part of coming to have the right pleasures and pains.

Perhaps more than Aristotle suggests, we should not assume that the direction of exchange flows solely from parent to child, for the child's vision may sometimes instruct the adult's. What the child sees so clearly and compellingly may be obfuscated in the adult by more tutored and abstract perceptions. In particular, the child's emotional vulnerability may make him alive to concerns the adult only inadequately or too dispassionately notices. Thus Aristotle himself remarks in the *Rhetoric* that youth often "prefer to do what is fine over what is advantageous, for they live more by their characters and emotions [*ēthei*] than by reasoning and calculation [*logismōi*]" (1389a32–5).

And so it is often the child who sees through his emotions, and who can attend to others in a way that is intense and empathic.[14] The child's example is an instructive reminder that we as adults may be at peril of losing our emotions, of over-intellectualizing them, of so protecting them that they become robbed of their spontaneity and candour. It suggests that there is something to be preserved in the child's emotional vulnerability, some (natural) virtue in the child's intense emotional responses that efforts at moderation must not eradicate.

There is good reason to believe Aristotle would applaud educational efforts that respected this resource. We have just noted a suggestion from the *Rhetoric* in this direction. In a passage which followed on the one quoted, the claim is more direct. Here Aristotle contends that the elderly no longer live by their emotions, that, hardened by life's misfortunes, they have made themselves invulnerable: "And they neither can love intensely or hate intensely, but as proposed by Bias, they both love as though they are about to hate, and hate as though they are about to love" (1389b23–5). This is clearly not meant as praise, but as a stern warning against what can happen when we stray too far from more candid, less protected responses. Virtuous activity falls short if, in the end, it disregards the passions, if behaviour fails to evidence the proper feelings and sentiments in addition to the proper actions and beliefs.

6. Learning to Make Choices

We have been focusing on the development of emotions and the role of perception and belief in this process. The training of the non-rational part thus has an essential cognitive dimension. But in what sense is the rational part itself cultivated? In what sense do deliberative capacities become trained? As we said earlier, the child is, on Aristotle's view, incapable of the sort of reasoned choices, or *prohaireseis*, that characterize mature virtue. This, however, will not bar the child from all deliberation. The child is capable of voluntary choices which may require a certain level of simple means–end reasoning and specification of ends. Also, to the extent that realization of an end requires various steps, the end may set up a certain agenda to be achieved in time. But what the child is excluded from—at least the child whose deliberative capacities are still quite immature—is the sort of "all things considered" judgement that comes with prohairetic reasoning. This will include an evaluation of alternative means as well as an assessment of ends in the light of other ends which might take priority. It is to judge an action best, given an agent's *overall* objectives and beliefs. This may further entail a revamping of acquired ends, in the light of considerations of fit and specific convictions. Now it seems eminently reasonable to assume that a child's rational capacities are not yet ready for this level of deliberation. As Aristotle conceives such deliberation, it shares much in common with the dialectical reasoning characteristic of the mature student engaged in justifying an account of good living.[15] Still, if, as I have contended, we need to make some sense of a transition to full rationality, then there must be a time when, in the more mature youth, these rational capacities are cultivated.

In a complete scheme, experience in this more complex sort of choice-making will constitute a later stage of development. It will precede the emergence of mature virtue and presuppose the sort of sensitive judgement and emotional response of the person who has been trained to notice the circumstances of moral action. But this is to recognize that even at the more intermediate stages of becoming virtuous, the learner does not simply perform some action-type, as one perhaps does in developing a skill, but *reacts* to the circumstances, and then *decides* how to act. This is itself a part of making voluntary, intentional choices. There is judgement and decision, even if not reflective evaluation (or justification) of the choice. To gain practice in the relevant actions is to come to work out, with appropriate guidance and models, what to do. For the more mature youth whose deliberative capacities are actively developing, the choice will be reflective and subject to rational justification. It will take into account the more complex and competing factors that need to be weighed in the balance, and represent a judgement as to what is best in the light of these varied factors. Practice in action is eventually, at the later stages, practice in choice-making of this sort.

But here it is important to remember that for full virtue, Aristotle requires not merely that actions be "chosen" in the above sense, but that they be chosen for their own sakes. Thus, in a passage in *NE* II. 4, Aristotle notes that there are three conditions of mature virtue: first, the virtuous agent must act knowingly; second, he must choose virtuous acts and choose them for their own sakes (*prohairoumenos di' auta*); and third, he must act from a firm and unchanging character (1105a30–4). I wish to focus on the second condition. Virtuous actions have, in some important sense, external ends. Generosity aims at alleviating need, temperance aims at health, battlefield courage aims at victory and, perhaps ultimately, peace. The actions are ameliorative and aim at certain external conditions which are valued within a human life. But, as Aristotle implies above, to be fully virtuous is not simply to choose actions which will tend to promote those ends. In addition, and perhaps more importantly, it is to find the actions which promote these ends, themselves valuable. Thus, while the actions derive their original value from external ends, in time it is the actions themselves that come to be valued.[16] They come to constitute their own ends. To act of the sake of the fine is just this: to value the actions which express virtue, even if these actions do not ultimately achieve their planned goals. From the point of view of cultivating virtue, the claim is that learning virtue is more than learning balanced deliberation, more than learning how to make certain general ends, such as peace and welfare, one's target. In addition, it is learning to value the actions which realize these ends, and the sort of person who reliably performs them. This, it is Aristotle's claim, cannot be learned apart from actual practice in virtuous action.

7. Habituation as Critical Practice

With these considerations as background, we are now in a position to interpret Aristotle's more explicit and well-known remarks about habituation. Character, on Aristotle's view, is the acquisition of states (*hexeis*) through habituation (*ethismos*). The process of habituation involves essentially practice and repetition:

> Now character [*ēthos*], as the word itself indicates, is that which is developed from habit [*ethos*]; and anything is habituated which, as a result of guidance which is not innate, through being changed a certain way repeatedly [*pollakis*], is eventually capable of acting in that way (*EE* 1220a39–b3, tr. Woods; cf. *Pol.* 1332b1 ff.)[17]

As Aristotle says more simply in the *Rhetoric*: "Acts are done from habit because individuals have done them many times before" (1369b6). Through repetition an acquired capacity becomes almost natural, or second nature: "For as soon as a thing becomes habituated it is virtually natural. For habit is similar to nature. For what happens often is akin to what happens always, natural events happening always, habitual events being frequent and repeated" (*Rh.* 1370a6; cf. *Mem.* 452a27).

Excellence of character or virtue, according to the above picture, is contrasted with abilities (*dunameis*) which are innate, which cannot be changed through habituation (*EE* 1220b4, *NE* 1103a20–3) and which exist prior to rather than consequent upon practice. This obviously does not entail that virtue will be independent of antecedent affective and cognitive capacities (1103a26–32). The point is rather that these are merely indeterminate capacities, not latent *dunameis* for virtue.

Character states thus arise through the sorts of activities that are involved in their exercise. This is the explicit point of a celebrated, though insufficiently analysed, passage from the *Nicomachean Ethics*:

> We acquire the virtues by first acting just as we do in the case of acquiring crafts. For we learn a craft by making the products which we must make once we have learned the craft, for example, by building, we become builders, by playing the lyre, lyre players. And so too we become just by doing just actions, and temperate by doing temperate actions and brave by brave actions . . . and in a word, states of character are formed out of corresponding acts. (1103a31–b21; cf. 1105a14, *EE* 1220a32)

But to say that we become just by doing just actions is to abbreviate a whole series of steps. As we have seen, action presupposes the discrimination of a situation as requiring a response, reactive emotions that mark that response, and desires and beliefs about how and for the sake of what ends one should act. We misconstrue Aristotle's notion of action producing character if we isolate the exterior moment of action from the interior cognitive and affective moments which characterize even the beginner's ethical behaviour.

These remarks prepare us for an understanding of the notion of repetition implicit in Aristotle's conception of habituation. Aristotle would clearly agree with the old saw that "practice makes perfect,"[18] that we become better at something by doing it repeatedly and persistently. But what is the real content of this sort of phrase? For one thing, to repeat cannot really mean to do the same action over and over again. Various considerations are pertinent here. First, as we said above, there is no external husk of all just actions that we can isolate and repeatedly practice. Any just action will be contextually defined and will vary considerably, in terms of judgement, emotion, and behaviour, from other just actions. It would be absurd to demand (and certainly run counter to the spirit of Aristotle's inquiry) some extractable piece of behaviour, training in which could form character.

Second, even if we take up the more straightforward case of practising a skill where there is some isolatable sequence of steps, repetition of that sequence cannot involve doing the same action, if by that is meant doing just what one did before. For repeating in that way seems to ensure that one will stay in a rut, do the same thing over and over again (mistakes included), rather than show improvement or progress. Indeed, it seems to make progress impossible.

A more plausible conception of repeating the same action, again within the simplified skill analogy, will involve trying to approximate some ideal action type that has been set as one's goal. Learning through repetition will be then a matter of successive trials that vary from one another as they approach this ideal way of acting. In each successive attempt, constant awareness of the goal is crucial, just as measuring how nearly one has reached it or by how much one has fallen short is important for the next trial. The practice is more a refinement of actions through successive trials than a sheer mechanical repetition of any one action.

On this view, then, practice achieves progress to the extent that repetition is critical. Whether the states to be acquired be primarily physical, intellectual, or emotional, and concerning *technē* or character, the rehearsal requisite for acquiring them must involve the employment of critical capacities, such as attending to a goal, recognizing mistakes and learning from them, understanding instructions, following tips and cues, working out how to adapt a model's example to one's own behaviour.

In the case of virtue, the practice of actions will obviously be more complex. Virtuous action, as we have said, will combine a judgement of circumstances, reactive emotions, and some level of decision about how to act. Here too the learner will follow the examples of emulated models, and may have in mind general precepts and rules of thumb. Following models and bringing to mind the appropriate precepts will in itself require cognitive skills. But these alone will be insufficient without the sort of imagination and sensitivity requisite for knowing how a type of action and dispositional response translate to the situation at hand. Becoming sensitive to the circumstances in which action is called for as well as flexible in one's conception of the requirements of a precept is all part of practising virtuous action.

The notion of critical practice is already implicit in Aristotle's discussion of habituation at *NE* II. 1. We learn how to play the lyre, he says, by practising not merely with persistence, but with an eye toward how the expert plays and with attention to how our performance measures against that model. Without the instructions and monitoring of a reliable teacher, a student can just as easily become a bad lyre player as a good one:

> Again, just as in the case of the crafts, the same causes and means that produce each virtue also destroy it. For playing the lyre produces both good and bad lyre players. And analogously, this is so for builders and all the rest; for building well makes good builders while building poorly makes bad builders. For if this were not so there would be need of no teacher. (1103b7–12; cf. 1104a27, 1105a14, *EE* 1220a32)

At issue here is how we make determinate more indeterminate capacities and actions. Since the capacities are not latent excellences, a teacher must be on hand to direct the progress. (This falls within Aristotle's general theory of *dunameis* at *Meta.* IX. 2 and 5 in which rational capacities—understood broadly as those which are not physical and as such do not have fixed ends—can produce contrary ends or effects. To produce one effect rather than another, desire or rational choice must guide the exercise of the capacity; *Meta.* 1046b1 ff., 1048a8–12.) In the case of virtue, unlike skill, it is more difficult to speak of a neutral action which is at once the means for virtuous or vicious action. The action cannot be separated from its end in this way.[19] Even so, occasions may be viewed in some sense as neutral, as being opportunities either for the development of a particular virtue or for its ruin, just as more basic abilities or dispositions can. So, Aristotle continues, just as danger is a moment for cowardice or bravery (*NE* 1103b16), so appetites and anger are at once the basis for temperance and gentleness or for indulgence and irascibility. The role of the tutor in helping us to see and respond aright is even more urgent here.

There are further sources of evidence in Aristotle's writing that support a critical conception of practice. The first requires looking again to the example of *technē* and to Aristotle's belief that to have *technē* is to have a skill that its possessor can teach to others. The claim now is not that beginners must have teachers, but that anyone who has sufficiently learned a skill must himself be (capable of being) a teacher of it. Thus, Aristotle argues that possessing *technē* differs from the possession of less systematic experience (*Meta.* 981b7–10), just as for Plato it differed from the possession of a mere knack.[20]

The capacity to formulate and teach a skill might thus require precisely defined procedural rules, or, what is pedagogically more plausible, a looser set of critical cues and hints as to how to proceed at each stage.[21] Though we would probably want to distance ourselves from Aristotle here and argue that even the latter condition is too strong a requirement for possessing a *technē*, its inclusion is still indirect evidence for the view that practice involves an awareness of what one is doing; for in order to teach others one must be aware of how one achieves certain ends. That awareness is deepened in the novice by attentiveness to the cues and comments of the expert, and in the expert, by the very process of formulating what one understands more implicitly.

Ethical action will not, of course, be procedural (*NE* 1140b22–5; cf. 1105a28–b4). Accordingly, cues and tips will not be expressive of some more systematic, longhand rules that a teacher can pass on to others. Even so, explicit teaching must take place, as we have argued above; but what is passed on will be ways of reacting, seeing, and understanding which will aim at establishing enduring patterns of action.

Significantly, Aristotle's views about musical education (*Pol.* VIII) support the same general picture of critical practice. Though we cannot address here, in any detail, the complex issues of ancient music or chronicle its time-honoured place in traditional *paideia*,[22] a few brief remarks should shed some light on the way in which music figures in Aristotle's own account. Training in music involves essentially, for Aristotle as for Plato, a mimetic enactment of poetry, song, and dance. (Thus the Greek term *mousikē* is only imprecisely translated by our term "music.") The performance is typically with accompaniment on lyre or *aulos* and is set to specific, highly conventionalized musical modes (*harmoniai*) meant to "express" the character or mood of the individuals depicted in the poetic text. Hence the modes are said by Aristotle to be ethical (i.e. to convey character). And the learner's mimetic enactment of them (through performance) is a way of coming to feel from the inside the relevant qualities of character and emotion. It is an emulative and empathetic kind of identification. Together with the positive reinforcement that comes from pleasure music naturally gives, the mimetic enactment will constitute an habituation, an *ethismos*:

> And since music happens to be a kind of pleasure, and virtue is concerned with proper enjoyment and loving and hating rightly, it is clear that there is nothing more necessary to learn and to become habituated in [*sunethizesthai*] than judging rightly and delighting in good characters and fine actions. Rhythm and melody provide keen likenesses of anger and gentleness, and also of courage and temperance and of all the opposites of these and of all the other states of character. (This is clear from experience. For in listening to such music, our souls undergo a change.) And

becoming habituated to feeling pain and delight in likenesses is close
to feeling the same way towards the things that are their models. (*Pol.*
1340a15–28)

The idea, then, is that music provides the child with exemplars of character, and allows the child to feel "from within" what the emotions and
actions of such characters are like. All this is complex and needs a fuller
account within a theory of mimetic education. What I wish to stress
here is Aristotle's own insistence that mimetic education requires not
merely that the child cultivate the mimetic powers of an *audience*, but
that the child be trained as a *performer*, as someone who himself must
act and practise (*Pol.* VIII. 6, esp. 1340b20–1341b15). And this, Aristotle
insists, is precisely because those who are to judge and delight correctly (*krinein kai chairein orthōs*) in fine actions and characters must
practise such actions themselves, making the sorts of judgements and
coming to have the sorts of emotional responses that are appropriate
to the characters. Thus, Aristotle says, "it is impossible or at least difficult for those who do not themselves perform to be good judges of
others" (1340b24–5). His principal point is *not* that they will be bad
aesthetic critics. That may be true too. What he means, rather, is that
they will be inadequately prepared to judge *ethical* character, in literature and in real life. For they will not have learned first hand, through
their own critical attempts at *mimēsis*, what sorts of emotions and responses characterize different sorts of states.

8. The Pleasure Intrinsic to Practice

Additional direct and compelling evidence for the notion of critical
practice comes from Aristotle's remarks about the relation of practice
to the pleasure consequent upon it. On Aristotle's view, practice would
be neither necessary nor sufficient for acquiring states and abilities if it
did not yield derivative pleasures. For it is the pleasure proper to a
particular activity that impels us to perform that activity the next time
with greater discrimination and precision:

> For the pleasure proper to an activity increases that activity. For those
> who perform their activities with pleasure judge better and discern with
> greater precision each thing, e.g. those finding pleasure in geometry be-
> come geometers, and understand the subject-matter better, and similarly
> also, lovers of music, lovers of building and so on, make progress [*epidi-*

doasin] in their appropriate function when they enjoy it. (1175a29–35; cf. 1175a36–b24, 1175b13–15, 1105a3–7)

Conversely, the pain derivative upon an activity impedes progress, just as alien pleasures from other activities distract from an appreciation of the activity at hand (1175b16–23).

More precisely, upon what does this pleasure depend? On the interpretation I shall offer, pleasure not only issues in but arises from discriminatory activity.[23] The model I ascribe to Aristotle is thus that of a chain of activities which increase in discriminated complexity as well as in derivative pleasures. On this model practice yields pleasure to the extent to which practice itself is critical. And pleasure, in turn, yields further critical activity.

These claims require further examination of Aristotle's account of pleasure. According to a unified account of pleasure in *NE* VII and X, pleasure is the perfect actualization of a state or faculty of the soul in good condition exercised upon appropriate objects (1174b14–1175a2).[24] It is activity that is unimpeded (1153a15), that is, without the impediments either of a defective nature or of external goods inadequate for the full exercise of a state. Thus, the pleasure of seeing requires both that the natural faculty of eyesight be in good condition and that it be exercised upon the finest perceptible objects (1174b15 ff.). Similarly, the pleasure which arises from virtuous activity (1104b3 ff.) is the pleasure of realizing a virtuous state without either internal impediments (i.e. insufficient or conflicting motivation) or external obstacles. In this way, the pleasure of virtue falls under the general account of the pleasure of excellent activity.

But there is an immediate problem. On this general view, the pleasure derived from a particular activity depends upon the capacities for that activity being well-developed and mature. Pleasure as perfect actualization requires a well-developed nature. But if this is so, then the account makes very puzzling the role of pleasure in learning virtue. For pleasure seems to arise only when a state is fully developed, and not when it is becoming so.

One reply to this objection is that this account of pleasure is consistent with the motivational role of pleasure at 1175a29–b24 in the following restricted way: the progress the geometer makes when he experiences pleasure in his activity involves the realization of an already acquired state or capacity in more precise and complex ways. Genuine development and improvement are involved here, though not the sort involved in initially acquiring a state.[25] Progress in the sense of refinement of an already existent state seems to be what Aristotle has in mind at 1172a12–15 when he says virtuous persons become better (*beltious*) through the company of virtuous friends. Although the virtuous person has already acquired a stable and firm character, that character is capable of further development and improvement through the activities of friendship.

But can pleasure attach to a broader notion of development, in particular one which includes the acquisition and habituation of states, such as virtue? If so, pleasure would arise not only from the exercise of developed capacities and states upon appropriate objects, but from the activity or practice which constitutes their development. Such pleasure derivative upon practice would be the pleasure of an imperfect actualization, imperfect not because of external impediments (though these might exist), but because of an imperfect state.

A preliminary answer to the above questions depends upon how we understand imperfect. On Aristotle's view a state or capacity may be defective in several ways. The state or capacity might be impaired temporarily, as in the case of an individual for whom sweet things taste bitter because of a cold; or impaired permanently, either because of some natural shortcoming, as in the case of those whose reason will always lack authority, or because of an irreversible illness, as in the case of those who cannot see in the light because of opthalmia; or impaired because it is not yet fully developed, as in the case of the (male) child. In this last case, although an individual's activities are imperfect, with the right opportunities and objects they can come to approximate the full potentialities of the species. The pleasure of this imperfect actualization is a real pleasure, that is, a pleasure specific to the capacities of a human being, though a pleasure lesser in degree than that of the most perfect actualization.

Aristotle raises the notion of degrees of pleasure in *NE* X. 4:

Hence for each faculty the best activity is the activity of the subject in the best condition in relation to the best object of the faculty. This activity will also be the most complete and the pleasantest. For every faculty of perception, and every sort of thought and study, has its pleasure; the pleasantest activity is the most complete; and the most complete is the activity of the subject in good condition in relation to the most excellent object of the faculty. (1174b18–24; tr. Irwin)

Exercise of the perceptual and critical faculties appears to admit of degrees. The more complete the actualization, the pleasanter the activity. But within that continuum, even the learner gains pleasure from the exercise of his abilities. The point is reminiscent of Aristotle's comment in *Poet.* IV, discussed earlier, that learning is pleasant not only to the philosopher but to all, whatever their capacity for it.

Our earlier problem still seems to remain, however: Aristotle's example at *NE* 1174b20 is of the individual who comes to use his perceptual faculties in more and more discriminating ways. Yet according to 1103a26–31, perceptual capacities, unlike states of virtue, exist antecedent to practice. Consequently, the pleasures derivative upon such activity do not refer to the process of habituation or acquisition, but once again to the process of actualizing an already existent state.

But does Aristotle ever relax the distinction between activities that engender states and activities that actualize states that are already formed? I shall argue that in a limited sense, he does.

At *NE* II. 4, after outlining his doctrine of habituation as the acquisition of states through corresponding actions, Aristotle raises the following puzzle familiar to readers of the *Nicomachean Ethics*: "The question might be asked, what we mean by saying that we must become just by doing just acts, and temperate by doing temperate acts; for if men do just and temperate acts, they are already just and temperate" (1105a17–20).[26] His solution in Book II is precisely to differentiate habituating actions from actualizations. Both actions will concern the same sorts of circumstances and external requirements (1104a28–b5), but the actions of the novice will lack the full structure of motives and reasons characteristic of the person who already has a stable character (1105a29–35).

But in *Meta.* IX. 8 Aristotle offers a different solution to a related (though distinct) problem. Here he describes a puzzle about the acquisition of craft knowledge:

> This is why it is thought impossible to be a housebuilder if one has built nothing or a lyre player if one has never played the lyre; for the individual who learns to play the lyre learns to play by playing it, and similarly in the case of all other learners. And so arose the sophistical puzzle, that one who does not possess a knowledge will none the less be producing the object of that knowledge: for he who is learning it does not possess it. But since, of that which is coming to be, some part must have come to be, and, of that which in general is changing, some part must have

changed (this will be clear in the case of change) so, equally, the one who is learning must, it would seem, possess some part of the knowledge he is learning. (1049b28–1050a2)

The force of Aristotle's remarks is to show that the learner, even at the very beginning stages of his apprenticeship, is already acquiring some of what the expert has. And to the extent that he is, he will receive the pleasures consequent upon exercising those states. Though no one would seriously hold that the apprentice becomes an expert in an instant, Aristotle goes to some pains here to make explicit the general sort of incremental process that must be involved.

Now the acquisition of craft knowledge, Aristotle insists, is distinct from the acquisition of character, so a solution to one sort of puzzle will not necessarily be a solution to another. Thus, shortly after Aristotle raises the ethical puzzle in *NE* II. 4, he distinguishes the case of the crafts and the virtues. I quote a passage to which we have already referred:

> But the case of the crafts and the virtues is not similar. For the products of the crafts have their goodness in themselves, so that it is enough that they should have a certain character when they are produced. But it is not true that if acts in accordance with virtue have themselves a certain character they will be done justly or temperately. The one who does them must also be in the right state of character when he acts. First, he must act knowingly, second, he must choose the acts, choosing them for their own sakes, and third, he must act from a firm and unchanging character. Except for the knowing, these conditions are not required for possessing a craft. But in the case of the virtues, the knowing has little or no weight, while the other two conditions count not for a little, but for everything. (1105a25–b3)

These remarks should serve to remind us once again of the limitations of Aristotle's own analogies between craft and virtue acquisition. The difference, Aristotle suggests here, is that acquiring an art, such as grammar, will be primarily a matter of internalizing certain procedural principles and producing a product that embodies that procedure (or knowledge). Virtue, on the other hand, will be a matter not of learning implicit procedures, but of having reliable motives, expressed in chosen actions which come to have intrinsic value. The actions will not be chosen by procedure, nor will what is brought about be valued apart from the actions which realize it.

Now habituating ethical action will not, at least at the early stages, meet these conditions. The learner's temperate actions may be directed at health, but the motive will neither be reliable nor the actions themselves chosen as a valued way of living. In a more dramatic way than in the case of the crafts, there may be qualitative differences between what the learner and the expert possesses; the development may be less smooth or continuous. This seems to be so simply in virtue of the fact that prohairetic capacities develop late. Even so, it can none the less be argued that what the learner does gain through habituating actions is not something externally necessary to full virtue, but itself a *part* (albeit an imperfect or not fully developed part) of what virtue is. To become aware of the circumstances necessary for the specific virtues, and to begin to form the right sorts of emotional responses and decisions for action, is itself a part of having virtue. It is not simply preparation for virtue, but doing something of what virtue requires. It might be in this way that we can make sense of the idea of pleasure which comes with learning virtue: though the habituating action is not itself an exercise of a perfected state, it is none the less an exercise of a part of virtue, and yields pleasure to the extent to which it develops that part. (Perhaps the case of convalescence and its pleasures (1154b14–21, 1152b34 ff.) provides a partial analogy for the pleasure of an imperfect character state. In both cases, some small part or the person continues to exist—i.e. the healthy part or the part that has the potential to develop—the activity of which is the proper focus of the non-accidental pleasure of "getting better" or "developing."[27] In the case of virtue, pleasure increases as the character state develops.)

This notion of degrees of pleasure[28] also offers the most natural reading of Aristotle's general view that moral habituation is the cultivation of fine (or noble) pleasures and pains. As already quoted: "We need to be brought up, right from early youth, as Plato says, to find enjoyment and pain in the right things" (1104b11–13, cf. 1105a3–8). By this remark, Aristotle might mean no more than that a student comes to enjoy the intrinsic pleasures of virtuous activity through essentially external pleasures and pains; the association of virtue with reward, and vice with reproof and castigation, makes virtue derivatively pleasant and vice, painful. As suggested earlier, this will be a part of Aristotle's account (cf. 1104b16–18). In general, he argues, the difficulty of learning virtue requires that the process be sweetened in various ways. Music serves this instrumental role in early *paideia* because of its natural pleasure and appeal for children (*Pol.* 1340b15–19). In a somewhat more complex way, the special affection children have for their parents makes the family a privileged and effective environment for ethical learning (*NE*1 VIII. 12; 1180b3–12).

But this conception of external pleasures and pains cannot exhaust Aristotle's notion of correct education. In addition there will be the intrinsic pleasure of approximating to virtue through action and emotion. Without some such notion, the idea of valuing virtuous action for its own sake would be curious indeed.

To summarize, then, good character arises through the sorts of judgements, emotions, and actions which approximate to the virtuous person's behaviour. Practice takes place not in a vacuum, but in response to the requirements of highly concrete, practical situations. A by-product of this sort of habituation, or what I have dubbed critical practice, is a sense of pleasure which stimulates further growth.

Aristotle's account, it should be obvious by now, is antithetical to any view which regards character as the maturation of internal capacities independent of significant interaction with the environment.[29] While Aristotle has a notion of natural virtues (i.e. the innate proclivity in some towards temperance, justice, courage, etc.), these are isolated capacities, he insists, which do not imply the presence of the other virtues (1144b33–1145a3), and which in the absence of proper habituation and guidance can lead to considerable harm (1144b8–14). . . .

We can confidently say at this point that Aristotle's account of habituation extends well beyond the truism expressed in the phrase that "we learn by doing." At issue is *how* we learn by doing, or, as Aristotle himself asks at the outset of the *Eudemian Ethics*, "how and by what sources does virtue arise?" This, he says, is the "most valuable" inquiry (1216b10–22). The inquiry, as conducted by Aristotle, leads to a rich and lasting theory which has at its centre the related beliefs that learning virtue is neither a mindless nor purely intellectual matter, and that the process requires practical reason and emotion working in tandem throughout.

Notes

1. A. Grant, *The Ethics of Aristotle* (Longmans, Green, 1885), 482–3; cf. 486, 241–2. J. A. Stewart concurs with Grant's view; see his *Notes on the Nicomachean Ethics of Aristotle*, i and ii (Oxford University Press, 1892; repr. Arno Press, 1973), 171.

2. Myles Burnyeat, 'Aristotle on Learning to be Good,' in A. O. Rorty (ed.),

Essays on Aristotle's Ethics (University of California Press, 1980), 69–92, esp. 73–4 (and in this volume), and Richard Sorabji, 'Aristotle on the Role of Intellect in Virtue,' *Proceedings of the Aristotelian Society*, 74 (1973–4), 107–29, repr. in Rorty, 201–19. I have benefited greatly from both these articles. For a comprehensive general history of Greek education, see Henri Marrou, *Histoire de l' éducation dans l' antiquité* (Editions du Seuil, 1948). I also found of interest, in thinking about general issues in ethical education, Joel Kupperman's *The Foundations of Morality* (George Allen and Unwin, 1983), ch. 12, and his 'Character and Education,' *Midwest Studies in Philosophy*, 13 (Notre Dame University Press, 1988).

3. Indeed, Aristotle too speaks of the boy arriving at manhood. So at *MM* 1194b15 ff. he says: 'For a son is, as it were, a part of his father, until he attains the rank [*taxin*] of manhood and is separated from him. Then he is in a relationship of equality and parity with the father.' And again at *EE* 1224a26–30 he speaks of the arrival at a 'certain age [*hēlikiai*] to which we ascribe action [*to prattein*]'; cf. *Problems* 955b22 ff., *NE* 1143b8–10. My general argument is that while such notions are a convenient way of marking maturity, they are not especially helpful in detailing moral growth.

4. I am grateful to Richard Kraut for urging me to take more seriously this last alternative.

5. Cf. *NE* I. 7, *Meta.* I. 1, *DA* III. 3, 9–11, *MA* 6–11. Very roughly, there is an "explanation of motion" common to all creatures, for both humans and animals are moved by critical and desiderative faculties. In the case of animals, however, critical faculties are limited to perception, memory, and perceptual imagination. Human capacities include these, but in addition belief, thought, the manipulation of belief through syllogism and deliberation, and choice.

6. Her deliberative part is *akuron*, or lacking in authority (*Pol.* 1260a13). Cf. W. W. Fortenbaugh, "Aristotle on Slaves and Women," and a reply by Elizabeth V. Spelman, "Aristotle and the Politicization of the Soul," in S. Harding and M. B. Hintikka (eds.), *Discovering Reality*, (Reidel, 1983), 17–30.

7. Cf. *Rep.* IX, 590d.

8. *Pol.* 1336b37 ff; cf. 1340b35–9. On this first passage, see the helpful discussion of Carnes Lord, in *Education and Culture in the Political Thought of Aristotle* (Cornell University Press, 1982), 44–8.

9. On other early signs of the child's capacity to discriminate, cf. *Ph.* 184b11–12 and *NE* 1161a25.

10. *MA* 702a18. Cf. Martha Nussbaum on a discussion of this passage in Essay 3 of her *Aristotle's De Motu Animalium* (Princeton University Press, 1978), 154 ff.

11. For a comprehensive discussion of *phantasia*, see Nussbaum, Essay 5 of *Aristotle's De Motu*, 221–67.

12. Cf. *Rh.* 1378a20–1, *NE* 1105a21–3, *EE* 1220b12–14.

13. Cf. *Pol.* 1260b6–8, which qualifies this picture and seems to run counter to the spirit of *NE* I. 13.

14. See *Rh.* I. 12 on the emotional intensity (and excess) of children's responses.

15. I defended this line of interpretation in the introductory chapter. It is

developed with considerable insight by Henry Richardson in *Practical Reasoning about Final Ends* (Cambridge: Cambridge University Press, 1994).

16. For an illuminating discussion of this issue, see Eugene Garver, 'Aristotle's Genealogy of Morals', *Philosophy and Phenomenological Research*, 44 (1984), 471–92.

17. *Aristotle's Eudemian Ethics*, Books, I, II, and VIII, tr. Michael Woods (Oxford University Press, 1982).

18. For an illuminating discussion of this old saw which has influenced my remarks, see Vernon A. Howard's *Artistry: The Work of Artists* (Hackett, 1982), 157–88.

19. This is the point of an otherwise obscure remark Aristotle makes at *NE* 1140b2 ff.: "And the person who voluntarily errs with respect to *technē* is more desirable than the person who voluntarily errs with respect to practical reason and similarly the virtues." The idea, I believe, is that whereas it may be desirable to use a particular *technē* for a non-standard end (as when a tennis coach uses his skill to demonstrate how to hit a bad forehand shot), it is less desirable to 'misuse' virtue. Indeed it is unlikely that full virtue *can* be misused.

20. Cf. *Gorgias* 465a, and *Meta.* 981a25–31: "And in general it is a sign of the man who knows and of the man who does not know, that the former can teach, and therefore we think craft more truly knowledge than experience is; for craftsmen can teach, and men of experience cannot."

21. Cf. Howard's excellent illustration, in *Artistry*, 9–116, of the language of coaching used in teaching singing.

22. Though *Pol.* VIII is the primary source for Aristotle's views on the place of music in education, additional remarks in *Poet.* 1447a18–b9 enhance the picture. Aristotle says here that *mimēsis* is produced in "rhythm, speech, and melody, and in these either separately or mixed together . . . flute and lyre playing, for example, using melody and rhythm alone'; dancers use rhythm alone for "through the rhythm of the dance figures, they imitate character, emotions, and actions." On difficulties in interpreting this passage, see Gerald Else, *Aristotle's Poetics: The Argument* (Harvard University Press, 1967), 17 ff. As regards the ethical character of music, the pseudo-Aristotelian remarks in *Problemata* IX. 27 are suggestive: "And in its rhythm and in its arrangement of high and low sounds, melody has a similarity to character. . . . And the motions [of sounds] are connected with practical action, and actions are signs of character" (919b26–37). For a detailed study of the place of music in Aristotle's educational curriculum, see Carnes Lord, *Education and Culture*.

On the general subject of ancient music, scholarly study is extensive, and I shall restrict myself to mentioning only a handful of works that are directly related to the issues raised above. (A more extensive discussion of the literature, and of the issues Aristotle himself raises, can be found in my Ph.D. thesis, "Aristotle's Theory of Moral Education" [Harvard University, 1982], ch. 4. There I discuss also the conception of *mimēsis* in tragedy.) First, there are the classic studies of D. B. Monro, *The Modes of Ancient Greek Music* (Oxford University Press, 1894), and R. P. Winnington-Ingram, *Mode in Ancient Greek Music* (Cambridge University Press, 1936). More recent discussion are provided by Donald Jay Grout, *A History of Western Music* (Norton, 1973), 27–34, and

Warren D. Anderson, *Ethos and Education in Greek Music* (Harvard University Press, 1968). Most recent is the comprehensive and penetrating study of ancient music undertaken by Andrew Barker, *Greek Musical Writings*, i. *The Musician and His Art* (Cambridge University Press, 1984) in which the author systematically compiles Greek writings on music and musical theory. On the subject of *mimēsis*, I have learned greatly from Göran Sörbom, *Mimesis and Art: Studies in the Origin and Early Development of an Aesthetic Vocabulary* (Scandinavian University Books, 1966). Finally, of related interest is Plato's theory of art and poetry; for a lively analysis that also illuminates more general issues about the role of poetry in ancient Greece, see Giovanni Ferrari, "Plato and Poetry," in *Cambridge History of Literary Criticism*, i (Cambridge University Press, 1987).

23. Although David Charles emphasizes only the first half of the process, his account, I believe, is essentially compatible with mine; cf. *Aristotle's Philosophy of Action* (Cornell University Press, 1984), 182–3.

24. This is a highly complex issue which I cannot take up here. Very briefly, the account is unified if we consider the perfection of activity at 1174b31 not to be something over and above the activity. In this way the notions of pleasure as unimpeded activity (*NE* VII) and as perfection of activity (*NE* X) both define pleasure as a form of activity. On Gosling's view, in particular, pleasure as the perfection of actualization is not additional to the fully actualized state, but its formal cause. J. G. B. Gosling and C. C. W. Taylor, *The Greeks on Pleasure* (Oxford University Press, 1982), 253.

25. In *DA* II. 1 Aristotle refers to the realization and cultivation of such a state through activity as its second actuality. The first actuality of an organism is the acquired, non-active state, which will itself be the actualization of some more basic potentiality.

26. There is of course the related paradox of learning in the *Meno*: in order to inquire about things we do not yet know, we must already know them.

27. The analogy was suggested to me by David Charles.

28. Gosling and Taylor detect in Aristotle's writings the notion of a continuum of activity whereby human beings approximate the most perfect activity of divine begins (*The Greeks on Pleasure*, 249). They cite *Meta.* 1072b13–30, *NE* 1154b24–8, 1178b7–28 in support of their case. Yet Aristotle's remarks elsewhere about our composite natures and necessarily human function (especially *NE* 1178a8–b8, I. 7) suggest that the point may be less well founded.

29. This has been taken by some to be Piaget's view. See Susan Isaacs, *Intellectual Growth in Young Children* (Routledge, 1930).

11

Being Properly Affected: Virtues and Feelings in Aristotle's Ethics

L. A. Kosman

I

A moral virtue, or as we might say, a good state of character, is for
Aristotle an established disposition for free and deliberate conduct of
the right sort, a *hexis prohairetikē,* as he puts it.[1] In providing an account of the moral life in which the concept of a virtue or state of
character is central, Aristotle reveals what is clear throughout the *Ethics:* that he, like Plato, thinks of the question of moral philosophy as
not simply how I am to conduct myself in my life, but how I am to
become the kind of person readily disposed so to conduct myself, the
kind of person for whom proper conduct emanates characteristically
from a fixed disposition. Of course the good life is a life of activity—a
life, that is, in which such dispositions are realized and not simply possessed by persons of worth. Otherwise a perfectly desirable life might
be spent asleep. But the good life is one whose activities are not simply
in accord with the virtues but are the appropriate realizations of these
virtues, and the virtues themselves are ready dispositions toward these
activities. The good person is not simply one who behaves in a certain
way, but one who behaves that way out of a certain character.

II

When we recognize the Aristotelian virtues to be dispositions toward
deliberate and proper human conduct, it becomes tempting to take

Aristotle to be thinking in terms of human action, of the virtues as fixed tendencies toward modes of *praxis*. But is that right? It is clear that no thoughtful reading of the *Ethics* can help but note the centrality of praxis in Aristotle's moral theory and its important connections to the other key notions in that theory—for example, responsibility, choice, and practical reasoning. But virtues are not in Aristotle's view dispositions solely toward modes of acting. Throughout his discussion of the moral virtues, and particularly in his earliest account of them in Book 2, Aristotle makes clear that the activities for which virtues are dispositions are of two sorts, actions and feelings, *praxeis kai pathē*. He rarely mentions virtue in Book 2 with respect to action alone, but rather in terms of this dual phrase. The first account of the notion of a disposition with which moral virtue will be identified, indeed, is exclusively in terms of feelings: *kath' has pros ta pathē echomen eu ē kakōs*.[2] So the virtues are dispositions toward feeling as well as acting.

Acting and feeling are not simply two modes of human conduct among others. This can be seen if we use the older and more etymologically parallel English renderings of Aristotle's *praxis* and *pathos* and describe the moral virtues as dispositions toward *action* and *passion*— toward characteristic modes of conduct, in other words, in which the virtuous person acts and is acted upon—is the moral subject, as it were, of active and passive verbs.

A view of feelings and emotions as passions or affections—that is, as instances of a subject being acted upon, of an agent, so to speak, as patient—is embedded in the very word which we translate by "feeling" or by "emotion," the Greek word *pathos*. This word, like the verb *paschein*, of which it is a derivative form, has an earliest sense of what is experienced or undergone by way of misfortune or harm—what is, as we say, *suffered*—but comes subsequently, as with "suffer," to have a general sense simply of what is experienced, a mode of a subject's being acted upon.[3]

Insofar as Aristotle sees fear, anger, desire, pleasure, and pain as pathē, as passions, he views what we would call feelings or emotions as modes of a subject being acted upon. This fact is further revealed in the list Aristotle offers us of emotions with which moral virtues are concerned and in which there can be excess, deficiency, and right measure. The majority of items on this list are described by passive verbs; in thinking of fear, anger, pleasure, or pain, Aristotle is thinking of being frightened, being angered, being pleased, being pained. When I am afraid, something is frightening me; when I am angry, something is angering me. When in general I am experiencing an emotion or feeling of the sort which Aristotle would call a pathos, something is affecting me; I am being acted upon in some way, where the concept of being acted upon is reciprocal to that of my acting in some way.[4] Actions and feelings are thus for Aristotle modes of human being—action and passion—seen in terms of reciprocal concepts basic to our understanding of entities in general, the concepts of acting and being acted upon.

The opposition between acting and being acted upon, that is, the praxis/pathos opposition, is, to be sure, peculiar to human activity, because praxis is according to Aristotle peculiar to human activity. But it is only a special instance of a more general structural duality, that of *poiein* and *paschein,* doing and being done.[5] This dualism is encountered early in and throughout Aristotle's writings, from its special appearance as an apparently reciprocal pair of relatively minor modes of being in the *Categories* to the important cosmological role recognized in the treatise *On Generation and Corruption.*[6]

This more general opposition of *poiein/paschein,* insofar as it governs and structures the most basic forms of being, understood as activity, is thus a central and fundamental structural principle of Aristotle's ontology. Action and passion then similarly represent terms of a fundamental structural principle of human activity. "Activity" here must take on a sense broad enough to include both acting and being acted upon—must, that is, include modes of active human being in which the human individual is both subject and object of the action, both agent and patient.

The notion of including as an aspect of human activity what an individual suffers, what is done to an individual in addition to what the individual does, may go against our intuitions. It is only an individual's actions, we might feel, which truly belong to the being of a human individual in its most basic sense. This intuition is something to which we shall have to return. But it should not blind us to the fact that the affections and passive sufferings of entities seem to be among the authentic characteristics which such entities have, and this is true for both human and nonhuman beings.

If the kinds of human activity now understood in this broader sense include not only what are, more strictly speaking, instances of human action but also instances of human passion in the sense of being acted upon, and these latter are understood as paradigmatic instances of feelings or emotions, then Aristotle's moral theory must be seen as a theory not only of how to *act* well but also of how to *feel* well; for the moral virtues are states of character that enable a person to exhibit the right kinds of emotions as well as the right kinds of actions. The art of proper living, we should say, includes the art of feeling well as the correlative discipline to the art of acting well.

III

Moral philosophy, then, should count as an important question that of sentimental education and should recognize the proper cultivation of our feelings as within the domain of our moral concerns. But how could this be? It appears to be a distinction between our actions and our passions that actions are within our control, whereas passions are not; we are the initiating principle of what we do, but not of what is done to us. Aristotle seems to make exactly this point in claiming that we are angered or frightened, for example, not by choice—*aprohairetōs,* as he puts it.[7]

But if we give allegiance to the meta-ethical dictum that "ought" implies "can," then it seems problematic how a moral philosophy could concern itself with questions of our feelings in contrast with questions of how we ought to act in response to or in light of those feelings. What is, as Aristotle would say, *eph'hēmin*—within our power—is surely what we do, but not what is done to us.

One way in which this objection might be met is by pointing out what I have emphasized earlier: the important role of the concept of *virtue.* Since we are primarily called upon by a moral theory not to act and be acted upon in certain ways but rather to be the kinds of persons disposed so to act and be acted upon, the question of what feelings are or are not immediately within our powers may be moot.

But could a moral theory be concerned with sentimental education even in this sense, namely, with the cultivation of proper sentimental dispositions? For in what sense might such dispositions themselves be said to be within the domain of choice or *prohairesis?* Why, in other words, wouldn't the question be pushed one step further back? And how then could we be said in the first place to have a *disposition* to be acted upon rather than to act in certain ways? Let me first say something preliminary about this latter question.

Aristotle's claim that virtues are dispositions toward feeling as well as action can be seen, in light of our recognition that feelings are passions, to rest upon a theory of potentiality which recognizes the existence of passive as well as active powers. For since a disposition is a power—that is, a potentiality that renders an entity capable of a mode of actual being—and since feelings are passions, the virtues in question must be passive powers—the potentialities, that is, for being actively affected in a certain way.

That Aristotle has a *general* theory of passive powers is evident. The discussion of potentiality in Book 9 of the *Metaphysics* makes this clear (in the context of a discussion that once again reveals the reciprocal relation and basic dialectical unity of *poiein* and *paschein*). Passive potentialities, we there learn, are elements within an entity's nature, not simply external to it, and are connected to other more obviously integral aspects of the entity's being. To say that oil is *burnable* is to ascribe to the oil a power that belongs to it and is a potentiality for being affected in a certain way, for having something done to it, and is at the same time to link this capacity to certain positive states and characteristics of the oil.[8]

More obvious forms of potentialities with respect to being affected are those by virtue of which an entity is capable of withstanding or not suffering a certain affection. Aristotle often refers to such a type of power both in the discussion in the *Categories* and in that in the *Metaphysics*.[9] In both cases, however, we are considering powers exhibited by an entity for discrimination among affections, for being affected in this way and not that.

Another class of such powers, and one that for Aristotle is paradigmatic and important, includes the faculties of the soul. The perceptual capacities, and the faculties of reason and thought as well, are potentialities of the sensitive and intelligent subject to be *affected* in certain ways, to be acted upon by the sensible and intelligible forms of objects in the world.[10] When we think of them in this way, there is nothing particularly mysterious about these powers: they are simply the abilities to be open to certain affections and closed to certain others—the reciprocal capacities, we might say, of being discriminatingly receptive and resistant.

The doctrine of passive potentiality enables Aristotle to envision a state of character by virtue of which an individual has the power to be affected in certain ways, the capacity to undergo certain passions and avoid others. A moral virtue with respect to feelings or emotions is just such a capacity; it is the power to have and to avoid certain emotions, the ability to discriminate in what one feels.

IV

But this suggests only how there might be said to be powers to be acted upon in certain ways; what concerned us was whether such powers might be said to be dispositions involving choice. We still therefore need to be concerned with the question of choice, and that question may now be put this way: how is it possible for Aristotle to see a virtue as a disposition toward a feeling or emotion, given the following facts about choice? In his first characterization of virtue Aristotle denies that virtues might be feelings themselves by pointing out that a feeling is not the sort of thing that is chosen; our anger and fear are, as he might have said, "aprohairetic," whereas the virtues are kinds of choice or at least not aprohairetic, not devoid of choice. But then we should ask: how could choice be involved in a fixed tendency toward that which does not involve choice, indeed for which we are in no wise praised or blamed? Won't there have to be a radical asymmetry between the relation among dispositions, actualizations, and choice in the case of feelings and that relation in the case of actions? For in the latter case a virtue appears to be a disposition toward prohairetic acts; the actions themselves are instances of choice, and it seems to be only by virtue of this fact that the hexis or disposition which is a virtue with respect to these acts is said to be prohairetic. But in the case of feelings, virtues would, on the view we are considering, themselves be chosen but at the same time be dispositions toward actualizations that are not chosen.

One solution to this problem which I hinted at before would be to abandon the notion that virtues are dispositions with respect to feelings in the sense of being fixed tendencies to feel in a certain way. It is not that courage as a virtue with respect to fear disposes us to feeling fear in certain ways or in certain circumstances or to a certain degree but rather that it disposes us to certain actions with respect to and in light of our fear. Some support may appear to be given to this reading by Aristotle's description of a disposition as a state by virtue of which we are ill or well disposed with respect to the emotions: *kath' has pros ta pathē echomen eu ē kakōs.*[11]

This is the view of Joachim in his commentary on the *Ethics;* he writes:

> In the development of the orectic soul there is a hexis when the soul *echei pōs* (viz. *eu ē kakōs*) *pros ta pathē:* i.e. when a permanent attitude

towards his emotions (towards any possible disturbances of his orectic self) has been reached—an attitude which expresses itself in actions which are either the right or the wrong response to such disturbances.[12]

But this reading is surely wrong: Aristotle, in the passage in question, immediately goes on to explain:

if for instance, with respect to being angered we do so excessively or insufficiently [*sphodrōs* or *aneimenōs:* if we're too violent or too easygoing] we're badly disposed, but if moderately [*mesōs*] then we're well disposed.[13]

Aristotle's more detailed discussions of the virtues make clear that it is with respect to how one feels and not simply how one acts in light of one's feelings that one is said to be virtuous. The courageous person is one who is frightened by the right things, in the right way, in the right circumstances, and so on, and who is not frightened when it is appropriate not to be. The temperate person is one who is pleased by the right things, in the right ways, and so on. The so-called "gentle" person (whose virtue Aristotle finds to have no proper name) is angered by the right things, in the right way, and so on.[14] There is here no indication that these moral virtues defined in terms of feelings are dispositions toward some range of actions appropriate in light of these feelings, and, on the contrary, every indication that they are dispositions toward appropriate feelings themselves.

What emerges in addition, however, is the recognition that these feelings are accompanied by concomitant actions. I have talked so far as though feelings could be understood as particular affects of an individual independent of anything else that might be true of the individual. In a sense this is exactly Aristotle's theory and is why he says that pathē are those things with regard to which we are said to be moved.[15] But considered more broadly, there is no way to identify a feeling or emotion without taking into account (1) what we might call the cognitive element in emotions and (2) actions on the part of the agent which are characteristically and naturally associated with such feelings.[16] Fearing is related to fleeing, desiring to reaching for, anger to striking out at, in no accidental way. In each of these cases, a certain action or range of actions is connected to a pathos in some important logical sense. That connection is defeasible, but it is not a merely accidental connection.

These considerations suggest that there may be two elements to the actuality corresponding to any given virtue. A virtue is a complex disposition in the sense that its actualization is complex, and specifically in that its actualization consists of a characteristic set of feelings *and* a correspondent characteristic set of actions.

But if this is true, our discussion of virtues has been seriously misleading. The fact that virtues are dispositions with respect both to actions and to feelings ought not to suggest to us that there are a number of virtues that are dispositions with respect to actions and a number of other virtues that are dispositions with respect to feelings, any given virtue being a disposition with respect to one or the other, but rather that a given virtue is a disposition with respect to a characteristic set of actions *and* feelings. These feelings are not, as in the view we have just been considering, merely the occasion for actions that are the proper realizations of the virtue; they are part of the concept of that virtue considered as a disposition. But neither are they the sole realizations of the virtue; they are part of the set of corresponding actions and feelings for which the virtue is a disposition.

V

With this understanding in mind, let us, as Aristotle would say, make a fresh start. Recognizing that virtues are dispositions toward feeling as well as toward action, we found ourselves perplexed by Aristotle's apparent claim that virtues involve choice, while feelings do not. It appeared to us that there was an unexplained asymmetry in Aristotle's understanding, such that virtues might involve choice without their appropriate feeling-realizations involving choice, even though virtues seemed to involve choice in the first place because they are dispositions toward actualizations that are deliberate and chosen. Is it possible to make sense of the notion that a virtue involves choice even though the feelings that are its realization do not? Could a person be said to be courageous in a deliberate and chosen manner without it being the case that the feelings which such a person characteristically exhibits by virtue of being courageous are themselves chosen?

Consider a parallel situation in the case of actions. A person may exhibit a vice such that the actions performed as a result of that vice are involuntary considered in themselves, and we may still want to say that the vice itself is voluntary. Thus someone, as Aristotle notes, may in one sense not be responsible for individual actions performed while he was intoxicated or ignorant of what he was doing or in general acting in accordance with some trait of character that made it impossible or extremely difficult for him to do the right thing, and yet in another sense clearly be responsible, at least for being in the first place unaware or drunk or in general of such and such a vicious character.[17]

These examples provide only a partial parallel to our case. In the first place, they concern the somewhat weaker notion of voluntariness, not that of choice. In the second place, they concern only instances of vice and the concomitant breakdown of moral action. Nowhere do we find an instance of Aristotle's characterizing as voluntary a virtue whose resultant actions could be said to be involuntary. Finally, the examples that come most readily to mind—cases of drunkenness, ignorance, or negligence—concern what seem to be in a sense "meta-vices": states that condition our general capacity for virtuous conduct. As a consequence the relationship between the action and the vice that occasions it is not a straightforward relationship of disposition to realization. Only under a partial description could an act of negligence be said to be the actualization of the vice of negligence in the same sense in which an act of courage is the realization of an agent's courageous disposition.

But we could extend the basic point to cases of specific vices. It seems a part of Aristotle's views on moral responsibility that vicious actions are in some important sense not chosen, and indeed under certain descriptions not voluntary, though the vices that occasion them *are,* and are therefore the responsibility, like their actions, of the moral agent.

This is an enormously complex and difficult topic in Aristotle's thought, and an important one for Aristotle and for moral philosophy in general; the respect in which vicious acts are not willed but nevertheless our responsibility may be central to an understanding of the moral life (compare Kant). I introduce the question here only because it suggests that certain predicates which we might think of as features of actions and only derivatively of characteristics or dispositions relative to those actions may be applied independently to one or the other in a variety of ways. Most importantly we see here a sense in which predicates appropriate to dispositions not only with reference to their actualizations but also with reference to the mode of their acquisition.

It is a part of Aristotle's moral theory which I have alluded to but not stressed that virtues are acquired. They are, as he says, not *phusei,* but neither are they *paraphusin:* neither natural nor contrary to our nature.[18] This is what makes them dispositions—*hexeis*—rather than simply potentialities—*dunameis*. They must therefore be acquired, and their acquisition cannot be effected simply by an act of choice; we do not decide to be virtuous and straightaway become so. Virtues are cultivated and not chosen in any simple sense, for it is not as a direct result of calculation, deliberation, resolution, or any other relatively simple mode of human activity that we become courageous, temperate, or wise. We become these through a process of *ethismos,* or habituation, through the habitual acting out and embodying of those actualizations which the dispositions are dispositions toward.[19] This mode of acquisition is part of the logic of a virtue, because it is part of the logic of a hexis, a disposition, and a virtue is a hexis. It is therefore part of the logic of a moral theory which, as I have suggested, places the notion of virtue at its center.

Note first that there is a sense in which a virtue might be said to be chosen, and on a specific occasion. A person might decide on such an occasion to act virtuously and see that act as the first in a series designed to effect a transformation in her life to being virtuous. So she chooses on this occasion to be virtuous and so acts, acting virtuously now this time, now another time, now another time, until the fixed disposition of virtue becomes a hexis that characterizes her moral self. Why shouldn't we say in such a case that the virtue has been chosen, from the beginning, and precisely because the acts that fix that virtue are chosen?

This notion accords well with the view of Aristotle's we have just been looking at. On this view one becomes virtuous by impersonating a virtuous person, and in that impersonation, through the process of habituation, becomes the virtuous person whom one impersonates. The direction of self-constitution is seen as leading from actions to states of character as well as the other way around; indeed, we should perhaps say that the other way around is subsequent, is only a logical feature of the relationship between our character and the individual moments of our conduct once they have been established.

But how does this help us with the question of virtues and feelings? For our initial problem with feelings was that they are said by Aristotle not to be chosen; an account according to which virtues are prohairetic because the acts that fix them are prohairetic seems therefore to be of little help in understanding the relation among choice, virtues, and feelings. This question supposes that virtues whose actualizations are feelings may be acquired only through the direct and deliberate choice of feelings. But given our recognition that the actualization of a virtue is a complex and related set of actions and feelings, a different view is now open to us. A person may act in certain ways that are characteristically and naturally associated with a certain range of feelings, and through those actions acquire the virtue that is the disposition for having the feelings directly. Acts are chosen, virtues and feelings follow in their wake, though in logically different ways.

On this view the structure of becoming virtuous with respect to feelings reveals itself to be of the following sort: one recognizes through moral education what would constitute appropriate and correct ways to feel in certain circumstances. One acts in ways that are naturally associated with and will "bring about" those very feelings, and eventually the feelings become, as Aristotle might have said, second nature; that is, one develops states of character that dispose one to have the right feelings at the right time. One does not have direct control over one's feelings, and in this sense the feelings are not chosen; but one does have control over the actions that establish the dispositions, the virtues, which are the source of our feeling in appropriate ways at appropriate times and in appropriate circumstances. Although we may in some narrow sense not be responsible for our feelings, we are responsible for our character as the dispositional source of those feelings.

This picture has much to recommend it. In the first place, it seems correct. My anger or jealousy may not be an emotion which I choose, and yet it may be true that I have become a person disposed to such anger or jealousy by a series of actions that would make it perfectly reasonable to describe my character as something I have chosen. In the second place, it points to what seem important differences between feelings and actions which become clear only when we talk about the modes of acquisition of virtues. Much of the picture I have sketched depends upon the fact that one can simulate an action but can only pretend to have a feeling. Thus the mode of inculcation with regard to feelings must be by some other method than that of habituation. There is, in other words, no way to come to feel a certain way by practicing feeling that way, and this is precisely because in some sense our feelings are not in our control. But it is nonetheless possible to engage in a certain range of conduct deliberately designed to make one the kind of person who will characteristically feel in appropriate ways, at appropriate times, and so on. And in this sense, feelings are deliberate and chosen, since the hexeis from which these feelings emanate are deliberate and chosen, since (in turn) the actions that lead to these hexeis are deliberate and chosen, and deliberately chosen to make one the kind of person who characteristically will have the appropriate feelings.

VI

This picture seems to me on the whole correct and, broadly speaking, faithful to Aristotle's vision of the moral life, but it fails in important respects as a solution to the problems that initially perplexed us. Note in the first place how far we have come from our initial characterization of a virtue as a disposition for deliberate and chosen conduct. That characterization interpreted Aristotle's description of a virtue as a *hexis prohairetikē* to mean that the virtue was the agent's ready capacity to act (in the broadest sense) prohairetically, not that the virtue had been acquired through some mode of prohairetic action. In the second place, the rather elaborate account into which we have been led seems curiously otiose; once we recognize that actions and feelings are linked together as the realizations of a virtue, why not simply say that a virtue is prohairetic because it is a disposition for those elements of its realizations which are actions? For there is no special problem, apart from the general problem of giving an account of what prohairesis is, about actions being prohairetic. Finally, the most important flaw in the account I have suggested is the following. The account depends upon actions that lead to the establishment of a virtue but are not the expressions of an already established virtue being prohairetic. But this is not a view which Aristotle seems to hold. Such actions are voluntary, but it is by no means clear that they are for him in the fullest sense prohairetic. Just as acts are in a sense virtuous when they are acts of the kind which a virtuous person would perform, but are fully virtuous only when performed by a virtuous person (one who performs such acts in the way that a virtuous person would perform them—that is, out of the fixed character that is virtue),[20] just so an act may be like a prohairetic act, but not be one because it is not properly embedded in the larger context of the character and disposition of a moral agent—because it is not a realization of that agent's virtue. There is, Aristotle says, "no prohairesis without intelligence and thought, nor without moral character."[21] Prohairesis involves, as we might say, not simply deciding, but willing, where the notion of will is sufficiently rich to demand reference to the larger context of central and properly integrated goals and habits of an agent's moral life.

The recognition that choice for Aristotle is a concept governing not individual actions in a life divorced from this framework of goals and habits, but rather actions only as moments within a larger context of the character and intentions of the moral subject, reveals our picture to be inadequate as a solution to the problems I have raised. But it should, I think, contribute to the dissolution of these problems. For it should suggest the necessity of rethinking our initial denial that feelings may be chosen. That denial arose, I think, from our attending to a description by Aristotle of passions without reference to the context of virtue and character in which they occur. But why should we not be prepared to say that a person of steadfast and cultivated virtue who exhibits appropriate feelings in circumstances which he understands correctly and in which those are precisely the feelings which he would want to exhibit, taking into account the entire fabric of his desires, goals, plans, and hopes for himself—why should we not be prepared to say that such a person has chosen those feelings?

Nowhere, I believe, does Aristotle say this. What we would like, but do not find, is an extension of the theory of deliberation and practical reasoning to account for the ways in which virtuous persons might be said to have the proper feelings which they have by prohairesis. Such an account would need to provide a sense in which we might be freed to feel what would be appropriate to feel by something like deliberation and choice, by some mode of coming to understand properly the circumstances in which our feelings arise, the place of these feelings and circumstances in our experience, and the ways in which we hold these circumstances and feelings in the larger contexts of our lives. In a sense, the theories behind certain religious traditions, psychoanalysis, and disciplines that promise self-transformation and self-mastery might be thought to represent attempts at such an account.

But any such account, I think, would have to recognize the primacy of praxis in the shaping and execution of our moral lives. It is this primacy that finally dominates the concerns of the *Ethics*. To say then that there is a strict parallelism for Aristotle between actions and passions would not be quite correct. On the one hand, he is led by the *paschein/prattein* structure and by the understanding of emotion as pathos to view virtue as a disposition equally for action and feeling, and as a consequence to recognize correctly the important place which our feelings occupy in the structure of our moral conduct. But on the other hand, the distinction between passion as something that happens to one and action as something that one does, coupled with the recognition that ethics must be concerned with prohairesis, leads him to turn his attention from feelings in the latter parts of the *Ethics*. It is not that he simply leaves the question of feelings out, but that their importance fades in the context of a particular theory of deliberation and choice and their place in moral conduct.

Nor is it the case, however, as I have argued, that feelings are for Aristotle simply not chosen. The reason for this, I have suggested, is that choice for him is not a concept having to do with individual moments in an agent's life, nor with individual single actions, but with the practices of that life within the larger context of the character and intentions of a moral subject, ultimately within the context of what it has become fashionable to call one's life plan.

The question of moral choice in the deepest sense finally concerns questions of creating the conditions in which our actions and our feelings may be as we would wish them. These conditions include our states of character—the virtues—which we acquire through the complex practices of our moral life. So long as we consider moral questions in terms of individual moments in the agent's life, we will not be able to understand this fact. This is why it should be clear that questions of virtue and feeling as moral categories are importantly connected.

Notes

1. *Nicomachean Ethics* 2.6. 1106b36; *Eudemian Ethics* 1.10. 1227b8.

2. *Nicomachean Ethics* 2.5. 1105b26; 2.2. 1104b14; 2.6. 1106b17, 1106b25, 1107a9.

3. See the article on *paschō* in G. Kittel, *Theological Dictionary of the New Testament* (Grand Rapids, Mich., 1964–1974), 5:904 ff.

4. *Nicomachean Ethics* 2.6. 1106b17 ff. Compare English *afraid* as originally the passive participle *affrayed*.

5. All this is on the assumption that *prattein* is a special case of *poiein* and not, as Aristotle comes to understand it, vice versa. Compare his uses of *kinesis* and *energeia* for a similar reversal of the common understanding.

6. *Categories* 9. 11b1 ff.; *On Generation and Corruption* 1.7. 323b1 ff.

7. *Nicomachean Ethics* 2.5. 1106a2.

8. *Metaphysics* 9.1. 1046a11 ff., 1046a19 ff.

9. *Categories* 8. 9a23; *Metaphysics* 9.1. 1046a13.

10. *On the Soul* 2 and 3. passim.

11. *Nicomachean Ethics* 2.5. 1105b26.

12. H. H. Joachim, *Aristotle, The Nicomachean Ethics* (Oxford, 1951), p. 85.

13. *Nicomachean Ethics* 2.5. 1105b26 ff.

14. See the table of the virtues in *Nicomachean Ethics* 2.7. 1107b1 ff., and the specific discussions of virtues in Books 3 and 4.

15. *Nicomachean Ethics* 2.5. 1106a4.

16. Thus *On the Soul* 1.1. 403a25, and the discussion of the emotions in the *Rhetoric*. See W. W. Fortenbaugh, "Aristotle: Emotion and Moral Virtue," *Arethusa* 2 (1969), 163–185.

17. *Nicomachean Ethics* 3.5. 1113b30 ff.

18. Ibid., 2.1. 1103a14 ff.

19. Ibid., 1103a28 ff.

20. Ibid., 2.4. 1105a26 ff.

21. Ibid., 6.2. 1139a33. See G. E. M. Anscombe, "Thought and Action in Aristotle," in *New Essays on Plato and Aristotle,* ed. Renford Bambrough (London, 1965).

12

Friendship and the Good in Aristotle

John M. Cooper

If the number of published discussions is a fair measure, the two books of the *Nicomachean Ethics* devoted to friendship (*philia*) have not much engaged the attention of philosophers and philosophical scholars. Yet such neglect is not easily justifiable. For both in his account of what friendship is and in the various considerations he brings to bear to show what is good about friendship, Aristotle displays psychological subtlety and analytical ingenuity of an unusually high order, even for him. In this paper I hope to show this for Aristotle's views on the value of friendship, by discussing his principal arguments in the *Nicomachean Ethics* and elsewhere bearing on this topic.[1]

I

In the *Nicomachean Ethics* Aristotle faces the question what the value of friendship is in IX.9; but before considering his answer it is important to be clear exactly what question he means to be asking. On Aristotle's theory of the good there is a distinction to be drawn between what is good absolutely and without qualification (good "by nature" he sometimes calls it) and what is good for a particular person or class of persons. A thing is good absolutely if it is good for human beings as such, taken in abstraction from special and contingent peculiarities of particular persons: these peculiarities may provide additional interests, needs and wants, and on the basis of them one can speak of additional, possibly divergent, things as good for this or that particular person. Hence in asking whether friendship is a good thing, and what the good of it is, Aristotle neglects the question whether, and how, it may be good for special classes of person (bad or weak or mediocre people, for example, of one kind or another). He wants to know instead whether it is a good for human beings, as such. Now the morally good, flourishing person is a perfect human being, leading the perfect human life; so anything that is a good for human beings as such (that is, good without qualification) will necessarily be good for him. So Aristotle's inquiry into the value of friendship takes the form of seeking an answer to the question whether or not a flourishing person, the perfect human being, will have any need of friends (*amphisbēteitai de kai peri ton eudaimona ei deēsetai: philōn ē mē, NE* IX.9, 1169*b*3–4).

This question itself is open to two sorts of misunderstanding. One of these Aristotle himself points out. To speak of someone's need for friends might be taken to imply some deficiency or defect in him and his mode of living—as if some essential element of his own good would be lacking to him unless he had friends to acquire or provide this for him. And of course to flourish is to be already leading a perfect, completely fulfilled life, so that, understood in this way, a flourishing person can have no *need* for friends. Since his life is already, *ex hypothesi,* perfectly complete he cannot, as Aristotle puts it, need any adventitious *(epeisakton)* pleasure (or other good) as a means of improving his condition (1169*b*23–28). When Aristotle asks, then, whether a flourishing person needs friends, he is inquiring whether the having of friends is a necessary constituent of a flourishing life—not whether friends are needed as a means of improving a life that was already flourishing.

In the second place, it is important to emphasize that the question to be pressed concerns the value to a person of his *having* friends. That is, one wants to be given reasons for believing that, so to say, anyone who sets out to design for himself a life that shall be a flourishing one, ought to arrange things so that he forms friendships—so that he becomes attached to certain people in ways that are characteristic of friendship, spends time with them, does them services out of unself-interested good will, and so on.[2] It seems clear that this is the question that Aristotle means to be asking in *NE* IX. 9 (and in the corresponding passage of the *Eudemian Ethics,* VII. 12, 1244*b*1–1245*b*19). At any rate it is possible, as I shall argue below, to discern in this chapter two quite profound, mutually independent attempts to answer this question, so understood.

Unfortunately, however, the largest part of Aristotle's response in the *NE* (the long argument beginning at 1170*a*13, honorifically described as the way people who consider the question "more scientifi-cally"—*phusikōteron*—will answer it) is hard to follow unless it is construed as answering a different question. The question seems to have become this: what need has a flourishing person for *his* friends?[3] That is, on the assumption that he will form friendships in the first place, the question Aristotle discusses is why he will need or want to do things for them or with them, what use he will have for them, and why. Why will he not simply pay them no special heed? Obviously this is not a very interesting question, nor particularly difficult to answer. Given what being someone's friend means, if one assumes that a per-son has made friends with someone else, it follows that he has come to have certain psychological propensities: he likes the other person, wishes him well, wants to help him when he is in need, wants to spend time with him; and so on. So of course he will have many uses for his friend: the friend will be needed in order for all these various desires to be fulfilled. Having these desires, his life will be defective unless he is able to satisfy them by engaging in the activities characteristic of friends; naturally, then, such a person will need his friends.

I take it, then, that a flourishing person's need for friends, under-stood as his need for *his* friends, is very easy to establish. Of course, it is easy to establish this only because in taking the question in this way one begs the more important question why one should suppose a flourishing person would make any friends in the first place. Yet, as I have just indicated, the most promising interpretation of the suppos-edly more profound argument with which *NE* IX. 9 concludes makes Aristotle guilty of taking this easy path to his conclusion. When one cuts through all the complications of a very convoluted argument (Ross sets it out in a series of eleven syllogisms)[4] Aristotle's final and grandest effort, on this interpretation, comes to the following:

(1) For a good person, life itself is a good and pleasant thing; it is always pleasant to be aware of oneself as possessing good things; therefore, the good person's awareness of himself as being alive is very pleasant and highly desirable to him (1170*b*1–5).

(2) A man's friend is to him a "second self," so that whatever is good for him as belonging to himself will also be good for him when possessed by his friend (1170*b*5–8).

(3) Since the good man's life and his awareness of it are pleasant and desirable to him, he will find the life of his "second self" and his awareness of it also pleasant and desirable (1170*b*8–10).

(4) But he cannot satisfy this desire to be aware of his friend's existence except by living in company with him, so he will need his friend "to live with and share in discussion and thought with—for this is what living together would seem to mean for human beings, and not feeding in the same place, as with cattle" (1170*b*10–14).[5]

Now it is quite plain that in step (2) of this argument Aristotle simply assumes, altogether without explicit warrant, that a good man will have friends. It is only if one assumes that he *will* have friends that one can apply to him, as Aristotle does in the remainder of the argument, the consequences that flow, or are alleged to flow, from the fact that a friend is to his friend as a second self. If the good man *has* friends, then of course, granted the "second self" thesis, he will take pleasure in being aware of his friend's life, as he also does in being aware of his own, and will want to be near him in order to have this pleasure. This I think is obvious and unobjectionable.[6] But until we are given some independent reason for thinking that the good man will need or want to form friendships in the first place, we are not entitled to assume that he will have the sort of attitude toward any other person which will enable him to get this pleasure and, in consequence, desire this close association. But there is not the slightest hint in this argument, so interpreted, of any reason for thinking *this*.[7]

It might be suggested that Aristotle has in mind (though certainly he does not say this here) that the pleasant self-awareness on which this argument turns is only satisfactorily obtainable through the awareness of a friend and his activities. On that basis one might be able to construct a more plausible looking argument for Aristotle's conclusion. Thus Stewart:[8]

> In seeing, hearing, walking, etc., a man is conscious of himself—of his own existence. . . . This perception of self, however, would hardly be possible to man if his only objects of experience were his own sensations. . . . [H]is experience of his own actions would be accompanied by only a dim consciousness of a self distinguished from them. But man is not confined to his own actions. He has a "sympathetic consciousness" of the actions of his friend—of actions which are still in a sense "his own" (for his friend is a *heteros autos*), and yet are not in such a way "his own" as to make it difficult to distinguish "himself" from them. . . . In other words—it is in the consciousness of the existence of another that a man becomes truly conscious of himself.

Why, however, should one believe this? No reason is given, and off-hand it does not seem true that merely in order to be distinctly conscious of oneself one needs to be aware of other persons first. But even granted that one cannot attain self-consciousness except through consciousness of another person and his actions, it would still not follow that one needs friends for this purpose. Why wouldn't a casual acquaintance do just as well? Stewart describes a psychological process whereby a person, having noted the fairly gross distinction between himself and the actions of another person, is able to make the same distinction, or make it more sharply, in the case of his own actions. I do not see how the step from others' actions to one's own is made any the easier by the fact that the other person in question is a friend; the purely verbal point that, on the "other self" thesis, one can call the actions of a friend "one's own" does not seem to me to add anything to whatever psychological plausibility the process as described without it might seem to have.

In any event, as already noted, Aristotle does not here (or, so far as I can discover, elsewhere) claim the priority of other-awareness to self-awareness. He argues instead from the assumption of robust, pleasant self-consciousness in the good man to the pleasantness of his consciousness of his friend—this latter consciousness is represented, as it were, as an overflow from the good man's self-consciousness, not as something needed to create it in the first place. Interestingly, however, in the chapter of the *Magna Moralia* corresponding to *NE* IX. 9 one does find the related point argued for, that self-*knowledge* depends upon knowledge of others:

> Now supposing a man looks upon his friend and marks what he is and what is his character and quality *(Ti esti kai hopoios tis ho philos)*; the friend—if we figure a friend of the most intimate sort—will seem to be a kind of second self, as in the common saying "This is my second Heracles." Since, then, it is both a most difficult thing, as some of the sages have said, to attain a knowledge of oneself *(to gnōnai hauton)*, and also a most pleasant (for to know oneself is pleasant)—now we are not able to see what we are from ourselves *(hautous ex hautōn . . . theasasthai)* (and that we cannot do so is plain from the way in which we blame others without being aware that we do the same things ourselves; and this is the effect of favour or passion, and there are many of us who are blinded by these things so that we judge not aright); as then when we wish to see our own face, we do so by looking into the mirror, in the same way when we wish to know ourselves we can obtain that knowledge by looking at

our friend. For the friend is, as we assert, a second self. If, then, it is pleasant to know oneself, and it is not possible to know this without having someone else for a friend, the self-sufficing man will require friendship in order to know himself (1213*a*10–26).[9]

It should strike one immediately that the focal point of this argument is self-knowledge and not, as in our *NE* passage, self-consciousness. Thus in the *NE* we find *to aisthanes thai hautou,* 1170*b*9, with repeated use of *aisthanesthai* and its derivatives throughout the argument, whereas in the *MM aisthanesthai* and its derivatives are wholly lacking, and we find instead *ho hauton gnōnoi,* 1215*a*15, 23, *eidenai a*16, 25, *gnōrizein a*23, 26. Nor are these mere stylistic variants: one can be conscious of one's self as an entity active in one's affairs even without knowing very fully or explicitly what kind of person one is, whereas self-knowledge as presented in the *MM* argument is precisely knowledge of one's character and qualities, motives and abilities. No doubt this kind of self-knowledge presupposes self-consciousness, but it is plainly not the same thing. The *MM* is arguing not that friendship is a necessary prerequisite to mere self-consciousness, but that it is necessary for self-knowledge.

One seems forced, then, to regard the "more scientific" argument of the *NE* as abortive.[10] The argument from the *MM,* however, seems more promising. Self-knowledge is certainly a more complex matter than mere self-consciousness, and the idea that it depends upon knowledge of others might strike one as plausible and important. But this argument, too, has its difficulties. First, how, exactly, is knowledge of others supposed to make possible self-knowledge? And, even more, why does self-knowledge (at any rate for the good and flourishing person) depend upon knowledge of one's friends—why wouldn't enemies or casual acquaintances do as well? Finally, it is not enough merely to say, as this text does, that self-knowledge is pleasant; for the argument to be sound self-knowledge must be actually indispensable to the good and flourishing person. But is it?

To take the last point first. It is certainly plausible to hold, and Aristotle presupposes throughout, that a person's life could not be called flourishing unless, in addition to leading the sort of life that is as a matter of fact the best (doing acts of kindness and courage and so on) he knew what sort of life he was leading and chose it partly for that reason. Human flourishing, in short, does not consist merely in conformity to natural principles, but requires self-knowledge and conscious self-affirmation. Self-knowledge is thus an essential part of what it is to flourish.[11] As such it is an extremely pleasant thing, and this is perhaps why in our text so much emphasis is laid on its pleasantness. But however that may be, there is no difficulty in granting on general Aristotelian grounds the indispensability of self-knowledge that the *MM* argument needs.

But how is self-knowledge to be attained? Notoriously, people tend to notice faults in others that they overlook in themselves; and they are equally inclined to attribute to themselves nonexistent virtues. Thus there is a double tendency to deny the presence in oneself of what one recognizes in others as faults, and to claim for oneself virtues that one does not really have at all. These threats to one's objectivity must be reckoned with by everyone, the person who in fact possesses all the good qualities of character and intellect and no bad ones no less than other people. To be sure, the qualities in himself he thinks virtuous are so, and he has no faults; but how is he to be sure that he is not deceiving himself in thinking these things, as he must be if he is to *know* what he is like? It is plausible to suggest, as our text does, that mistakes of this kind are not so apt to occur where one is observing another person and his life; here the facts, both about what are faults and what are virtues, are more likely, at least, to speak for themselves. But that just points to the problem: how attain the same objectivity about oneself that is so comparatively less difficult about others?

This is where friendship is supposed to come in. At least in friendships of the best sort, where the parties love one another for their characters, and not merely because they enjoy or profit from one another's company, intimacy (it is alleged) bespeaks affinity: my friend is, in the *MM*'s striking phrase, a second me (*toioutos hoios heteros einai egō*, 1213*a*12), myself all over again. Now no doubt the sense of kinship among friends, even among character friends, can be exaggerated. Some people are certainly drawn together partly by the presence of character-traits in the one that the other lacks. Even in such cases, however, it seems reasonable to think that there must be a strong underlying similarity of character and views, and that this similarity, intuitively felt by each in the other, forms an important part of the bond between them. In any event, on Aristotle's theory (compare 1156*b*7–8) the perfect friendship is one where the parties are fully good persons who are alike in character. If one supposes that in this perfect character-friendship, as in other lesser ones, the friends may feel a sense of their own kinship without necessarily knowing antecedently, on both sides, in what their similarity consists, then such a friendship could well serve as the needed bridge by which to convert objectivity about others into objectivity about oneself. For knowing intuitively that he and his friend are alike in character, such a person could, by studying his friend's character, come to know his own. Here the presumption is that even an intimate friend remains distinct enough to be studied objectively; yet, because one intuitively knows oneself to be fundamentally the same in character as he is, one obtains through him an objective view of oneself. In the *MM*'s image, one recognizes the quality of one's own character and one's own life by seeing it reflected, as in a mirror, in one's friend.[12]

This is the nub of the argument. It is certainly ingenious, but is it cogent? The principal weaknesses would seem to be two. First, one might doubt whether, if, as seems true, people tend to be biased in favor of themselves and blind to their own faults, they are any less so where those with whom they are intimate are concerned. And secondly one might feel uneasy about the weight apparently being laid on the effectiveness and reliability of one's intuitive sense of kinship with another person. Plainly the argument only works if one can justifiably have more initial confidence in these feelings than in one's own unaided attempts to judge the quality of one's life and character. But however difficult the latter may be, is one any less open to deception through the former?

Although these are genuine doubts, not easily allayed, I think the argument nonetheless contains considerable force. For it must be admitted that self-knowledge is, under any conditions, an extremely precarious accomplishment. Neither this nor any other argument is likely to show the way to an absolutely assured knowledge of what one is really like, proof against all possible doubt. The question is just whether character-friendship provides the best means available to a human being for arriving at as secure a knowledge of his own life and character as such a creature can manage. Considered in this light I think this argument has a certain weight. For it does seem fair to believe that objectivity about our friends is *more* securely attained than objectivity directly about ourselves. And the reliance we are being invited to place on our intuitive feelings of kinship with others is not, after all, either unchecked or unlimited. For it is the sense of kinship as it grows up, deepens and sustains itself within a close and prolonged association that the argument relies on. And it does seem right to trust such tried and tested feelings. They are not "*mere* feelings" but are developed through long experience both of the other person and of oneself. This is, indeed, one reason why knowledge of one's friends might make self-knowledge possible where knowledge of a mere acquaintance, however detailed, would not: the sense of affinity, if it existed at all, could not be relied upon in this latter case, since it would not be based on prolonged and deep familiarity with him.

On the other hand, while granting some weight to the considerations advanced here, one may well feel that this argument hardly exhausts the sources of self-knowledge, or even the most important ways in which friendship might help to advance it. Still, the recognition, which lies at the center of this argument, of the social bases of a secure self-concept and of the role intimacy plays in providing the means to this, is a notable achievement.

In any event, it deserves emphasis that this argument from the *Magna Moralia,* unlike the professedly more profound argument from *NE* IX. 9 examined above, does give reasons, however strong or weak, why one ought in designing one's life to make explicit provision for friendships. It would be wrong, of course, to conclude that in the *Nicomachean Ethics* Aristotle argues only ineffectively for this conclusion. For there are other arguments in *NE* IX. 9 and one of them (1169*h* 28–1170*a*4), though certainly not without obscurities of its own, has pronounced affinities to the *MM* argument just examined.

> For at the outset it was said that flourishing is an activity, and an activity clearly exists as something continuous and is not possessed like a piece of property. If flourishing consists in living and being active, and the activity of a good person is good and pleasant in itself, as was said at the outset, and what is peculiarly one's own is pleasant, and we can study *(theōrein)* our neighbors better than ourselves and their actions better than those that are peculiarly our own, and the actions of good persons who are their friends are pleasant to good people (for they are characterized by both the natural marks of pleasantness)—if so, then the fully flourishing person will need friends of this kind, given that he chooses *(prohairetai)* to study *(theōrein)* actions that are good and peculiarly his own, and the actions of the good person who is his friend are of this kind.

Here, as in the *MM* passage, we find two principal claims: that the good and flourishing man wants to study *(theōrein, 1169b33, 1170a2; theasasthai 1213a16)* good actions, and that one cannot, or cannot so easily, study one's own actions as those of another.[13] But why does the good person have reason to want to study good actions? Here the *NE* is silent. This gap in the argument can, however, naturally be filled in from the *MM:* it is because, for reasons we have already noted, the self-knowledge that is a prerequisite of flourishing can hardly be attained by other means. And, at the same time, it is clear, as it would not otherwise be, why the other person whose actions these are must be an intimate and not merely a casual acquaintance. If I am right, then, this passage of the *Nicomachean Ethics* is intended to convey essentially the same argument in favor of friendship as we find set out in full in the *Magna Moralia.* The claim, here again, seems to be that it is only or best in character-friendship that one can come to know oneself—to know the objective quality of one's own actions, character and life.

II

A second argument, independent of this one, follows in the *NE* immediately after the passage just quoted. At 1170*a*4-11 we read:

> Further, people think a flourishing person should live pleasantly. Now life is hard for a solitary person: for it is not easy to be continuously active apart by oneself, but this is easier together with others and towards them. So, [in living with others] his activity, which is pleasant in itself, will be more continuous, as it ought to be for a fully flourishing person (for the good man, *qua* good, takes pleasure in morally virtuous actions and dislikes vicious ones, just as a musician enjoys beautiful melodies and is pained by bad ones).[14]

Aristotle's central claim here is that living in isolation causes one to be less continuously active at the things one cares most about than is consistent with leading a flourishing life. By contrast, he claims, one can be more continuously active at these pursuits if one engages in them together with others, by which he clearly means not just living in their company—sitting by the side of others, as it were, but absorbed in one's own private pursuits[15]—but making one's fundamental life activities themselves activities shared in common with others: *meth'heteron de kai pros allous, rhaion* (1170*a*6). Why should there be this difference in continuity of activity between a life made up of shared and a life made up of purely private activities? Aristotle does not say. Several things might be in his mind. Perhaps in a solitary life, where one has to see to all one's needs by oneself and cannot rely on others, or the products of others' work, one is simply forced to be too busy too much of the time at menial and uninteresting things for one to be free to concentrate uninterruptedly on one's most cherished pursuits. But, though this might well be true, it is hard then to see the point of Aristotle's proposed remedy: one does not have to *share* one's activities with any one in order to have the benefits of others' assistance. Again, it might be suggested that if one tries to complete one's favorite projects all on one's own it may simply require physical exertions of such magnitude that one has to take many pauses for rest, thus rendering one's activities intermittent and discontinuous.[16] But again this cannot be all that Aristotle has in mind, since the natural remedy here would be to induce someone else to cooperate by making his skills, interests, and so on, available for one's private purposes, perhaps in return for occasional assistance from oneself: sharing one's projects with anyone else would surely not be necessary. In order to give Aristotle a reasonably plausible case for the preferability of a life of shared activities one must, then, at least supplement these points. A natural suggestion is this: Aristotle may be thinking that living in isolation causes one to lose the capacity to be actively interested in things. Even if the activity that delights one most is something that can be enjoyed by a solitary person (as is true of most intellectual pursuits) it tends not to be pursued with freshness and interest by someone living cut off from others. One tends to become apathetic and inactive without the stimulation and support which others, especially those whom one likes and esteems, provide by sharing one's goals and interests. If so, then one can see why Aristotle claims a special and essential place in any truly satisfactory human life for the sort of shared activities that only friendship makes possible: it will only, or especially, be through such activities that a human being finds his life continuously interesting and pleasurable.

Now whether or not this is what Aristotle has in mind, it is at any rate an interesting idea, and one that merits quite extensive consideration. I shall not attempt such a full-scale treatment here; still, the following points should be noted.[17]

First, by "shared activities" here I mean (and understand Aristotle to have in mind) activities that are performed by two or more persons together, and not just activities that are common to more than one person, or mutually known to several persons to be common to them all. Thus two persons might be solitaire devotees, and so have a common interest, and each might know of the other's attachment to the game, so that one could speak of their mutual interest in solitaire; but neither of these conditions is sufficient to make their attachment to the game count as a shared interest (nor of course would their solitaire games count as shared activities), for the reason that solitaire is not a game that they play together. The playing of the game is not something in which they jointly share. Now some activities are shared activities, in this sense, by one sort of necessity or another. Thus perhaps games like baseball and tennis are so defined by their rules that they cannot be played at all unless some specified number of persons, greater than one, is actively involved. In other cases, such as playing a string quartet, or doing many industrial and agricultural jobs, the work will normally have to be done together by more than one person, simply because of the physical limitations of the human body. Many activities, however, that can perfectly well be performed by single individuals in private (so far, at any rate, as the definition of what is being done, and physical capabilities, go) can also be shared. One can worship in private, or together with others; solve a mathematical problem, or write a book, alone or jointly; bathe by oneself or in company. Artistic and cultural activities are an especially interesting case. Here many activities that, narrowly considered, might seem to be personal and private are nonetheless engaged in by those who do them in such a way as to make them shared. Thus even although a single author may be solely responsible for a scholarly article, he presumably wrote it as a contribution to an ongoing subject of study to which he thinks of himself as attached jointly with others. His attitudes to his own work may be construed on the model of a game in which there are various positions, occupied from time to time by different persons, linked together by a common set of rules and shared purposes. The individual player's move, looked at in isolation, may well seem quite private to himself, but given the system of positions, rules, purposes, and so on, it is thought of by him as a contribution to the game in all the moves of which all the players share. Thus the individual author's acts of writing can be seen as part of a shared activity, namely the shared activity of advancing the discovery of the truth in the subject in question. In general, where an activity is shared one finds the following features: (1) there is a shared, and mutually known, commitment to some goal (whether something to be produced or something constitutive of the activity itself), (2) there is a mutual understanding of the particular role to be played by different persons in the pursuit of this common goal, and (3), within the framework of mutual knowledge and commitment, each agrees to do, and in general does do, his share in the common effort.

What then is there about shared activities that might make Aristotle think them in general more continuously interesting and enjoyable, in comparison with strictly private pursuits? Two things come to mind. First, the fact that others, especially if they are people one likes or admires, share with one in a commitment to the goal which gives the activity its sense is likely to strengthen one's own perception of the worth or value of the activity and thereby enable one to engage in it with interest and pleasure; that others, too, find a thing worth doing will be at least a welcome confirmation of one's own attitudes. Of course, it is possible to know that others agree in finding a thing worth doing even although each engages in it in a completely private way, so that if it is a good thing to know one's own views confirmed by the experiences of others, this good is available even if one does not share one's activities with anyone. On the other hand, what is in question here is not a person's mere abstract knowledge that something is valuable and worthwhile but his actual direct experience of it *as* worthwhile. And it must not be overlooked that it is possible to know on sufficient grounds that something is good, but be unable to actually experience it as such; and it is the latter that is crucial to the enjoyment of one's own life. In a shared activity one knows of the commitment of others to the goodness of the activity in no mere abstract theoretical way. It is concrete and immediate. Hence it is only through participation in such activities that the confirmatory knowledge of others' evaluations is likely to be both constantly and directly present to one's consciousness. It seems not unreasonable to suggest, then, that the sort of confirmation of the worth of one's endeavors and pursuits that is so valuable, perhaps necessary, to a human being if he is to sustain his interests is hardly available outside of the context of a shared activity.

Secondly, where an activity is shared each of the participants finds himself engaged in a number of different ways and at a number of different points: to be sure, he participates directly only in the parts of the enterprise to which it falls to himself to contribute, but indirectly he is, in principle, involved in every stage of the process, whoever the direct agent may be. What others do as their share of the joint activity he experiences as his doing as well, insofar as he is a member of the group, and it is the group that is the agent primarily at work in it. Admittedly, in not all shared activities does every participant retain a very full sense of his own involvement in all the varied operations that go to make it up; but it follows from my characterization above of shared activities that in some degree this sense of extended participation must be present in any person who conceives of himself as engaging with others in a joint activity. One's involvement in what one is doing is thus much broader in a shared activity than it is in the case of a completely private one: there are, so to speak, many more places and types of contact with a shared activity than there can be for a private one. In a shared activity one's enjoyment, and so one's interest in what one is doing, is not limited just to what one directly does oneself. This fact has two consequences that support Aristotle's claims for shared activities. First, insofar as the agent sees his own personal activity as a contribution to a larger whole, to which he is attached and in which he is interested also through the contributions of others, the sources of his continued interest in what he directly does are much expanded. His multiple involvements in the whole activity naturally enhance the interest which he can take in the activities that he personally undertakes as a participant in the larger group activity. He is thus much more likely to sustain his interest in his own personal doings and to get pleasure continuously from them. Imagine, for example, some one who enjoys mathematics as a purely private exercise. Numerical relationships fascinate him, and he wants to spend a lot of time exploring them. Such a person is likely to neglect this pursuit after a time, and be only intermittently active at it; but if he comes to regard his activity as part of a larger group activity—so that he takes an interest not just in his own but also in others' research—he will be much more capable of sustaining his active interest in his own work because of its connection with the group activity of which he now sees it as part and in which he also has an interest. The tendency of anything long continued to become boring is thus avoided, to some extent, by finding in it additional things to be interested in. Secondly, insofar as he participates at second hand in the doings of others engaged with him in the shared activity he can be said to be active—indirectly—whenever and wherever any of the group is at work. In this sense one could say that a participant of a group activity is active even when he is not himself directly making any contribution. So, if one takes into account the activities that a participant is indirectly sharing in, one can say that those who engage in shared activities will continue to be active even when they are not directly active at all—that is, not active at all in the only way in which one can be active in a purely private pursuit.

Now I do not claim that these considerations were actually in Aristotle's mind when he said that it is easier to be continuously active with others and towards others than it is in isolation. His failure to explain why he held this view makes it impossible to say with certainty what his reasons were. On the other hand, it is hard to imagine what he could have meant if he did not have in mind at least some of these points. In any event I think the account I have just given does show that Aristotle's view, whatever exactly he may have rested it on, is sound. Shared activities are especially valuable for any human being since they, more than purely private activities, enable one to be continuously and happily engaged in things. This is so, in sum, for three reasons: (1) they provide one with an immediate and continuing sense that what one finds interesting and worthwhile is really so, since the experience of others is seen to agree with one's own in this respect; (2) they enhance one's attachment to and interest in one's own personal, direct activities by putting them within the context of a broader group activity which is itself a source of pleasure and interest; and (3) they expand the scope of one's activity by enabling one to participate, through membership in a group of jointly active persons, in the actions of others. It is reasonable, I think, to assume that human nature is inherently such that no human being can provide entirely from within himself the sources of his interest and pleasure in his life and the activities that make it up. Nothing can be made, as it were, automatically and continuously interesting for any human being, just because of what *it* is like. A human being has to invest things with his interest, by responding in appropriate ways to them; but these responses, though no doubt subjective, are not for that reason under one's own control. They depend in part upon the firm and continued sense of the value of what one is doing and, as Aristotle's argument plausibly suggests, this can hardly be secured except through the sense that others agree with one in this. If this is so, then I think one is entitled to infer, with Aristotle, that no life can be satisfactory for a human being that does not make explicit provision for a considerable range of activities shared with others. Only by merging one's activities and interests with those of others can the inherent fragility of any human being's interests be overcome.

Now this is obviously an extremely important conclusion to reach. But Aristotle must go even further, and hold, not just that shared activities, but that activities shared with friends, are a necessary ingredient in the flourishing human life, if he is to derive from his emphasis on the greater continuousness of shared activity a defense of friendship. For even if, as I have implied, the benefits to be derived from shared activities are in many cases dependent on one's esteeming or respecting the judgment of one's fellow participants, this does not mean they must be one's friends. At any rate one does not need to have character-friendship, which is the fundamental kind and the kind which Aristotle wishes to defend, with those with whom one enjoys playing games, or performing music, or, notoriously, having sex. On the other hand, it is clear enough that the satisfactions that derive from shared activity are especially needed in connection with those activities, whatever they may be, that are most central to a person's life and which contribute most decisively to his flourishing, as he himself conceives it. For here the flagging of one's commitments and interests will be particularly debilitating; here more than anywhere else one needs the confirmatory sense that others too share one's convictions about which activities are worthwhile, and the other benefits of sharing pointed out above. Now on Aristotle's theory of *eudaimonia* the flourishing human life consists essentially of morally and intellectually excellent activities. So the flourishing person will have a special need to share *these* activities, if his own interests in life are to be securely and deeply anchored. But according to the account of shared activities that I have given, it is an essential condition of a shared activity that the parties to it should not just be committed to the goal or goals that give the activity its sense, but should know about each other that they share this commitment. This requirement of mutual knowledge has substantial consequences where the activities to be shared include morally virtuous ones. For in order to know that some one is genuinely committed to moral values one must know him and his character pretty closely, since commitment here just is a matter of moral character or its absence. Superficial acquaintance is for this purpose quite insufficient, as it is not where there is question of some one's interest in music or baseball, because genuinely good moral character is what is required and this is not easily distinguished from feigned or half-hearted attachment. So before one can share activities where the common pursuit of moral values is essential to what is to be done, one must come to know, and be known by, the other party or parties quite intimately. But this sort of mutual knowledge is hardly available outside of character-friendship. Hence, a human being cannot have a flourishing life except by having intimate friends to whom he is attached precisely on account of their good qualities of character, and who are similarly attached to him: it is only with such persons that he can share the moral activities that are most central to his life.

It is possible, then, to defend both Aristotle's claim that shared activities are essential to any satisfactory human life, and his implied conviction that true friendship is a necessary context within which at least some of these essential shared activities should take place.

III

I conclude that there are to be found in the Aristotelian Corpus—and, if I am right about the purport of 1169*b*28 ff., in the *Nicomachean Ethics* itself—two interesting and telling arguments to show that true friendship is an essential constituent of a flourishing human life. If my interpretations are correct, Aristotle argues, first, that to know the goodness of one's life, which he reasonably assumes to be a necessary condition of flourishing, one needs to have intimate friends whose lives are similarly good, since one is better able to reach a sound and secure estimate of the quality of a life when it is not one's own. Secondly, he argues that the fundamental moral and intellectual activities that go to make up a flourishing life cannot be continuously engaged in with pleasure and interest, as they must be if the life is to be a flourishing one, unless they are engaged in as parts of shared activities, rather than pursued merely in private; and given the nature of the activities that are in question, this sharing is possible only with intimate friends who are themselves morally good persons.

Three points about these arguments should be noted. First, in a certain way they both emphasize human vulnerability and weakness. If human nature were differently constituted we might very well be immune to the uncertainties and doubts about ourselves that, according to Aristotle, make friendship such an important thing for a human being. As it is, we cannot, if left each to his own devices, reach a secure estimate of our own moral character; nor by ourselves can we find our lives continuously interesting and enjoyable, because the sense of the value of the activities which make them up is not within the individual's power to bestow. The sense of one's own worth is, for human beings, a group accomplishment. Hence we need each other because as individuals we are not sufficient—psychologically sufficient—to sustain our own lives. For a god things are different; the goodness of the divine activity of contemplation is continuously evident to a god, and he needs no other person or thing to enable him to see this or reassure him that it is so: as Aristotle says in the *Eudemian Ethics,* god is his own good activity, but human good consists in relationship to others *(hēmin men to ev kath'heterom ekeinōi de autos hautou to ev estin)*, 1245*b*18–19). To argue thus the need of human beings for friendship from deficiencies in our psychological makeup both illuminates the nature of friendship and gives what I think is an entirely accurate account of its status in human affairs. Properly understood, there is nothing in this that should be construed as undermining or detracting from the intrinsic goodness, for human beings, of friendly relations with others. For Aristotle's point is that the deficiencies which make friendship such a necessary and valuable thing are inherent in human nature itself. There is no basis in his argument for one to accept one's friendships in a regretful, still less a provisional, spirit—pining away, as it were, for the day when one's deficiencies might be made up and one could live entirely out of one's own resources without having to depend upon others at all. Since the deficiencies in question are essential to being a human being—that is, essential to being what one is, to being oneself—it is irrational to form one's attitudes in the hope of adjustments in these respects. The only reasonable attitude is to accept one's nature as it is and to live accordingly. The arguments we have considered profess to show how and why someone who adopts this attitude will be led to form friendships and to value friendly relations as fundamental and intrinsically good ingredients of the life that is best for himself.[18]

It is worth emphasizing that although in these arguments Aristotle defends the value of friendship only by showing that, for human beings, it is a necessary means to attaining certain broadly valuable psychological benefits, nothing in them commits him to denying that friendship is or involves anything intrinsically valuable. Indeed, in a few passages (1167*b*31–33 with 1168*a*5–9, and 1159*a*25–33), though they are not backed by much in the way of argument, Aristotle insists on the worthwhileness-in-itself of the active expression of love and on the direct pleasure that human beings take in the experience of being loved by others. These remarks are plainly not inconsistent with the arguments we have been examining, since there is no reason why something that is itself intrinsically good should not also be valued for other reasons. In fact, however, I think it is a mistake to see these two trains of thought even as separable, much less as competing, defenses of the place of friendship in a satisfactory human life. For, clearly, it does not follow from the mere fact that the active expression of love is found intrinsically good by human beings that a person who did not form friendships would be lacking something essential to his own good: there are lots of intrinsically good activities and no human life can, in any event, contain them all (see note 5 above). To show that the active expression of love is necessary in any satisfactory human life requires further argument establishing the fundamental importance of *this* intrinsically good activity vis-à-vis others with which it might compete for a place in a person's life. Again, and for the same reason, it does not follow from the fact that people delight in being loved that one who had all the other goods in life would still want and need the love of others. This claim could only be made good by further argument showing why, for human beings constituted as they actually are, *this* experience in particular is indispensable.[19] The arguments we have examined (and, in the *NE,* only these) attempt this essential task— which is why I have focussed principally on them. What they do is to characterize friendship from several points of view in such a way as to make it clear why human beings should find friendship and the activities and experiences that constitute it so interesting and valuable, in themselves, as they do. According to Aristotle, we value, and are right to value, friendship so highly because it is only in and through intimate friendship that we can come to know ourselves and to regard our lives constantly as worth living. It must be granted, of course, that someone who was so constituted that he could achieve these results without forming friendships, as Aristotle plausibly thinks no actual human being could, would have been given no strong reason to form them; he would at most have been told that the active expression of love is something intrinsically good and, as we have seen, this is no more than a prima facie, defeasible reason to form friendships. Hence anyone who thinks that, nonetheless, such a friendless person would be leading a less than fully satisfactory life will not find in Aristotle anything to support his view. It may be that such a view cannot be defended; but even if it can, I think it must be granted that Aristotle's arguments capture an important part of what there is in love and friendship that is so valuable for human beings.

Finally, this emphasis on the psychological benefits of friendship is not at all incompatible with the claim that, necessarily, a friend cares for and about another person's good in the same way in which that other person himself does so. If Aristotle is right, the psychological benefits he appeals to are not available to human beings unless one takes up the altruistic attitudes towards others which on his theory are essential to friendship. This is obviously true for the argument that only within the context of a friendship can one establish and maintain active interests that are sufficiently secure and constant so that a continuously active life can be constructed round them. This argument professes to show why one should want to become the sort of person who shares with others, on a basis of equality, his chief interests in life: the life of such a person, Aristotle argues, is more continuously active and interesting to him than anyone's life can be who lives in the sort of psychological isolation that the absence of friendship implies. But I think it is equally, though perhaps less obviously, true for his other argument, from the need for self-knowledge, as well. Admittedly, on this argument the benefit which accrues to a person from being someone else's friend is the firm sense that his own preferred activities are morally good. On the other hand, Aristotle's point is that this sense is only achievable insofar as one first and more distinctly recognizes the moral goodness of the similar life and similar activities of another person. This means that one must regard the association with one's friend, through which one first comes to know him and in which one constantly renews one's knowledge thereafter, as an association with someone who is objectively good and whose life is worthwhile in precisely the same sense as one's own. The motif of the friend as a mirror, which is indeed at best implicit in the *Nicomachean* argument, is not to be interpreted as meaning that on Aristotle's view a flourishing person treats his friend as a mere instrument by which to enhance his own self-esteem. On the contrary, this image implies that his self-esteem only gets the support he seeks insofar as he first has precisely the same esteem for the other person and his life, taken by itself, as he will come to have for himself and his own life. Aristotle's argument, in short, is that *in* loving and valuing the other person for his own sake one becomes able to love and value oneself, and this he offers in explanation and illumination of the fact that a friend loves and values his friend for his own sake, and places a high value on doing so. There is no reduction here of friendship to narrow self-love, nor, properly understood, does the need for self-knowledge emphasized in Aristotle's argument in any way undermine or render doubtful the recognition of the worth of the other person and his life which we think (and Aristotle emphasizes in his opening account of what friendship is) is essential to any relationship deserving of that name.[20]

Notes

I wish to thank Robert H. Bolton, G.J. Massey, Alexander Nehamas, Mae Smethurst and Charles M. Young for helpful comments on an early draft of this paper, and Richard Kraut for his forthright criticisms of a version of it read at a University of Minnesota conference on Aristotle's ethics held in March, 1976.

1. For a treatment of Aristotle's theory of what friendship is see my "Aristotle on the Forms of Friendship" (*Review of Metaphysics,* vol. 30, June, 1977).

2. For these (and other) essential conditions of friendship see "Aristotle on the Forms of Friendship" (n. 1 above).

3. The same contrast is found in the *EE.* The topic is introduced (1244*b*2–3) as follows: *aporēseie gar an tis poteron, ei tis eiē kata panta autarkēs, estai: toutōi philos.* Plainly, this question addresses itself to the need of the flourishing man to have friends in the first place. Yet here too, when he comes round to answering his question (*b*21 ff.) Aristotle apparently shifts his ground, and discusses instead why the man who has friends will spend time with them, etc.

4. See the footnote to 1170*b*19 in his translation (*The Works of Aristotle Translated into English,* Oxford: Clarendon Press 1915, vol. IX).

5. Alternatively, the argument might be interpreted as follows (I state just the main points): Everything that is good by nature is choiceworthy in itself, and everything choiceworthy in itself is worthy of the good man's choice. Furthermore, the good and happy man must possess everything that is worthy of his choice, since without even one of these things his life will be lacking in something it ought to have (cf. 1170*b*14–19). But association with people who are one's friends is by nature a good thing: this is so because in being aware of a friend and his activities one is, given that friends are "other selves," aware of one's self, and being aware of oneself is admittedly good by nature. Hence it will be worthy of a good man's choice to have a friend, and therefore he must have a friend if his life is to be completely fulfilled and lacking in nothing.

This argument is unsound. First, it is not true that the good person's life will be defective if he lacks any of the things that are good by nature and in themselves. No one can have all the things that are good in themselves; there are too many such things, and of too many distinct types (cf. my *Reason and Human Good in Aristotle,* Cambridge: Harvard University Press, 1975, pp. 129–130). Card games are good in themselves, but it does not follow that a person who never learns to play cards leads a less than flourishing life for that reason. If having friends truly is necessary to the flourishing life it must, then, be because friends are more than merely good in themselves to have. Secondly, even if it was granted, as perhaps it ought to be, that self-awareness is a sufficiently important good-in-itself to be a compulsory component of the flourishing life, it would still not follow that friends are a compulsory component of this life. To show that, one would have to show that self-awareness is only or best obtainable through the observation of one's friends, and (see below, p. 295) this does not seem true.

6. Despite the remarks of W.F.R. Hardie, *Aristotle's Ethical Theory* (Oxford: Clarendon Press, 1968), pp. 331 f. It is doubtless true, as Hardie points out, that Aristotle pays no attention in this argument to the fact that, however closely one may be attached to another person, one can never experience his thoughts and actions in just the way one experiences one's own. But it is not clear how this is supposed to matter to Aristotle's argument. It remains true

that friends do take interest in and derive pleasure from one another's thoughts and actions, and that the interest they take in them is akin to the interest they take in their own.

7. Nor is there a hint in this direction in the *EE* argument, 1244*b*23–1245*b*9.

8. *Notes on the Nicomachean Ethics* (Oxford: Clarendon Press, 1892), p. 392.

9. Translated by St. G. Stock (*The Works of Aristotle* . . . , vol. IX), except for the first sentence, which is taken from G. C. Armstrong's translation (Loeb Classical Library, *Aristotle,* vol. XVIII [Cambridge: Harvard University Press, 1935]).

10. Thus I concur with Gauthier in his judgment that "toute cette argumentation, prétendue plus profonde et qui n'est que plus laborieuse, tourne court" (R.-A. Gauthier and J. Y. Jolif, *Aristote: L'Ethique à Nicomaque,* Louvain and Paris: Publications Universitaires de Louvain, 1958, p. 693). Our reasons for this conclusion are, however, not the same.

11. It should be borne in mind here and in what follows that having a good character, on Aristotle's theory, requires not merely correct practical *judgments* (having a certain reasoned conception of how one ought to live) but also, and even more, having this conception embedded in one's desires and thereby making it effective in one's actions. Thus to know one is virtuous requires knowing (1) what the desires are that in fact motivate one's actions, and (2) that these desires depend upon the same scheme of ends as one's reasoned conception defines for one's life. And while it may not be hard to know what one's considered view of how to live is, and even that this view is the correct one, it is quite another, and much more difficult, thing to know what conception of how to live is embodied in the desires that actually motivate one's actions. In any event, it is essential to keep in mind that the self-knowledge required for flourishing is knowledge of what actually motivates one's actions, not just of what intellectualized theory of living one is prepared to defend.

12. For the theme of self-knowledge through examination of a reflection of the self in the mirror of another self, see Plato, *Alcibiades* I, 132*c*-133*c.* This passage may be the source of the *MM*'s analogy. In explicating the *MM*'s use of the analogy I have built especially on two features emphasized in the text. First, the good man is represented as looking at another person and his life in order to see a reflection of himself. And second, by observing this person's life he sees clearly what his own life is actually like: one cannot see what one is from oneself (1213*a*16), but one can see this, i.e., one can overcome this bias, by looking to another who is one's friend. The author plainly is not saying that one evades the effects of bias by trying to find out by observing from someone's behavior towards oneself what his opinion of one is. It is by observing *his* personal qualities, not by guessing his judgment of one's own, that one receives the sort of confirmation that is at issue here. And it is impossible to see how this can be supposed to happen unless, as in my expansion, one takes the knowledge acquired in looking at the "mirror" and refers it back to oneself: knowing that this other person has the same or very similar qualities to oneself (this follows from his being a true friend, one's "other self"), and having ob-

served that his character is virtuous, one now knows that one's own personal qualities are virtuous as well.

13. I translate *theōrein* here as "study" (instead of "see" or "observe" or "contemplate") in order to make it clear that Aristotle is saying something much stronger here than merely that the good man wants to be aware of good actions and takes pleasure in that. In this context *theōrein* is no mere equivalent of *aisthanestha:* as often in Aristotle, even where it implies the use of the senses, the word carries overtones of concentrated study, of the sort involved in theoretical knowledge (its other principal meaning in Aristotle). So neither of the two central claims of this argument is found in the later argument at 1170*a*13-*b*19; nor, for the same reason, is the further claim made here, that the good man enjoys (i.e., enjoys studying) the good actions of his friend, equivalent to the later claim that he enjoys (i.e., enjoys perceiving) them. If *MM* 1213*a*10-26 corresponds to anything in *NE* IX. 9 it must be to 1169*b*28–1170*a*4; certainly not to 1170*a*13 ff.

14. I take it that the clause in parentheses *(ho gar spoudaios . . . lupeitai)* is meant to explain why one should expect the morally good person to be continuously active. A morally good person enjoys virtuous action and (cf. 1175*a*30-36, *b*13-16) what one enjoys doing one tends to keep on doing; hence a virtuous person should tend to be continuously active when engaged in virtuous pursuits. But, as Aristotle has just pointed out, a solitary person cannot manage to be continuously active at anything. It follows that a solitary does not really enjoy anything very much. Hence the principle that virtuous action is pleasant for thc virtuous person must be understood as carrying with it the tacit assumption that such persons live their lives in social union with others.

15. Cf. 1170*b*10-14: "[The flourishing person] needs, therefore, to be conscious of his friend's existence, and this would come about in their living together and sharing in discussion and thought: for this would seem to be what living together means for human beings, and not, as for cattle, feeding in the same place." Evidently the solitariness Aristotle finds so debilitating is at least as much a matter of psychological as of physical isolation.

16. I owe this suggestion to Richard Kraut.

17. Throughout the discussion which follows I am indebted to a paper of Annette C. Baier's ("Intention, Practical Knowledge and Representation," presented at the May, 1975, Winnipeg Conference on Human Action and due to appear in *Action Theory,* ed. Myles Brand and Douglas Walton, forthcoming from D. Reidel), and to conversations with her.

18. Of the arguments of *NE* IX. 9 I have omitted to discuss the three found in 1169*b*8-22, since these, although they are put forward as supporting the view, which Aristotle himself favors, that a flourishing person needs friends, belong to the setting up of the dialectical problem and are not part of the solution to it. Strictly speaking, Aristotle's defense of his view is to be looked for not in these preparatory remarks, but in the official response which follows. (As usual, some aspects of the preliminary arguments are preserved in the solution.) I have omitted to discuss also the brief argument, which does form part of the solution Aristotle proposes, that by living together as friends good persons sharpen and train their moral sensibility (1170*a*11-13): this ought to

hold only, as indeed its source (Theognis) makes clear, for the association between a young and not fully formed person and someone older and morally more mature. It does not apply to all friendships, nor, apparently, to those that Aristotle wants most especially to defend, the friendships between equally good, fully developed persons.

19. Richard Kraut in "The Importance of Love in Aristotle's Ethics," available now from the *Philosophy Research Archives,* goes seriously astray in supposing that from these isolated remarks taken by themselves one can construct an adequate defense of the value of friendship (see sect. III of his paper, esp. p. 13, and further remarks at pp. 14, 16, 24). For the reasons noted in the text, they are quite inconclusive.

20. I am grateful to Michael Bratman for forcing me to clarify the argument of the last two paragraphs.

13

Feminism and Aristotle's Rational Ideal

Marcia L. Homiak

Several years ago, as part of a meeting of the Society for Women in Philosophy, I was asked, along with two other feminist philosophers working on canonical male figures in the history of philosophy, to participate in a panel entitled "What's a Nice Girl like Me Doing in a Place like This?" The title reflected the organizers' view that there was something politically suspect about feminists working on established male figures—and something particularly suspect in this case, where the three philosophers in question (Aristotle, Hobbes, and Kant) were well-known for their benighted views on women.[1] How could we reconcile our commitment to feminism with a scholarly life devoted to the study of philosophers who explicitly describe women as inferior to men, as unfit for the best life available to human beings, as incapable of being full moral agents?[2]

In addition to these long-acknowledged problems regarding women, there have recently come to be other difficulties associated with working on Aristotle, Hobbes, and Kant. With the growing interest in revising and reorganizing the "canon" of the humanities, so as to include works by and about not only women, but also non-Western and non-white peoples, devoting one's scholarly life to the study of Aristotle, Hobbes, and Kant seems to be an even more egregious departure from progressive values and ways of life. For the use and teaching of canonical works, which are predominantly white and male, has encouraged an ignorant and prejudiced view of works, writers, and subject matters outside the canon. Moreover, many of the values associated with canonical works have, historically, been used to denigrate and oppress women, nonwhite men, and the uneducated in general.[3] Thus teaching the works of the traditional canon has encouraged not only ignorance and elitism but also sexism and racism.

I have said that the values associated with the traditional canon have historically been used to denigrate women, nonwhite men, and the uneducated. One might think this historical fact renders these values themselves suspect. They may be thought skewed and incomplete or, worse yet, inherently Western, Eurocentric, or masculine. I want to explore one value in particular that is associated with most of Western philosophy and with much of the traditional humanistic canon. I am referring to the value of reason and to the value of exercising one's rational faculties. Aristotle, Kant, and Hobbes each recommends, as the best life available to human beings, a rational life, though each has a different view about what this life requires and includes. I shall discuss only Aristotle's views on these matters, and I shall argue that his picture of the rational life is neither inherently masculine nor inherently exploitative. Instead, I shall claim, his ideal is worthy of emulation by both women and men.

Ethical systems that promote rationality as an ideal have recently come under considerable criticism from feminist scholars. Much of this criticism has been influenced by Carol Gilligan's work comparing girls' and boys' ways of reasoning about ethical questions.[4] In her work *In a Different Voice,* for example, Gilligan suggests that males and females have, in general, different orientations or perspectives toward moral values and moral strategies. Women tend to adopt a "care" perspective, in which what matters to them is the preservation of relationships and connection with others; men tend to adopt a "justice" perspective, in which what matters is acting on impartial and universalizable principles. Since relationships are matters of intimacy and personal feeling, the care perspective is associated with a focus on emotion, especially on the altruistic emotions. Since impartial and universalizable principles are a result of reasoned reflection about what to do, where such reflection is carried out without the distractions of emotion and without a prejudiced concern for one's own interests or the interests of specific others, the justice perspective is associated with rationality and with the value of one's status as a rational being capable of such reflection.[5]

Thus the basis of the feminist criticism of rational ideals is that such ideals, in their application to moral questions, ignore the role of emotion and of the nonuniversalizable particularity of human life.[6] But these domains, of emotion and of specific and particular relationships, are the domains historically associated with women. Hence, the rational ideal suggests that the concerns most typical of women's lives are irrelevant to the best human life and to reasoning about what to do. Lawrence Blum has described the type of philosopher whom Gilligan's work has been used to attack, the type Blum calls the "moral rationalist": "It is the male qualities whose highest expression he naturally takes as his model. In the same way it is natural for him to ignore or underplay the female qualities as they are found in his society— sympathy, compassion, emotional responsiveness. . . . The moral rationalist philosopher thus both reflects the sexual value hierarchy of his society and indirectly gives it a philosophic grounding and legitimation."[7] Not only are the concerns of women irrelevant to the rational ideal but they also may be thought to be incompatible with it. If that is so, then the rational ideal suggests that women are not capable of living moral lives.

In effect, the rational ideal suggests that the best human life and a moral life is available only to those who engage in the kind of rational reflection necessary to determine properly how to live. We have seen how such an ideal tends to exclude women's concerns from the moral life, or women themselves from the moral life, if women are thought incapable of the necessary rational reflection. As I have mentioned, the rational ideal can also be taken to exclude other persons whose lives tend not to be associated with the rational. In Aristotle's view, for example, menial laborers are not fit to be citizens of the best state, since Aristotle believes that menial labor is a deterrent to engaging in the rational activity characteristic of human beings. More broadly, the rational ideal can be taken to exclude persons who have been associated with the body and bodily functions rather than with rational activity, however rational activity is to be understood. Oppressive stereotypes of "inferior" peoples have tended to include images of their lives as determined by what is animal or bodily. This is a way in which the rational ideal can support prejudiced views of nonwhites and uneducated people.

But the fact that the rational ideal has been, or can be, used to exclude particular groups from that ideal does not show that the rational ideal is defective. Even assuming one could establish that particular groups actually possessed the characteristics on which their exclusion was based—for example, that they were more "physical" or more "compassionate"[8]—one would have to show that their having these characteristics is incompatible with the rational ideal. And even if it could be shown that having these characteristics is incompatible with living according to the rational ideal, *that* would not be sufficient to show that the rational ideal is suspect or even that it is incomplete. The problem might lie, instead, with the way these "non-rational" characteristics are being understood. It is possible that, upon examining them carefully, they may not be found worthy of emulation. The rational ideal may emerge as a more attractive model after all.

I want to examine Aristotle's picture of the rational ideal, and to explore its worthiness to serve as a model for a good human life, by looking at three groups that fail, in Aristotle's opinion, to embody the rational ideal. These groups are menial laborers, slaves, and women of varying political status. Once we see how these people fail to embody the rational ideal, we can understand more clearly what we are committed to in living according to that ideal. Then we will be in a better position to determine whether Aristotle's rational ideal is incompatible with the traits of character typically associated with women (for example, with being more caring, more compassionate, more altruistic) and whether it is incompatible with a more "physical" or "bodily" life.

I shall argue that his ideal is not incompatible with being altruistic or with performing physical labor. But, I shall claim, if altruistic traits of character and physical work are not themselves to become oppressive, they must include precisely the activities Aristotle describes as rational. I shall treat the compatibility between the rational ideal and physical work relatively briefly, since the main focus of my concern is the relationship between caring for another and being rational, as Aristotle understands it. On the view I shall propose, being caring and compassionate must be expressed within a life lived according to the rational ideal, or else these traits become destructive and unhealthy. To explicate destructive care, I use examples of contemporary women's lives, since they are often structured so as to preclude women from exercising the rational activities Aristotle most valued. Thus some of Aristotle's reservations about women's lives are sustained, though not, of course, for the reasons he offered. If my interpretation of the rational ideal is correct, and the activities Aristotle considers rational are critical components of a nonoppressive life, then we have good reason to embrace his ideal rather than to reject it.

Psychological Freedom in Aristotle's Ideal State

Aristotle recognizes different sociopolitical classes or categories of women and men. These classes are ordered along a spectrum that reflects the different degrees to which individuals have realized the capacities and traits characteristic of human beings, where these capacities and traits are understood to be rational. To the extent that one fails fully to realize these capacities and traits, one fails to be fully human. At the extreme end of this socio-political spectrum, some individuals—namely (natural) slaves—aren't really human beings at all and hence are not women and men, properly speaking.[9] Because they lack crucial rational characteristics, Aristotle thinks they can justifiably be treated differently from other individuals who more completely realize human capacities and traits. There is, in effect, a hierarchical ordering of different human natures, according to which those who completely realize their human nature rule all those who do not or cannot.

In Aristotle's ideal state there are three broad categories of men: citizens; free persons who are not citizens, including artisans, tradesmen, and day laborers[10] (for the sake of convenience, I shall refer to these persons simply as menial or manual laborers); and persons who are neither free nor citizens (slaves). Male citizens spend the major portion of their adult lives in democratic decision-making (after serving in the military when young and before becoming priests when too old). (*Politics* [hereafter *Pol.*] 1329a2–34). They are members of the assembly, members of juries, city officials of various kinds, and so on. They take turns ruling and being ruled (*Pol.* 1332b26–27; 1295b14–27). Ruling is the activity that distinguishes these men from other groups of men in the political community. The suggestion is that through participatory democracy with other citizens like themselves, they alone fully realize their characteristic human rational capacities and traits. These rational powers, associated with the rational part of the soul (*Nicomachean Ethics* [hereafter *EN*] 1139a12), consists of deciding, choosing, discriminating, judging, planning, and so forth (*EN* 1170b10ff.).[11]

Menial laborers should not, according to Aristotle, be citizens in the best state, presumably because menial labor, in Aristotle's view, impedes the full exercise of one's rational powers (cf. *Pol.* 1277b2–6; 1278a20–21). How is this so? (i) One answer might be that menial labor involves much routine and monotonous work, in which little use is made of choosing, judging, deciding, and discriminating. There is little room for the personal style and self-expression that characterize more interesting and challenging activity. But obviously this need not always be the case. Though the sculptor Pheidias counts as a menial laborer, his work involves highly sophisticated decision-making and discrimination. If his doing manual labor impedes the full expression of his rational powers, it must do so in some other way. (ii) We must consider not only the work Pheidias does but also the conditions under which he does it. Like other menial laborers, Pheidias's decision-making powers are constrained by his need to survive. He must travel to the cities where his skills are needed, and the building projects he oversees must fit the constraints imposed by city officials or private citizens. The exercise of his rational powers is limited by, and therefore dependent upon, other people's decisions and desires. In this way he does not have complete control over his own decisions and actions.

This lack of control is evidenced in at least two ways. First, the fact that Pheidias's decisions and actions are constrained by his need to earn a living may require him to compromise his moral principles. He may be "compelled" by his superiors (cf. *EN* 1110a25) to act in ways he would not ordinarily choose. His actions are then a combination of the voluntary and the involuntary (*EN* 1110a11–19). Second, even if Pheidias is not required to take "mixed" actions (*EN* 1110a11), the fact that his decisions and actions are constrained by the desires of others means that he cannot fully express his conception of what is worth sculpting, how it is to be done, and so on. He cannot design and direct the project according to his own ideas of what is interesting and important. He must accommodate his creations to the values of others.[12]

In Aristotle's view, then, the citizen and the menial laborer (in contrast to the citizen and the slave) have the same psychological capacities. What distinguishes them are the circumstances under which they choose and decide. The menial laborer does work that often does not require much decision-making. More important, however, is the fact that the laborer's concern for economic survival constrains his decision-making, in that he does not have complete control over what work he is to do and how it is to be accomplished. On the other hand, a natural slave, in Aristotle's view lacks the very capacity for deliberation and decision (*Pol.* 1260a12). So, presumably, if he were not a slave, he would not be able to control his own life even to the extent that a menial laborer can. A slave acts wholly in the interests of another person; this is why he is not free (*Pol.* 1278b32–37). To the extent that a manual laborer lacks control over his life and must act in accordance with what others desire and require of him, his life is slavish (*Rhetoric* 1367a32–33).

Indeed, to the extent that any person's life is not the product of his own decisions and desires and is overly or improperly dependent on the desires, decisions, and opinions of other people, Aristotle deems that person's life slavish. In the *Nicomachean Ethics,* for example, Aristotle is able to say of various nonvirtuous male citizens in nonideal states that their lives are slavish. Of course, it is difficult to be precise about what constitutes "too much" or the "wrong kind" of dependence on others' decisions and desires. Surely every person who is not self-sufficient is dependent on others' actions and decisions. But many forms of dependence that arise from the absence of self-sufficiency are innocuous in that they do not undermine one's status as a rational being. I may not be able to fulfill my desire for hazelnut ice cream if there is no one to make it available to me; however, because I do not produce it myself and must rely on others to do so does not render me unable to make the sorts of decisions that serve to realize my specific rational abilities or the rational abilities I share with other rational beings. What Aristotle wants to avoid, and which he thinks only the virtuous person successfully avoids, is the kind of dependence on others that impedes, rather than encourages and extends, the full realization of one's rational abilities.

Let me illustrate with some examples from the *Nicomachean Ethics.* Aristotle tells us that the inirascible person is slavish in that he is willing to accept insults to himself and to overlook insults to his family and associates (*EN* 1126a7–8). He does not have enough self-esteem to allow himself to get angry at others' ill treatment of himself, his family, and his friends. He lacks confidence in his own judgments and perceptions and will have a tendency to accept the judgments and perceptions of others as correct. Hence, he is apt to allow others to make decisions for him. Flatterers are another example of servile persons (1125a2). They want to improve their position by gaining the favor of more privileged people (*EN* 1127a7–9). To do this, they must accept the correctness of the privileged person's desires and decisions, and thus they must accept a situation in which many of their decisions are, in effect, made for them by others. Flatterers and inirascible people are in a psychological situation analogous to that of skilled menial laborers like Pheidias.

Aristotle describes intemperate people as slavish too, but not because others make decisions for them. Indeed, intemperates may control their lives in just the ways that inirascible people and flatterers do not. They may make their own decisions, and they may be able to implement their decisions without having to accommodate others' preferences and interests. But they misuse their rational powers and undermine their development in that the activities they enjoy make too little use of these powers. Intemperate people enjoy physical sensations rather than the discriminating and choosing that surrounds tasting and touching (*EN* 1118a32–b1). Their psychological situation is like that of menial laborers whose work is routine and monotonous. There is so little decision-making going on that even natural slaves, who lack the powers of deliberation and decision, can experience the intemperate person's enjoyments (*EN* 1177a7).

In contrast to these various slavish types is the male citizen of Aristotle's ideal state. He is different even from a Pheidias who has full control over the specific sculptural projects he is engaged in. On Aristotle's view, not even such a Pheidias would have fully realized his powers of choosing and deciding. The male citizens of Aristotle's ideal state fully realize their characteristic human powers in the political activity of democratic decision-making. They realize their human powers fully in these circumstances because the deliberations involved in democratic decisionmaking are comprehensive and overarching. Here the exercise of the human powers is not restricted to specific decisions about what statues to sculpt, what materials to use, and so on. Rather, these are higher-level decisions about what is best for the community itself. So they would include decisions about other, more specific activities (cf. *EN* 1094a27). The exercise of the human powers is *generalized* and extended to cover virtually every aspect of human life, including, for example, questions of war and peace, finance, legislation, public works, cultural projects, and sexual matters.[13]

As far as men are concerned, then, we can determine a ranking from the complete human being who is able to actualize his powers fully because he is a politically active citizen of the ideal state, to a slave who cannot actualize the characteristic human powers because he is without them to begin with. In between are various types of incomplete, slavish persons, ranging from wealthy aristocrats (in nonideal states) to manual laborers.

What about the women who are the wives or companions of these different men, the wives of free citizens in the ideal state, the wives of free citizens in nonideal states, the wives of manual laborers, and the female companions of slaves? (I do not discuss unmarried daughters, since, for our purposes, their situations will not differ markedly from those of married women and married female slaves.)

Although Plato seems to have had moderately progressive views about some women (namely, those he thought capable of ruling the state),[14] Aristotle's views on women's nature are, without exception, objectionable. Aristotle claims that free women cannot be fully actualized human beings, no matter what their political status, since they are, like slaves, naturally defective. Although free women do not lack the capacity for deliberation and decision, as slaves do, their capacity for deliberation, Aristotle says, is not "authoritative" (*Pol.* 1260a13). Women are contrasted with (presumably male, free) children, whose deliberative capacities are merely "incomplete" (*ateles, Pol.* 1260a14). The deliberative capacity in women, then, we may assume, is permanently stunted. Unlike free, male children, no amount of education and practice in decision-making, and no change in their economic or social circumstances, will enable women to deliberate properly about what is best. They may give too much weight to what is pleasant or to what appears to be good. In effect, a woman may give over the rule of her soul to its non-rational part and thereby endanger the proper functioning of the household (cf. 1254b4ff.).[15] Hence, decisions about what is best must be made for her by men. A free woman's life will always, then, be slavish, since her life is not controlled by her own decisions.

Because natural slaves lack one of the features characteristic of human beings, they cannot, strictly speaking, be human beings, and hence they cannot be women or men—that is, they cannot be adult members of the human species. (I say they cannot "strictly speaking" be human beings, because it seems clear that Aristotle be *EN* 1161a34ff., where Aristotle admits that there can be friendship and justice between masters and slaves "to the extent that a slave is a human being."[16]) But despite this species difference between free persons and slaves, it is hard to see the extent to which the life of any free woman is relevantly different, in regard to her departure from the ideal of fully realized human being, from that of a slave (male or female). Although a free woman presumably can deliberate about how best to carry out the decisions of her husband, or father, her actions are ultimately determined by the decisions of free men, as are those of slaves. Perhaps this is why Aristotle does not bother to discuss female slaves in any detail. As far as their legal status is concerned, it is the same as that of male slaves. As far as their psychological status is concerned, it seems no different, relative to the ideal, from that of free women.

Is Aristotle's Ideal Exploitative or Musculine?

I have sketched a view of psychological freedom in Aristotle, according to which a complete human being is one who fully realizes his characteristically human powers (the powers of judging, choosing, deciding, planning, discriminating, and so on) in the political activity of democratic decision-making. Democratic decision-making is characterized by a political structure that is egalitarian (each citizen participates equally in decision-making) and comprehensive (each citizen participates equally in the same, broad type of decision-making). Citizens participate in decisions about matters that fundamentally affect the course of their lives. These higher-level decisions influence the lower-level decisions individuals make about the specific life-plans they pursue (cf. *EN* 1094a27).

Two questions arise about the life Aristotle admires and recommends. First, does the realization of this ideal life *require* that some segments of the political community exploit the labor of other segments so that they (the exploiters) have time for the decision-making involved in ruling? And, second, is this ideal life inherently masculine? If we answer either question affirmatively, we have good reason to reject Aristotle's recommendations. I think there is a fairly straightforward response to the first question. I shall indicate that briefly here.[17] Most of my attention will be directed to the second question.

Aristotle believes that the realization of the life he admires does require that rulers exploit menial laborers, since he believes that the conditions under which menial labor is performed will involve the laborer in relations of dependence that prevent the full actualization of the rational powers. Hence, rulers cannot be menial laborers. As I have suggested, Aristotle is not crazy to believe this. But it is important to distinguish between a menial life (a life whose main activity is menial labor performed under conditions of dependence) and a life that may involve menial labor but is not restricted to it. Aristotle may be correct to think that a life restricted to menial labor (where such labor can be monotonous, routine, exhausting, and carried out for the sake of an end external to it—housework is a good modern example) will demand little use of the human rational powers and will impede the development of the type of character one needs to exhibit the moral virtues. But surely he would not be correct to think that engaging in some menial labor, as part of a life that is devoted to the full expression of the rational powers, will have a devastating effect upon character. Indeed, as he notes at *Pol.* 1333a9–11: "Actions do not differ as honorable or dishonorable in themselves so much as in the end and intention of them."[18] Just as citizens take turns ruling and being ruled, then, they could take their turns at menial labor, while preserving for themselves the type of life that Aristotle considers fully human. Thus, as far as I can tell, the best kind of life, from Aristotle's point of view, does not require, even given his views about the dangers of menial labor, that some persons take up lives of menial labor to provide the necessities for others who live political lives.[19]

I have considered whether the ideal described by Aristotle is necessarily exploitative. I have argued that if citizens determine how the menial labor is to be carried out, they will not involve themselves in the dehumanizing relations of dependence Aristotle found so objectionable. And if the menial labor is distributed among the citizens in ways so as not to absorb much of any one citizen's time, then there is no reason to think that the possible monotony of some menial labor will impede the continuing exercise of the human rational powers.

One point should perhaps be emphasized. Aristotle's citizens enjoy the complete exercise of the human rational powers that participation in ruling provides. Therefore they want to avoid both the slavishness of a menial life and the slavishness of a Pheidian life. For, as we have seen, Pheidias's life, though involving sophisticated and subtle uses of the human powers, remains seriously limited and incomplete. Just as Aristotle is not crazy to think that a life of routine menial labor is incompatible with his rational ideal, so too he is not crazy to think that a "physical" life of the Pheidian type is also defective and incomplete. But this does not commit Aristotle to the view that physical activity itself is dehumanizing. There is nothing to prevent Aristotle's democratic decision-makers from being artisans and tradespeople, as well as farmers and warriors.

I now consider the second issue I raised above—that is, the issue of whether Aristotle's ideal is masculine, and, if so, whether this is reason to reject it. I take it that the ideal is considered masculine because the life considered most worth living is the life in which the characteristic human powers, considered as rational powers, are fully realized. Since, as I suggested at the outset, reason and rational deliberation have, in the history of Western thought, been associated primarily with men, and since the non-rational (which includes passions, emotions, and feelings, all of which are thought to have some relation to the body) have been associated with women, to recommend a way of life that praises and prizes reason over all else is implicitly at least to denigrate what has traditionally been associated with women. And, historically, to accept a view that prizes and praises reason above all else provides room not only for sexist views but also for racist views—views that denigrate other peoples because they have traditionally been thought more bodily or more physical than white males. Indeed, we have seen this tendency to be true of Aristotle, whose view of slaves and women as less than fully rational enables him to justify their low status in the political community.

I want to consider whether Aristotle's view of the rational, in particular, requires a devaluation of the non-rational side of the human being. This might be true if his view were a simple one, in which reason "rules" in some straightforward way over the passions, emotions, and feelings. But his view is not simple. I shall suggest, instead, that in Aristotle's virtuous person, the proper development of the nonrational side of the person can be seen to constrain and limit the operations of the rational side. In effect, it is as if to say that the rational part of the virtuous person's soul cannot work properly unless it is properly guided by the non-rational part.

Both Plato and Aristotle insist that the non-rational part of the soul (which includes appetites, feelings, emotions, and passions) must be educated—in the case of Plato, before one can begin to think sufficiently abstractly ultimately to see the Form of the Good, and, in the case of Aristotle, before one can learn how to deliberate properly about the contents of the best life (before, that is, one can acquire practical wisdom). For Aristotle, many of the individual virtues involve feeling or responding in the appropriate way. For example, it is a vice to take too much pleasure in eating, drinking, and sexual activity; it is also a vice to take insufficient pleasure in these activities. It is a vice to get too angry, or angry at the wrong times, or angry toward the wrong persons, and so on. But it is also a vice not to get angry or to exhibit anger at all, or not to do so when the situation is appropriate for anger./ It is a vice to feel too much fear or not enough, or to feel it on the wrong occasions or toward the wrong persons. Reason, by itself, cannot create these feelings; nor can reason, by itself, destroy them. If reason could create or destroy feelings, then Aristotle would not be faced with the problem of *akrasia* (*EN* VII.1–3). Thus the first things to note about Aristotle's rational ideal are that it does not involve the suppression of feeling and emotion and passion and that if reason does rule over passion, its rule does not consist either in producing or in destroying passion. Nor does it consist simply in offering some general directives to the non-rational side of the soul, since there are no rules or rational guidelines for determining how much of an emotion or feeling is appropriate in different situations (*EN* 1109b21–24).

More important, however, is the psychological basis for all the different virtues. I have argued elsewhere[20] that they can be viewed as expressions of what Aristotle calls true self-love. The virtuous person is characterized by a love of what is most himself—that is, by a love of the exercise of the human rational powers, where these are the powers of judging, choosing, deciding, and discriminating that I have listed before (*EN* 1168b34–1169a3; cf. 1168a7–9 and 1170b10ff.). In enjoying the exercise of his rational powers, the true self-lover enjoys rational activity in general rather than a particular kind of rational activity. His life is therefore broadly based; it is not devoted to the pursuit of specialized goals or to the completion of specialized projects. The true self-lover enjoys the intricacies and subtleties of different intellectual endeavors and also the intricacies and subtleties of endeavors not considered intellectual: he enjoys playing, or watching, a good game of baseball or tennis; he delights in telling a story others will appreciate or in finding just the right gift for a special occasion; he enjoys pleasing and benefiting his friends.

In loving what is characteristic of himself, the virtuous person enjoys who he is and what he can do. His self-love is thus a kind of self-esteem and self-confidence. But as my examples of self-expression have indicated, true self-love is to be distinguished from the self-love that we associate with selfishness and that we normally condemn (*EN* IX.8). Given that the virtuous person enjoys rational activity in a general way, he is able to take pleasure both from the exercise of his own rational powers and from others' exercise of these powers.

The self-love Aristotle admires becomes even more generalized and more stable when a person exercises the human rational powers in political activity where decision-making is shared and evenly distributed. Self-love is more generalized because its source, the exercise of the human rational powers, is now extended to cover comprehensive, higher-level decisions, as well as decisions about activities specific to one's own life. And because the decision-making has been extended in this way, it is flexible and less vulnerable to changes in circumstance and fortune than a more specialized exercise of rational activity would be. Democratic decision-makers can adjust to changes in circumstance and can redirect the use of their abilities to meet these changes. Hence the more stable and continuous their self-esteem will be. But for someone whose decision-making powers have been focused on a particular activity, self-esteem is tied to the success of that particular activity. Hence, this person's self-esteem is precarious and easily upset. This person is like Aristotle's professional soldiers who, though (improperly) confident from past success, turn and run when circumstances are against them (*EN* 1116b15–17).

The enjoyment that a person takes in who he is and in what he does, though its source and basis is the exercise of the rational powers, is not itself an instance of such exercise. Although enjoyment may be produced by rational deliberation, the pleasure taken in rational deliberation, like the enjoyment we take in any other activity, is non-rational. This affects the extent to which my enjoyment can be altered by rational deliberation, even if rational deliberation is what I enjoy and even if that deliberation produces *rational desires* for what I enjoy. When, for example, I want to play tennis because I enjoy it, I desire to play because I find it pleasant, not because I believe playing tennis is good for my health. In this sense, my desire to play tennis is non-rational. I might also want to play tennis because I think it is good for my health, and I might have reached this conclusion on the basis of deliberation about what conduces to my good overall. The desire to play tennis that arises from such deliberation is therefore rational, and it can be altered by further such deliberation. If I cease to believe that playing tennis is good for my health, I will cease to *want* to play tennis for that reason. My newly acquired beliefs produce a rational aversion to tennis. But no such deliberations will undermine my general non-rational desire to play tennis. If I somehow come to believe (correctly) that I no longer enjoy playing tennis, my having that belief is an indication that I have already stopped liking tennis. In this case, my beliefs do not produce my non-rational aversion. It comes about in some other way. The same holds for my non-rational enjoyment of rational activity itself, which, on Aristotle's view, accounts for my having self-love.

On the assumption, then, that Aristotle's virtues require self-love and that they can be understood as different ways in which self-love is expressed, being virtuous is importantly a matter of having one's non-rational desires properly structured. Without the appropriate background of non-rational desire, the agent will not perceive correctly the nature of situations calling for practical decision and action and will thus respond in ways that Aristotle describes as non-virtuous rather than virtuous. Aristotle's notoriously vague remarks at *EN* 1144a34–36 are consistent with the idea that the structure of one's non-rational desires crucially affects one's ability to perceive practical situations correctly: "[The highest end and the best good] is apparent only to the good person; for vice perverts us and produces false views about the origins of actions."

There is a second aspect to the role of the non-rational desires in Aristotle's conception of virtue. The enjoyment taken in the expression of the human powers in cooperative democratic activity not only produces a stable self-confidence; it also produces stable feelings of friendship between the parties involved in the decision-making. Feelings of friendship arise from the fact that the democratic activity is self-expressive, that it is beneficial to the parties engaged in it, and that it is itself enjoyable (*Rhet.* 1381a30 and *EN* 1168a7–9). Friendship includes a care and concern that friends have for each other for each other's own sake (*EN* 1155b31), a tendency to rejoice and take pleasure in each other's good fortune, and a tendency to help when friends need assistance (*EN* IX.4). Feelings of friendship are maintained over time by continuing the activities that originally produced them or the comparable activities that have come to sustain them. Like enjoyment itself, friendly feelings are not produced by beliefs about what is best or about what contributes to my overall good. They thus belong to the non-rational part of the soul.

In the case of democratic decision-making, the relevant feelings of friendship are particularly stable. A combination of factors explains why this is so. First, the feelings of friendship are produced by a form of self-expression that is especially enduring in that it is overarching and generalized. They are not the product of the expression of some contingent features of the self that might disappear in a change of circumstance or fortune. Hence, the friendship is not "coincidental" and easily dissolved (*EN* 1156a14–21). Second, the democratic decision-makers share their most basic values and goals in that they are committed to engaging in cooperative activities that promote and sustain the development and exercise of the human powers (cf. *Pol.* 1280a31–34). Thus each decision-maker can view the deliberations of the others as expressions of his thinking and reasoning self (*EN* 1168b34–1169a3). Deliberators identify with each other's decisions and actions, so that each deliberator's actions become the expression of the others' rational activity. This form of self-expression, now even more generalized, is especially enduring. Citizens in the ideal state are thus tied together by feelings of friendship that are long lasting and strong.

The care, concern, and sympathetic attachment that partly constitute these ties of friendship encourage a healthy dependence among citizens. Citizens are not uninvolved with each other or contemptuous of each other in the way several of Aristotle's vicious types are (*EN* IV.3). Nor are they overly concerned with others' opinions—that is, concerned in a way that would upset their self-esteem if they were to face criticisms or obstacles. Their concern for each other does not produce a self-destructive dependence; their autonomy does not preclude enduring ties of association. Along with the self-love of virtuous citizens, these ties of friendship will influence what citizens perceive to be central to the type of life they want to maintain. They will not act to jeopardize the activities and relationships they value and enjoy.

In summary, citizens' understanding of what is best to do, their rational deliberations about how to live and act, take place within the limits imposed by educated passions and feelings. They take place within the limits imposed by a stable self-esteem that derives from an enjoyment in rational activity and within the limits imposed by strong ties of friendship that involve care and concern for other citizens for their own sakes. If this is a rational ideal, it is one in which the proper operation of reason is guided and constrained by feeling and emotion, that is, by the non-rational side of the soul.

Feminism and Reason

I have argued that Aristotle offers a picture of a rational ideal that does not exclude the emotions, passions, and feelings. In particular, the proper operation of reason is limited and constrained by the specific feelings constitutive of true self-love and civic friendship. In describing this ideal, I have not discussed the nature of the actual deliberations virtuous persons will make in specific practical contexts. But it is reasonable to suppose that virtuous persons will recognize the importance of producing and sustaining true self-love and stable ties of civic friendship that are based on enduring features of the self. When citizens come to decide how best to govern their city, these values, one would think, would be paramount in their deliberations. Specific decisions would be made with a commitment to, and appreciation of, the critical role these values play in the lives of every citizen. This does not mean that all civic decisions will be made from an "impartial" perspective, where that is taken to imply that a consideration of the specific circumstances of particular individuals is inappropriate. Nor does it mean that deliberating from such a perspective is never appropriate.

I now want to discuss in more detail the nature of the care and concern I have attributed to Aristotle's virtuous citizens. For it is "care and concern" that have come to be associated with feminist ethics and women's moral experience, where such care includes an interest in preserving relationships and commitments to others. In feminist ethics, an interest in applying impartial rules or comprehensive principles becomes secondary.

Assuming it is true that women's moral experiences focus more on questions of care and on preserving relationships and commitments, ought we to accept these experiences as a general model for our behavior toward others or as a more specific model of our moral behavior? What type of care and concern is appropriate? Is care and concern always to be preferred over more emotionally detached ways of relating to others?[21]

The care and concern that constitutes a virtuous citizen's friendship with other citizens resembles in important ways the care that Aristotle's "complete friends" have for each other. Complete friends, according to Aristotle, are virtuous, know each other well, and spend much of their time together in shared activities (*EN* IX.10). As a result, it is not possible to have many complete friends, whereas political (or citizen) friendship holds among many. Yet, even though citizen friendship and complete friendship have different characteristics, it is not hard to see a resemblance between them in regard to the care that the friends extend toward each other. For though citizen friends may not know each other to the extent that complete friends do, and though they might not spend much time together, they know each other well enough to know that they share the major aims and values that guide the decisions and practices of their community. Citizen friends perceive each other as Aristotle's complete friends do, that is, as "another oneself" (*EN* 1166a32), meaning that they value and enjoy about each other what they value and enjoy about themselves. They take pleasure, for example, in the exercise of each other's rational powers as they do in their own. In this way they are like each other and take enjoyment in the exercise of the powers they share. Each is, then, a self-lover who takes pleasure in the self-love of the other, since the exercise of self-love in one is like the exercise of self-love in the other. Their ties of friendly feeling are firm and strong and long lasting because they are grounded in the pleasure they take in who the other is as a realized human being.

The care and concern they have for each other comes from the affection that arises from their sharing in each other's rational activity.

That is, they share over-arching and higher-level interests and goals, and they each participate in the activities associated with these higher-level interests. This does not mean that they share each specific interest and desire.[22] The contents of their individual life-plans might be surprisingly divergent. But each has an individual plan that realizes the human powers in a specific way, and this fact is a source of enjoyment for them. So each takes an interest in the other's interests, rejoices in the other's successes, grieves with the other's losses, and so on.

None lives through the lives of the others or acquires a basis for self-esteem and self-confidence through the activities of the others. Each is independent in the sense that each enjoys the activities in her individual life-plan as well as the higher-level activities her plan shares with the plans of her friends. None is dependent on the praise and admiration of specific individuals for the maintenance of self-love, so each can endure the loss of particular friendships. Aristotle's citizens are likely to be involved in a number of relationships, since their shared general commitments and goals give them a basis for association and affection. Their emotional eggs are not all in one basket, and hence their sense of their own value and importance is not undermined by the loss of specific relationships.

The care they extend to others, then, in times of difficulty and need, is not likely to involve a sacrifice of what they take to be valuable for the sake of someone else. Care does not take the form of altruistic action, where this is thought to require self-denial or a willingness to meet another's needs without consideration for one's own. Thus, among Aristotle's citizens, one would not find relations of unhealthy dependence in which some gain a sense of their own worth only through the assistance they give to others.[23]

But in our contemporary, non-Aristotelian socioeconomic circumstances, women who live with men are often in precisely this position of unhealthy dependence in regard to them. Given the still prevailing ideology, which does not consider it deplorable that most employed women have low-paying, dead-end jobs and even that some women choose to remain unemployed, women tend to find themselves in positions of low self-esteem. Even if they are employed, they are usually economically dependent on men.[24] This dependence undermines the realization of their decision-making powers in various ways. Important family decisions, for example, are often left up to the men on whom women depend. Even women's decision-making authority over matters connected with child care and household maintenance is upset by the extent to which the market has successfully penetrated the household. Many household decisions are now made for women by men through commercials in which men promote one product or another. Women are thought to be good (that is, easily manipulated) consumers, and most commercials are directed toward women, because women often lack the self-esteem necessary to make their own decisions about how to provide the proper physical environment for their families.[25]

These problems apply to the emotional environment as well. In the context of unequal economic power, whatever care and compassion is extended to family members is likely to be distorted and unhealthy. Since family relationships are often the only means through which women obtain a sense of their own worth, preserving these relationships may take place at the cost of encouraging psychologically harmful ways of treating family members. Care within the context of unequal power relations can generate more harm than good.

In such circumstances, where the preservation of a relationship may take priority over the content of the relationship, kindness and emotional supportiveness may be offered when other emotional responses might be more appropriate. Women in these circumstances, for example, may tend not to show anger, at least toward those family members with power and control over decision-making. Women may get angry at children, since this anger does not threaten the relationships that sustain women's sense of self-worth. But women in subordinate circumstances who have little self-confidence will be much less likely to feel that they are in a position to judge adult male family members. But a belief that another has acted wrongly or improperly is part of what provokes anger; therefore, to feel angry, one must have at least enough self-esteem to be able to judge another's actions as improper.[26] But judging another in this way is difficult for persons who have survived their oppressive circumstances by encouraging calm relations with those who have power over them. A lack of confidence in their own assessments will make them tend to accept the judgments and perceptions of others as correct, just as Aristotle's inirascible persons do. Kindness in such circumstances would seem only to sustain inequality, to obscure recognition of what is best, and to undermine further the decision-making powers of the person who shows kindness.[27] In these ways, care within the context of unequal power relations can harm both the person who gives it and the person to whom it is given.

These examples suggest that altruistic actions can be damaging when undertaken in circumstances in which the altruistic person lacks self-esteem. By showing kindness and compassion when other responses might be more appropriate, the kind person can act to sustain oppressive and unhealthy ways of relating to others. Through kindness, the kind person can make the acquisition of self-esteem even more difficult. Kindness seems least likely to damage oneself or another, however, when it is offered from a position of healthy independence. But healthy independence is precisely the psychological condition of Aristotle's virtuous person, who has true self-love. Because such a person has the appropriate confidence in who he is, he need not live through the achievements of another. This kind of dependent relationship will not be of interest to him, and he will not feel the need to act in ways to develop and sustain such a relationship. If kindness can be thought of as a concern for another's good for that person's own sake and as a willingness to act to contribute to that good, then Aristotle's virtuous person will act kindly, because this is the attitude he has toward fellow citizens. Yet Aristotle's virtuous citizen knows that another's good is not equivalent simply to what another wants. He knows that another's good includes the performance of activities that will nurture and sustain the other's self-love. So Aristotle's virtuous citizen recognizes that showing concern for another's good for the other's own sake may take all sorts of forms, only some of which will look like mere behavioral niceness.

I have been suggesting that if compassion and a concern for relationships constitutes some kind of model or ideal, it is not a simple one according to which we simply act to preserve the relationship or act to help another achieve what he might want. If compassion and concern are directed toward another's good for that person's sake, then for them to be proper objects of an ideal, they must operate against the background of some sound recognition of what another's good consists in. If not, compassion and concern can serve to promote oppressive or destructive relationships. Moreover, if the compassionate person is an ideal, she must be someone whose concern for another is ungrudging and noninstrumental. Aristotle's virtuous person is most likely to offer that kind of concern, since she is secure enough in who she is not to begrudge others' successes and not to rejoice spitefully in others' losses.

Aristotle's ideal has been considered masculine because it deems the best life to be that which fully realizes the rational powers characteristic of human beings. I have argued that Aristotle's emphasis on rational powers should not deter anyone, particularly feminists, from embracing his model. Although Aristotle organizes the best life around the pleasures of rational activity, this does not commit him to a model in which the non-rational is suppressed or even subordinated. As I have argued, the realization of the virtuous person's rational powers are constrained by properly educated non-rational feelings and emotions. Moreover, Aristotle offers a way to explain how reason and emotion (and passion and feeling) can operate together to produce psychologically strong and healthy individuals—individuals who take pleasure from their own lives and from the lives of others, who are caring and concerned but not in ways that are destructive of their own self-esteem, who are independent while retaining strong and enduring ties of friendship and relationship. He offers us a view of compassion and care that is positive and constructive, not oppressive and debilitating.

There are various ways in which reason can be offered as an ideal. I think Aristotle's model of how to organize one's life around the pleasures of rational activity is worthy of emulation by both men and women.[28]

Notes

1. The title also suggests that the organizers thought it appropriate, even in this special context, to refer to the three of us as "girls." I leave aside the problems associated with the use of this term in relation to adult women.

2. For Aristotle's views on women, see *Generation of Animals* 728a17ff., 732a1ff., 775a15; *Nicomachean Ethics* [hereafter *EN*] 1162a19–27; *Politics* [hereafter *Pol.*] 1259b28–1260a24, 1277b20. For Kant, see *Observations on the Feeling of the Beautiful and Sublime,* sec. 3. For Hobbes, see *Leviathan,* chs. 19–20.

3. For a useful discussion of these issues, see Elizabeth V. Spelman, *Inessential Woman: Problems of Exclusion in Feminist Thought* (Boston: Beacon Press, 1988), esp. ch. 5.

4. See Carol Gilligan, *In a Different Voice: Psychological Theory and Women's Development* (Cambridge, Mass.: Harvard University Press, 1982). In her more recent writings, Gilligan has softened her position, to claim that though women can have the "justice" perspective as well as the "care" perspective, men are more likely to have only the "justice" perspective. See "Adolescent Development Reconsidered," in *Mapping the Moral Domain,* ed. C. Gilligan, J. V. Ward, and J. McLean Taylor (Cambridge, Mass.: Harvard University Press, 1988). For the influence of Gilligan's work on moral theory, see Lawrence Blum, "Gilligan and Kohlberg: Implications for Moral Theory," *Ethics* 98, 3 (1988): 472–491; and Eva Feder Kittay and Diana T. Meyers, eds., *Women and*

Moral Theory (Totowa, N.J.: Rowman & Littlefield, 1987). For a different approach to these issues, see Owen Flanagan and Kathryn Jackson, "Justice, Care, and Gender: The Kohlberg-Gilligan Debate Revisited," *Ethics* 97, 3, (1987): 622–637.

5. See, for example, John Rawls's account of the principles of justice as chosen in special circumstances of rational deliberation in *A Theory of Justice* (Cambridge, Mass.: Harvard University Press, 1971).

6. For a discussion of the role of "particularity" in the moral life, see Lawrence Blum, "Moral Perception and Particularity," forthcoming in *Ethics* 101 (1991): 701–725, and the works cited therein.

7. Lawrence Blum, "Kant's and Hegel's Moral Rationalism: A Feminist Perspective," *Canadian Journal of Philosophy* 12 (1982): 296–297.

8. Claudia Card questions whether it is appropriate to associate care and compassion more with women than with men, and offers some helpful criticisms of the care perspective in "Women's Voices and Ethical Ideals: Must We Mean What We Say?" *Ethics* 99, 1 (1988): 125–135. See also Catherine G. Greeno and Eleanor E. Maccoby, "How Different Is the 'Different Voice'?" and Carol Gilligan's reply in *Signs* 11, 2 (1986): 310–316.

9. For considerations in favor of the view that even natural slaves are men and women for Aristotle, see W. W. Fortenbaugh, "Aristotle on Slaves and Women," in *Articles on Aristotle,* vol. 2, ed. Jonathan Barnes, Malcolm Schofield, and Richard Sorabji (London: Duckworth, 1977), p. 136.

10. For an enumeration of the various different types of non-citizens in Aristotle's ideal state and for a discussion of their legal status, see David Keyt, "Distributive Justice in Aristotle's *Ethics* and *Politics,*" *Topoi* 4 (1985): 23–45.

11. What to make of Aristotle's views in *EN* X.7–8 and how to integrate them into the rest of the *EN* and *Pol.* are not matters I shall discuss here. I shall be concerned only with Aristotle's broadly based view of human good, which includes the goods of social, political, and family life (*EN* 1097b8–11), as well as various intellectual goods.

12. It should be clear that Aristotle's implied and stated reservations about manual labor are not dissimilar from some of Marx's criticisms of wage labor under capitalism, in particular, from Marx's view that such labor alienates the worker from the activity of production and from his species-being. See *The Economic and Philosophic Manuscripts of 1844,* in vol. 3 of Karl Marx and Friedrich Engels, *Collected Works* (New York: International Publishers, 1971–1978), pp. 274–277, and *Communist Manifesto,* vol. 6 of *Collected Works,* passim.

13. I discuss the nature of these higher-level decisions in more detail in "Politics as Soul-Making: Aristotle on Becoming Good," *Philosophia* 20, 1–2 (July 1990): 167–193.

14. For a helpful discussion of Plato's views on women, see Julia Annas, "Plato's *Republic* and Feminism," *Philosophy* 51 (1976): 307–321; and her *Introduction to Plato's Republic* (Oxford: Clarendon Press, 1981), pp. 181–185.

15. Fortenbaugh draws a similar conclusions in "Aristotle on Women and Slaves," p. 138.

16. I use the translation by Terence Irwin of Aristotle's *Nicomachean Ethics* (Indianapolis: Hackett Publishing, 1985).

17. I follow, in broad outline, the more detailed argument for the same conclusion offered by Terence Irwin in *Aristotle's First Principles* (Oxford: Clarendon Press, 1988), pp. 411–416.

18. As translated by B. Jowett in the Revised Oxford Translation, vol. 2, ed. Jonathan Barnes (Princeton, N.J.: Princeton University Press, 1984).

19. It is not clear that one could provide the same type of argument for Plato. This is in part, I think, because the content of the good life is less well articulated in Plato than in Aristotle and also because, however we are to understand the content of the good life, it does not include democratic decision-making as a good in itself. For the philosopher-rulers, ruling is a burden they would prefer to be without, since they would prefer to be without the responsibilities and activities that take them away from a continual contemplation and love of the Forms. They accept the burdens of ruling only because there is no other way to replicate the beauty they see in the Forms. Although it is best for the state as a whole that they rule, their interest in ruling is purely instrumental. And since menial labor is often monotonous and routine, requiring little use of the rational powers, it would be inefficient for rulers to take it up. It is therefore better left to others.

20. In "Virtue and Self-Love in Aristotle's Ethics," *Canadian Journal of Philosophy* 11, 4 (December 1981): 633–651, and in "The Pleasure of Virtue in Aristotle's Moral Theory," *Pacific Philosophical Quarterly* 66, 1–2 (January–April 1985): 93–110.

21. See Card, "Women's Voices and Ethical Ideals"; Greeno and Maccoby, "How Different Is the 'Different Voice'?"

22. For a related discussion, see Sharon Bishop, "Love and Dependency," in *Philosophy and Women,* ed. S. Bishop and M. Weinzweig (Belmont, Calif.: Wadsworth, 1979), pp. 147–154.

23. Cf. Nancy Chodorow's description of healthy dependence in "Family Structure and Feminine Personality," in *Woman, Culture, and Society,* ed. Michelle Rosaldo and Louise Lamphere (Stanford, Calif.: Stanford University Press, 1974), pp. 43–66, esp. pp. 60–63; and in *The Reproduction of Mothering: Psychoanalysis and the Sociology of Gender* (Berkeley: University of California Press, 1978), pp. 211ff.

24. For current wage differentials between full-time working women and men, see U.S. Department of Labor, *Employment and Earnings: July 1987* (Washington, D.C.: Government Printing Office, 1987).

25. See Margaret Benston, "The Political Economy of Women's Liberation," in *Feminist Frameworks,* 2d ed., ed. Alison Jaggar and Paula Rothenberg (New York: McGraw-Hill, 1984), pp. 239–247, esp. pp. 244–245.

26. For further discussion of anger in the context of unequal power relations, see Elizabeth V. Spelman, "Anger and Insubordination," in *Women, Knowledge, and Reality,* ed. Ann Garry and Marilyn Pearsall (Boston: Unwin Hyman, 1989), pp. 263–273; and Friedrich Nietzsche, *On the Genealogy of Morals,* tr. Walter Kaufman and R. J. Hollingdale (New York: Vintage, 1967), passim.

27. For more discussion of these and related points, see L. Blum et al., "Altruism and Women's Oppression," in Bishop and Weinzweig, eds., *Philosophy*

and Women, pp. 190–200; and John Stuart Mill, *On the Subjection of Women* (Cambridge: MIT Press, 1970), ch. 2.

28. I am grateful to David Copp, Jean Hampton, Janet Levin, and the editors of this volume for helpful comments on earlier versions of this paper.

Suggested Readings

Ackrill, J. L. 1981. *Aristotle the Philosopher*. New York: Oxford University Press.

Annas, Julia. 1992. "The Good Life and the Good Lives of Others" in *The Good Life and the Human Good,* ed. E. Paul, F. D. Miller, and J. Paul, 133–48. Cambridge: Cambridge University Press.

———. 1993. *The Morality of Happiness*. New York: Oxford University Press.

Broadie, Sarah. 1991. *Ethics with Aristotle*. New York: Oxford University Press.

Burnet, John. 1900. *The Ethics of Aristotle.* London: Methuen.

Charlton, William. 1988. *Weakness of Will.* Cambridge, Mass.: Blackwell.

Cooper, John. 1975. *Reason and Human Good in Aristotle.* Cambridge, Mass.: Harvard University.

———. 1985. "Aristotle on the Goods of Fortune." *Philosophical Review* 94: 173–97.

———. 1987. "Contemplation and Happiness: A Reconsideration." *Synthese* 72: 187–216.

———. 1988. "Some Remarks on Aristotle's Moral Psychology." *The Southern Journal of Philosophy* 27, Supplement: 25–42.

———. 1998. *Reason and Emotion*. Princeton: Princeton University Press.

Dahl, Norman. 1984. *Practical Reason, Aristotle and Weakness of Will.* Minneapolis: University of Minnesota Press.

Davidson, Donald. 1969. "How Is Weakness of the Will Possible." In *Moral Concepts,* ed. J. Feinberg. New York: Oxford University Press.

Frede, Michael, and Gisela Striker, eds. 1996. *Rationality in Greek Thought*. New York: Oxford University Press.

Gauthier, R. A., and J. Y. Jolif. 1970. *Aristote, L'Éthique à Nicomaque,* 2nd ed. Louvain: Publications Universitaires.

Gomez-Lobo, Alphonso. 1989. "Aristotle." In *Ethics in the History of Western Philosophy,* ed. R. Cavalier. New York: St. Martin's Press.

Gottlieb, Paula. 1991. "Aristotle and Protagoras: The Good Human Being as the Measure of Goods." *Aperion* 24: 25–45.

Grant, Alexander. 1885. *The Ethics of Aristotle.* London: Longmans, Green, and Co.

Greenwood, L. H. G. 1973. *Aristotle, Nicomachean Ethics: Book Six.* New York: Arno Press.

Hardie, W. F. R. 1978. "Magnanimity in Aristotle's Ethics." *Phronesis* 7: 63–79.

———. 1980. *Aristotle's Ethical Theory.* New York: Oxford University Press.

Hirsthouse, Rosalind. 1997. "Virtue Ethics and the Emotions." In *Virtue Ethics: A Critical Reader,* ed. D. Statman. Washington, D.C.: Georgetown University Press.

Irwin, T. H. 1975. "Aristotle on Reason, Desire, and Virtue." *Journal of Philosophy* 72: 567–78.

———. 1985. *Aristotle's Nicomachean Ethics.* Indianapolis: Hackett.

———. 1986. "Aristotle's Conception of Morality." *Proceedings of the Boston Area Colloquium in Ancient Philosophy,* ed. J. Cleary, 115–143. Lanham, Md.: University Press of America.

———. 1988a. *Aristotle's First Principles.* New York: Oxford University Press.

———. 1988b. "Disunity in the Aristotelian Virtues." In *Oxford Studies in Ancient Philosophy*, supplementary volume, 61–78. Oxford: Oxford University Press.

———. 1989. *Classical Thought.* New York: Oxford University Press.

Joachim, H. H. 1951. *Aristotle, The Nicomachean Ethics: A Commentary.* New York: Oxford University Press.

Kenny, Anthony. 1992. *Aristotle on the Perfect Life.* New York: Oxford University Press.

Keyt, David. 1983. "Intellectualism in Aristotle." In *Essays in Ancient Greek Philosophy,* ed. J. P. Anton and A. Preus, vol. 2. Albany: State University of New York Press.

Kraut, Richard. 1989. *Aristotle on the Human Good.* Princeton: Princeton University Press.

Lear, Jonathan. 1988. *Aristotle: The Desire to Understand.* Cambridge: Cambridge University Press.

Leighton, Stephen. 1982. "Aristotle and the Emotions." *Phronesis* 22: 144–74.

MacIntyre, Alasdair. 1981. *After Virtue.* Notre Dame, Ind.: Notre Dame University Press.

McDowell, John. 1980. "The Role of *Eudaimonia* in Aristotle's Ethics" in *Essays on Aristotle's Ethics*, ed. A. O. Rorty. Berkeley: University of California Press.

———. 1996. "Incontinence and Practical Wisdom in Aristotle." In *Essays for David Wiggins: Identity, Truth and Value*, ed. S. Lovibond and S. G. Williams. Cambridge, Mass.: Blackwell.

Nussbaum, Martha C. 1986. *The Fragility of Goodness: Luck and Ethics in Greek Tragedy and Philosophy.* Cambridge: Cambridge University Press.

———. 1993. "Non-Relative Virtues: An Aristotelian Approach." In *The Quality of Life,* ed. M. Nussbaum and A. Sen. New York: Oxford University Press.

———. 1994. *The Therapy of Desire: Theory and Practice in Hellenistic Ethics.* Princeton: Princeton University Press.

———. 1995. "Aristotle on Human Nature and the Foundation of Ethics." In *World, Mind and Ethics: Essays on the Ethical Philosophy of Bernard Williams,* ed. J. E. J. Altham and R. Harrison. Cambridge: Cambridge University Press.

Pears, David. 1980. "Courage as a Mean." In *Essays on Aristotle's Ethics,* ed. A. O. Rorty. Berkeley: University of California Press.

Price, A. W. 1989. *Love and Friendship in Plato and Aristotle.* New York: Oxford University Press.

Richardson, Henry. 1994. *Practical Reasoning about Final Ends.* Cambridge: Cambridge University Press.

Rorty, Amelie O., ed. 1980. *Essays on Aristotle's Ethics.* Berkeley: University of California Press.

Santas, Gerasimos. 1969. "Aristotle on Practical Inference, the Explanation of Action and Akrasia." *Phronesis* 14: 162–89.

Sherman, Nancy. 1988. "Common Sense and Uncommon Virtue." In *Midwest Studies in Philosophy,* vol. 13, ed. P. French, Th. Uehling, and H. Wettstein, 97–114. Notre Dame: Notre Dame University Press.

———. 1989. *The Fabric of Character: Aristotle's Theory of Virtue.* New York: Oxford University Press.

———. 1997. *Making a Necessity of Virtue: Aristotle and Kant on Virtue.* Cambridge: Cambridge University Press.

Stewart, J. A. 1973. *Notes on the* Nicomachean Ethics *of Aristotle*. New York: Arno.

Stocker, Michael. 1986. "Dirty Hands and Conflicts of Values and of Desires in Aristotle's Ethics." *Pacific Philosophical Quarterly* 67: 36–61.

Walsh, James. 1963. *Aristotle's Conception of Moral Weakness*. New York: Columbia University Press.

Watson, Gary. 1977. "Skepticism about Weakness of Will." *Philosophical Review* 86: 318–39.

White, Stephen. 1992. *Sovereign Virtue*. Stanford, Calif.: Stanford University Press.

Wiggins, David. 1980. "Weakness of Will, Commensurabilility, and the Objects of Deliberation and Desire." In *Essays on Aristotle's Ethics,* ed. A. O. Rorty. Berkeley: University of California Press.

Woods, Michael. 1982. *Aristotle's Eudemian Ethics* (translation and commentary). New York: Oxford University Press.

Young, Charles. 1988. "Aristotle on Temperance." *Philosophical Review* 97: 521–542.

Authors

J. L. Ackrill is Professor Emeritus of the History of Philosophy in University of Oxford. He is the author of *Aristotle's Categories and De Interpretatione* (translation and commentary), issued under the Clarendon Aristotle Series, of which he serves as the General Editor. He is also the editor of the *New Aristotle Reader* and author of *Aristotle: The Philosopher*. His most recent work is *Essays on Plato and Aristotle* (1997).

Julia Annas is Regent's Professor of Philosophy at the University of Arizona. Her publications include *Aristotle's Metaphysics, Books M and N* (translation and commentary); *An Introduction to Plato's Republic*; *Hellenistic Philosophy of Mind*; *Modes of Scepticism*; and *The Morality of Happiness.*

M. F. Burnyeat is Senior Research Fellow in Philosophy, All Souls College, Oxford. He has taught in London and in Cambridge, where he was Laurence Professor of Ancient Philosophy. He is the author of *The Theaetetus of Plato* as well as many articles in classical and philosophical journals.

John McDowell is University Professor of Philosophy at the University of Pittsburgh and emeritus fellow of University College, Oxford. He is the author of *Mind and World*; *Mind*; *Value and Reality*, and *Meaning, Knowledge, and Reality.*

John M. Cooper is Stuart Professor of Philosophy at Princeton University. He is the author of *Reason and Human Good in Aristotle* and of numerous articles on diverse aspects of ancient philosophy. He is also the editor of *Plato: Complete Works* and coeditor and cotranslator of *Seneca: Moral and Political Essays*. His most recent book, *Reason and Emotion*, is a collection of his essays.

Marcia Homiak is Professor of Philosophy at Occidental College. She has written articles on Aristotle's moral theory and is currently working on a book on that subject, entitled *Virtue and the Limits of Reason*.

Rosalind Hursthouse is a member of the Philosophy Department at the Open University in Britain. She is author of *Beginning Life*, is coeditor of *Virtues and Reasons: A Festschrift for Philippa Foot,* and has written extensively in the area of virtue theory. Her forthcoming book is *On Virtue Ethics*.

Terry Irwin is Susan Linn Sage Professor of Philosophy at Cornell University. His books include *Plato's Gorgias* (translation and notes), *Aristotle's* Nicomachean Ethics (translation and notes), *Aristotle's First Principles, Classical Thought,* and *Plato's Ethics.*

Aryeh Kosman is John Whitehead Professor of Philosophy at Haverford College. He is the author of a number of essays on the history of philosophy, mostly on Plato and Aristotle.

Richard Kraut is Professor of Philosophy and Classics at Northwestern University. He is the author of *Socrates and the State, Aristotle on the Human Good,* and *Politics: Books VII and VIII* (translation and commentary), and the editor of the *Cambridge Companion to Plato.*

Alfred R. Mele is Vail Professor of Philosophy at Davidson College. He is author of *Irrationality, Springs of Action,* and *Autonomous Agents.* He is the editor of *The Philosophy of Action* and coeditor of *Mental Causation.*

Martha C. Nussbaum is Ernst Freund Professor of Law and Ethics at the University of Chicago. She is the author of numerous books, including *The Fragility of Goodness, The Therapy of Desire, Love's Knowledge, Poetic Justice, Cultivating Humanity,* and editor and translator of *Aristotle's De Motu Animalium*.

Nancy Sherman is Professor of Philosophy at Georgetown University and inaugural holder of the Distinguished Chair of Ethics at the U.S. Naval Academy. She is the author of *The Fabric of Character* and *Making a Necessity of Virtue*. She is coeditor of *Ethics for Military Leaders*.